NEVER GIVE AN INCH

NEVER GIVE AN INCH

★ Fighting for the America I Love ★

Mike Pompeo

BROADSIDE BOOKS
An Imprint of HarperCollinsPublishers

All quotations from the Bible have been sourced from the New International Version.

Page xvi: Secretary Pompeo and American hostages freed from North Korea, Joint Base Andrews, Maryland; May 10, 2018, AP Photo/Alex Brandon

FIRST EDITION

Library of Congress Cataloging-in-Publication Data
Names: Pompeo, Mike, 1963– author.
Title: Never give an inch: fighting for the America I love / Mike Pompeo.
Description: First edition. | New York, NY: Broadside, [2023] | Includes index.
Identifiers: LCCN 2022044384 (print) | LCCN 2022044385 (ebook) |
    ISBN 9780063247444 (hardcover) | ISBN 9780063247468 (ebook)
Subjects: LCSH: Pompeo, Mike, 1963– | Politicians—United States—
    Biography | United States. Department of State—Officials and
    employees—Biography. | United States. Central Intelligence
    Agency—Officials and employees—Biography. | United States—
    Politics and government—2017–2021 | United States—Foreign
    relations—2017–2021.
Classification: LCC E901.1.P66 A3 2023 (print) | LCC E901.1.P66 (ebook)
    | DDC 973.933092 [B]—dc23/eng/20221104
LC record available at https://lccn.loc.gov/2022044384
LC ebook record available at https://lccn.loc.gov/2022044385

23 24 25 26 27 LBC 5 4 3 2 1

To my wife, Susan, who—when fighting for those she loves, her Lord, our family, and America—never gives an inch.

We must be ready to dare all for our country. For history does not long entrust the care of freedom to the weak or the timid. We must acquire proficiency in defense and display stamina in purpose. We must be willing, individually and as a Nation, to accept whatever sacrifices may be required of us.

—PRESIDENT DWIGHT D. EISENHOWER,
FIRST INAUGURAL ADDRESS, JANUARY 20, 1953

CONTENTS

FOREWORD

The Great American Experiment began in 1776. At the time, its success seemed implausible, but we prevailed. Ever since, the American Republic has delivered for its people. And its people have delivered for one another. Throughout our history, everyday people—farmers and printers, traders and carpenters, even machine shop operators—have stepped forward to defend the things that matter.

Our forty-fifth president, as with each of his predecessors, faced countless challenges. He was an unlikely president, whose ways were as unique as the team that he assembled. Donald Trump was a real estate guy from New York; Mike Pompeo was a guy who had run machine shops in Kansas. This unusual combo set out to lead America's national security team.

Lead they did, and well. This book narrates and provides the backstory for the four years of the Trump administration's work on behalf of everyday Americans. You'll hear about the geopolitical challenges it faced, how the team translated "America First" into policy, and, of course, a few good stories. Best of all, it's told from the perspective of Mike Pompeo, who served as America's CIA director and secretary of state. He also happens to be my father.

I was raised in Kansas by two wonderful parents. After retiring from a long career at a regional bank, my mother was always busy—she volunteered at our church, bused me to practices, helped with my homework, and took care of everything in between. My dad worked tirelessly, running a couple of small manufacturing companies, but still managed to be at all my basketball games and school functions. We were a normal family leading a simple midwestern life. Then my father lost his mind and decided to run for Congress in 2010. Like many sons, I've always looked up to my dad. He is a special man. He imparted to me the importance of faith, family, honesty, hard work, and what it means to never give an inch.

As I was beginning my adult life, I was a typical twentysomething: impatient, thought I knew more about the world than I actually did, and eager to make my mark. From time to time, I would lament to my dad that my career wasn't progressing fast enough, or that I wasn't accomplishing as much as I'd hoped, or that my true value was not being rewarded. Every time, my dad had the same response: "Put your head down, work hard, and good things will follow." I would roll my eyes so hard that I was worried he might hear it through the phone line. But, as it turns out, parents *do* know best.

I'd seen my dad live out these words countless times in his own life. In business, he devoted everything to the companies he ran and his teams. As a CEO, he shouldered the burden of protecting the livelihood of every single employee and his or her family, knowing that if he failed, he'd be failing them. He made tough and bold decisions when necessary, but they were always in the best interest of the people he served.

When he ran for Congress, I knew he wasn't doing it for the fame. If you want to run for office for celebrity or esteem, I recommend singing or acting instead. He wasn't doing it for the elitist DC cocktail parties. To this day, I've never seen my dad drink more than two Sam Adams in a twenty-four-hour period. He did it because he felt our nation was wandering from our essential principles and that the people in Kansas's Fourth Congressional District deserved better.

When then President-elect Trump nominated him to be the director of the CIA, well, that surprised us all. But my dad didn't think twice—it was God's plan, and he answered the call to serve his country at that moment, and then again as secretary of state. All my life, I'd watched my dad diligently focus on whatever task was at hand: serving the team, the people, or the country he represented. He was never thinking about what was next. He just put his head down, worked hard, and, I'll be damned, good things followed.

While one can never *plan* to be nominated by a president to lead America's intelligence and diplomatic teams, he was fully prepared for the opportunity. I knew this for a multitude of reasons, but it was evident, even in the smallest of ways, throughout my childhood. Whenever we watched the Army-Navy football game with my buddies (something we never missed), my dad would educate us on the military unit patches as they flashed across the screen. While shooting hoops together in the driveway, he'd ask for my opinions on things like Middle East peace in between jumpers. One night, I had my friend Stephen over for dinner. Seemingly out of nowhere, my dad asked him, "Do you know who Hans Blix is?" Blix, at the time, was the UN weapons inspector leading the monitoring and inspection of Iraq's weapons arsenal. Of course, my friend had no idea who he was—after all, we were sixth-graders. I apologized to Stephen and then coached him onto the answer, as this was not my first Hans Blix rodeo.

In high school, my dad would often distribute his own pop quizzes, usually around eight on Saturday mornings. I specifically remember once being handed a blank map of Europe, the Middle East, and Asia: "You won't be able to grasp global issues if you can't even point out the countries on a map," he would say. Thanks to him, I know the difference between Bangladesh and Ukraine. An eerie—yet, in hindsight, obvious—foreshadowing of my dad's future role as America's chief spy came when I was eleven or twelve years old. I asked him what his dream job was. "Deputy director of the CIA," was his response. "You get to run the spies and don't have to deal with the bureaucracy." I guess he overshot his dream job by a hair—and, as predicted, ended up dealing with *plenty* of bureaucracy.

Of course, knowing who Hans Blix is or being able to fill out a blank map doesn't qualify you to be director of the CIA or the US secretary of state. But in these instances—no matter how embarrassing or bothersome they may have been to this teenager at the time—I understood my father's passion and deep understanding of the world and America's place in it. I came to revere his ferocious and dogged work ethic, whether he was running his company, fighting for Kansans, or teaching fifth-graders at our church. I listened to him talk about his time at West Point and in the Army—his love for America was clear, and I could see how it shaped him into the incredible leader that he is today.

I've always known that my dad was a fierce defender of the Great American Experiment and the essential principles upon which our Founders set the course. And I've always known that, when it comes to fighting for the America he loves, he would never give an inch.

Now the world knows it, too.

Nick Pompeo
September 2022

Be on your guard; stand firm in the faith; be courageous;
be strong.

—I CORINTHIANS 16:13

At roughly 2 a.m. on May 10, 2018, white-and-blue American planes returned from Pyongyang, North Korea, to Andrews Air Force Base in Maryland. We were greeted by President Trump, Vice President Pence, and their spouses. My team and I were happy to be home, but the men of the hour were Kim Dong-chul, Tony Kim, and Kim Hak-song—American hostages released from North Korean detention. It was one of the most joyous days of my life. In my hand is the index card those men gave me with words from Psalm 126 written on it: "The Lord has done great things for us, and we are filled with joy."

WORDS FROM KIM HAK-SONG

I was arrested by the North Korean authorities while leaving Pyongyang for Dandong, China, on May 6, 2017. I was in Pyongyang to serve as a manager of an experimental farm at Pyongyang University of Science and Technology for three years. They had accused me of blaspheming the dignity of the supreme leader, which is considered the most serious crime in North Korea. The ordeal began immediately as I was consistently interrogated and mentally harassed. This hopeless and fearful situation continued for a year. On the morning of May 9, 2018, an inspector of the prison told me to pack my bags. Without knowing the reason, I packed my luggage and waited, like an animal waiting to be taken to the slaughterhouse. It wasn't until around 6 p.m. that evening that they dragged me to a hotel conference room, where they declared: "We are deporting the anti-DPRK criminal Kim Hak-song at the request of the US government!"

Hearing this deportation order, I couldn't help but doubt my ears. It happened so unexpectedly that it felt like a dream. When I exited the room and stepped into a North Korean police van, I recognized my fellow Korean American detainees, Mr. Kim Dong-chul and Mr. Kim Sang-duk, already sitting in the van.

Soon after, the van arrived at the Pyongyang Sunan International Airport beneath an airplane with a large marking of United States of America. Only then did I admit that this was not a dream but reality. We soon headed for the ladder to board the plane. Next to the ladder, a tall, gentle-looking white male hugged and shook hands with each of us. I will never forget what he said then: "America has not forgotten you!"

When I heard this, I burst into tears. I survived because I am an American, even though I am not good at English. I heard his words as the voice of God. Yes, America has not forgotten us. Because America is on God's side!

It was only when I arrived at Andrews Air Force Base in Washington, DC, that I realized that Secretary of State Mike Pompeo was the one who had hugged us at the Pyongyang Sunan International Airport the day before. He risked himself to become God's ambassador to our rescue! He is the benefactor who gave me a second life!

And America is the country that gave me true freedom! Hallelujah!

—*Kim Hak-song, pastor, former hostage held by*
the Democratic People's Republic of Korea

INTRODUCTION

As a young cavalry lieutenant in the late 1980s, I was training with my tank platoon at Grafenwöhr, Germany. One day, I took my M1A1 Abrams tank down to a gunnery range where we practiced maneuvers and firing. My gunner was Specialist 4 Martinez. He was on the main gun, and I was just above and behind him. We rumbled at high speed while blasting 105-millimeter rounds. In our second engagement, Martinez hit two moving wooden tank targets in rapid succession, at a total distance of just under three miles. The smell of cordite filled the turret, and the beastly machine's Lycoming AGT 1500HP turbine engine whirred. Over the crackling tank intercom, Martinez shouted, "Sir, America is f——ing awesome!" Unapologetic Americanism from the turret of an American fighting machine.

America is indeed, in a word, awesome. I have been reminded of this in every opportunity I've had to serve the United States of America. By God's grace, over the course of the Trump administration, I became the only person ever to have served as both America's most senior diplomat and the head of its premier espionage agency. Growing up, this son of a mom from Kansas and a dad from New Mexico never dreamed of such a future for himself.

Advising the president, leading America's intelligence officers and diplomats, and negotiating with the world's toughest leaders is difficult under any circumstance. But adding to those challenges was an adversarial domestic political climate that included two impeachments, riots ignored by public officials because Black Lives Matter, and a progressive-activist media that asserted, among other falsehoods, that President Trump was a Russian asset. Oh, and the Chinese Communist Party (CCP) foisted a virus on the world that has killed more than a million Americans and paralyzed the world's largest economy for nearly the entire final year of my service. These developments changed how America was seen in the world and how we saw ourselves. They shaped the Trump administration's foreign policy decisions in no small ways. And, still, when it mattered most—on the big things, on the American idea—I never gave an inch.

Notwithstanding these challenges, I had some real advantages that helped me along the way. My mother, Dorothy Mercer Pompeo, was the most decent woman I have ever known, full of the same motherly affections I admire so much in my own wife, Susan. When I was a boy, we didn't have much money, but we had plenty of love, and my parents raised us right. They couldn't afford to fly with me in June 1982 to drop me off at college, so as I left home for the US Military Academy at West Point, New York, she pulled me in close. I don't think she wanted my dad to hear what she wanted to tell me. "Michael," she said, using my full name as she always did, "I know you're a grinder. Don't ever let them wear you down. You wear *them* down."

In the days that followed, I took my first real steps of adulthood in government-issued boots. Like many cadets, I was amazed and grateful that a total unknown could gain admission to the world's most elite leadership institution without special connections, a bribe, or an august family name. That realization was a critical seed of my lifelong belief in America as the greatest nation in the history of civilization. America is where grinders of no special background or privilege can rise like nowhere else.

But American greatness depends only in part on great Americans. Thanks to the Declaration of Independence and the Constitution, our republic honors human dignity, unalienable rights, and the rule of law more completely than any other country in history. We use our unmatched power and resources to be a force for good in the world, even if we misfire on occasion. We are the most brilliant star in the darkest skies of the world, showing humanity that life in a free society is superior to life under the evil wardens of Communism or Islamism or thieving strongmen who rule by the crooked principle of might makes right. But none of this happens if our leaders aren't prepared to put our nation first and honor our American principles and history.

★ ★ ★

My entire life's experience, through His grace, had prepared me to continue defending this extraordinary American way of life as the director of the Central Intelligence Agency (CIA) and as America's seventieth secretary of state. That experience started as a student at Los Amigos High School in Orange County, California, where I was the captain of a highly mediocre basketball team and the assistant manager of a Baskin-Robbins. They were leadership roles with small responsibilities, but if you learn to be faithful in the small things, you'll be faithful in the big ones.

My chances to lead got bigger with time. Spending four years as a cadet at the nation's premier foundry of leadership, and then commanding tank and scout platoons as a young lieutenant, provided me boundless opportunities to learn about brutal choices. I learned how to follow and to lead, and to realize that, although each of us will fail often, failure must not prevent us from grinding on. My time in law school gave me the chance to read widely about power, law, and human dignity, and I came to appreciate the difference in approach between those who teach about such concepts and those who have the responsibility of executing on them in public service. As the senior leader of two small businesses in Kansas, I shouldered the responsibility of running complex organizations and making sure that our teams executed our business plan ruthlessly. The well-being of my employees' families depended on that.

Then, convinced our nation was coming unmoored, I lost my mind and decided to reenter public service. In 2010, voters elected me to the US House of Representatives as part of the Republican conservative wave. My time as a member of the House Permanent Select Committee on Intelligence and the Select Committee on Benghazi improved my understanding of the world, the US Department of State, and the US intelligence community—knowledge that later aided my decision-making in the administration. Leading our intelligence warriors was the finest experience of my life. Leading the State Department was, well, fascinating.

The most immediate challenge, and the subject of my daily work, was the world we confronted. Our outgoing president was distinguished for espousing moral equivalence among nations of deeply unequal decency and apologizing for our country. Global news providers such as the BBC and CNN International reinforced his foul narrative as they spewed hatred of America on TV screens to an international audience. Newer, cheaper, and more powerful cybertools for warfare, chaos, and extortion were now in the hands of not only nations but cartels, terrorists, and even simple hoodlums such as Julian Assange and Edward Snowden. America was nearly two decades into a global war on terrorism, and our strategy in Afghanistan had grown long in the tooth. And then there was Xi Jinping and the CCP. Few times in history has such a dangerous colossus bestrode the world.

I am grateful to have confronted these challenges under a president who was prepared to break glass, recognize reality, and accept risk—and to give this former cavalry officer, machine shop CEO, and congressman from Kansas the authority to execute his vision. Not that Chairman Kim, Xi Jinping, Ayatollah Khamenei, Nicolás Maduro, or Vladimir Putin gave a rip about my background. Indeed, prior to 2017, I doubt the name Pompeo had ever tripped off any of their tongues unless they were fans of Ellen Pompeo, an actress on *Grey's Anatomy*. (We are not related, but she did once call me a "maniac," which I accept as a compliment from a Hollywood celebrity.)

Today the murderer's row of America-hating leaders know who I am, not because I'm Mike Pompeo, but because, for exactly one thousand days, I served the greatest nation in the history of civilization as its top diplomat. I've now been sanctioned by Iran, Russia, and China, which means I don't have vacation plans for Tehran, Moscow, or Beijing. On the plus side, my understanding of the world and its risks is greatly expanded. This book does not merely serve to entertain, although I hope it does. It is also a blueprint for ensuring America's future security, prosperity, and liberty against the designs of evil actors.

My task, for four years, was to listen to President Trump and what the American people had asked us to do, then to translate those demands into sound intelligence and diplomatic plans. I built teams that relentlessly, and often coldheartedly, delivered for the president and our nation. Executing my mission was made easier because my strategic compass pointed directly to a set of principles that were never in doubt: put America first, champion our values, and never apologize for our country. Embracing this civic trinity was not only right as a matter of honoring our constitutional order but also right in delivering good outcomes for the American people and the world. What mattered most, however, was the continued grace and wisdom that the good Lord provided to me and my teams.

While I own all that is written here, this book is ultimately not about me. It's about our team. We led. We worked. We kept grinding. And we wore down our adversaries—my mother, God rest her soul, would have been proud. We imposed crushing pressure on the Islamic Republic of Iran, executed shrewd diplomacy to avert a nuclear crisis with North Korea, and held the banner of international religious freedom higher than any administration in American history ever has. We delivered unmatched support for Israel and expanded peace in the lands of Abraham. And, in what I regard as the most important mission of all, we led a much-needed generational transformation of America's relationship with China. My Christian faith, my commitment to the American way of life, and my belief that the dignity of every human being matters drove my decision-making every day. In the end, our team left America more secure and more respected—even if not always more loved—in the world. And we did it in the face of a political establishment that hated what we stood for. Sadly, that establishment too often loathes the citizens it purports to represent and seeks to destroy our nation's Judeo-Christian founding and all it has bequeathed to our people.

★ ★ ★

People ask me all the time if I ever came close to quitting during my Trump administration years. Easy answer. Not once. A major inspiration for why is captured in some words I once heard a great American speak.

When I was a student at Harvard Law School, the hearings on Clarence Thomas's nomination to the Supreme Court dominated nearly an entire semester. Every leftist student donned an "Anita Is Right" T-shirt.

For me, there was one searing moment during that whole circus that I will never forget. Many Democrats, with a senator named Joe Biden as their chief inquisitor, were mounting a withering assault to convince this great American to withdraw from the confirmation process. Having been attacked unfairly and ruthlessly because he is both black and conservative, Justice Thomas looked directly at his Senate accusers and uttered these words: "I would rather die than withdraw. I will not be scared. I've never run from bullies."

I've come to know Justice Thomas only a little bit, but I cannot tell you how many times in the past decades his example of strength under fire that day has emboldened me in my own moments of pressure. Indeed, whenever I held a hard line in a meeting with the likes of Kim, Xi, or Putin, I often prayed I would possess the strength Justice Thomas did.

Whenever I'd watch a cabinet member resign, whenever the leftist media would slander me as the worst secretary of state in history, or whenever some third-rate numbskull from the administration would leak that I was insufficiently on board with the Trump agenda, I thought about Justice Thomas's words: "I would rather die than withdraw." I thought about my classmates from the West Point Class of 1986, some of whom sacrificed everything for our country in the deserts of Iraq and the mountains of Afghanistan. If I had left to protect my reputation or because I was tired or because I had "done my time," how could I have told them I had lived up to our class motto: "Courage Never Quits, '86"? It would have been un-American. Nor could I have looked my wife, Susan, or our son, Nick, in the eye.

The privilege to be an American, with all it connotes and bestows, required me to soldier on. It would have been immoral and unfaithful to relinquish a once-in-a-lifetime stewardship of power and opportunity to do good for my country. I did not get things right every time. It was a massive thrill and a staggering burden. On the things that mattered most, I never gave an inch. I'd do it all again with no second thoughts. And I may.

Mike Pompeo
Virginia
August 2022

NEVER GIVE AN INCH

CHAPTER I

FIND THE RISK-TAKERS

It wasn't the Easter weekend I had planned.

My clandestine mission began on Good Friday, March 30, 2018, as I departed Andrews Air Force Base. My destination: Pyongyang, North Korea. I was headed to one of the darkest places on earth to meet with Chairman Kim Jong Un, its darkest inhabitant. The mission was a complete secret, known only to a few. My objective: correct the failed efforts of the past that had not eliminated North Korea's nuclear weapons of mass destruction (WMD), and had, in fact, led to the current heightened threat. President Trump had told me he was prepared to take risks—and as director of the CIA, I was ready to take them, too.

As our aircraft entered North Korean airspace, our foreign adversary's fighter jets shadowed us. Normally, this action would signal hostility and perhaps an imminent attack. But our crew and I had confidence that it was just typical North Korean bluster. Still, this special mission's pilot informed me that if the North Koreans did anything stupid, a US rescue team would arrive soon to recover our remains. I think it was an Air Force guy giving an Army guy a good joke. The dark humor was welcomed.

On final approach, I saw the dismal concrete blocks of government-built housing that littered the surroundings of the capital of the Democratic People's Republic of Korea (DPRK). The country's very name is a lie: it's not democratic, it's not a republic, and it certainly doesn't serve the interests of its people. When the wheels hit the tarmac, I peered through my cabin window to see Pyongyang Sunan International Airport, a retrograde structure that was only a bit more cheerful than the ram-shackle apartment complexes I had just seen. The airport was completely deserted—no people, no vehicles, no other aircraft, no ground equip-ment. At least it looked clean.

As soon as the plane came to a halt, a convoy of very-low-mileage black Mercedes-Benz sedans, a couple of military trucks, and a few equip-ment vans pulled up beside us. When they had settled in formation, my head of security got off the plane to speak with his North Korean coun-terpart. After a rather lengthy conversation, undertaken with the aid of a translator, my security chief came back up into the aircraft and broke some news to me:

"Mr. Director, they're not gonna let us take our weapons downtown."

About one beat after he finished his sentence, we burst out laughing. We had both instantly come to the same conclusion: if it all went to hell, our weapons would make it interesting, but probably only extend a valiant last stand by minutes. I had no problem leaving the guns on the plane. In for a penny, in for a pound—or at least a worthless North Korean won.

I headed for the exit of our airplane. At the bottom of steps, as I expected, was Kim Yong Chol, one of the nastiest men I've ever encoun-tered. Chol is a retired general who serves as vice chairman of the Work-ers' Party of Korea—the Communist Party of North Korea. He was also the head of the DPRK's external propaganda machine, the United Front Department. He had previously headed the Reconnaissance General Bureau—the DPRK's primary intelligence service. Among his résumé highlights is his role in killing forty-six South Korean sailors in 2010, when the North sank a South Korean naval vessel.

From our first interactions, it was obvious Chol wanted to intimidate me. He greeted me and Andy Kim, the CIA's top North Korea expert and my only aide on this mission, with a military guard force flanking him. I reached out to shake his hand. Mid-grip, through a translator, he said, "We have eaten grass for the last 50 years. We can eat grass for the next 50 years." No hello, no welcome—simply his own personal message that the regime had the will to survive even if the North Korean people had to suffer famine. Of course, Chol wasn't eating grass. Like all other klepto-maniac North Korean elites, he was drinking top-shelf booze and dining on Wagyu beef. Eating grass was for ordinary people. I knew Chol didn't run the show in the Hermit Kingdom, so I gave him a salty response: "General Chol, nice to see you too. I can't wait for lunch. And I prefer my grass steamed." He didn't laugh, but Andy did. That comment, like this entire trip, was a calculated risk.

Andy and I were escorted to a black Mercedes-Benz. We climbed into the backseat with no real idea of our precise destination. The thought briefly crossed my mind we could be taken hostage. At that moment, in fact, the DPRK was unlawfully detaining three Americans. Other than making progress on the mission, my biggest concern was for the safety of my team. Thankfully, I knew Chairman Kim Jong Un—the man I was there to see—desperately wanted this meeting to succeed.

I was also worried that the DPRK would use the trip for propaganda. It was a real possibility that Andy and I would get what we called "the Albright dolphin treatment." In 2000, Secretary of State Madeline Albright had gone to meet with Chairman Kim's father, Kim Jong Il. She was taken on a long and involuntary sightseeing tour that included performing dolphins—I guess the DPRK wanted to use a picture of a Western leader marveling at animal tricks for propaganda. In the negotiations leading up to my visit, we'd made clear that a stunt like the dolphin act or forcing us to lay flowers and bow down to the statues of Kim Il Sung and Kim Jong Il would cause us to leave immediately. I wasn't interested in whatever the hell a North Korean Sea World looked like. The whole country was already enough of a poorly run zoo. We were fixated exclusively on deterring North Korea's nuclear program and convincing the country's leaders to fully and verifiably dismantle all their WMD programs.

US visits in years past had also resulted in American teams folding under the North Koreans' extortionate yet petty demands that the United States make cash payments on the tarmac for "landing rights" and "fuel." I had given my team clear instructions: "Not one f——ing nickel. If they demand cash, tell them to ask me personally for it, and remind them that we can invoice them for the fuel cost to come to see their crappy little country if we want to." Not very diplomatic, but I wasn't officially a diplomat—at least not yet. And it wasn't about the money. We wanted to make sure they understood that we were not like the American teams they had met with before. I learned later they never asked us for a thing. It was clear that they already knew we were different.

Speeding into downtown Pyongyang, we traveled through blocked-off roads in the heart of the city, past the city's most beautiful buildings—a low standard for sure. Our driver never so much as turned his head or glanced into the rearview mirror at his cargo of CIA leaders. I tried to imagine what this soldier, perhaps a couple of years younger than my son, Nick, might have been thinking. What lies had the regime told this young man about the United States?

Eventually we turned into a tunnel. This led into an entrance to what we later learned was an office of the Korean Workers' Party that Chairman Kim sometimes used for office work and meetings. Along the final quarter mile of the route, the North Koreans had posted a line of stern-faced soldiers, standing at attention in immaculate ranks, gripping massive machine guns. I am confident that I have now seen every North Korean male who stands over six feet three inches tall—a small number to be sure. Due in large part to widespread and severe malnutrition, the average height of a North Korean male is less than five and a half feet.

We stopped, and a North Korean bruiser opened my door. Standing there to escort us inside was Chairman Kim's sister, Kim Yo Jong. She was known to us as a potent figure within the regime, but her presence at this meeting caught our attention. Given the Kim family's history of killing each other, we couldn't be sure who we'd see.

We walked through massive doors, crossed rooms with high ceilings, and saw lots of dreary Communist art. All the while, martial music played in the background.

Then we saw him.

Chairman Kim, ever the showman, was standing at the end of a long red carpet, wearing his signature black Mao suit before a brilliant orange wall. The colors and the lights created the appearance of a halo above his head—something he was the least deserving person on earth of wearing. The epic setting and heavy theater caused my mind to flash back to President Trump's stage entrance at the Republican Convention in 2016, one adorned with backlighting and a smoke machine, before he introduced his wife, Melania. The language of power and image is universal, and leaders in both democracies and dictatorships put a premium on it. The world's worst dictator greeted me with a smile. I was determined not to smile back, not with North Korean cameras everywhere.

This small, sweating, evil man tried to break the ice with all the charm you would expect from a mass murderer. "Mr. Director," he opened, "I didn't think you'd show up. I know you've been trying to kill me." My team and I had prepared for this moment, but "a joke about assassination" was not on the list of "things he may say when he greets you." But I was, after all, director of the CIA, so maybe his bon mot made sense.

I decided to lean in with a little humor of my own: "Mr. Chairman, I'm still trying kill you."

In the picture taken seconds after that exchange, Kim is still smiling. He seemed confident that I was kidding. Soon the photographers were shooed away. Apart from some security personnel, only Chairman Kim, Andy Kim, Kim Yong Chol, Chairman Kim's interpreter, and I remained. Virtually no one in the world had any idea that this meeting was happening. There was a substantial chance it would end in disappointment and disengagement, perhaps even escalating a nuclear peril to America and the world. But given the way Chairman Kim had been firing off missiles and making threats, the meeting was worth the risk.

LEADERSHIP MEANS TAKING RISKS

For American leaders, risk is ever present. You can't hide from it. The world, as I said when I became secretary of state, is a "mean, nasty" place. America's commander in chief must reduce risks for the American people. Sometimes that means embracing other risks. Knowing which ones to accept requires courage, strength, intellect, and the good Lord's blessings.

When I became the CIA's director, I was determined to help the national security team understand these nuclear risks and help President Trump diminish them. We came into office not a moment too soon. With Donald Trump's election as president, America had found the risk-taker in chief it had long needed—especially in our foreign policy. Before Trump, America's foreign policy priorities had become climate change,

LGBTQ rights, and begging forgiveness for alleged transgressions. In the words of an Obama administration official, we had been "leading from behind."

Indeed, America's situation in the world was not an encouraging one at the close of the Obama-Biden years. While we had largely remained the world's only superpower, we had achieved few true foreign policy victories since the first Gulf War. Our leaders seemed incapable of addressing the geopolitical problems of our time. Our enemies were gaining on us. North Korea, with its improving nuclear arsenal, was just one problem. China had quietly eroded our edge in power, influence, and economic strength, while we kept hoping without cause in its evolution toward democracy, freedom, and true friendship. Iran, the world's largest state sponsor of terror, was more aggressively seeking hegemony in the Middle East, and still proclaiming its desire to wipe Israel off the face of the earth. Russia had marched into Crimea in 2014, with barely a hoot of protest from Washington. Meanwhile, we'd been mired in Afghanistan for nearly two decades, focusing our resources to fight terrorism, not military threats from potential great powers. We had failed to adapt our strategies to conflicts involving technology, currency control, economic power, and cyberwar. More of the same was not going to break any of these trends. Nor could we continue to ignore them.

In many ways, by the final years of the Obama administration, we had lost our tolerance for risk. The costly outcomes of the Iraq and Afghanistan wars discouraged commitments of American military troops around the globe, even as deterrent forces. American diplomats and business leaders worried that a break from a policy of unconditional engagement on China would destroy the American economy. And politicians in Congress avoided hard choices and just kept spending money on the same old weapons and programs. Perhaps most of all, national security experts simply didn't want to hurt their reputations by advocating for actions—such as meeting with our most dangerous adversaries—that were at odds with the American foreign policy establishment's conventional wisdom, even if that wisdom was wrong.

It's always tempting to stick to the status quo as the "safest" option. Yet avoiding risk is quite often more damaging than confronting it is.

That's true in warfare, diplomacy, business, and any other field. Quite simply, nothing can change for the better if you won't accept risk. And it's never in your interest for your foes to believe that you cannot or will not pursue a goal as aggressively as they will. If your opponents know that you have at least the capacity to do something a little wild, it will cause them to recalculate what they think they can get away with.

Passivity is especially deadly for an intelligence service. America must maintain a qualitative edge in its ability to collect intelligence, so that the best possible information guides our military and diplomatic calculations. If you shy away from taking risks, you're giving up inch by inch, mission by mission. Such failure is nearly always justified by the empty refrain of "we'll be bolder next time."

I loved that the CIA was full of doers who didn't mind rolling the dice a bit, especially because we have the biggest stack of chips. I couldn't always say the same about the State Department. I use "rolling the dice" intentionally. It has the connotation of a shot in the dark, but any craps player, or, for that matter, any good Yahtzee pro, knows that rolling the dice delivers a precise set of outcomes. Dice are predictable. You can do the math. In many cases, sound analysis and excellence in operations can give you a known set of odds, too. If you know the odds beforehand, and they favor you, throw the dice. That's what we did.

My service in the Trump administration was aided by the fact that I am by experience a risk-taker. Much of my appetite for taking chances came from my years in the military. Every mission proceeds from an analysis of what is to be gained or lost—and serving in uniform trains you to prepare for some level of attrition in live-fire scenarios. You assume that things will go wrong once you start the mission. This idea of acceptable danger is often anathema to leaders who try to come out of every fight without a scratch.

Risk-taking had also proven to work in one of the biggest challenges of my life: starting the company that would become Thayer Aerospace with three of my best friends from West Point. In 1996, I was working at Williams & Connolly as a junior attorney litigating complex criminal cases, mostly on behalf of major US companies. One day I received a call from Mike Stradinger, who graduated with me in 1986.

"Pomps," he said, using my old nickname, "practicing law sucks. Let's start a business together."

"Strads, what business are you thinking about and with what money?"

He responded, "If you keep getting caught up in the details, this will never work."

I told him I was in.

Risky? Maybe. But we prevailed on two more of our classmates, Ulrich Brechbühl and Brian Bulatao, to join us. We ended up buying a small machine shop at 7330 North Broadway in my mother's hometown of Wichita, Kansas. We borrowed most of the money to get started. Knowing you are on the hook for a big bank loan is a scary feeling. But taking the entrepreneurial plunge comes with a multitude of rewards. Risk-taking is a part of the American character, and we should never lose that advantage.

In public service, I've also taken inspiration from the risk-takers who have come before me. We have all heard the old adage "Nothing ventured, nothing gained." The American republic was founded and secured by the courage of those who took bold plunges. The signers of the Declaration pledged "our lives, our fortunes, and our sacred honor" to one another because they knew that if their just revolution failed, they would all go to the gallows as criminals and traitors. Courage spurred Colonel Jimmy Doolittle to launch his daring bombing raid over Tokyo during World War II, just as Lieutenant Commander Butch O'Hare took on a wave of Japanese bombers by himself to save the aircraft carrier *Lexington*. Corporal Jason Dunham dove on a grenade to save the lives of his fellow US Marines in Iraq in 2004, for which he received the Medal of Honor. We in the Trump administration cannot be spoken of in the same breath as those brave men. But we understood that accepting risks was the only way to keep America from continuing a comfortable but costly glide toward being a second-rate power. That diminished status would be bad for every American.

Fortunately, we had elected a president who was willing to make bold moves to reverse bad foreign policy trends. In turn, he had built a team that refused to get bogged down in conventional ways of thinking. Motivating us was an adherence, as best we could, to the wisdom of the American Founders, who appreciated the tensions of executive command: Lead, but be restrained. Project power, but do not chase trouble. Understand that our nation is exceptional, but not perfect. Were there risks involved in putting America first? Every day. But our country is worth it. That's why I fought so hard for the America I love.

FROM CONGRESS TO THE CIA

When I met Congressman Mike Rogers over a beer at an Army-Navy football game in December 2010, never in my wildest dreams did I imagine that I would one day lead that critical Easter diplomatic mission to Pyongyang. I wasn't even officially a congressman yet; I would be sworn in to represent the people of south-central Kansas on January 3, 2011. As a former Army officer, I thought I'd be a good fit to handle national security issues as a member of the Intelligence Committee. So I told Congressman Rogers, then the chairman of the House Permanent Select Committee on Intelligence, that I was the right man for the job. Mike was polite about it, but he essentially, very politely, replied, "Yeah, you and everyone else."

Despite this rebuff, I kept at it during my first term, learning the issues and building my case. As luck would have it, in 2013, a spot opened up for one new Republican on the committee. Speaker of the House John Boehner filled it with yours truly. John gets a bad rap sometimes, but there's no doubt about his love of country and home state of Ohio, as well as his gifts for navigating complex political environments. I'll never forget when there was a piece of legislation that Speaker Boehner regarded as essential. Thirty or forty Republicans, including me, had decided not to vote for it. In the wee hours of the morning before the vote, around one thirty, I received a phone call summoning me to the Capitol. When I arrived in the speaker's grand office about a half an hour later, John was in his usual back-corner spot, where he liked to hold court, drink red wine, and smoke cigarettes.

"Mikey," he sighed, "I understand you're voting against me."

"No, Mr. Speaker, not against you. I'm voting against the spending bill. This is a bad piece of legislation. We're spending too much money."

Unamused by my quaint distinction, he said, "Mike, why do you think I put you on the Intelligence Committee?"

I was smart enough to know his question was actually a statement. I cracked an impish smile and said, "John, I assumed it was because of my good looks and smarts."

He laughed. "I need your vote. Get the f——out of here."

I thanked him for his time and went back down the hall. I appreciated the fact that he sent his message but didn't twist my arm. Ultimately, I voted no the next day, but that encounter gave me a better appreciation of how difficult it is to lead and achieve results in the face of political complexity. The bill I voted against was as good as it could get given the makeup of the House and the grandstanding that would follow its passage. The speaker had a tough job. A junior member of the House, not so much.

Even though I couldn't vote with him on that occasion, I don't think John regretted putting me on the Intelligence Committee, as he would later include me on the Benghazi Committee. I worked my tail off, and I'm sure I drove the CIA and other intelligence agencies crazy. I always wanted more from them: more briefings, more documents, more materials. I logged plenty of hours reading classified intelligence in the secure rooms in the basement of the Capitol. My goal was to round out my understanding of America's challenges and the most effective ways to respond to them. Just as importantly, I was trying to gain a deeper understanding of how decisions are made, both in our country and among our allies and our adversaries. I wanted to know how to effectively reduce and manage risk to American lives. Those long hours taught me to recognize good intelligence analytic work, as well as to know that not every piece of analysis was politically neutral or well-reported. I had zero understanding of how important that knowledge would one day prove to be.

Then, out of nowhere, that experience truly mattered. I had just been reelected to my fourth term in Congress, on Tuesday, November 8, 2016—the same day Donald Trump was elected president. No one but Susan and I knew at the time that I intended that race to have been my last. Years earlier, she and I had agreed that if we were blessed to win our first campaign, then somewhere between six and ten years in Congress seemed right. By this time, we had concluded that I would run in 2016, complete that term, and then head back to real life: back to Kansas, back to our church and family and friends in Wichita, and back to earning a living in the world of free markets and economic risk-taking.

On Sunday, November 13, I received a call from Vice President–Elect Mike Pence. I knew Mike from his time in Congress. During his final term, which was my first, his office was nearly straight across the hall from mine. From time to time, we would walk to votes together when the bells at Cannon 107 rang. He was a senior member from Indiana; I was a backbencher from Kansas. Our wives had been members of the same Bible study group. While we weren't close, he was always willing to lend wisdom and advice, and we shared a conservative, midwestern vision of America. He went off to be governor in Indiana and I hadn't spoken to him until the summer of 2016, when his team asked me to brief him on national security topics for his debate against Tim Kaine, the Democratic senator from Virginia who was Hillary Clinton's running mate.

"Mike," he began, "if we found the right thing for you, would you be willing to join the administration?"

Humbling. Flattering. Surprising.

"Mr. Vice President–Elect, you may recall that I campaigned very hard for Senator Rubio to be the next president. And I just spent $1.5 million being reelected myself."

Pence stopped me mid-thought and reiterated the same question: "If we found the right thing for you, would you be willing to join the administration?"

Easy answer. "Of course, Mr. Vice President–Elect. It would be an honor."

He gave his thanks and hung up. I thought next to nothing of this three-minute phone call. At that time, there were so many names being thrown around and so much noise surrounding every senior position that it was impossible to know which conversations were serious and which were done as box-checking exercises.

That same evening, I received a call from Reince Priebus, the man who would become President Trump's first White House chief of staff. His line of questioning was nearly identical.

"Mike, if we found the right opportunity for you, would you be willing to join the administration?"

I said yes, he said thanks, and the call ended. While I told Susan
about the short calls, I thought little about them.

On Monday morning, Pence called again. "Mike, how about CIA
director?"

Did I hear that right?

I don't recall my precise response, but I know I believed that it would
be a great fit. The CIA desperately needed good leadership. The director
at the time, John Brennan, was a total disaster, more than I even knew
at the time. The call lasted less than two minutes, with me telling Pence
I'd be thrilled to speak further about that opportunity. I told Susan that
it looked like I might be considered to run the CIA. We laughed, fully
expecting that even if the vetting continued, a dozen other people were
working the phones to get that plum assignment. I didn't even know who
I'd call if I'd wanted to do so.

It's hard to convey how odd it seemed that I was being considered to
be Donald Trump's CIA director. First, I had never met President-Elect
Trump. Second, during the primaries, I had supported the presidential
campaign of Senator Marco Rubio of Florida. I had known Rubio for a
few years, respected him a great deal, thought he would be a great president, and believed he could win the general election. Third, I was a white
guy from Kansas—the administration wasn't going to rack up any diversity brownie points there. Fourth, there were several capable leaders out
there with more intelligence experience than I had. Finally, President-
Elect Trump was skeptical of the federal bureaucracy in general and of
the intelligence community in particular. Would he pick someone like
me, who believed that sound American national security leadership entailed empowering high-risk espionage and clandestine operations?

The only time I had been in a room with Trump was during the
primaries. I was set to speak on behalf of Senator Rubio at a Republican
caucus in Wichita. Several thousand people crowded into the convention
center on a Saturday morning, after Trump had held a rally across the
street. I was supposed to speak third, after Ted Cruz and Trump—an order based on how we drew lots the night before. When I arrived, the state

party chairman came up to me sweating and broke some news: "Mike, you'll be speaking first."

"Why?" I said. "I drew for third."

"Yes, but Trump says he will not go on stage if he doesn't get to speak last."

I immediately got the joke and replied, "I guess he doesn't get to speak?" In the end, I spoke first. I let it rip. When the nomination was Trump's, I worked hard for him. I voted for him, and to this day, I remain convinced that his presidency put America in a radically better place than one commandeered by Hillary Clinton would have.

Two years later, standing in the Oval Office, Trump said to me (the first time he'd ever mentioned it), "Mike, you were a mean son of a bitch that day."

"Mr. President, when I'm in a fight, I'm all in. I've done that for two years for you and America now, too."

"That you have, my Mike. That you have." No higher praise. I was also glad to have earned a favorable nickname: the president often called me "My Mike." I still don't completely understand why he chose this un-usual locution, which he has also used with others. But it was better than many other nicknames Donald Trump has bestowed on people. Perhaps, one day, I'll get an updated moniker.

My work in the 2016 primary gave the president a stock answer whenever we disagreed on an issue: "Oh, yeah, you're the Rubio guy." I would often respond by saying, "Oh, yeah, you're the Hillary guy," as he had given her numerous campaign contributions. He would always break into a small smile.

That was all in the future, however. Back in 2016, the remote chance of becoming CIA director was a lot to think about, but for the time being, I had other business to attend to. I had just been reelected myself, and my team and I continued to prepare for year-end congressional duties and the new term that would commence in January. It would be the first time in my career that Republicans controlled both the legislative and executive branches. There would be opportunities to do new good work.

But on Tuesday morning, a call from a young lady with the presi-dential transition team directed my attention back to this fast-moving interview process. "Congressman, I'm calling to see if you are available to be in Bedminster on Saturday to meet with President-Elect Trump?" I was not then aware that Bedminster was his golf club in New Jersey.

With zero consideration of my actual schedule for Saturday, I blurted out, perhaps too eagerly, "Of course!"

"Excellent, plan on being in Bedminster late morning."

I said, "I'll be there, but someone is going to have to tell me where Bedminster is."

Her response was perfect. "If you can't find Bedminster, I don't think you're qualified for the job I understand you're coming to interview for."

"Touché. I'll find it." We both had a good laugh.

It was an exciting moment, but my hopes were still muted. I was pleased to have the courtesy of a meeting, but I still figured Trump would select someone else. I also believed it would be a good chance to share with him my thoughts on two very important topics that would loom over our next four years together: China and Iran.

One thing was for sure: the personnel team was in a hurry. Less than two weeks after Trump's election, the media was asking why he had not announced any cabinet nominees. Those questions may have produced another call that came later that same day, again from the transition team's scheduler. "If you're on the East Coast, Mr. Trump would like you to meet him tomorrow at Trump Tower. Can you make it?"

"I know I can find Trump Tower," I joked. "I'll be there."

So it began. Susan and I took the train to New York City early the next morning and hung out at a friend's office for a few hours. We had called our son, Nick, who worked in the city, and delivered a cryptic message: "Your mom and I are headed to New York so that I can speak with Mr. Trump about a potential role on his team. More in person." Shortly before two in the afternoon, I arrived at the corner of Fifty-Seventh Street and Fifth Avenue to scout out my post, just as any good soldier or case officer always does. Susan headed to St. Patrick's Cathedral to pray. We were both in position. No one recognized me as I walked past the enormous amount of media thronging the now-famous pink-marbled and gold-trimmed lobby.

An assistant brought me to the Trump Organization executive suite, which now doubled as the nerve center for the man who would soon be the most powerful individual on the planet. As I waited in a receiving area, I was greeted by Donald Trump Jr., Steve Bannon, and Kellyanne Conway as each of them passed in and out of the reception area. They all said, "You're going to be great." Huh. It was almost as if I had already been selected.

After some time, I was led back into the inner sanctum. The president-elect—flanked by Jared Kushner and Steve Bannon—didn't get up from his desk. He was holding court, with Mike Pence on the phone. When he saw me enter the room, he blurted out, "Mike, how come you are so wrong on Russia? We should try to be nice to them! Maybe it's because you're an Army guy." He would go on to say a variation of this same line about US-Russia relations in public innumerable times.

He had clearly been briefed about me at least a bit, so I replied: "Sir, I'm not wrong on Russia. Putin is a very smart, bad guy." It was risky to push back against the views of a potential new boss, but that exchange of banter helped. We actually agreed that Putin was a bad guy, but that we should try to find a way to coexist peacefully with Russia. Little did either of us know that Hillary Clinton's smear campaign that led to the "Russia Hoax" was going to make that effort damn near impossible.

The ensuing discussion on national security matters was fine, but the conversation really became interesting when the president-elect asked me to name my favorite general. I replied in an instant, "I'm from Kansas, so General Eisenhower is my favorite."

Bannon couldn't help himself and chimed in. "That's bullshit! Who's your favorite Civil War general?"

Again, quickly, I said, "Easy! Sherman. In fact, we named our dog General W. T. Sherman." In 1864, Union general William Tecumseh Sherman led a famous slash-and-burn march in Georgia from Atlanta to Savannah, destroying everything in his path to break the Confederacy's will to fight. It was brutal. Sherman took lots of risk, and he never gave an inch when it mattered.

At this point, at least in Bannon's eyes, he had a winner. He said that they had built their campaign on a paper he wrote about Sherman and the need to be willing to burn it all down to achieve the strategic objective of reclaiming American greatness. I think Mr. Trump enjoyed my response, too, and I pulled out my phone to show them a picture or two of our golden retrievers, just to make the point. "Let's talk again soon," said Trump.

As I left Trump Tower on Wednesday afternoon, I assumed that there would be other interviewees and that I would hear back in a week or two. Dinner with our son that night left us all dizzy with the thought of the potential burden and opportunity. Still, we didn't share the fact of the interview with anyone else.

The next morning, I was back at work in my congressional office, meeting with constituents. In the middle of a discussion on farm policy, my phone lit up with a call from a 212 area code—New York City. Rudely and uncharacteristically, I excused myself to take the call inside a little closet at the back of my congressional office. I don't think I'd interrupted a conversation with constituents even once in the previous five years.

"Hello, this is Mike."

"Hi, Mike, this is the Donald. How'd you like to be my CIA director?" It wasn't so much a question as a confirmation.

"Sir, it would be a privilege to serve America in that role."

"Jeff!" barked Trump, apparently to Jeff Sessions, who was sitting with him in Trump Tower. "We have offer and acceptance; he can't back out now!" Then, turning back to me, he continued.

"Mike, someone will call you later. It's going to be great and wild!" Then he hung up.

I called Susan to tell her that it appeared we were indeed headed for great, important, and wild times. I was going to be the nominee to become the director of the CIA—something I told her she could tell Nick and no one else. I returned to the office, finished my meeting, and then asked Jim Richardson, my highly capable chief of staff, to clear the calendar as best he could for the rest of the day. That evening, the media-affairs folks from the transition team asked for a biography they could use, as the plan was to make the announcement the next morning at eight o'clock. We sent them a document that could not have been more than one or two pages.

Once the news popped, I called a friend at a law firm that has helped other Republican nominees through the confirmation process. Within half an hour, I got a call back from his law partner who would guide me through it. His first question was "Can you send me the paperwork you submitted for the transition team's due diligence so I can review it?" I told him I had already sent him the entirety of what I sent the transition team—my publicly available biography. He asked if I was kidding. When I replied in the negative, he asked, "Did they at least interview you and ask you the sex, drugs, and rock 'n' roll questions?"

"Nope."

The transition team had done virtually no vetting on me. I could almost hear the lawyer's beads of sweat dripping when he said: "I'm on my way over to see you now. I'm going to need a few hours with you. Where are you?" The transition team was, at this point, moving so quickly that it had relied only on the votes of Kansas's Fourth District and my time on the Intelligence Committee to inform its risk calculus on my confirmability. Less than forty-eight hours after the interview and less than five full days after my first conversation with Pence, I was the president-elect's choice to lead America's CIA. While I still don't know for sure, I believe I was the only person interviewed for the job. Talk about an appetite for risk.

I did a quick count of votes in the Senate and fully expected I'd be confirmed if I didn't screw it up. I also returned to my military training and began to develop my plan for how I would lead the CIA. Even writing this brings back the daunting nature of the task. I'd read histories of the CIA, met hundreds of officers while serving on the Intelligence Committee, and loved spy movies. But to run the world's premier spy outfit was a completely different kettle of fish. I began to gather books on Wild Bill Donovan, the founder of the Office of Strategic Services (OSS). The OSS, founded during World War II, was the precursor to the CIA and represented the core mission of collecting and delivering critical information, as well as conducting espionage operations around the world. I began to think about building a team that was loyal to America and ruthlessly focused on excellence. I would seek to help crush our adversaries by taking informed risks.

JOHN BRENNAN'S RISK-AVERSE CIA

My confirmation hearing began on January 12, 2017—eight days before President Trump's inauguration. It's a credit to the American system that we strive to preserve continuity in our national security operations, because America's enemies are always looking to exploit gaps. I was grateful to have one of Kansas' most honored sons, the retired Senator Bob Dole, introduce me to his former colleagues. He and Elizabeth were among the very first to call me after my nomination. On the phone, they sounded like two happy grandparents: "Another great Kansan leading our nation; we are so happy for you and Susan!" they gushed. They are two of the most lovely public servants I've ever met. As a couple, Susan and I have sought to model and honor them.

Senator Dole had become a friend after I was first elected to the House. Even in 2016, at age ninety-three, he asked me to accompany him to the Kansas State Fair as part of his work to help candidates across the state. Not even the brutal summer heat could sap his desire to shake the hands of patriots in uniform. After eight long hours of greeting well-wishers, he said, "Mike, let's go find the military recruiting booth." To his last breath, he never ran out of energy, and he never stopped believing in America and her people as a force for good.

I wish every senator who questioned me that day had been as nice to me as Bob Dole was. I received tough inquiries about protecting national security and honoring civil liberties. What limits should be applied to collecting intelligence on Americans? Should the federal government have access to encrypted information in the name of national security? Would the Agency abide by the *US Army Field Manual*'s prescribed, lawful interrogation techniques? It was here that I made my first stand to affirm a Trump administration foreign policy rooted in the American tradition. I told the Senate that I would always honor Americans' constitutional rights, follow the laws of the land, and ask Congress to change those laws if I felt they weren't serving our people well.

Some questions were stupid. Instead of asking meaty questions about how I might confront our adversaries, Senator Kamala Harris first parroted a media-pleasing query about the Russia Hoax. Then she tried to cast me as a bigot over my voting record against gay marriage, pretending she was concerned I would treat our LGBTQ workforce differently. I shot her down by saying, "I can't imagine putting in place any policy that was discriminatory with respect to any employee." Then she wanted to know, in not so many words, if I would make a priority of analyzing climate change as a driver of instability. Really, she was just trying to burnish her own green street cred. My answer: "It seems my role is going to be so different and unique from that. It is going to be to work alongside warriors, keeping Americans safe." What a wasteful use of a seat on a committee dedicated to protecting America.

Some senators tried to take me down by claiming I didn't have enough experience. And Senator Ron Wyden of Oregon tried to scotch the nomination over my alleged support of "torture." But eleven days after my hearing, and two days into the Trump administration, I was confirmed by a 66–32 margin, with two abstentions. Telling the truth and standing on constitutional principles have never let me down. I don't think they ever will.

My time on the Intelligence Committee showed me the talent and dedication of the team at CIA headquarters in Langley, Virginia, and around the globe. Yet one of the earliest conclusions I drew after being on the job a while was that the most skilled and stealthy intelligence service in the world was simply far too risk averse. Though Brennan was a former career CIA analyst, he publicly said, "We don't steal secrets." What? Nor did he like the word *spy*. Let me tell you something: if you are a clandestine service officer tasked with breaking into a vault of documents in a Middle Eastern country in order to expose a lethal nuclear program, I am quite confident that the country whose materials you are taking thinks you are a "spy" who is "stealing secrets." I realized that if the world's most elite clandestine service was too timid to merely *describe* our work in terms known to everyone, surely the team was also being too conservative on actions that no one would ever know about. It was important to America to fix this problem. Operating according to the eastern elite's penchant for nicety, order, and Marquess de Queensberry rules is dangerous for an espionage organization. To be timid and weak when evil roams the earth would be a dereliction of duty.

There were other problems, too. At the time I became director, Brennan had just completed an overhaul of the Agency, spearheaded by McKinsey & Co.—the same consulting firm that counts the CCP as a client and previously advised certain pharmaceutical companies to boost sales in ways that helped fuel the opioid crisis. The firm's report provided Brennan with a basis to defang the greatest spy agency the world has ever known. In exchange for what were massive taxpayer-funded fees, and with the Agency's approval, McKinsey spent nearly two years redrawing lines on the organizational chart to make sure that nothing happened before convening an interagency panel. While pockets of OSS-style pugilists and risk-takers remained, they were largely exiled to the basement in Langley to conduct historical reviews of past agency failures. I was determined to put them back on the field.

Finally, a top-down ideological campaign led by Brennan himself had wasted our people's focus and resources on the wrong things. Brennan has publicly admitted he previously voted for the Communist Party USA, and he was a de facto commissar of the progressive movement as director. Rainbow lanyards? Check. Diversity-and-inclusion bullet points in nearly every slide deck? Check. Support for the terrorists in Palestine? Check. Raise climate change to the number one intelligence-collection priority? Check. Despite being a career CIA officer, Brennan was wildly political.

The irony is that eventually I was accused of being too political as director, just because I was a Republican member of the House prior to taking the job. Sign me up for diversity, because I want excellence everywhere; I want the brilliant kid from Appalachia who can fix anything and the female wrestling champion from inner-city Chicago who fears nothing. But the CIA's broader culture had begun to rot from within and suffer mission drift, and it had to be fixed. This isn't partisan. Director Leon Panetta— a Democrat, who, like me, served in the House of Representatives— is rightly one of the most admired and effective directors in the history of the Agency. He ran the organization with a clear sense of purpose and always had the back of a team whose jobs can be tougher than old leather. This is what matters on the seventh floor at Langley, and I turned to him for his thoughts on how I could be effective. Just as Panetta had been focused on serving his president and his country, so would I be.

SHIFTING THE AGENCY TO EMBRACE RISK

I shared the president's concerns that our adversaries no longer feared what America could do *to* them and that our friends didn't know what we would do *with* them. Taking risks meant there would be failures. I worked tirelessly to make sure that those inevitable failures fell on me and not the president. I could be fired and blamed when things went wrong. To maintain effective American leadership, he could not. We had to develop a much higher tolerance for risk. I knew the American people would respect this approach if we did it right. Americans had just entrusted the presidency to a man who had pledged to shake things up. After eight years of President Obama's foreign policy of "Apologize First," they had told us to put "America First." They had given our administration the green light to aggressively and unapologetically pursue American interests.

To start, I knew our patriots at the CIA needed direction from the president. The main media narrative during my time as the nominee to run the Agency asserted that Trump hated the intelligence agencies. I knew better. I knew Donald Trump would love the CIA's clandestine service. He might not love Comey or Brennan or Clapper—second the motion—but would love the guys who operated around the world in secret on America's behalf. I wanted those warriors to know that, too.

So, one day in early December at Trump Tower, I told the president-elect that he was going to love the CIA and that he should visit its headquarters on Inauguration Day. He loved the idea and said, "Done." I told Bannon, and he thought it was great too. I then went and told Priebus, who was managing the opening hours of the administration. He was not happy: "You did what? He can't go to Langley on Inauguration Day!" I had apparently committed a faux pas by asking the president-elect before asking the chief of staff–elect. In any event, we compromised and agreed that President Trump would go to Langley on Saturday morning—the day after his inauguration. I then shared the plan with the Agency. They resisted: "It's a Saturday; no one will be there . . . How could you commit us to this? You're still just a Congressman." And on and on.

The day before the inauguration, we hit a snag. It became clear that Senator Wyden was going to use a procedural tool to prevent me from being sworn in on Friday afternoon. That meant that when the president went to Langley on Saturday, I'd still be just the congressman from Kansas. I told Meroë Park, the number three official at the Agency and the person who was slated to be acting director on Saturday. She said we needed to cancel. "Too late," I said. Park again said she didn't think we could get any CIA officers to be at Langley on the weekend. I said, "Well, you could be right, but send out an email inviting anyone who wants to attend a gathering with the president to do so. First come, first served." She did that, and hundreds of agency officers signed up. I knew that Trump and the CIA clandestine service were a match made in heaven— personalities who weren't afraid to let it rip despite the risks. The event on Saturday was incredibly productive for America and our team. The president met privately with the senior leaders. "Mike is my guy," he said. "Tell him what you need. I'll get it for him and for you."

This attitude was in marked contrast to that of the standoffish and risk-averse Obama, who, through his henchwoman, National Security Advisor Susan Rice, had killed dozens and dozens of important operations. In fact, from her small office in the White House, Rice had become a shadow CIA director, without whose approval no action moved forward. Her knee-jerk dislike for espionage created a verb among CIA officers. Whenever something risky was on the table, someone might say, "No, we can't do that. It will be SR'd." "SR," of course, stands for Susan Rice. It should not be forgotten that two CIA officers perished on her watch during the Benghazi disaster, and she proceeded to lie to Americans about the events of that tragic night and the actions of those American heroes.

On his first Saturday as president, when he walked into the hall that is known around the world for its CIA logo on the floor, the assembled officers cheered. They loved him. President Trump, hearing the ovation and seeing the horde of cameras, treated the event a bit too much like one of his campaign rallies. The press pounced on him, saying he had dishonored the fallen heroes by speaking in front of the wall of nameless stars commemorating CIA personnel killed in the line of duty. If he did dishonor them, that's my fault, because the president's team chose the location in front of the memorial wall. But none of that should take away from the fact that Trump and our clandestine teams were kindred spirits from day one.

The president reinforced the idea that it was time to be risk-takers once again: "We have not used the real abilities that we have. We've been restrained," he said in his remarks. He added, "We're going to start winning again, and you're going to be leading the charge." It was clear he was issuing a directive—take the gloves off against America's enemies. Now it was my job to translate his vision into action through a bureaucracy composed of thousands of people.

I knew I needed help to implement this vision throughout the organization. The CIA was far bigger than either of the two manufacturing companies I had led, to say nothing of my tank or scout platoons. So I set about finding the right risk-takers. My first hire was my old friend Brian Bulatao. "Friend" is not really the word to describe Brian, who is more like a brother. We first met on July 1, 1982, riding a bus en route to a hazing during our first day as cadets at West Point. He went on to a six-year career in the 82nd Airborne Division. We once boxed each other in our cadet days. I won't tell you who won, but I knew from very personal experience that Brian isn't afraid to hit hard.

Minutes after my nomination to be CIA director hit the news, Brian called. I hadn't told a soul outside my own family and two members of my staff what had transpired over the past few days. Giving me crap as only friends can do, he started out by asking, "Hey Mike, anything new?"

I apologized and told him about the speed with which this had all unfolded. He chuckled and said: "I'm happy for you. You'll be great."

"Not so fast!" I retorted. "There's an upside and a downside for you. The upside is that you can now say you're best friends with the next CIA director, assuming I get confirmed. The downside is that you are going to be my chief operating officer."

Brian asked, "Does the CIA have a COO?"

"No idea, but I'm going to have one. And you are going to be it!"

The correct response to this ridiculous request would be to hang up. Instead, after about two beats, Brian replied: "OK, can you give me till noon? I have to run a couple of traps." A couple of hours later he called back to say he was in. I told him to be ready to start on Inauguration Day.

This wasn't an easy ask. Brian had a family, as well as a great job in Texas he would have to drop almost immediately. Nevertheless, he agreed to serve without even knowing much about what his service would entail. He trusted me, but this was more about Brian being a patriot of the highest order. Whenever I hear people say they don't make them like the Greatest Generation anymore, I point to Brian. Our conversation that day reminded me of my favorite line from the movie *The Town*, starring Ben Affleck and Jeremy Renner as a couple of ne'er-do-wells. Affleck's character says to Renner's: "I'm asking for your help. I can't tell you why, you can never ask me about it after, and it involves hurting people." Renner responds simply, "Whose car we gonna take?" That was Brian and me. No questions. No doubts. Total understanding that if I asked, it mattered. He became one hell of a COO at CIA.

I also needed a deputy director, preferably one who, to paraphrase a biblical concept, was "in" the bureaucracy but not "of" it. I recalled that on a previous congressional visit to Europe, I had met a razor-sharp officer named Gina Haspel. She was aggressive, patriotic, and brilliant. To this day, I joke that I fear only two women: my wife, Susan, and Gina.

I knew Gina's history: three decades at the Agency, all in the clandestine service. Moreover, she had stood with the Agency during the controversies over enhanced interrogation. She even had been punished for her commitment to America in the course of working on this program that saved American lives. I wanted to right that ship and show the Agency that laying it all out for America would not mean professional relegation but in fact be rewarded. My choice of Gina was also a message to the workforce: "We're back in the espionage business." I also had come to know Gina as a conservative's conservative in the way she viewed her life and her duty. I interviewed half a dozen people to be my right hand, but I knew she'd fit our administration better than any of the others. I brought her in to meet the president for the first time, and he loved her, too. The risk-takers were assembling.

CHAPTER 2

PIVOT QUICKLY FROM FAILURE

M r. Director, Director Cohen needs to speak with you immediately."
The call from Yossi Cohen, the head of the Mossad, arrived
shortly after I had stepped off a plane in a European capital. I turned
around and went back onboard, where we had communications equipment suitable for a classified conversation with the leader of Israel's intelligence agency.

The voice on the other end was calm but serious: "Mike, we just had
a team complete a very important mission, and now I'm having a bit of
trouble extracting some of them. Can I get your help?"

Whenever Yossi called, I took it. He did the same for me. In my
mind, it was another Affleck-Renner conversation. I was there to help
our friends, no questions asked, no matter the risks.

My people swung into action across the world. We connected with his
team, and within twenty-four hours we had guided them to safe houses.
Within the next two days, they were back in their home countries without the world ever knowing that one of the most significant clandestine
operations ever conducted was now complete. The team members from
our two countries were now at home with their families, safe and ready
to do it all over again.

This is a story that never could have been told during the Obama
administration, because it wouldn't have happened. The fact that the
United States and Israel were able to pull off such a maneuver reflected
smart risks, close partnerships, and a willingness to pivot quickly from
overarching policy failures.

FIXING OBAMA'S MIDEAST FAILURES

On January 23, 2017, I was sworn in as CIA director. I got to work welcoming smart risks and populating the Agency's ranks with those willing to take them. And I immediately started to assess the various areas where we needed to break from what wasn't working. Time was absolutely of the essence. There were no guarantees of how long I'd last in the job, and I knew there would be plenty of work ahead to roll new policies up the mountains of CIA and federal bureaucracies. Some policies, after careful assessment, proved to be working, and we kept those. But where various initiatives had obviously not yielded results, we had to cut our losses and move on.

I'd learned this lesson over and over again in life. If you make a bad decision, don't get gun-shy or lost in analysis paralysis over another big decision to correct the first one. This is how many businesses go under—they waste time admiring the problem and avoiding embarrassment rather than accepting sunk costs and moving on. In the meantime, their competitors are moving fast, day and night, to steal market share.

I think of one of my favorite teams, the LA Rams. They made a quarterback named Jared Goff the number one overall pick in the draft in 2016. He was fairly successful—even taking them to a Super Bowl—but management judged that, in spite of his lofty draft status and the credibility and money invested in making him the top pick, he was not the guy who would lead them to a championship. In 2021, the team made the hard decision to upgrade at quarterback with a fellow named Matthew Stafford. Much to my delight, the Rams became Super Bowl champions that very next season.

The need to pivot quickly from failure—in this case, the Obama administration's—immediately applied to our Middle East policy. Other than North Korea, the biggest item on my plate in the first days of the administration was helping the team reassert American power in the vacuum the Obama administration had left behind in the region. American support for the 2015 Iran nuclear deal had a ripple effect throughout the region of empowering an adversary. The deal created massive danger for Israel and America, and the Israelis felt that America had betrayed them. Iran couldn't figure out if it was happier about its economy growing after sanctions were lifted or happier that it would have a legal green light to build nuclear weapons in a few short years.

That wasn't all. Iran-backed Syrian dictator Bashar al-Assad had invited Russia to the neighborhood and used chemical weapons on his own people, and Obama had sent a bad signal to America's adversaries by weakly walking back from his own redline there. Half of the Syrian people were either living as refugees in places such as Turkey, Lebanon, and Iraq, as well as Germany, or were displaced inside their own country, creating massive threats to Europe and the region. Iraq and Yemen were Iranian subsidiaries. Lebanon was one, too; Iran's proxy militia Hezbollah had developed and placed thousands of Iranian precision-guided missiles on Israel's northern border. The Gulf States, while trying to appear poised in public, were also frightened by American support for Iran. They were in full-on hedge mode, as their confidence in the United States had sunk to an all-time low.

Our Mideast strategy, therefore, depended on a few key pillars: Build policies that reflect a basic fact—Iran is the Middle East's greatest troublemaker. Restore the relationship with Israel. And create new Gulf-Israeli security partnerships. By pursuing these goals, we sought to diminish risk to the American people from the Iranian regime and jihadist terrorists alike. We sought to stabilize the region and create economic opportunities for Americans in the form of new markets for our businesses and lower energy prices. And most critically, new security ties would mean that fewer American sons and daughters in uniform would have to risk their lives in the bloody sands of the Middle East.

Because of ancient animosities, tribal clashes, differences of faith, raw power politics, and authoritarian rule, rivalries in the region are as common as sand and falafel. Much of America's involvement in many of the region's conflicts has been costly and poorly executed. Our administration didn't want to get America into another protracted military engagement, and we didn't. As CIA director, I was determined to build out knowledge and capabilities that the president could use to achieve American security objectives in the Middle East without committing additional troops to that theater. We would not repeat past failures.

The Mideast mission that demanded our immediate attention was dealing a death blow to the caliphate of the Islamic State in Iraq and Syria (ISIS), the successor network to al-Qaeda in Iraq. Despite the valorous efforts of America's warriors, diplomats, and intelligence agencies since 9/11, radical Islamist cells from Libya to Pakistan, and everywhere else, were still active. When President Obama withdrew troops completely from Iraq in 2011, he allowed ISIS to fill the void. In 2014, as ISIS moved from conquest to conquest, President Obama belittled it as a "JV team." His words demonstrated a combination of ignorance, failed intelligence, and hubris.

Far from incompetent amateurs, ISIS was stacked with diehard, seasoned jihadists, who by 2015 had established a genuine Islamist government that ran schools, collected taxes, and enforced Sharia law in a territory equal in size to that of Great Britain. ISIS extremists were hacking off the heads of Christians and raping non-Muslim women and girls. Gulf leaders were terrified of the caliphate expanding into their countries or inciting their own populations to revolt. ISIS also assaulted Americans and Europeans as its agents radicalized people online and helped orchestrate deadly attacks. Massacres such as those in Paris (130 dead in 2015), Brussels (32 dead in 2016), and Orlando (49 dead in a 2016 ISIS-inspired shooting) were the ghastly results of ISIS's ability to motivate and perpetrate attacks. And war zones in Iraq and Syria proved fertile ground for recruiting impressionable and desperate Muslim men into their fighting ranks.

I'd often heard intelligence professionals speak of the root cause of terrorism as being "disillusioned Muslims." OK, but why do disillusioned Muslims build massive jihadist organizations and conduct mass acts of violence in the name of religion while disillusioned Buddhists and Sikhs seldom do? The networks built around Islamist extremism almost certainly contain young people who are there for kinship in jihadist groups or even for a steady wage. But a nebulous idea of "disillusionment" is not the motivation for terrorism in the name of Islam—a radical form of political Islam is.

The Obama administration eventually woke up to the problem of ISIS, but it still hadn't done enough to beat back the caliphate. In January

2017, ISIS still controlled massive portions of Iraq and Syria. President Trump set a new tone when he spoke about the problem to the CIA team on his first full day as president: "We have to get rid of ISIS," he said. "Radical Islamic terrorism . . . has to be eradicated just off the face of the earth."

Those words set the course for a policy direction of breaking from past failures quickly—and it started with President Trump's willingness to take the risk of delegating and trusting the people who worked for him to make the right call. In March 2017, President Trump gave the CIA additional authorities. We were able to give top jihadi leaders their death wish more quickly. And it wasn't just ISIS killers who we could take out faster. During the Trump years, by my own personal estimation, the administration oversaw the elimination of more than thirty leaders of al-Qaeda and similar jihadist groups, such as Jama'at Nasr al-Islam wal Muslimin in West Africa. Many of those confirmed kills came from good work by my team.

And on the uniformed military side of things, the president, knowing that speed is vital, delegated greater authority to America's commanders to pursue our enemies in the field more aggressively. Day by day, America and her allies in the Global Coalition to Defeat ISIS worked to claw back parts of Iraq and Syria. While the United States continued to supply intelligence, military advice and training, and air support, Kurdish fighters fought on the front lines to defend their homes. Thus, we continued to crush our adversary in concert with our allies. A quick pivot from failure paid off.

CONFRONTING IRAN AT THE CIA

As we put on the brass knuckles for our fight against ISIS, we also took the first steps to pivot from the failed Obama-Biden policy of appeasement and confront the Iranian regime. Task number one for me as CIA director was to make sure we had the tools we needed to take on the ayatollah and his minions. While President Trump stated that regime change was not our mission, and I followed that directive, I knew that putting pressure on the regime would massively increase the possibility of its collapse, and the Iranian people would have a fair shot at governing themselves for real. My mission at the CIA was to collect sound intelligence on what would help drive that change, figure out how to push back on Iranian proxies in the region, and develop ways to undermine the regime's authority.

Overshadowing my mission set was a dispute within the administration. President Trump had promised on the campaign trail to abandon the Iran nuclear deal, signed by Obama in 2015 and known formally by a bland title: the Joint Comprehensive Plan of Action (JCPOA). Regrettably, we did not break from this past failure as quickly as we should have. The president's entire national security team—Secretary of Defense Jim Mattis, Secretary of State Rex Tillerson, and National Security Advisor H. R. McMaster—believed staying in was the right call. Mattis and Tillerson argued to the president that even if the deal wasn't great, withdrawing was too risky, and we might end up in a war. To this CIA director, that sounded exactly like John Kerry, John Brennan, and Joe Biden.

My instinct to never give an inch kicked in. There is a long tradition at both State and Defense of "kicking the can down the road"—putting off the hard decisions and giving one inch at a time, all the while swearing that next time will be different. The JCPOA was unsound policy, and we needed to get out. We couldn't meekly plod along in the deal, promising that eventually we would exit once conditions were right (an objective with moving goalposts if there ever was one). I had worked my tail off trying to stop the deal when I was in Congress. Now that I had even more intelligence to fill out my understanding of it, I became even more convinced we had to break from this failure and get out.

The first step to counter Iran's nuclear threat was tuning out the overwhelmingly pro–nuclear deal analysts at Langley and creating the Iranian Republic Mission Center. This brand-new task force was intentionally named to be only one letter off in its acronym from the Islamic Revolutionary Guard Corps. The IRGC is Iran's elite military unit. But it's also something of a domestic mafia in its brutality and corrupt control over the Iranian economy. I wanted one of the Agency's finest, most seasoned Middle East operators to lead the IRMC, a fellow named Mike, whom I knew came to work every day with a figurative knife in his teeth.

When I told my deputy, Gina, of my plan to choose Mike, she reminded me that many people thought he was an "asshole," "a shithead," and "impossible" to work with. I had known Mike from my time on the House Intelligence Committee, and I could see her point. But I believed he would take appropriate risks to confront Iran, just the kind of invigoration the Iran team needed. Brennan had banished him into bureaucratic oblivion—an action that was as indecent and counterproductive as I could imagine—and Mike was chomping at the bit to get back out on the field. I knew what he had already done for America. I had made up my mind.

When I interviewed him and told him about the task force's mission set, his eyes lit up, confirming he was the right man to lead a fast course correction. But I also wanted to confront him on what I had heard, since he had to build a team: "They tell me you're an asshole, a shithead, and impossible to work with." He smiled and gave a perfect reply: "Mr. Director, I am *not* impossible to work with." I hired him on the spot and never regretted it. We loaded up the team with seasoned operators who had worked on hard targets in Iraq, Afghanistan, and Russia. We identified the regime's vulnerabilities. And we built the capabilities President Trump and future commanders in chief would need to employ to protect America. I pray that work is ongoing.

YOSSI AND ME

The second step in confronting Iran was building out international partnerships. No relationship was more critical than the one America had and must continue to have with Israel and the Mossad. Director Yossi Cohen got that agency's top job by working his way up through the ranks. Unlike me, he was a real spy, with a storied career that began in the early 1980s. Fearless, creative, and charismatic, he had been Prime Minister Benjamin Netanyahu's national security advisor. I knew that his deep relationship with Netanyahu would matter. I also knew that he was eager to meet: for the CIA, the Iranian regime is *a* problem; for the Mossad, it is *the* problem.

We first met in February 2017 at the legendary King David Hotel in Jerusalem, on my first international trip as CIA director. As my wife will confirm, Director Cohen is handsome—he is even known as "The Model Spy" for his good looks. So, when I walked into a conference room for our breakfast meeting, I greeted him with a joke: "You're even better looking than in our surveillance photos of you!" He laughed out loud and replied that I seemed even smarter than he had expected. I could tell right away that I was going to like working with him. We soon got on a first-name basis as "Yossi" and "Mike" rather than "Director Cohen" and "Director Pompeo."

We designed a plan to deliver excellent outcomes for our respective agencies by working in unison. The CIA and Mossad viewed each other with a bit of suspicion, but that's what good intelligence agencies do. Spying is tough. Even your best friends want to know what their friends are up to, and that's understandable. But Yossi and I agreed that our shared work on crushing Iran must be 100 percent complementary.

Later on that trip, I stood with Yossi in front of his senior Iran team. He told them that we were going to work closer together than ever in history: no egos, no secrecy, just teamwork. He said that he would fire anyone who didn't get on board. Then we flew back to Langley, and he and I stood in front of my CIA team and delivered that same message. The teams were thrilled that we had cut through the bureaucracies, provided them with clear commander's intent, and given them the green light to do real espionage. We set the tone that risk-taking would be welcome. This was a monumental and necessary recasting of our relationship from where it had been under the Obama administration.

A few months later, Yossi and I spent a weekend at a CIA training facility, where we plotted more strategy. On the first morning, we laid out the Iran-related projects each of us had been working on separately and the resources each of us could commit to the cause. Our teams had developed a blueprint for action; it was our job to refine it and figure out its execution. Then we spent the afternoon doing James Bond spy stuff: racing and crashing cars and firing exotic weapons. It was certainly fun, but also humbling as it became clear that I had spent my life as a tank commander and machine shop CEO, not as a streetwise operative like Yossi, who outperformed me on the track and at the training range. With my ego only slightly bruised, we spent the remainder of the time mapping our plans. Those two days strengthened the foundation for four years of productive collaboration.

Being men of deep faith also solidified our bonds. Yossi and his wife, Aya, are Orthodox Jews. As evangelical Christians, Susan and I understood that our tradition wasn't just Christian—it was Judeo-Christian. Yossi and I each understood the importance of Israel within our respective faith traditions and why this remarkable land was worth fighting to preserve. Talking with Yossi helped me realize, contrary to the later baying of the media hounds, that being open about my faith life didn't scuttle my efforts on behalf of America—it *strengthened* them. Our abiding respect for one another flowed directly from talking about our imperfect, lifelong journey to honor God. It made the late nights when Yossi and I shared good bourbon and cigars together even more special. During my time in the administration, there would be no more capable partner and, as it turns out, no better friend in the world than Yossi.

While much of the work that Yossi and I did must remain secret, I can tell you that the model we developed has saved countless American and Israeli lives. We were able to build a scaffolding that let President Trump and Prime Minister Netanyahu work with our friends and partners in the region and take risks that, absent this clandestine work, they might not have been able to accept. It was a 180-degree pivot from what had preceded the Trump administration.

NORTH KOREA: ALL-IN RISK-TAKING

The issue on which the Trump administration had to pivot most quickly from past failures was North Korea. We broke from a quarter century of conventional diplomatic strategies that had failed to deliver any meaningful progress—and not a moment too soon, given how Chairman Kim was threatening nuclear disaster. There were plenty of twists and turns along the way.

By the time I became director, the Kim regime—which has ruled North Korea since 1948—had conducted scores of nuclear tests and built increasingly accurate and long-ranging nuclear warhead delivery systems.

These developments had given the regime new confidence to coerce the world into accepting its nuclear capabilities as well as its economic and political demands. The national security threats from North Korea's nuclear program included the launch of a nuclear weapon, the mishandling of one in a catastrophic way, and the spread of materials and technology on the black market in exchange for desperately needed cash.

North Korea had a fairly new and young leader, Chairman Kim Jong Un, general secretary of the Workers' Party of Korea and president of the State Affairs Committee. Despite his relative youth, Chairman Kim had already demonstrated an uncommon level of ruthlessness and ambition. When his father, Kim Jong Il, died in December 2011, it was not a foregone conclusion that Kim Jong Un, then age twenty-seven, would be able to emerge victorious from any power struggle inside the North Korean regime's brutal inner world. Within weeks, however, he had consolidated nearly total power inside his country. He was no pushover.

Whenever I'm asked about the intelligence or skills of a foreign leader, I remind people that no matter the nation or its system of government, a person who rises to the top of the pile usually has demonstrated some level of excellence as an orator, thinker, politician, warrior, or bureaucratic knife fighter. In Kim Jong Un's case, he had wielded the threat of violence against his military commanders so adroitly that North Korea held parades of goose-stepping soldiers in his honor within two months of his father's passing. In 2013, Kim had his uncle executed as a traitor. Kim Jong Un's half-brother, Kim Jong Nam, who some in the West believed would succeed Kim Jong Il, was assassinated in a Malaysian airport by North Korean agents in 2017, following five years on the run. Clearly, Chairman Kim had already mastered the art of maintaining authority by killing his rivals. And he made sure everyone knew he had done it.

I couldn't wait to meet this nice young man.

Between North Korea's growing capabilities and Kim's ruthlessness, the threat of a nuclear confrontation with the country consumed a great deal of the president's time and thought. His preoccupation with this issue was due in part to President Obama's closed-door warning to him that North Korea would pose a "first test"—words that Trump, as president, took seriously. I learned quickly that my briefings on nuclear weapons focused President Trump's attention much more tightly than did other topics, and with good reason. He often said that a tank division can create a bad day for America, but nuclear weapons present an entirely different level and complexity of risk.

The president and his national security team settled on an ambitious objective of the final, fully verified denuclearization of North Korea. I took it as my mission to build a set of clandestine capabilities that could be deployed in case the president found diplomacy and conventional military power insufficient. I was very concerned that the intelligence community had allowed its efforts to understand North Korea, and Asia more broadly, to lapse. We needed two things: First, we needed a collections and operations effort capable of providing sound information and options to the commander in chief. Second, we needed to reallocate resources toward tracking the Chinese—not just inside China but in every country in which they operated. China was essential to the success of any effort to enforce economic sanctions against North Korea. It also had a vested interest in using its relationship with North Korea as a chess piece against the US presence in Asia.

To expand our capabilities, I needed a pipehitter: someone willing to stare down the little demon in Pyongyang holding twenty-five million North Koreans and, just as importantly, four Americans hostage. I asked around and discovered that the perfect person for this role, Andy Kim, a North Korea ace, had just retired four months ago. I asked him to return and promised that we would build a massive campaign under his leadership. I promised that he would have a direct line to me and Deputy Director Haspel. Of course, the mission meant Andy would have to postpone his retirement to work for the country one more time. After I made my pitch, Andy deadpanned, "Will you be the one to tell my wife?"

With Andy at the helm of the Korea Mission Center, some of the Agency's finest leaders, operators, and analysts developed intelligence to share with the entire world in support of a new diplomatic initiative. When North Korea spent the first few months of 2017 launching a barrage of missiles, the Trump administration decided to bring them to the negotiating table by imposing the most crushing set of diplomatic and economic pressures the country had ever felt—an effort that we knew only

the United States could lead. The Japanese were only somewhat supportive of the idea of a pressure campaign, at least in private, and the South
Koreans endlessly emphasized all carrots and no sticks. It was up to us.

So we threw out the old playbook and began putting the screws to
the regime. Beginning in the spring of 2017, thanks to a diplomatic
campaign constructed by Secretary Tillerson, the United Nations—
including Russia and China—unanimously began to implement sanctions that would deprive the regime of revenue from exports such as oil,
coal, and seafood. We also constricted the regime's ability to confiscate
wages from North Korean laborers the country had sent to work abroad
in slavish conditions.

The CIA's job was to produce information we could share with other
countries to let them know what North Korea was doing and the areas
in which each country needed to improve sanctions enforcement. It was
disheartening to know that the North Korean people, already emaciated
and oppressed, would be feeling some effect of the campaign. But the
truth is that while the ordinary people starve, thieving regime elites in
Pyongyang grab almost all external revenues to sustain their own lavish
lifestyles. If their leaders were miserable because they ran short on Grey
Goose vodka and BMWs, all the better. We knew that if we could put
enough stress on North Korean leaders, they would beg for mercy. It
was also a key opportunity to gauge Xi Jinping's willingness to solve the
North Korean problem and work with us on nonproliferation issues. It
came as no surprise that we ultimately expended enormous diplomatic
energy urging the Chinese to plug their leaky sanctions enforcement.

In June 2017, the North Koreans gave us even more motivation to
succeed. A young American named Otto Warmbier, who had been imprisoned inside North Korea for seventeen months, was returned to his
family in Ohio in a vegetative state. He died less than a week later. I was
infuriated when I discovered the North Koreans had the audacity to bill
the United States for the costs of Otto's medical "care" inside North Korea. At the CIA, I convened the leadership of the Korea Mission Center
for an emotional meeting. We vowed to avenge his death. His family and
America deserved it.

Meanwhile, things were heating up publicly, too. In August 2017,

President Trump made his famous statement that if North Korea continued to threaten the United States, the country would be "met with fire and fury like the world has never seen." North Korea responded to the "fire and fury" talk by announcing that it was entertaining an attack on the US territory of Guam. Later that week, Trump leaned in again: "If [Kim] does something in Guam, it will be an event the likes of which nobody's seen before, what will happen in North Korea."

A month later, the president kept pouring it on with a brilliant speech at the UN General Assembly: "Rocket Man is on a suicide mission for himself and his regime," he said from the grand platform. Short. Crisp. Clear. Factual, not bellicose. The next week, the president went to Huntsville, Alabama, and reiterated his position: "We can't have madmen out there shooting rockets all over the place." Kim responded in his 2018 New Year's Day address: "The entire United States is within range of our nuclear weapons, a nuclear button is always on my desk. This is reality, not a threat." This in fact *was* a threat, and the president was not at all happy at being threatened publicly. Like night follows day, he counterpunched with a tweet: "North Korean Leader Kim Jong Un just stated that the 'Nuclear Button is on his desk at all times.' Will someone from his depleted and food starved regime please inform him that I too have a Nuclear Button, but it is a much bigger & more powerful one than his, and my Button works!"

While Secretary Tillerson urged calm, I thought the strategy of matching Kim's incendiary rhetoric was brilliant. No other administration would ever have done this. We could see that North Korean senior leaders were surprised by it, and it actually had the effect of settling Kim down—in the months following the UN meeting, North Korea conducted only one missile test. Our language was not just for Kim either. Xi Jinping, the ayatollah, and Vladimir Putin also needed to know that America was back in the game and willing to take risks. To borrow a line from one of my favorite movies, *Watchmen*, "I'm not locked in here with you" was effectively our message. "You're locked in here with me."

But even amid these verbal salvos, we left the door open for negotiations. The president, always willing to break from convention for the good of the country, decided that he was open to meeting Chairman

Kim personally, something no US president had ever done. Some members of the national security team discouraged it, fearing, among other things, that we would be legitimizing a rogue regime through high-level diplomatic contact. But the world already knew Kim was a bloodthirsty toad. If granting him a little "legitimacy" lowered the possibility of a nuclear attack or mishap, it was worth the risk. I'm confident most Americans would see it the way we did.

We also had our detractors among Democrats and the self-appointed elites of the foreign policy establishment, who worried that the president and his fiery tweets were undiplomatic. President Trump and I would often read these critiques and chuckle that many of the same national security elites who criticized us were the very people whose diplomatic failures had allowed North Korea to develop a nuclear program in the first place. Take Richard Haass, former State Department director of policy planning in the Bush administration and today the president of the Council on Foreign Relations. The Bush administration's "Six-Party Talks" with North Korea accomplished nothing, but that didn't stop Sir Richard, whom I otherwise like, from belittling our efforts: "Effectiveness is not the word that comes to mind," he sniffed. Yet his preference for having midlevel diplomats engage in endless rounds of negotiations for three successive administrations had allowed the North Korean threat to grow like a weed. It was time to pivot from past failures. If accusations of diplomatic unorthodoxy were our cross to bear as the result of trying to deliver outcomes for the American people, then so be it. I'll take that over respectable mediocrity any day.

One day, near the end of 2017, the president requested that I stay back alone after a briefing in the Oval Office. He asked me, "Do we have a way to communicate with the North Koreans?" In other words, did we have a communications channel to get a message to Chairman Kim? I confirmed that we did. "Good, call them," he said. "Tell them you want to come see them."

I sent the message and waited for an answer. A few weeks later, I informed President Trump that the North Koreans had replied that they would consider my visit, but they had laid down a few preconditions: Bring only a tiny team. Keep the visit fully clandestine. And provide them with what we would say in talks ahead of time. We met the first two requests, but not the third. We responded only by saying, basically, "You'll like our ideas."

Pulling off the operational aspect of this mission was uncommonly complex. With no State Department presence inside North Korea to prepare for the visit, we had to roll with whatever the North Koreans would decide to do once we were on the ground. Not that we would have enlisted State's help, anyway. This had to be a secret mission with no leaks to the press, and it's not easy to keep a cabinet member's travel out of the news. Andy and I therefore decided early on to cut out the rest of the national security team except for briefing National Security Advisor H. R. McMaster a few days before departure. I told President Trump that's how we intended to proceed, but also asked whether Secretary Tillerson ought to know about the trip. "Why would we tell Rex?" he shot back. "What's he going to do? He screwed up the Otto Warmbier thing with them already." I honored his direction until before I departed, as I was certain that Tillerson—and his pal Secretary Mattis—likely would have already known. After all, Mattis's department was providing our team the plane to get me to Pyongyang.

As the logistical plan came together and we set the date for Easter weekend 2018, I spent much of that winter and early spring building a negotiation strategy. Andy fed me a steady diet of all the information we had on Kim himself and previous failed negotiations, and I devoured all of it. We knew that after almost seventy years of the regime justifying totalitarian control, global isolation, and mass destitution, Kim would need a credible explanation for massive changes to sell to his military brass, who were true believers in clinging to nuclear weapons as the sine qua non for regime survival.

The reality that I would soon set foot on North Korean soil really sank in when a South Korean delegation visited the White House in March 2018 and passed a message to President Trump that Chairman Kim wanted to meet with him. The first step to achieving that meeting would be a successful visit on my end. No pressure.

Finally, the big day came. I was to leave early on Good Friday and, as we joked, "return to the US on the third day." It was the first time, but not the last, that the death and resurrection of Jesus Christ would provide cover for action. In my final in-person conversation with President Trump before I left, I reminded him that this was a very secret trip—*hint hint*. He predicted word of it would leak like everything else. But to my great surprise, it was one of the few missions in which I personally participated over four years that did not get into the media.

As I was turning to walk out of the Oval Office, President Trump asked me one more thing.

"Have you spoken to Dennis Rodman about Kim?"

I looked back at him, and we both grinned. I said I hadn't, but that I was nevertheless well-prepared for the mission. He said: "Oh, you should call him! He loves me, and he knows Chairman Kim really well." Trump, of course, knew the former NBA star from their time together on *The Apprentice*, and Rodman had traveled to North Korea several times for basketball exhibitions. I took the directive to speak with Rodman as an order and began to head out. Just as I was leaving, the president shouted behind me: "Make sure to call him before noon! He's usually drunk or stoned after that."

Unfortunately, I was unable to reach Mr. Rodman before I departed. But as it turns out, he had spent more time with Chairman Kim than had any other American, and he had provided us with the most detailed knowledge of Chairman Kim we had in our collection, including many insights about Kim's personality. And on a related note, one day I am going to publicly do an imitation of President Trump doing an imitation of Dennis Rodman doing an imitation of Chairman Kim. Yes, that really happened.

At some point during the Trump administration, I surpassed The Worm, as Rodman was known in his playing days, as the American record holder for the most time spent with Chairman Kim. As a guy who loved to play basketball as a boy, I'd always dreamed I would break the records of NBA greats. This wasn't exactly what I had in mind.

DIALOGUE WITH A DICTATOR

A long plane ride across the Pacific Ocean later, in Pyongyang, I met Chairman Kim face to face. Our session lasted for hours, interrupted every forty-five minutes or so for the dictator to take an "important phone call." These "calls" were in fact a summons from the Marlboro Man—Kim has a serious smoking habit.

Kim began by saying that he understood precisely why I was there. He said that he intended to redirect his country's focus to economic development and the welfare of his people over military spending. For the first time ever, a North Korean leader would try to make North Koreans more self-sufficient at home. He wanted me to know, too, that Kim Yong Chol was his point man on talks with the United States, and that the North Korean foreign ministry would not join the discussions. Apparently, diplomats across the world aren't well-trusted by their leaders, not just in the United States.

Kim remarked that he had studied me and deduced that President Trump had chosen me to be the CIA director because I was powerful, loyal, and brutal. I was not about to disabuse him of any of these notions, hoping that such a perception would provide an advantage in future talks. I shared with him that I was on a mission from President Trump to eliminate North Korea's weapons of mass destruction capabilities, including its uranium enrichment and plutonium processing, and to establish a broader peace between North and South Korea. When those actions were complete, I made clear, we would release the global economic chokehold on his country and work on getting Japan and South Korea to make massive investments. Kim was extremely curious about Donald Trump and told me that he believed Trump was the first American president the North Koreans could trust. I said that President Trump and I were peacemakers and that Kim had a short but open window to change the course of history.

A big part of the meeting required the sales pitch of my life. Andy and I knew that Kim needed to believe in an alternative vision for North Korea that also took his interests into account. We knew that complete denuclearization would not happen unless Chairman Kim came to believe three propositions: First, Kim needed to believe that he could survive a dramatic North Korean transition from a nuclear to a non-nuclear state—something that other dictators, such as Iraq's Saddam Hussein and Libya's Muammar Gaddafi, had failed to do. Second, he needed to be able to reassure his military leaders that a non-nuclear North Korea would survive and prosper and that the elites' kleptocracy could continue. On that point, I described for Kim the investments that could go to his dreamed-of projects, like a beautiful international tourist resort at Wonsan. Somewhat humorously, at one point, Chairman Kim told me that he loved good cigars, and I reminded him that if we got this deal done, I'd host him on the nicest beach in Miami and smoke the best Cubanos in the world. He told me, "I already have a great relationship with the Castros." Of course, he did.

The third point of reassurance involved China. Kim needed protection—and I had underestimated how much this mattered to him. The memory of past Chinese domination of the Korean Peninsula burns deeply in the North Korean mind, and to this day China maintains a sizable military presence along an 880-mile-long disputed border. During our discussion, Kim raised the issue of the joint military exercises America routinely conducts with South Korea. I insinuated that he was a little hypocritical to get worked up about them, given how his planes and rockets could within minutes, or perhaps seconds, lay waste to the city of Seoul, South Korea, a city of ten million people and a few dozen kilometers from the demilitarized zone (DMZ). I also told him that the CCP consistently told the United States that American forces leaving South Korea would make Chairman Kim very happy. At this, Kim laughed and pounded on the table in sheer joy, exclaiming that the Chinese were liars. He said that he needed the Americans in South Korea to protect him from the CCP, and that the CCP needs the Americans out so they can treat the peninsula like Tibet and Xinjiang. Policymakers take note: expanding US missile and ground capabilities on the Korean Peninsula won't bother the North Koreans at all.

In the end, Chairman Kim made three commitments to me on that Easter trip. He committed to completely getting rid of his nuclear weapons, saying that they were a massive economic burden and made his nation a pariah in the eyes of the world. He further committed to putting a moratorium on his nuclear and missile development programs. He also committed to meeting with President Trump. We agreed that I would return after our teams had exchanged next steps on the potential for the two leaders to meet. I closed by reminding him that Otto Warmbier's death was still on my mind as well as the minds of many Americans and that he continued to hold Americans hostage. These detentions, I said, made a meeting very difficult for President Trump. Kim did not respond other than to gesture toward our departure door. On the way out, he told me that he loved the beach and that I should "visit our beautiful beaches." I told him I grew up in Huntington Beach, California, and would be happy to do so when the time was right.

Following the meeting with Chairman Kim, Kim Yong Chol insisted that we stay in Pyongyang a little longer. I had already accomplished what I came for and, wanting to set the tone for this old general who wanted to showcase his control, I demanded that we leave immediately. It intimidated him significantly. As he walked away, he pulled his phone out, but could only stare at it with shaking hands. One of his aides had to approach him and dial a phone number for him. In that moment, I told Andy that DPRK's military capabilities may be overrated, as its senior general couldn't even operate his phone under stress. Andy laughed.

That day, I left Pyongyang having made progress on nearly all our objectives. Pivoting quickly from past failed diplomatic strategies had made Americans safer. Our risk-taking paid off.

Curiously, Kim, in his parting words to me, said the day was "the last time I hope to meet an American CIA director." I was not sure whether he meant me specifically or whether he was hoping I'd have a different job by the time of our next meeting. Either way, I did think it was likely to be the last time I'd meet him in my current role.

After all, President Trump had just asked me to be his secretary of state.

CHAPTER 3

"IT'S A MEAN, NASTY WORLD"

Y ou. Your ass. In the seat. Monday. POTUS won't take the briefing without you."

I'd been CIA director for only a few days, and this was the second time Steve Bannon had called to request my presence at the president's daily intelligence briefing. The first time, I'd waved him off. "Steve, I'm still learning my way around the building," I had said. "I'll make sure the team briefing him is killer good."

This time, I knew I needed to show up—and I probably never would have become secretary of state if I hadn't made a habit of attending these briefings. I likely wound up spending more time with the president than did any other cabinet member in the first twelve months of our administration.

Whether out of distrust of the Agency or confidence in me, clearly the president wanted his CIA director to be the voice of the intelligence community's products developed for him. So, most weekdays, I crossed the Potomac River from Virginia to present the president with the CIA's best findings and recommendations for action. The conversations were both freewheeling and focused on America First. They were also deeply informed by a reality the president and I both recognized: it's a mean, nasty world out there.

I didn't do the briefing alone. Two very capable professional intelligence officials did the heaviest lifting. The affable director of national intelligence, Dan Coats, frequently joined as well. The lineup of other senior staff for the briefings varied but almost always included whoever was the national security advisor at the time and, often, Vice President Pence and the president's chief of staff.

We rarely brought good news. Most days, we were deciding which various pieces of bad news to prioritize. Director Coats and I directed the team to begin with "news of the day." Then we'd present the material the president should know or hear because of upcoming events such as a visit from another world leader. And then we'd present a deeper piece about a longer-range issue that would shape the hard decisions on big challenges.

One morning the president asked me to stay behind. We had briefed him that day on a rogue nation's efforts to eliminate another country's access to food. It put him in a sober mood. He understood that just as every subcontractor working on a building must rightfully protect his own interest, America needed to defend ours from countries such as China and Iran, which wanted America to fall and fail.

He shook his head. "Mike, it's a mean, nasty world out there."

★ ★ ★

I've known that the world is a mean, nasty place most of my adult life. That reality first really began to sink in for me on Sunday, October 23, 1983, during my sophomore year at the US Military Academy. The news seemed to sweep down the Hudson River on a cold wind: a terrorist attack had killed and wounded hundreds of US Marines in their barracks in Beirut, Lebanon. Many of these men were probably my age, if not younger. As a cadet expecting a commission as a second lieutenant after graduation, I expected deployment into a danger zone. Could that be my fate someday?

The event also unlocked many other questions in my mind, ones concerned with far more than my own welfare.

Who would do this to American soldiers? What was their motivation?

What is America's role in the world that we think it necessary to put our service members in harm's way? In Beirut? How many Americans even know where Beirut is?

What does it take to keep Americans safe?

We soon learned that an early incarnation of the Iran-backed terror-ist organization Hezbollah had carried out that bombing, killing 241 US military personnel and wounding 128 more. I never forgot that moment when Iranians killed American service members, as well as what all of this meant to America and regarding the use of the American military.

Fast forward a few years, after my graduation in 1986. I was posted to West Germany. On a freezing-cold night at three forty-five in the morning, in a place called Bad Berneck, the phone rang. The voice on the other end told me that Soviet forces were poised to flood across Europe. I grabbed my gear and sprinted to my green car, a soldier-to-soldier hand-me-down 1974 BMW 5 Series. I floored it toward headquarters.

As I drove, my mind moved faster than the speedometer.

It's got to be a drill, right?

Are we ready?

Once there, I mustered with my unit: Second Platoon, B Troop, First Squadron, Second Armored Cavalry regiment. It became clear when I arrived on post that it was only a drill—evaluators were everywhere—but we trained as if it were real: meet at the motor pool, rally at the Quick Reaction site, load the tank rounds and Bradley munitions, convoy to our initial battle positions. This was an exercise I would perform often as a small-unit leader. Our mission was to conduct reconnaissance and patrol the border areas of what were then called East Germany and Czechoslo-vakia. On duty, we peered across the Iron Curtain to see East German dogs, border guards, and Mi-24 Hind helicopters doing their part for their comrades.

I rotated out in October 1989, just weeks before the Berlin Wall came down. "Mike, you should have stayed a few more weeks," said Lieutenant Jeff Boobar, a soldier whom I had served with in Germany. Speaking to me right after the Berlin Wall fell, he said, "The roads we were blocking are now wide open, and we're playing traffic cops for thousands of Tra-bants." (A Trabant was a cruddy little car manufactured in East Ger-many.) After a pause, and without thinking, he said, "Mike, the cars are going in one direction, towards freedom!"

Between the terrorist attack in Beirut and my active-duty posting in Germany, my days in the US military drilled in me an understanding that America's adversaries are, in ways big and small, always looking to do us harm. I took comfort in the fact that my commander in chief, President Reagan, understood that, too. My service coincided with his Cold War buildup of the US military, and we had all the fuel and ammo we needed to train and prepare. If the Commie bastards tried to roll across the German plain, we would crush them. I cheered the president as he lauded America as a redoubt of freedom and goodness, while executing a merciless mission to smash the totalitarian Soviet Union. I think all the time about a set of words he uttered about America in 1964: "If we lose freedom here, there is no place to escape. This is the last stand on earth."

THE FOUNDERS HAD IT RIGHT: THE
WORLD IS A ROUGH PLACE

The American Founders also played a major role in shaping how I assessed threats. I still have my copy of *The Federalist Papers* from my time as a cadet. Its pages are a little more dog-eared and yellowed now, having gotten extensive use ever since my days as an undergraduate. Pondering this collection of arguments, published in 1787–1788 in support of the ratification of the new US Constitution, caused me to grow more confident in my thinking about America and the world. The Founders knew the world was a cruel place, not ultimately because of specific ideologies or policies—although some are much worse than others—but because of human nature. Their thinking was very much rooted in a Judeo-Christian worldview that recognized mankind's fallen, sinful ways— think of Romans 3:23: "For all have sinned and fall short of the glory of God." In Federalist no. 6, for example, Alexander Hamilton claimed, "Men are ambitious, vindictive, rapacious." He wasn't just speaking about the editorial staff at MSNBC. He was talking about all of humanity. It's part of the greatness of the American experiment that the Founders conjured up a system of government designed to prevent one person from accumulating too much power and using it for evil ends.

But the Founders also believed that mankind had inherent dignity and unalienable rights granted by God, among them the rights to "life, liberty, and the pursuit of happiness," as the Declaration of Independence describes them. As one of my predecessors as secretary of state, Thomas Jefferson, put it, "Almighty God hath created the mind free." As a result, the Founders undertook a bold experiment in government—one still ongoing—that afforded citizens an unprecedented amount of freedom. But because freedom without any constraint whatsoever tends toward anarchy and injustice—look at how crime rates go up when police are defunded—the founders also knew that some regime of laws was indispensable. As James Madison, the father of the Constitution, summed it up in Federalist no. 51: "If men were angels, no government would be necessary."

Men aren't angels, sure. But some of them are devils. I saw this reality as I led the CIA. Day after day, I scrutinized the world's most sensitive intelligence, which confirmed that our planet is a messy one, filled with wild, evil people. The most well-intentioned or well-executed policies can't change or erase human nature. Those that assume the best of human beings—especially of authoritarian leaders with track records of inhumanity and aggression—are doomed to fail. The calculations and methods that democratic leaders apply to managing situations with allies don't work with rogue regimes and terrorists. Thus, the progressive philosophy that wars will cease and harmony will reign if we just have more talks, more tolerance, more concessions, more UN governance, and less American presence in the world is completely naive. It causes wicked men, such as Kim, Xi, and Putin, to salivate.

I'm proud to say the Trump administration took on the world as it was, not as we wished it to be. We knew that protecting Americans rarely comes with neat and tidy options. I think of President Trump's first trip overseas, a strategic visit to Saudi Arabia designed in part to shore up majority-Muslim nations' support for our counterterrorism efforts. The leftist media gave the president a hard time for doing a photo op on that trip with King Salman of Saudi Arabia and President Sisi of Egypt, leaders whose histories put them out of step with American values. But we knew partnering with these terror fighters to protect the lives of the American people must take precedence over favorable "optics"—a loathsome DC term. It was an easy calculation to make in a mean, nasty world.

Noting that America would now "make decisions based on real-world outcomes, not inflexible ideology," the president told America's Middle East partners that "Muslim nations must be willing to take on the burden, if we are going to defeat terrorism and send its wicked ideology into oblivion."

"YOU ARE GOING TO BE THE NEXT SECRETARY OF STATE"

As I continued to brief President Trump throughout 2017, I apprised him of the threats and opportunities the United States had before us. He and I were in sync on issues such as North Korea and Iran—you can't give dictators something for nothing. We also agreed on the importance of crushing ISIS. The president asked thoughtful questions about the world and how intelligence works. He consistently delivered the resources I requested, provided I made a strong enough case for them. And we both loved Diet Coke.

From the outset, I had some ability to read the president well. Bill Barr claims in his book that whenever President Trump got angry at me or someone in the room, I would distract him by bringing up the Russia Hoax. This isn't an accurate recollection of how I engaged with the president. I simply had developed, by experience, a sense of when and how to try to steer the conversation in ways that would help the president and our team toward a sound outcome.

Sometime in early 2017, after the daily briefing, I was alone in the Oval Office with President Trump.

"Mike, I've made my living figuring out what people's side hustle is. I can't figure out your side hustle."

I wasn't sure what he meant. "Mr. President, I don't think I have a side hustle."

"Everyone has a side hustle, and I know every one of them. But I can't figure out yours."

I smiled, not knowing if this line of conversation was good or bad. Then I told him the truth: "No side hustle. Just a hard-working American." He chuckled.

Given the number of folks in his orbit who were trying to ride the

Trump Train to personal glory, my protestation that I was strictly in it
for America must have seemed a little insincere to him. But it was the
truth. I had not expected to have the privilege to serve at the highest level
of my country's government, so I never took my job for granted, nor did
I think of myself as intrinsic to our mission's success. A commitment to
American exceptionalism and our Judeo-Christian heritage mattered a
hell of a lot more to our success than Mike did.

One person who was not gelling with President Trump was Secretary
of State Rex Tillerson. In my experience, Rex was a very decent, intelligent man and skilled diplomat. But he never accepted the president's style
and leadership. He consistently teamed up with Secretary Mattis to save
the Iran deal, and he refused to accept the importance of defending our
policies in the press. The proud Texan put the final nail in his coffin by
reportedly calling the president "a f——ing moron" in a fit of anger after
an intense strategy session during the summer of 2017. Two days after
the "moron" story broke, I encountered rumors about Secretary of State
Pompeo for the first time in a *New York* magazine article published on
October 6, 2017. I assumed that it was just gossip and people making stuff
up—it happens all the time in Washington. But the whispers seemed to
grow louder. A few weeks later, Deputy National Security Advisor Dina
Powell told me, "The boss can't stand Rex and is done. You are going to
be the next secretary of state."

I mostly tried to ignore it, keeping my head down and running the
Agency as well as I could. Being the director was an incredible privilege.
I had built a very good team and was on my way to building a great one.
My goal was to make it the best ever. I enjoyed coming to work to kill
terrorists and generally make life miserable for America's enemies. I'm a
simple man.

In early February 2018, Chief of Staff John Kelly told me that President Trump was thinking about making me the secretary of state. He
gave me that look that said, "I'm sure this sounds great, but you might
want to take a beat before leaning in too hard." That gave me pause. Kelly
was a serious person, whom I came to love and still do. I first met him in
Munich, Germany, at a security conference in 2014, if I recall correctly.
He was standing at the bar in his Marine uniform. Then-Representative

Tom Cotton and I decided to go up and say hello to a general we had never met. Kelly was brilliant and as funny as you would expect for a guy who grew up in the Brighton section of Boston. We spent a half hour explaining how two junior members of the House of Representatives were going to change the world. He told us, merely by describing his time of service, how he already had. Who would have dreamed that a handful of years later, he'd be telling me I was likely to be the next secretary of state of the United States of America?

Given my respect for his judgment, I wanted to heed Kelly's warning. A CIA director works in the quiet places. The ratio of time spent doing real work versus being forced to address media madness was really high at State. Fending off reporters is a daily chore there. I wouldn't enjoy that.

A couple of days later, the president asked me to stay behind in the Oval Office after the briefing. He said he was thinking about firing Tillerson and asked if I would be up for being his replacement. I gave a version of the same answer I've given for decades when asked to serve: "It would be an honor, Mr. President." President Trump told me I'd be great and that I should start thinking about who should replace me at CIA.

In mulling over who would succeed me at Langley, President Trump asked about Gary Cohn, the former president and COO of Goldman Sachs who was at the time leading the White House economic team. I had already made the case for my deputy, Gina Haspel. I repeated that recommendation and added that I thought Tom Cotton—now Senator Cotton of Arkansas—would also be great. I guess the president was tired of reading in the press that Goldman Sachs alumni were running the White House, because he responded: "Too many Goldman people. Gina has balls. Let's do that."

On March 9, 2018, the president called to tell me that he was "pulling the trigger" on firing Tillerson, who was at that moment on a trip to Africa. "My Mike, most people say I should wait until he gets back from Africa. I say f——him." Not long after, on March 13, a tweet appeared: "Mike Pompeo, Director of the CIA, will become our new Secretary of State. He will do a fantastic job! Thank you to Rex Tillerson for his service! Gina Haspel will become the new Director of the CIA, and the first woman so chosen. Congratulations to all!"

I never anticipated becoming secretary of state. I wasn't angling for the job. I was simply doing the one I currently had to the best of my ability. I still have the same philosophy today that I did when I won employee of the month at Baskin-Robbins in high school: Work hard. Tell the truth. Keep your faith. If you perform every task with excellence, conduct yourself with integrity, and keep trusting God through the ups and downs, good things will almost certainly come your way.

RUNNING THE CONFIRMATION GAUNTLET

Before I became secretary of state, my musings on policy were not particularly relevant—I was the "just the facts" intelligence leader. But, now, as the head of the State Department, I would be at the center of policy formulation for the president. The president had given me not only a promotion but a very public attaboy in another tweet: "Mike Pompeo is outstanding. First in his class at West Point. A top student at Harvard Law School. A success at whatever he has done. We need the Senate to approve Mike ASAP. He will be a great Secretary of State!"

The president's confidence proved important, but *not* for whipping up votes on my confirmation; the senators had their own political angles that would determine how they voted on me. No, it was *extremely* important because leaders all around the world saw that I would represent him and America as his top diplomat. The team at State could see it, too, as could the others in the Trump foreign policy world. I knew that little in life was permanent, especially life in the zaniness of DC. But at that moment, as they say in the Arab world, I had *wasta*—clout. And I knew I had to earn it every single day. The ability to speak for the president would be one of my most important assets in standing up for the America I love in a mean, nasty world.

To his credit, Secretary Tillerson was gracious and helpful during the transition period. He knew as did I that the State Department careerists considered him a scalp. Many of them wanted me to fail, too. He also knew that I had learned to work within the Trump model and therefore stood a better chance of success. The press had driven Tillerson to distraction in a way that he didn't have to deal with as CEO of ExxonMobil.

In the moment, I was also reminded of a great lesson given to me by a company commander back in Germany: "Lieutenant, always make sure you take over the worst platoon. Surest way to look like a genius." State was certainly in the running for worst platoon, so if I could just figure out how to be measured on a standard of performance that was relative, not absolute, I ought to be just fine.

I was also grateful for the wisdom that every living secretary of state shared with me, both Republicans and Democrats. I was a bit surprised former secretary Hillary Clinton took my call. The last time she and I had spoken was across the dais during the Benghazi hearings in 2015, when we clashed over the Obama administration's actions—or lack of them—during a murderous assault on Americans by Islamist militants in Libya. My call as the nominee was a much friendlier exchange. I respected her for sharing her experiences. Her willingness to be helpful to me was, in retrospect, all the more surprising now that we all know that she was at the center of the Russia Hoax through her campaign's commission of the lie-ridden Steele dossier and that she personally approved a dump of unverified information about a connection between a Russian bank and the Trump Organization.

My most important conversation with former secretaries of state was with Jim Baker, who had served under George H. W. Bush. He wanted to meet in person. I offered to travel to him. "No," he said. "You're busier." Visiting with me in my office in Langley, he offered three valuable ideas. First, he told me: "The secretary's relationship with the president must be seamless—both to the outside world and in the eyes of the other players in the president's circle. If the perception arises that the president and the secretary are not on the same page, it will be fatal to your ability to deliver for the president." He reminded me that he had enjoyed the advantage of being the godfather to one of President Bush's daughters. As far as me replicating that relationship with President Trump, he joked, "You'll have to figure that out."

Baker continued with a second observation: "The State Department is primarily an implementing institution. It doesn't create or make foreign policy; it delivers on the president's guidance." By this he meant the rank and file; obviously I would have some say in advising the president on what to do. It sounded good in theory, but I was confident that very few of the ten-thousand-plus Foreign Service officers agreed with that idea in practice! Finally, he urged me: "Savor every minute. You have great power. Use it for good—for your team, for President Trump, and for America."

Not everyone was as eager to see me become secretary of state as Secretary Baker. Once again, I had to run the gauntlet through a Senate confirmation, a trip that proved much more fraught than my first one fifteen months prior. Democrats on the Senate Committee on Foreign Relations tried to nail me every which way. Senator Bob Menendez, a left-winger who, save for a hung jury in a corruption case—which I find incomprehensible, given the evidence—would be in jail, was particularly aggressive. I guess they weren't moved by my opening statement, a part of which I used to mention my love for golden retrievers, Broadway musicals, and my father's recipe for meatballs—the secret is to add extra breadcrumbs and consume lots of vodka while it simmers.

The hearing was one of the biggest moments of my life, but the world didn't know I was struggling to stay focused that day. Just before it began, I learned that terrorists had shot one of our CIA operatives in the head during an operation in Afghanistan. This hero was at that very moment being medically evacuated to Ramstein Air Base in Germany. His prognosis was uncertain. I was thinking of his wife and children, as well as the risk that my teams accepted every single day to stand against the storms of a hard world. Taking a few questions in an air-conditioned Senate hearing room, with a massive entourage and security detail in the gallery, suddenly and paradoxically felt both completely trivial and desperately urgent. We had to get our foreign policy right so that fewer Americans—including those who had served so long in Afghanistan— would be put in harm's way.

I also had to survive incoming flak from members of my own party. Senator Rand Paul thought President Trump shared his isolationist tendencies, so he went golfing with him on the even weekends. Meanwhile, Senator Lindsey Graham, a known hawk, golfed on the odd weekends, thereby providing President Trump with a full spectrum of foreign policy ideas. There was some speculation that I would need Senator Paul's vote to win confirmation. The president said he could call the senator and get him to vote for me in committee, an essential step for proceeding to a full Senate vote. I was on the call with the president when he told Paul: "Look, you gotta vote for Pompeo. He's going to be a lot more successful as secretary of state than you were as a presidential candidate." Boom. In the end, Paul flipped and voted for me in committee.

Of course, the media wanted to see me go down, too. I chuckle now at so many headlines that turned out to be dead wrong more than four years later. The *New Yorker* fretted, "With Mike Pompeo at the State Department, Are the Über-Hawks Winning?" Likewise, the *Financial Times* declared, "Regime Change Leaves Hawks Ascendent in U.S. Foreign Policy." No new wars started while I was secretary of state. And we responsibly drew down all but 2,500 troops from Afghanistan by the time we left office. How's that for hawkish?

Nahal Toosi of *Politico*, the State Department beat reporter, would go on to be one of the reporters fueling false narratives about me and our team throughout my four years. She embodied the lazy thinking and partisanship with which many reporters approach their work. Let me dissect some of her reporting from my confirmation hearing:

> Asked about a huddle with Pompeo and Director of National Intelligence Dan Coats where Trump reportedly complained about the investigation into his campaign's ties to Russia, Pompeo demurred on providing any details about closed-door discussions with the president.
>
> "I don't recall what he asked me that day precisely," Pompeo told Menendez, adding, nonetheless, that Trump "has never asked me to do anything that's improper." Critics immediately seized on this contradiction and his repeated unwillingness to share details.

First, it may well be the case that critics questioned what I had to say. But adding that line functions as adding spin under the guise of "reporting both sides." It is the injection of a counternarrative, one that does not even put one of my critics on the record. Anyone reading this should take note of how common it is for many news stories to editorialize by starting a sentence with a construction such as "Critics say . . ." Adding that little phrase merely gives reporters cover against accusations of failing to be neutral.

There is also a slant to the idea of my "unwillingness to share details." Toosi frames this as a bad thing. Of course, she is a reporter, so she wants dirt on privileged conversations and to see fireworks in the form of my contradicting the president. Did it ever occur to her that refusing to share details of privileged discussions with the leader of the United States of America is in fact a greater statement of respect for the American constitutional order than is blurting them out in the name of the journalistic Holy Grail of transparency?

Finally, there is a failure of logic in her claim that I had contradicted myself. One can both be blurry on the exact specifics of a meeting that was little different from countless similar ones and also have certainty on never being asked to do something illegal—a moment that would be undeniably seared in any conscientious person's memory.

Despite the best efforts of many to take me down, on April 26, 2018, the Senate confirmed me with a vote of 57–42, which was much closer than that of my confirmation at CIA. My son joked that the trajectory of the decline suggested that this would be the last time I'd be confirmed for anything.

In the course of service in the military, four elections to Congress, and running the CIA, I'd taken the oath of loyalty to the United States on nine occasions. The tenth time was my first having a Supreme Court justice administer it. My friend, Justice Samuel Alito, swore me in. Standing in his chambers, with my Susan and Nick by my side, I became America's seventieth secretary of state. A few weeks later, we had a ceremonial swearing in at State that both the president and vice president attended. My family and I took part of the day to walk down the hallway of Mahogany Row, a corridor near the secretary's office named for its rich wood lining. Portraits of every former secretary of state hang on its walls. They inspired me every day. But they also could have a humbling effect, as Nick reminded Susan and me. As we walked by the historic faces, he read the names out loud: "Jefferson, Adams, Webster . . ." He paused. "Pompeo." He paused again. "Dad, I don't know." It was a great joke.

PUSHING NATO FOR MORE

I had no time to celebrate my confirmation. The foreign ministers of the North Atlantic Treaty Organization (NATO) were scheduled to meet the next day in Brussels, Belgium, so my commute for my first day on the job required me to cross the Atlantic Ocean. Busting my tail to get to the gathering would send an important message, too. We were pushing these countries to step up their defense spending. They needed to understand how much this mattered to the Trump administration. For them, my physical presence would matter as much as anything I said.

After the swearing-in ceremony, I hustled to a waiting US government aircraft. Following quick introductions to the new team at the State Department, I shooed them away and burrowed into some briefing books. That plane—usually a Boeing C-32, a variation of a 757—became a home away from home for my thousand days as America's top diplomat. Every time I embarked on a trip, my team and I swelled with pride when pulling up on the tarmac to see an aircraft with "United States of America" emblazoned on the side. Those words, by the way, are printed on the plane in the same font as one used in certain copies of the Declaration of Independence.

The NATO meeting was important on multiple levels. The president had been outspoken about the need for all NATO allies to spend what they had promised on common defense. As the world's leading military power after World War II, it made sense that America had provided a security umbrella for Europe in the fight against Communism—indeed, we were the only nation that could muster the proper financial support and military capabilities in the years when Europe was rebuilding from total destruction. But the world had changed a lot since the days of President Harry Truman and Secretary of State George Marshall. The nations of Europe—especially Western Europe—were now some of the richest on earth. They contributed billions to a bloated welfare state, but they refused to pony up to defend their people adequately from Russia, terrorism, and cyberattacks? In addition, the threat of China wasn't even on their radar. Their desire to piggyback on the United States without paying their fair share, all while trashing President Trump, wasn't going to cut it.

My experience as a veteran also informed how I thought about defense commitments. Having served in Europe as part of a NATO force, I knew money mattered. But just as important was the need for European nations to build their own forces with their own boys and girls. It's one thing to pay taxes; it's quite another to send your son or daughter to storm a beach, knock down the door of a terrorist safehouse, or tote a rifle. As much as we focused on money, I also reminded them that our alliance needed a fair share of their real treasure.

Despite substantial tension, my fellow foreign ministers received me warmly, and some of them went on to become terrific partners. But the diplomatic niceties didn't knock me off course from saying what needed to be said. I leveled with them in our meetings, making it known that America's new secretary of state would be forthright in urging our partners to face the realities of a dangerous world. I made this clear publicly, too. In my first press conference, a reporter from the *Washington Post* asked if I thought Germany was doing enough to meet the 2 percent of GDP target all NATO nations had agreed to in 2014. My answer was blunt: "No."

I said it with a chuckle, but the diplomatic pressure I was applying was serious. Vladimir Putin and his ilk are constantly looking to weaken our defenses and split our alliances. The Trump administration put our Western allies on notice that we would make them live up to their promises about providing for the common defense. In our cutthroat, mean, nasty world, we depend on a posture of combined strength. Ultimately, we achieved our goal: NATO allies agreed to boost spending by $130 billion by the end of 2020 and $400 billion by 2024. For justification of our insistence that NATO harden its defenses, look no further than the Russian invasion of Ukraine in 2022.

FIXING FAILURE ON IRAN

As my plane left Brussels, it didn't head back west across the Atlantic—it continued toward the Middle East. It was time to strengthen another constellation of American allies to meet the challenges staring all of us in the face. And in the world's toughest neighborhood, there is no challenge like the one posed by the Islamic Republic of Iran.

Ever since the Islamic Revolution of 1979, which was in fact a coup carried out by a band of feverish radicals and hijacked by religious fanatics, a radical Shia Islamist government has dominated Iran and its people. Led by Ayatollah Khamenei since 1989, this ruthless theocracy exists to impose what it calls the "Islamic Revolution" at home and abroad. That's why former secretary of state Henry Kissinger once remarked, "Iran has to take a decision whether it wants to be a nation or a cause." There was proof enough of the regime's warped worldview back in 1979, when thugs under the command of a previous supreme leader, the Ayatollah Khomeini, assaulted the US Embassy in Tehran and seized fifty-two hostages for 444 days. Today, the Iranian regime is the power behind a network of terrorist groups fighting to create a "Shia crescent" of Iranian-controlled territory arcing through not only Iran but also Iraq, Lebanon, Syria, and Yemen.

The regime keeps Americans in its crosshairs: the Beirut barracks bombing that was so formative for my own outlook was masterminded by a nascent form of Iran's top proxy militia, Hezbollah. Other examples of Iran's viciousness include the nineteen American airmen slain in the Khobar Towers bombing in Saudi Arabia, in 1996, and the ten American sailors humiliated and taken captive by Iran during the Obama administration.

In our time, the Shia Iranian regime has even made common cause with Sunni al-Qaeda. Forget what you thought about a Sunni-Shia rivalry preventing cooperation. As I exposed definitively in January 2021, Tehran is today the home base of top al-Qaeda leadership. That's right. Al-Qaeda's operational headquarters is *not* in Tora Bora, Afghanistan, or in Pakistan. It's not in Syria or Iraq. It's in the capital of Iran. The ayatollahs are harboring the leaders of a group that murdered nearly three thousand Americans on 9/11. Years before his death at the hands of Navy SEALS in 2011, Osama bin Laden himself wrote: "Iran is our main artery for funds, personnel, and communication . . . There is no need to fight with Iran unless you are forced to."

The Iranian regime is a de facto terrorist group. But unlike most terrorist groups, the regime—with the protection of the IRGC—possesses all the tools of statecraft: internationally recognized borders, diplomats at the United Nations, a fiat currency, and total command of massive oil fields, banks, and other sectors of the Iranian economy. Attempted attacks on Jews worldwide and abominable rhetoric about the destruction of Israel and America are routine—I wish Twitter's woke censors would put as much time into censoring the ayatollah's genocidal rhetoric as they would the words of ordinary conservatives. "My Mike," the president would ask, "why is it that when you tell me about problems in the Middle East, it's always 'Iran' with you?" I told him with confidence: "Easy, Mr. President, because it is Iran." His mission guidance was clear: "Let's fix it, Mike. No soldiers, but let's fix it."

In the Trump administration, fixing it meant first undoing the damage done by the Obama administration's preposterous nuclear deal. In the early years of this century, Iran started laying the groundwork for producing a nuclear weapon—a nightmare scenario for the United States, Israel, and the Sunni monarchies in the Persian Gulf region, where many Americans live and work. Beginning in 2006, the international community responded with a sanctions and monitoring campaign that severely restricted, but did not end, the regime's nuclear work. Then the Obama administration's overeducated liberals with no understanding of power politics decided that they knew better and sought to cut a deal with Iran. They believed that they could transform die-hard Islamists into responsible partners in peace, and even one day turn the regime into an ally. It was sheer madness.

In keeping with this fantasy, in 2013, the Obama administration began to negotiate sweeping sanctions relief for Iran in exchange for what amounted to, at best, a mere postponement of its nuclear progress. In 2015, the deal was done. Secretary of State John Kerry, joined by his deputies Wendy Sherman and Rob Malley, traded American and Israeli security for a bag of magic Iranian fava beans. At the strategic level, the JCPOA was staggeringly stupid in myriad ways. The removal of sanctions meant the regime had more money to oppress its own people and build ballistic missiles, which were completely unrestricted under the deal. Sanctions relief also meant that the regime gained gobs of cash to advance the Islamic Revolution by force, bankrolling the likes of Hezbollah, Hamas, Palestinian Islamic Jihad, and the Houthis in Yemen. A mastermind of this sinister project was an IRGC leader named Qasem Soleimani, who would become a focus of our determined efforts to thwart Iran's agenda. More on him and why he mattered to every American later.

But the most boneheaded move of all was that the West had allowed Iran to sit back, count its cash, enrich fissile material, and wait patiently until nuclear restrictions expired in ten to fifteen years, at which point it could lawfully resume its development of nuclear weapons. This, too, was a sellout of American national security. Secretary Kerry himself had previously said in 2013, "We do not recognize [Iran's] right to enrich." Yet, in the end, desperate for a deal at any cost, he moved his diplomatic goalposts all the way from Nantucket to Martha's Vineyard. It was a lesson in negotiations the Trump administration vowed not to repeat in our dealings with Chairman Kim or any other tyrant.

I was serving in Congress during the years the JCPOA was crafted. I spent that time banging the table as hard as I could to call attention to this gigantic mistake. I gave floor speeches, wrote opinion pieces, and, in the summer of 2014, called every single colleague in the House of Representatives—all 434 of them. I told them that, as constructed, this deal would lead to a nuclear Iran, with real missile capabilities, flush with the money to expand both of those programs. To this day I am proud that I forced the State Department to admit that the "deal" was not actually a treaty or even an executive order but rather a press release coauthored by America and other nations. As the State Department's assistant secretary for legislative affairs Julia Frifield wrote me in a formal response that had been months delayed: "The Joint Comprehensive Plan of Action is not a treaty or an executive agreement, and is not a signed document. The JCPOA reflects political commitments between Iran, the P5+1 (the United States, the United Kingdom, France, Germany, Russia, China), and the European Union."

That letter also contained the claim that the Obama administration had made no "secret deals" with Iran. The administration was lying. In the summer of 2015, within days of the JCPOA having been put forward, I traveled to Vienna with my fellow representative Tom Cotton to meet with the International Atomic Energy Agency (IAEA)—the organization responsible for conducting the mandated inspections of Iranian nuclear facilities. Our expectations were low. First, we were surprised IAEA officials had even agreed to meet with two of the fiercest opponents of the Iran nuclear deal. We fully expected the Obama State Department to nix the meeting. When we arrived, a member of the IAEA protocol team began with an apology: "I'm sorry, Director General Amano will not be able to meet with you today." Tom and I grimaced and shook our heads, believing we had just flown 4,400 miles for nothing. But we realized we had misunderstood why Amano couldn't meet with us when the IAEA staffer continued: "He has had a bicycle accident and is in the hospital. He has directed his deputies to brief you."

Over the course of the two-hour meeting, we stumbled onto the fact that the IAEA and the Obama administration were not telling the world the whole truth about the deal. The IAEA and Iran had crafted two secret addenda governing verification measures at an Iranian military complex. These addenda were not available for public review. This was a stunning admission.

I demanded to know, "Which Americans have actually seen these side deals?"

The reply said it all. "We are not permitted to answer that question."

Our State Department handler sprinted from the room in terror, probably to inform his superiors that we had learned of these additional provisions. We appealed to a CIA station chief, asking if he could help us see these documents. But he just shrugged. "That's way above my pay grade. You'll have to ask the State Department." In truth, neither the State Department nor any other Americans were permitted to see the secret side deals either. The Obama administration had made the outrageous decision to do a deal without knowing how certain elements of Iranian compliance would be verified. Call me crazy for not wanting to stake a nuclear war on the ayatollah's trustworthiness.

Within a few days, Tom and I announced that we had discovered the Iranian secret side deals, even though we were blocked from reading them. Once the deal came into effect, the cheating began. Despite the JCPOA crowd's claims that the Iranians had shuttered their nuclear program long ago, the Iranians had secretly kept it going. They dispersed their facilities across the country, built deeper tunnels into harder mountains, buried their nuclear scientists in schools and military programs, expanded their "space" program to develop missile capability, and kept their most senior nuclear scientist, Mohsen Fakhrizadeh Mahabadi, at the top of the effort. The Iranian Ministry of Intelligence had also structured the JCPOA to allow Iran to exploit its "dual use" civilian nuclear capabilities and creep quietly toward a nuclear weapon without crossing the legal line.

Fortunately, I wasn't the only one who knew the Iranians were cheating. So did my friend, the director of the Mossad, Yossi Cohen. His team eventually pulled off an amazing clandestine operation. They stole vital documents from Iran's nuclear archives that were held in an incredibly secure facility. History will one day convey the head-spinning details of how they executed this remarkable raid. But more importantly, in April 2018, Israeli prime minister Netanyahu revealed to the world the knowledge gleaned from that daring feat. The seized documents showed that Iran had never abandoned its nuclear weapons program, as it was required to do under the JCPOA. The whole deal was founded on a lie. I claimed it. Yossi proved it. The world now knows it.

During the 2016 presidential campaign, I was heartened to hear candidate Donald Trump deride the JCPOA as a charity program for the ayatollahs, who received $400 million in cold, hard cash in exchange for four American hostages as an incentive to seal the deal. I recognized he was seeing the deal and the regime for what they were, not for what we wanted them to be. Once I became CIA director, I couldn't wait to help reverse this diplomatic blunder.

Getting America out of this foolish bargain, however, was easier said than done. For one thing, I was fighting headwinds within the CIA. Nearly the entire Iran analytic unit had spent the two years before I became director working to justify the JCPOA. The team had developed an elaborate claim, later disseminated in a public briefing, that the JCPOA's verification regime increased inspections, enhanced our understanding of Iran's activity, and prevented Iran from increasing its centrifuge capacity. But what that analysis never addressed adequately was the lies on which the JPCOA was built, or an Iranian track record of cheating that would make Lance Armstrong look like an amateur.

Fulfilling the president's campaign promise to get out of the JCPOA also faced vociferous opposition from two of his most senior national security cabinet members: Secretary Tillerson and Secretary of Defense Jim Mattis. They both believed that we should not directly take on Iran. Secretary Mattis warned that it would "create the conditions for war, Michael." I'm not sure why he always called me by my Christian name, but this was his habit. For months and months, debate raged over the JCPOA. As a condition of the deal, every six months the president was required to sign a waiver to prevent the reimplementation of economic sanctions on Iran. Like clockwork, Secretaries Tillerson and Mattis would come into the Oval Office together and lobby the president that he needed to sign the waiver. This made the president most unhappy.

The international consequences of a withdrawal were significant, too. It would ruffle feathers across Europe. It might well trigger a burst of Iranian aggression—not that the ayatollah was acting like Mother Teresa to begin with. The Trump administration made a good-faith effort to convince our allies to join us in renegotiating the deal with permanent restrictions on Iran's nuclear activities and more. Sadly, the British, French, and Germans weren't interested. There was too much money at stake for their companies now doing business with Iran and too much pride on the line for the rosy-eyed diplomats and leaders who had brokered this useless pact. Like Mattis, they, too, were captive to the fear that leaving the deal would mean war. But we could not leave a bad decision in place—one built on an unrealistic hypothesis of the deal's power to transform the Iranian regime into something kinder and gentler.

REVIVING MIDEAST ALLIANCES

One set of allies understood what was at stake and encouraged us to do the right thing. Israel and her Arab neighbors had seen with clear eyes for decades Iran's path of destruction. After a year of Tillerson and Mattis pressuring President Trump to stay in the corrupt deal, I wanted them to know that America now had a secretary of state who saw the situation as they did. I was now speaking for the president when I expressed my hatred for the agreement and a desire to revamp it or—better yet—get out if it completely.

Thus, my first stop after the NATO meeting in Brussels was Riyadh, Saudi Arabia, where I met with my counterpart, Foreign Minister Adel al-Jubeir—not a royal but a man with influence whom I had known since I was in Congress. He was clear and unambiguous about what the Gulf States could and would do if America provided them with the simple assurance that we would no longer underwrite the Iranian regime with sanctions relief. It was a good conversation. I also had the occasion to meet with my former counterparts in the Saudi intelligence services—great guys who understood the dark world of espionage and how to operate in it. My engineering of Gina as my successor also gave them confidence— they were happy to see one of their kind get promoted. US-Saudi relations would turn out to be very important for American national security.

After Saudi Arabia, I was thrilled to head to my next destination, Tel Aviv, to meet with Prime Minister Netanyahu of Israel. He and I went back a bit as mutual critics of the Iran deal. I was also pleased to see my friend Yossi Cohen. The foursome of Trump-Netanyahu-Pompeo-Cohen might only have had one good golfer in the group, but it had four leaders who were determined to build security alliances that mattered and to do it without thinking that the deployment of American military forces would solve every problem.

As I got to know Netanyahu, I could see that he was like my boss: a force of nature. Yet they were men of different temperaments and backgrounds. Bibi, as he is known to all, was a veteran of both political fights and real warfare. He was a decorated hero, as was his brother Yonatan, who was killed in 1976 during the rescue of Israeli hostages at Entebbe International Airport in Uganda. In private, Bibi was calm and loquacious. Always thinking, always pushing, and always happy to hear various points of view, he was a capable manager, but also one who could burn through team members with lightning speed. Hardworking, he'd call me at any time of day or night. He once flew to meet me face to face in a cramped hotel room in Brussels to share one tiny message. It was that important for him to work with America's secretary of state in person. He had a capable national security advisor and a firm grip on his entire national security apparatus. Like me, he was often frustrated with his Ministry of Defense and its unwillingness to use the tools they had been provided.

My final stop on the trip was Jordan, another longtime American friend and important source for stability in the region. As CIA director, I had built relationships with King Abdullah II and my intelligence counterparts. As secretary of state, I wanted them to know that we were working on a plan for peace and we needed them on board, details to follow. They were underwhelmed about what they thought we were going to propose. This never changed.

It had been a busy first week, but as the plane began to glide homeward over the dusty expanse outside of Amman, Jordan, I was confident my missions had succeeded. I wanted America's allies in Europe and the Middle East to understand that so long as it was in my power as secretary of state, American foreign policy would proceed from a realistic assessment of the threats that my country and our allies and partners faced. Our foreign policy would recognize that we live in a mean, nasty world in which the coddling of America's enemies only made them more dangerous. We would confront them and, if necessary, crush them.

DITCHING THE DEAL

On May 8, 2018, twelve days after I became secretary of state, the United States withdrew from the Iran deal. The days that preceded that decision were filled with simpering, whimpering, and begging from nearly the entire transatlantic national security establishment. The first call came from Mattis, who consistently argued that withdrawal from the JCPOA would draw us and Israel into a war with Iran. The second call was from my British counterpart, Boris Johnson, who served as the UK's foreign secretary before becoming prime minister. He was quite funny in that he prefaced his appeal with classic British style, understating the importance the JCPOA had for the British people. The third call came jointly from the Germans and the French, imploring me to work with them to develop an amendment to the JCPOA that would "address our concerns." This was a futile effort. For one thing, the Trump administration had already spent months urging the Europeans to rework this garbage deal, to no avail. For another, any amendment to the deal that would address our concerns had exactly zero chance of acceptance by the Iranians. The JCPOA crowd wasn't dumb, just hopelessly naive.

Many also failed to appreciate the fact that withdrawal from the JCPOA wasn't the end of our Iran strategy. Withdrawal was simply a mechanical necessity to deliver on the Trump administration's broader objectives, which had yet to be detailed publicly. To articulate those objectives, I gave my first major address as secretary of state on Monday, May 21, at the Heritage Foundation, a conservative think tank in Washington, DC. I worked all day on Sunday to get the text exactly right. Helping me was Brian Hook, a policy advisor I had inherited from Secretary Tillerson. He was at a Washington Nationals baseball game with his kids when I summoned him to the office, and he arrived wearing a red baseball cap and a lime-green polo shirt. Brian had worked the Iran file extensively in the George W. Bush administration under UN ambassador John Bolton, so I knew he had a good understanding of both the Iranian nuclear program and the UN sanctions architecture that we would soon try to scale back up. We were joined by my new speechwriter, David Wilezol. I called him to talk though a draft of the speech as he was helping run Sunday-school classes at his church. He knew I had been a Sunday-school teacher myself back in Kansas. He sheepishly appealed to my own experience in asking if he could finish up before he headed into the office. I gave him my benediction.

The next day I rolled out a hard-hitting speech that laid out both how the deal had failed and that a new maximum-pressure campaign would take its place. The goal was to force Iran back to the table for a much better deal than the one drawn up under the Obama administration. But that wasn't all. Only after Iran met twelve basic requirements—including completely ceasing nuclear weapons work and releasing Americans held hostage—would we be ready to lift sanctions. Our Iran strategy also sought to rally the Iranian people against the regime, so I told the truth about how the regime had stolen their money to fund terrorism: "The regime reaps a harvest of suffering and death in the Middle East at the expense of its own citizens."

This maximum-pressure campaign would take years, and I needed a trusted point person who understood the problem and wouldn't be cowed by State Department bureaucrats who had clung to the deal. At the end of the summer, I appointed Brian as my special envoy for Iran. He and his team—Nick, Danielle, Matt, Gabe, Mike, Jason, Len, and Emily—spent the next two and a half years executing commander's intent on everything from driving new sanctions to rescuing American hostages, such as Michael White and Xiyue Wang, from Iran. At no time did they mimic the Obama administration and deliver pallets of cash to the mullahs in Tehran.

Brian was also instrumental in working with allies to marshal international pressure on the evil regime in Tehran. Among other necessary steps, we had to remove Iranian oil from the global market to deplete the regime's top source of revenue, but we also knew that that effort would cause the worldwide price of oil to jump. I was on the horn constantly to convince the Saudis and Emiratis to keep their pumps operating at high capacity. Even more frequently, I got an earful from oil-poor nations that depended on Iranian crude. I tried to be diplomatic, but they essentially heard a few words I've learned to live by: "Life isn't fair."

The biggest challenge in denying wealth to the Iranians was a recalcitrant China. The CCP cannot on its own produce enough energy for its economy. It depends on the Middle East, including Iran. This is an immutable fact of geopolitics that is too often forgotten. Consequently, the CCP was constantly busting our sanctions. I pushed to sanction China just as we did other countries, but the Treasury Department worried about losing the dollar as a reserve currency—a valid concern. In any case, President Trump was clear about the need to cut off Iran's financial flows—money was almost always the first prism through which he evaluated national security matters. In May 2018, Iran exported nearly 2.5 million barrels of oil per day. By May 2020, Iran's oil exports had fallen to just 70,000 barrels per day. This may well have been one of the most successful sanctions campaigns in world history. And, importantly, we did it without driving up global crude prices, requiring European cooperation, or, most importantly, causing a war.

THE KHASHOGGI CRAZE

Executing on a maximum-pressure campaign that lived up to its name meant growing partnerships with countries in every corner of the world. The Left *hated* us for cultivating ties with Middle Eastern regimes whose human rights records were dismal. I couldn't believe the level of hypocrisy from Democrats and the media, given that the Obama administration had attempted to make the Islamic Republic of Iran, among the world's worst abusers of human rights, America's top partner in the Middle East. Moreover, there is a world of difference between forging permanent friendships with America-hating ideologues and cultivating transactional relations with authoritarian regimes willing to work with the United States. As Ronald Reagan's great UN ambassador Jeane Kirkpatrick wrote in her famous essay "Dictatorships and Double Standards," "Only intellectual fashion and the tyranny of Right/Left thinking prevent intelligent men of good will from perceiving the facts that traditional authoritarian governments are less repressive than revolutionary autocracies, that they are more susceptible of liberalization, and that they are more compatible with U.S. interests."

What really made the media madder than a vegan in a slaughterhouse was our relationship with Saudi Arabia. We wanted to help the kingdom move forward to modernity, but this had to be done slowly and with great care. Our close association with the Saudis set up one of my first diplomatic crises as secretary of state.

On October 2, 2018, the Saudi government lured a critic of the regime named Jamal Khashoggi into the Saudi consulate in Istanbul, Turkey, where agents of the Saudi regime quite literally chopped him into pieces. This grotesque butchery was outrageous, unacceptable, horrific, sad, despicable, evil, brutish, and, of course, unlawful.

This episode was ugly, but it wasn't surprising—not to me, anyway. I'd seen enough of the Middle East to know that this kind of ruthlessness was all too routine in that part of the world. That doesn't make it righteous or good, but the reaction of many evoked the faux outrage of the corrupt police chief played by Claude Rains in the film *Casablanca*, who interrupts his own gambling when he needs a pretext to shut down Rick's café: "I'm shocked, shocked to find that gambling is going on in here!"

Much of the disproportionate global uproar was fueled by the media, which hammered the story extra hard because Khashoggi was a "journalist." To be clear, Khashoggi was a journalist to the extent that I and many other public figures are journalists. We sometimes get our writing published, but we also do other things. The media made Khashoggi out to be a Saudi Arabian Bob Woodward who was martyred for bravely criticizing the Saudi royal family through his opinion articles in the *Washington Post*. In truth, Khashoggi was an activist who had supported the losing team in a recent fight for the throne in Saudi Arabia, and he was unhappy with having been exiled. And as even the *New York Times* reported, Khashoggi was also cozy with the terrorist-supporting Muslim Brotherhood. His very public expression of sorrow for the death of Osama bin Laden shows, at least, a situation far more complex than has been acknowledged. He didn't deserve to die, but we need to be clear about who he was—and too many people in the media were not.

Just as the media spent years trying to drive a wedge between me and President Trump, they spent the ensuing weeks trying to fracture America's relationship with Saudi Arabia. Much of this had to do with Mohammed bin Salman (MBS), the crown prince of Saudi Araba and the heir to the Saudi throne. The progressive Left hates MBS, in spite of the fact that he is leading the greatest cultural reform in the kingdom's history. He will prove to be one of the most important leaders of his time, a truly historic figure on the world stage. The *Post* led the charge for weeks in trying to sever American-Saudi ties, running columns with titles such as "America's Hypocrisy on Saudi Arabia" and "Trump Telegraphs a Soft Line on Jamal Khashoggi—Even as Evidence Becomes More Damning." The media was more invested in complaining about MBS than in investigating how Turkish president Recep Tayyip Erdoğan had let his country become a very permissive environment for Iranian hit squads.

The Left also shamed Republicans into decrying Khashoggi's murder as a singularly horrible event. Senator Lindsey Graham, with whom I have worked closely, told me he was "never going to speak with the kingdom again until MBS is destroyed." At one point, I called Senator Graham to ask if he was indeed demanding that the Trump administration make regime change in the Kingdom of Saudi Arabia our official policy. He demurred, saying only, "Mike, this is bad." Deep down he knew we couldn't, and shouldn't, cut ties.

As information about the butchery inside the consulate developed, I continued to share it with President Trump. Intellectually, the president had the same reflex I did: it wasn't good, but it wasn't remotely the kind of action that should cause the United States to abandon an important partner. We both chuckled that Erdoğan and his intelligence services were leaking the details of what had transpired inside the consulate to masterful effect. And Erdoğan was a near-dictator. What business did he have complaining about a government-sanctioned killing?

So, what to do? Jared Kushner, then working on Middle East peace, wanted nothing to do with our policy choice on this issue. It was the president and me on this one. My proposal to him was "Lead. Do the right thing for America. Suck up the noise and put America first." I went to the Oval Office, and we drafted a statement:

AMERICA FIRST!
The world is a very dangerous place!

The country of Iran, as an example, is responsible for a bloody proxy war against Saudi Arabia in Yemen, trying to destabilize Iraq's fragile attempt at democracy, supporting the terror group Hezbollah in Lebanon, propping up dictator Bashar al-Assad in Syria (who has killed millions of his own citizens), and much more. Likewise, the Iranians have killed many Americans and other innocent people throughout the Middle East. Iran states openly, and with great force, "Death to America!" and "Death to Israel!" Iran is considered "the world's leading sponsor of terror."

On the other hand, Saudi Arabia would gladly withdraw from Yemen if the Iranians would agree to leave. They would immediately provide desperately needed humanitarian assistance. Additionally, Saudi Arabia has agreed to spend billions of dollars in leading the fight against Radical Islamic Terrorism.

After my heavily negotiated trip to Saudi Arabia last year, the Kingdom agreed to spend and invest $450 billion in the United States. This is a record amount of money. It will create hundreds of thousands of jobs, tremendous economic development, and much additional wealth for the United States. Of the $450 billion, $110 billion will be spent on the purchase of military equipment from Boeing, Lockheed Martin, Raytheon and many other great U.S. defense contractors. If we foolishly cancel these contracts, Russia and China would be the enormous beneficiaries—and very happy to acquire all of this newfound business. It would be a wonderful gift to them directly from the United States!

The crime against Jamal Khashoggi was a terrible one, and one that our country does not condone. Indeed, we have taken strong action against those already known to have participated in the murder. After great independent research, we now know many details of this horrible crime. We have already sanctioned 17 Saudis known to have been involved in the murder of Mr. Khashoggi, and the disposal of his body.

Representatives of Saudi Arabia say that Jamal Khashoggi was an "enemy of the state" and a member of the Muslim Brotherhood, but my decision is in no way based on that—this is an unacceptable and horrible crime. King Salman and Crown Prince Mohammad bin Salman vigorously deny any knowledge of the planning or execution of the murder of Mr. Khashoggi. Our intelligence agencies continue to assess all information, but it could very well be that the Crown Prince had knowledge of this tragic event—maybe he did and maybe he didn't!

That being said, we may never know all of the facts surrounding the murder of Mr. Jamal Khashoggi. In any case, our relationship is with the Kingdom of Saudi Arabia. They have been a great ally in our very important fight against Iran. The United States intends to remain a steadfast partner of Saudi Arabia to ensure the interests of our country, Israel and all other partners in the region. It is our paramount goal to fully eliminate the threat of terrorism throughout the world!

I understand there are members of Congress who, for political or other reasons, would like to go in a different direction—and they are free to do so. I will consider whatever ideas are presented to me, but only if they are consistent with the absolute security and safety of America. After the United States, Saudi Arabia is the largest oil producing nation in the world. They have worked closely with us and have been very responsive to my requests to keeping oil prices at reasonable levels—so important for the world. As President of the United States I intend to ensure that, in a very dangerous world, America is pursuing its national interests and vigorously contesting countries that wish to do us harm. Very simply it is called America First!

The blowback in the media from this missive was precisely what one would expect. But we were right to not give an inch. We could not afford to lose a critical American security ally ready to help reduce the threat of Iran. Stable and affordable energy prices depend on Saudi Arabia's output. Political instability in the kingdom would be a nightmare scenario for the region and American national security. We also hoped to keep the Saudis involved in the conversations surrounding new Middle East peace, an outcome that, I argued to the president, depended upon the youthful and open-minded MBS staying in power. One transgression, even an egregious one, shouldn't upend our entire policy. Today the kingdom continues to come under attack from both the Right and the Left, despite its effort to support America under presidents from both parties. Under the leadership of the crown prince, Saudi Arabia, which President Biden once hoped to make a "pariah state," continues to support US security and economic interests. It has demonstrated leadership in building relationships with our country that I can only wish for from wealthy, capable European nations.

Sticking with the Saudis wasn't a hard decision, but the ordeal of cleaning up the mess publicly wasn't over yet. President Trump told me, "I want you to travel to Saudi Arabia." This would make me the first Westerner to meet with MBS since the crime. I told him yes, I'd be the right one to go. In some ways, I think the president was envious that I was the one who gave the middle finger to the *Washington Post*, the *New York Times*, and other bed-wetters who didn't have a grip on reality. He said, "My Mike, go and have a good time. Tell him he owes us."

The content of my meeting with MBS will remain private, but suffice it to say we were focused on how to keep America and the kingdom safe. I've been asked the same question a hundred times and in dozens of ways: "Mr. Secretary, did you tell him that murder is bad and the United States doesn't approve?" It betrays no confidences to answer with a question of my own. Does anyone think for one minute that I wouldn't have said that, that he wouldn't have known that I was going to say it, and that he wasn't deeply aware that what happened to Khashoggi was damaging to our relationship?

Afterward, almost every newspaper in America ran a big picture of me meeting with the man whose sole identity, in their minds, was the murderer of Jamal Khashoggi. There are two things worth noting about that: First, contrary to what has been reported, there is nearly zero intelligence that directly links MBS to ordering the murder. The Office of the Director of National Intelligence report released in February 2021 that claimed to demonstrate his guilt said little more than "surely he must have known." Second, I met with many people who had ordered killings. Were it to be proven that MBS had ordered this one, it would have meant only that he was one more ruthless leader in a pretty damn ruthless part of the world. To say these two things is not to greenlight bad behavior. It's just the opposite. We used that dire moment to chart a course forward to a peace whose benefits, I pray, will last for generations.

When I returned, the administration faced a choice of how to punish the perpetrators. In November, we levied visa bans and economic sanctions on seventeen Saudis connected with the incident. But we decided against punishing MBS himself, and frankly, it wasn't a close call. Even the bureaucrats at State thought that would be dumb. We could impose accountability for what happened, while not rupturing a key relationship.

As I said in a press conference addressing the matter on November 20: "It's a mean, nasty world out there—the Middle East in particular. It is the president's obligation . . . to ensure we adopt policies that further America's national security." It wasn't a pleasant series of events, but I'm proud that our administration didn't make an emotionally rash choice that would have jeopardized American lives and our strategic objectives in the Middle East. The Khashoggi episode was also one of my first experiences in the secretary of state's chair reaffirming something I had always heard: if you wait for the perfect option in foreign policy, it will never come. It's just too much of a mean, nasty world out there.

The coda to this episode for me took place some months later. I was invited to a recurring dinner party where the members of the establishment media sit for a chat. The dinner started off nicely enough, as I told a few stories and answered a few questions. But the dam could only hold back the flood for so long. The evening descended into an inquisition on the one topic they all agreed on: How could I possibly defend Jamal Khashoggi's killer? I made a pass at explaining. Then I endured the same question a second time. And then another.

I lost it.

I turned to the group and shouted what I was really thinking: "You crazy Lefties have lost your minds! You all should be thanking me for protecting your Georgetown cocktail parties from radical Islamists and defending our Jewish friends from Qasem Soleimani!"

It got really quiet. Susan exclaimed out loud, with as much cheer as she could muster, "Well, it's been lovely!"

We hastily made our exit from that dinner party—a mean, nasty world of its own.

CHAPTER 4

PIPEHITTERS WANTED

W e'd been chasing a piece of data.

The work on this project had begun before my time as CIA director, but the team needed more heft to make it successful. In time, we found the right gal to lead the effort to get that data, and we equipped her with the resources to pursue it. Her leadership would pay dividends.

Just before I departed the CIA to become secretary of state, I was at a station headquarters, and the team said they had a surprise for me. A young and talented CIA officer came forward. His hands were sweating as he told me a harrowing story of how, after months of working an asset for a long time, he "got to do one old school."

The night before, he had been in the jungle, to meet his mark. Then, he said, "He gave me a thumb drive, and I gave him money." With the exchange of Benjamins for intelligence complete, he walked back to a rendezvous point, hopped in a helo, and made his way back to where I was at that moment. He had obtained the critical intelligence that we'd been trying for months to acquire. Not a typical day, even by CIA standards. I joked that he should have been sweating in the jungle, not in an air-conditioned office with me.

Perhaps one day the world will know more about this daring operation. It was a great success, due to the leader of character we put in charge of the operation and the courage of the young man who executed it. I am confident that the outcome saved lives. These are the results that accrue to the benefit of the American people when you build teams full of pipehitters.

THE DEFINITION OF A PIPEHITTER

I read lots as a kid. Among my favorite books was *Nice Guys Finish Last*, the autobiography of Leo Durocher, the firebrand second baseman and manager who never gave an inch to his opponents. He coined the famous phrase from which his book takes its name. That title, along with a famous line from the book—"I come to play! I come to beat you! I come to kill you!"—captures the competitive fire with which I've approached many parts of life.

Good teams and good teammates have common characteristics. Earlier, I used the term *pipehitter* to describe somebody with a mentality focused on winning, and I like having as many of them on my teams as possible. Being a pipehitter doesn't mean being brash or disrespectful to others—in fact, that approach is fatal in business, diplomacy, and personal relationships. It means having your head in the game, doing everything with excellence, and not avoiding a necessary fight. A high level of intensity should come standard in all those who handle US national security affairs, because there is no more weighty responsibility in public service than helping safeguard the lives and material welfare of more than 330 million Americans.

Being a pipehitter doesn't mean swinging wildly. In fact, it often means patiently gathering up the facts so you can make the right move. Thus, listening is one of the most important skills anyone can develop. When I arrived in Germany for my first posting as a young second lieutenant, a grizzled staff sergeant quite a few years my senior picked me up in a Jeep and brought me to base. I guess I was eager to show him that I was a hotshot young officer, and I talked a lot during the ride. Then he turned to me and told me something I've never forgotten. Even though I outranked him, he had a lot more experience than I did, and he firmly conveyed with a few four-letter words that I'd do well to "just shut up and learn a thing or two." It was good advice that I've shared with people time and again. Leaders should listen more than they speak, so that they can properly collect information and diagnose problems before giving direction.

For those who know Donald Trump, they know that when you're

with him, you get to listen. You get to listen a lot. For me, that was no problem. But for so many others on the team, that was unbearable. Yes, I heard the same stories multiple times, but Nick and Susan say I do the same thing. Sometimes the president's rants were colorful. Other times they were off-color. They were always no-holds-barred, and I loved that. It could take patience and stamina to stay focused, but he was the president. The older I get, the more I know that the absence of the ability to listen is the hallmark of weak minds. I reminded my national security colleagues—four national security advisors, four chiefs of staff, and four secretaries of defense—of this repeatedly. Listen. Learn. When the time is right, vigorously make your case. When necessary, make it viciously. Then execute the plan.

Pipehitters also embrace accountability. In the Army, every member of our unit had a job to do. In a live-fire scenario, the success of the mission could depend on a single soldier performing a role to perfection. The military raises standards and kills laziness by training soldiers to take responsibility for everything in their control. That's how I have always led my teams in business, in Congress, and at the CIA and the State Department. I make no apologies for setting high bars of performance, insisting people rise to them, and demanding explanations for failure.

My approach has caused nearly everyone who has ever worked for me to admit that I can be a tough son of a gun. To adopt a line from Shakespeare, there is method to my madness: enforcing rigorous accountability causes people to perform at high levels and even beyond what they believe are their capabilities. My people can say without hesitation that they show up for work to win for the American people every day. They can say they belong to teams where a commitment to excellence comes standard. I wish I could tell you that most members of Congress are this way, but they aren't. Too many of them are grandstanders, just trying to make it to their next successful reelection bid—they're show horses, not workhorses.

I was pleased to serve with a president who shared my fixation on winning. He took to heart the famous quotation "Winning isn't everything. It's the only thing." For a man shaped by the relentless world of New York real estate, winning is as essential as oxygen, in everything from Twitter fights to sham impeachment proceedings. In 2016, President Trump ran for office largely on the lament that America wasn't winning anymore. Gone were the days of America First, ceded to what he called the "false song of globalism" and the whims of a self-enriching political class. The fact that millions of voters rallied behind his message told me that the American people were ready to fight to win, too.

Our shared love of competition and winning undergirded an America First foreign policy. We both despised it when people in the federal bureaucracies demanded credit for *how* things are done as much as the outcomes themselves. Anyone who has ever run a business knows this foolhardy approach is an express train to failure. It boggles my mind that educated people often prize process and outcomes equally. That's not how pipehitters view the world.

EMPOWERING THE PIPEHITTERS AT THE CIA

When I became CIA director, I knew I had a once-in-a-lifetime opportunity to win for the Agency and for America. Seizing that opportunity meant, first of all, tuning out the noise and focusing on what matters. Busy people must target essential work. I've thought often of something my friend Brian Mulroney, the former prime minister of Canada, has told me: "Mike, history only remembers the big-ticket items. Everything else is forgotten. Don't waste any more time than you must on the forgotten."

Concentrating on what I must do has been the story of my life. I am an engineer by training. In my introductory electrical engineering and physics classes, nearly every problem set began with the caveats "Assuming no friction . . ." or "With all noise eliminated . . ." That was good enough for EE-301 or PH-201, but in real life friction and noise is everywhere. The best leaders overcome these obstacles through both personal and organizational discipline. Members of our own team in the Trump administration became consumed by the noise generated by a progressive media that operates like a home crowd when the visitor has the ball: they scream and holler, hoping to jam your play calling so that you'll fail.

Consequently, my first task at the CIA was to hire people who would be outstanding human filters—people who would have good judgment on which problems to bring to my attention and which to solve on their own.

That's why I hired Gina Haspel and Brian Bulatao for the top jobs—I trusted these pipehitters to handle what was important work for which I simply did not have time. When I arrived at the Agency, the stack of "approvals" that hit my desk was staggering. For the vast majority of those decisions, I had neither the knowledge nor the expertise to second-guess the team. If I couldn't add value, I'd push it down to Haspel, Bulatao, or someone else. If I had to touch it because of legal obligations, I'd devote thirty seconds to it and no more. I estimate that by the time I left the Agency, I reduced the amount of paperwork coming to my desk for approval by somewhere between 40 percent and 70 percent. By eliminating myself as a choke point, the Agency got better and faster.

I had delegated responsibility to leaders who were good enough to own it. And I could apply more of my energies to the items that truly mattered. It was also critical for me to set an example for the entire CIA team that we should eliminate bureaucracy whenever possible. We must always move faster than our adversaries do. I wanted to be faster, more agile, and more operational. And I wanted my team to know I trusted them. With only a few exceptions, they never let me down. Nor did they give an inch—an essential pipehitter quality.

Most federal agencies have scores of political appointees. At the CIA, we had only four: director, deputy director, general counsel, and inspector general. Because of this, building a winning team at Langley also meant finding out who the pipehitters were among the career officials and empowering them. This is just what I did with Andy Kim and the gentleman who led our Iranian Republic Mission Center.

I especially put the Agency's paramilitary operators, the Special Activities Division (SAD), in the pipehitter category. These patriots—mostly men who had previously served as special operators at the Defense Department—took enormous risks across the entire world every day. They worked with our allies and partners to project American power into the toughest places. I was blessed to have Brian Carbaugh run SAD. I got to know him as my chief of staff when I first arrived. He, Gina, and I built our team. We'd review a résumé, and I'd say, "I like her, I think she'd be great." He'd say, "Chief, she's a pipehitter, can't go wrong." The next one, he'd say, "Mmm, good guy, not a pipehitter." America needed pipehitters in the field, and Brian helped me find them, give them guidance, and then send them out to execute for our country. As head of SAD, Brian empowered his warriors to do their dangerous jobs and kept them as safe as he could. He implored me to alter their rules of engagement in Syria and elsewhere, and we did. We can't talk about much of what we did—but we saw the positive effects of building a good team.

I was blessed to find that many in the Agency's rank and file were true pipehitters with a clear-eyed view of the world and an appetite for risk. This was most true among the members of the Ground Branch Operators. Almost all of them were veterans of elite military units. They are frequently the first force to confront our country's most immediate and vexing problems, which makes these heroes the most brilliant and fearsome operators on the planet.

When the Trump administration showed up, Ground Branch was a shadow of its former self—thanks in large part to John Brennan's evisceration of a risk-taking culture. My senior team did three things that allowed them to turn things around: First, we made sure they got the long-term physical and mental health care that they needed and deserved—a big morale boost for them and their families. Second, we got them helicopters and other stocks of equipment that had been underfunded or depleted. And third, we let Ground Branch start filling out its roster again. At one point, I had to call the head of human resources and raise my voice: "If you don't let Ground Branch hire, I will personally f——ing crush you." It wasn't the nicest thing to do, but there weren't any problems afterward. The Ground Branch unit's leader thanked me and Brian Bulatao for having their backs, providing them resources, and—dare I say it?—making them great again. I regret I didn't have more time at CIA to work with them.

I also worked to build up the human-resources capacity. Perhaps the best example resulted from a review of high turnover rates on a CIA team. I interviewed a couple of the outgoing team members. Their stories made clear to me that we were missing something. Those who suffered from marital discord or excessive drinking often had nowhere to turn—in part, because they were undercover or working extremely sensitive files that caused waves of stress to crash down on them daily.

I changed that by setting up a faith-based counseling program. It took nearly a year because I had to overcome a bunch of lawyers who resisted the idea. But I had seen the power of the Chaplain Corps in the Army and how it made my team better. We borrowed a couple of retired military chaplains and built a model that fit the CIA. By the time the administration left, CIA officers had a cadre of trained professional faith leaders who were cleared to hear the secrets that needed to be heard. Our officers could find refuge, emotional sustenance, and faith-driven assistance. In my four years in the administration, that CIA Chaplains Corps was among the best team-building outcomes.

I can't tell you the names of most of the great Americans who compose the best intelligence service in the world, but that team that ran the Counterterrorism Mission Center, the brassy women who ran my Counterintelligence Mission Center, the head of the Special Activities Center, and my head of Clandestine Operations all crushed it. Even with families of their own, these men and women were on call and on a mission. History and the good Lord will know their important work. I had many good intelligence counterparts overseas, too. In Japan, Shigeru Kitamura was always a force. In the United Kingdom, Andrew Parker, now Lord Chamberlain, at MI5 and Alex Young at MI6 shared my mission and my intensity. Partners in Switzerland, Australia's services, and a handful of others who will thank me for not naming them likewise did great work that helped save American lives.

I don't regret becoming secretary of state, but I was bummed to leave behind a winning team at the CIA—and gratified to know that much of it would remain in place for my successor, Gina Haspel. Yet she wasn't happy with me because I was taking Brian Bulatao with me to State. Brian had earned enormous respect inside the Agency and had demonstrated the ability to execute large projects on time and on budget. In the words of one CIA officer, the Agency had "never been close to this good" in his thirty-plus years there. I don't take personal credit for that accomplishment. It was because I had a team of pipehitters that knew how to win.

TRANSFORMING THE CULTURE OF THE
STATE DEPARTMENT—GOOD LUCK!

Upon becoming secretary of state in 2018, I was put in charge of an organization of about seventy-five thousand people and a budget of more than $50 billion. I had a universe of operational and financial resources at my disposal, but that also meant the number of vectors for potential failure increased. Additionally, I was deeply aware that President Trump was the forty-fifth president and I was the seventieth secretary of state. It was simple math: there is a lot more turnover in my gig than in his. I was appropriately on thin ice from day one, and not just because of the president's proclivity to fire people who don't do what he asks. When things go wrong, secretaries of state are a heck of a lot more expendable than presidents are.

I had already had many experiences with the State Department during my time in Congress. Most of them were characterized by deceit and stonewalling—not the hallmarks of pipehitters or of a winning diplomatic corps. As a member of the House Select Committee on Benghazi investigating fatal terrorist attacks on an American diplomatic outpost in Libya in 2012, I sought to get to the bottom of how Secretary of State Clinton had allowed Libyan jihadists to kill Ambassador Christopher Stevens, a State Department information management officer named Sean Smith, and two patriots from the CIA, Glen Doherty and Tyrone Woods. The State Department opposed every single effort we made to obtain the answers that the American people demanded. The then–undersecretary for management, a crab of a man named Patrick Kennedy, was placed in charge of State's response on Capitol Hill. At every turn, Kennedy was dishonest, incompetent, and nasty in the way he dealt with our congressional team. I felt that Kennedy sought to cover up for Hillary Clinton, Susan Rice, and Huma Abedin by lying about their roles and burying the documents we requested.

I also remembered how much opposition I had received as a member of Congress from the State Department's embassy in Tel Aviv, and then the so-called consulate in Jerusalem, which might as well have been a community center for the Palestinians. On one visit, I had arranged to walk around the top of the wall that surrounds the Old City. I was to be escorted by Mickey Rosenfeld, a great Israeli cop. The goal was to evaluate security issues concerning the Israeli police forces whom I'd come to know as amazing heroes. Literally minutes before my inspection was to begin, the State Department official who was managing my trip placed me in a van. To call it kidnapping would be too much, but to my shock, I was dropped off at my hotel rather than at the Old City. The stated reason? "Sir, this would be provocative to the Palestinians and create diplomatic risk. No senior American has ever done this. We regret we cannot support your effort." I knew that as secretary of state, I'd have to fix this timid attitude.

Finally, I'd worked closely with the State Department during my time as CIA director. I'd encountered some excellent leaders but could also see that this was a union-led, passive-aggressive, establishment leak-machine that had resolved from day one of our administration to obstruct the goals of our America First agenda. They loathed President Trump for many reasons, not the least of which was that he had romped to victory in the election over their former leader, Secretary Clinton, a person whom most of the senior leaders at State had come to love and admire.

I observed the effort to thwart the Trump administration before I even made it to the secretary's desk. In 2017, I traveled to the United Arab Emirates as CIA director to visit with the Emirati crown prince, his team, and my intelligence counterparts—highly capable operators who were and are great partners of the United States. I was at a casual dinner that night, a short, nonbusiness affair to which my wife, Susan; several diplomats from the embassy; and Barbara Leaf, a career official then serving as the temporary US ambassador to the United Arab Emirates, had been invited. About twenty minutes into the evening, she began to rip into the Emiratis in the most rude and arrogant fashion I have ever seen in a public setting. At a purely social gathering, she called out Emirati officials by name, recounted stories about American officials that I felt were not appropriate to share with the group present, and made a slew of statements clearly demonstrating to me that she was not on board with current US policy. Not a pipehitter.

I was pissed and decided to cut the evening short. As we left, I apologized to our host—the Emirati ambassador to the United States. Then I let Secretary Tillerson know what had happened and asked to see Leaf in her office the next morning. While it was not my place to do so, I demanded she apologize to the Emirati ambassador, which she never did. I warned her that I was going to do all that I could to make sure she never represented America at so much as a game of tiddlywinks. All she could do was stare at me with the self-satisfaction of a careerist who intended to outlast the Trump administration. In a normal organization, violating both decorum and policy in the way Barbara Leaf did would result in her getting fired and never working there again. But the State Department is not a normal organization. After hitting the think-tank circuit for a few years, Leaf is at this moment the Biden administration's assistant secretary of state for Near East Affairs. She is the US government's highest-ranking official overseeing Middle East policy.

In my very first days as secretary of state, I was concerned about not getting rolled by the likes of Leaf—seasoned operatives hostile to the agenda who know how to pull the right levers within the bureaucracy to frustrate objectives. I needed people to help me navigate the State Department bureaucracy and diplomatic conventions. I needed people I could trust to win every day for America. I needed pipehitters.

The first piece of the puzzle was to drag in my brothers. I brought Brian Bulatao over from CIA to be the undersecretary of state for management, essentially the State Department's chief operating officer. I then reached for secret weapon number two: Ulrich Brechbühl. Ulrich has had a successful business career in his own right and, like Brian, dropped everything and moved to DC to help me in the job of my life. "Brechs" and I met in July 1982 as brand-new cadets. As with Brian, Ulrich is practically family. My son knows him as Uncle Ulrich. To know Ulrich and his wife, Michelle, is to love them. They are kind, generous, and massively competent. I would have brought them both on board, but their three boys needed momma to keep the home fires burning. Next time.

Ulrich has the virtue of being among the hardest working and most diligent, organized, and patient leaders one will ever encounter. At West Point, he was part of the senior cadet military leadership team—already demonstrating at age twenty-two his ability to lead and earn the respect of his peers in ways the rest of us knuckleheads had not done. Right after graduation, Ulrich served with me in the 2nd Armored Cavalry Regiment. We reconnected at Harvard and then partnered in Wichita on our airplane-parts business. We used his Swiss meticulousness and demeanor to great effect as the company's CFO.

At State, I gave him the role of counselor, a historically important post. But his title belied his role as my enforcer. Every time a big problem arose I'd tell my team, "Get Ulrich in here." He made the problems go away, and he made me better every day. He was a builder, a coordinator, and, when required, the deliverer of bad news. Because he is neither easily impressed nor intimidated, nor one to get caught up in DC status games, I knew he could succeed in the Trump administration. He helped triage untold personnel jams and referee bureaucratic disputes, very often thankless work that was nonetheless crucial for allowing me to do what only the secretary of state can do. He knew me so well that often, before others on the team approached me with a problem, they would say, "Let's check with Ulrich." A first-rate pipehitter.

Just as Gina Haspel was my eyes into the CIA's organization chart, David Hale became my most senior career officer at State. Like I had done with Gina, I had first met him while I was in Congress. A US diplomat since 1985, he had been the US ambassador to Jordan, Pakistan, and Lebanon, teaching me a great deal of what I know about that wonderful country and its place in the Eastern Mediterranean. I'd also worked with David when I was running the CIA, and he was the US ambassador to Pakistan. He is so professional that I couldn't tell you whom he voted for in 2016, even though he'd worked closely with Secretary Clinton. I wish there were more like him, doing their work in a nonpartisan way for whomever the American people elect. David and I shared an understanding of the Middle East, and of our responsibility to deliver for President Trump. His career suffered for having worked for me. I regret that. It says more about the State Department than anything I can write.

I picked Lisa Kenna as my chief of staff—the person responsible for my frantic schedule. Lisa had already been battle-tested over years in the national security world, and I trusted her competence and dedication. Even as she balanced serious family commitments, she stuck with me for all one thousand days of my tenure as a critical conduit between my office, the rest of the State Department, and the entire US national security apparatus. Like David, I think Lisa was kicked out of the Foreign Service cool-kid clubhouse for agreeing to work alongside Donald Trump's secretary of state.

★ ★ ★

As I settled into the seventh floor, I knew that fixing morale at the department was a top priority. The headquarters building, to quote Ecclesiastes, became a "house of mourning" the moment Hillary Clinton lost the 2016 presidential election. It was especially hostile to the idea of a president ready to reject the Iran deal and other obsessions of the establishment. The Foreign Service officers weren't going to care for whomever the president chose as his secretary of state, but the deck was stacked against Secretary Tillerson, a foreign policy outsider who had run America's largest fossil-fuel company. Rex made things worse with an ill-fated effort to restructure the department, and his decision to freeze the hiring of new Civil Service and Foreign Service officers also hurt him. The department's morale suffered more when he hit pause on the practice of embassies hiring family members of Foreign Service officers into clerical jobs overseas—a common practice that tried to balance difficult service obligations with family life. The career workforce, always prone to overreact to well-intentioned proposals, revolted by anonymously complaining to the press about what they thought was Rex's horrible leadership. Rex complicated things even more by engaging only with a handful of top advisors, creating the impression that he didn't need the building's expertise, which, in some instances, is crucial.

Consequently, by the time I arrived, esprit de corps had sunk to a low point. Tradition holds that every secretary of state is welcomed into the building by throngs of State Department employees. I greeted them with assurances that I wanted them to be active in every corner of the world, executing on behalf of America. Later that day, I lifted the hiring freeze on family members. Another directive followed soon after reauthorizing the hiring of Foreign Service and Civil Service officers.

In May, I held a town hall meeting for employees and invited them to ask me (almost) anything. In my opening remarks, I said that there are tests for which you cannot cram. These are the tests of character, courage, and honesty, and you must pass them every time. I advised that the failures that come with taking risks are steps toward becoming a high-performing team. I cautioned them that producing paper is not an outcome. I demanded that they not leak and warned them that I would try to throw leakers in jail. To me, it was common sense that our diplomats be expected to uphold the American rule of law they represented worldwide. I reminded them that our mission is not about them but about America.

Those first days at State also saw the beginning of the "swagger" campaign. I wanted everyone to know that risk-taking would be rewarded, that pride in America was a prerequisite to success, and that everyone should support President Trump and me every single minute. Though mocked by the hyenas in the diplomatic press, the concept of swagger matters. I wanted our diplomats to be unflinchingly proud of America and to treat every encounter—whether they were engaging with the king of Jordan or a poor Guinean mother trying to visit her grandchild in America—as if it were the first and last impression someone would ever have about our country and its people. That meant no apologizing for our actions. That meant no whispers about how Mike Pompeo is a right-wing, Christian zealot. No whining, just winning. Sadly, after one thousand days at the top, I doubt that I left behind much swagger at all.

I also sought to build a team of pipehitters by pushing more of the Trump administration's nominees through Congress. At the time of my arrival, 56 percent of our ambassador posts were unfilled. Fifty-seven percent of the leadership jobs at headquarters, including many important assistant secretary and undersecretary slots, were also vacant. Senior leaders such as David Schenker (assistant secretary for Near East Affairs) and David Stilwell (assistant secretary for East Asian and Pacific Affairs) were ultimately stalled for a year or more because of petty objections and demands. Brian Bulatao's nomination to be undersecretary for management was held up, too, thanks to Senator Bob Menendez. I was annoyed that Democrats were delaying confirmation of the man who would make sure our Diplomatic Security units were protecting our people all over the world, even as they cried that the State Department was in disarray because they read quotes from anonymous leakers in *Politico*. I made more than a few phone calls to chew out the Hill for slowing down confirmations.

In addition to swagger, we wanted the members of the State team to have a common understanding of their purpose and the core ideas that should drive their commitment to service. Nearly every major organization in the world has a mission statement and a creed, so I told Ulrich to create one for State. He led the implementation of the *Ethos*—a code of professional ethics we developed to help set the culture of a winning State Department. Ulrich didn't write it himself. He spent months with a team of State leaders conducting focus groups, taking internal polls, and building consensus. Here's the whole thing:

I am a champion of American diplomacy.

My colleagues and I proudly serve the United States and the American people at the Department of State, America's first executive department.

We support and defend the Constitution of the United States.

We protect the American people and promote their interests and values around the world by leading our nation's foreign policy.

As a member of this team, I serve with unfailing professionalism in both my demeanor and my actions, even in the face of adversity.

I act with uncompromising personal and professional integrity.

I take ownership of and responsibility for my actions and decisions.

And I show unstinting respect in word and deed for my colleagues and all who serve alongside me.

Together, we are the United States Department of State.

Most of these dictums may seem like common-sense principles to apply in any workplace, but the truth was that the State Department was in especially desperate need of them. The aim of the *Ethos*, ultimately, was to push the department's culture toward a greater embrace of professionalism, integrity, and accountability. That transformation would begin with a special *Ethos* session to put every new State Department hire on the same page. The blowback to this nonpartisan statement was staggering. We realized we were attempting to build culture in an organization that didn't want it. The unions that represented State Department employees didn't want anything that held them accountable. The department was also simply hostile to any notion of reform led by what they saw as an evil Trump administration. This was evidenced by the fact that the department pulled down an enormous placard of the *Ethos* principles from the State Department headquarters' lobby before the Biden administration even took office on January 20, 2021.

People say it's impossible to turn around the culture of the State Department. I know one thing: At the end of my tenure, I didn't leave much change behind. But I had to try to turn more of the team into pipehitters. I know the *Ethos* inspired more than a few career employees who want to work for an organization that can win for America. Even if the *Ethos* doesn't live on by name, my hope is that those who took it to heart will perform in such a way that its principles rub off on their colleagues. I do believe the State Department can be fixed. But building a team of pipehitters will take more than a thousand days. It will take a president prepared to do it. And it's not just the State Department within the federal government that will require a teardown and rebuild.

Despite these frustrations, I was truly blessed to work with many great Americans who distinguished themselves as patriots and pipehitters. I am indebted to my Diplomatic Security detail, led by Roy Stillman and Lon Fairchild. They kept me and my family safe every day. Morgan Ortagus was a savvy department spokeswoman who had real foreign policy experience as a Navy reservist and former Treasury Department and USAID official. This made her a true weapon at the podium and on TV. Katie Martin, who ran media relations, was a warrior who pushed back on lazy reporters and urged them to write better stories that reflected the reality of our work. Joe Semrad, my body man, was more attentive to detail than any person I have ever met. He kept me running early for every meeting, just how I like it. Howard Van Vranken spared no effort in coordinating our overseas trips with the Air Force. As much as the State Department's ideological biases and petty internecine wars can be a detriment to America, the department does have a deep bench of highly conscientious and mission-first people, and I served with many of the finest of them.

Sadly, for every David Hale, a career officer who kept partisanship out of diplomacy, there are ten State Department officials driving a left-wing agenda. Let's start with the unions—principally, the American Federation of Government Employees and the American Foreign Service Association. You, the American taxpayer, provide office space and full-time staff for union bosses to do their work. They specialize in creating inefficiencies. They draft work rules that make fast processes and teamwork very difficult. They file grievances on behalf of workers who were harmed by paper cuts and cold coffee. They leak. They complain. And then they cash their paychecks, underwritten by citizens with real jobs. Among the reasons government fails so epically is because incentivizing high performers, and the inverse of that proposition, is nearly impossible. A good start for fixing the State Department, and much of our federal government, is simple: at-will employment and no unions. This is what millions and millions of us who work outside of government sign up for. What makes federal service so different as to deserve protection of your job for nearly a lifetime? My answer: nothing.

The Foreign Service Officer Corps is also overwhelmingly hard left in its cultural sympathies. One thing I encountered at State and CIA was a self-congratulatory culture of diversity in which people patted themselves on the back just for existing. Far too many man-hours were spent on planning, announcing, and executing celebrations for all kinds of groups. This effort—and it truly was an effort—to promote diversity was a far cry from the easy blending that we had at my machine shop in Kansas. German rednecks and Mandarin-speaking engineers, mothers with a half dozen children, and African American grandmas who loved the factory all worked side by side. This environment created space for fun, too. Together, we just made stuff.

In some ways, running the machine shop was easier than leading diplomats, because you could measure each team member's performance every day. How many good parts did he or she make on the lathes or mills or deburr machines? Sure, a diplomat could say he or she helped negotiate nine treaties or managed $600,000 worth of taxpayer money in some program. But most outcomes in diplomacy are qualitative. What is the standard for a "productive phone call" or "solid conversation?" How do I measure the payoff for spending two hours drinking tea with a Middle Eastern sheikh? The results are far less tangible and may not be known for months down the line. I'm a numbers guy, so I sometimes found this tough to come to terms with.

At both State and CIA, there were scores of people focused exclusively on things not directly related to the core mission. Massive diversity programs, huge training sessions on work-life balance, and climate change bureaucracies at both outfits were just some of the extraneous lines of effort. The goal of elevating these peripheral causes to be the central foci of our national security institutions—an impulse that was cultivated among the workforce—was to make these agencies more woke. No one disputes the need for finding the best talent from the broadest set of Americans. But when feeling good about oneself supplants achievement based on merit, excellence will be lost. When group identification based on unalterable traits is exalted above individual competence, the best of the best will find another place to ply their trade. America will be the loser. As a corollary to the department's loss of focus on delivering winning outcomes, my management team swam hard against the tide in getting our workforce to come back to the office during COVID-19, when they preferred to "work" from home.

The department's mission drift and hard-left orientation were evident during the summer of 2020, at the height of the Black Lives Matter madness. Harry Harris, a former admiral who had commanded the US Pacific Fleet, is a true patriot. After I was nominated to be secretary, I met Admiral Harris on the tarmac at two in the morning at Ramstein Air Base in Germany. He was then the nominee to be US ambassador to Australia.

"Harry, we are going to be deeply engaged with North Korea. I need you as my ambassador in Seoul."

"Mike, there's two problems with that. First, I'm of Japanese heritage. And second, my wife thinks Sydney and Melbourne are special."

While acknowledging that both reasons created risk, the first for smooth diplomacy with both Koreas, the second for his marriage, I asked him to think about it. He agreed to do so and, in a few days, agreed to serve as the ambassador to South Korea instead of Australia. As I said, a true pipehitter who understands winning.

In June 2020, I saw on CNN, as best I recall, that a massive Black Lives Matter banner had been hung from our embassy building in Seoul. I immediately asked Ulrich and Brian to call Harry and find out why he had unfurled a message on diplomatic property from a Marxist group whose supporters have advocated for killing police officers. Harris, ever the leader, took full responsibility and, at my direction, had it removed. The banner was so large that he needed forty-eight hours to take it down because, as someone explained, "the crane that installed the banner has already been returned to its owner."

The buck stops with the ambassador, no doubt. But I'm guessing Harry's team played him. He told us he assumed this message was nothing more than a neutral assertion of the equality of every human being—a laudable foundational principle of the American tradition. His team took advantage of Harris's goodwill to broadcast a politically loaded message. Black Lives Matter is a Marxist organization credibly accused of corruption, having spent millions on things that have nothing to do with activism, such as a $6 million Los Angeles mansion. Senior State Department officials put up their banner as if it were an American flag sewn by Betsy Ross herself.

I found this insertion of partisanship and left-wing orthodoxy masquerading as US policy dangerous to our diplomacy. I don't know how many similar incidents like the one in Seoul I would have had to handle personally had Brian and Ulrich not been riding shotgun with me. For example, American diplomats, for years, displayed Gay Pride flags from American embassy flagpoles. It's a political statement that sends a confusing message to the host country. What activist diplomats fail to realize is that loud displays of identity politics can alienate people in other countries—especially in strategic arenas of competition in the

Middle East, Africa, Latin America, and South Asia. Injecting identity politics into diplomacy also telegraphs to our enemies that our priorities are very much focused on generating affirmation at home rather than figuring out how to win at geopolitical competition. I prohibited every other political message from being flown from that flagpole—Christian flags, Trump 2020 flags, even POW flags. One pole, one mission, one flag. Defending liberty is a necessary imperative for a winning American foreign policy. Indoctrinating the world on International Pronouns Day, which the Biden State Department has promoted, is not.

PERSONNEL IS POLICY

I didn't just lead teams for four years; I was a part of one: Team Trump. As a member of the cabinet, I depended on sound relationships and deep connections with my peers and the president's staff. Some were pipehitters. Others were not. I came to understand better than ever that "personnel is policy."

The cabinet, more often than not, was filled with people who, like myself, had experience in areas of life where winning and losing mattered. The Obama administration was a taxpayer-funded work program for activists, academics, and government careerists. For them, funding tends to flow no matter what outcomes they achieve. By contrast, many of the Trump administration's senior leaders had either served our country in uniform or successfully run a business: Rex Tillerson (ExxonMobil), Jim Mattis (Marine Corps), John Kelly (Marine Corps), Steve Mnuchin (Dune Capital Management), and Gary Cohn (Goldman Sachs) to name just a few. The Biden administration to date has two veterans in the cabinet: Secretary of Defense Lloyd Austin and Secretary of Transportation Pete Buttigieg. None of the Biden team have run a major corporation, and it's hard to figure out which, if any, have signed the front side of a paycheck or spent much time as part of a significant business enterprise that didn't involve consulting. The attendant detachment from reality in both economic and national security matters is obvious.

If you want to put America first, you want people who know America, love America, and operate with competence. Take our onetime deputy

national security advisor Ricky Waddell. A humble man from Benton-
ville, Arkansas, Ricky graduated four years ahead of me at West Point.
He later became a Rhodes Scholar and earned a PhD at Columbia University. Even more impressively, after he served America on active duty,
he became a US Army Reserve officer who deployed to places such as
South Korea, Iraq, and Afghanistan, often while juggling a busy career
as a business executive in South America and raising three children with
his equally servant-hearted wife, Donna. As President Trump's deputy
national security advisor in 2017 and 2018, he helped formulate policy.
I worked with this pipehitter closely when he served as the official liaison between the chairman of the Joint Chiefs of Staff and the secretary
of state. I wish every American had a chance to see this man's integrity, brains, and dignified bearing in action. General Waddell had been
working on national security issues for decades and had seen warfare up
close—real-world experiences you would expect of someone who regularly briefs the president, the chairman of the Joint Chiefs of Staff, and
the secretary of state on national security.

Contrast General Waddell with Ben Rhodes, one of President
Obama's deputy national security advisors. Rhodes grew up on the Upper
East Side of Manhattan and got a master of fine arts degree in creative
writing from New York University in 2002. He joined Barack Obama's
campaign as a speechwriter in 2007. There's nothing wrong with a communications staffer making a jump into the policy lane, but to elevate a
novice thirty-two-year-old writer into a position of making crucial diplomatic decisions and steering the president is insane. Rhodes, according to
his own website, "led the secret negotiations with the Cuban government
that resulted in the effort to normalize relations between the United
States and Cuba" and "supported the negotiations to conclude the Joint
Comprehensive Plan of Action (JCPOA) with Iran." These were terrible
decisions for America that increased risk to our people and put Cubans
and Iranians further under the thumb of brutal regimes. Rhodes's taking the pen on foreign policy speeches explains why President Obama's
foreign policy tried to sell fictional grand narratives based on his own
messianic self-conception rather than explain the cold, hard truth of a
mean, nasty world. I did a double take in 2018 when I saw that Rhodes

came out with a book titled *The World as It Is.* A man who was willing to take a deal that let the ayatollah continue enriching uranium most assuredly lives in a fantasy world.

Treasury Secretary Steve Mnuchin and I didn't see eye to eye on every decision—but I always regarded him as a friend and understood that he had a different set of American interests to represent than I did. Moreover, the president and I both respected Steve because he had made money in the world of finance, putting his own cash on the line in risk-taking ventures. Smart, capable, calm, and determined, he knew what it took to unleash the capital flows that make our economy hum. He knew the players and how markets operated. State, CIA, and Treasury work together on many national security projects, and he was an incredibly solid partner for me.

President Obama, by contrast, employed career government official Tim Geithner as his Treasury secretary, a man who spent the great majority of his formative years growing up outside the United States and then worked almost exclusively in a series of government jobs. Succeeding him was Jack Lew, another individual who spent nearly his entire career in government and academia. As of this writing, Janet Yellen, another member of the lifelong government-academic class, is running the Treasury Department for the Biden administration. At every level, an administration will set its priorities according to the people it chooses. My colleagues in the Trump administration could win for America because so many of them had firsthand experience defending our country, not criticizing it, and creating wealth, not regulating it.

Yet the Trump administration was not without its own warts. A series of self-inflicted personnel wounds held us back. Turnover was way too high, and as the months went on, loyalty to President Trump became the sole criteria for being hired. The personnel office was eventually led by Johnny McEntee, who saw himself as the keeper of the MAGA flame. I don't know Johnny well. The president liked him, and I'm sure McEntee was competent in executing on what he was asked to do. But he failed to understand that while loyalty was a necessary qualification for service, it was not sufficient. When he started appointing unqualified people into positions of power and influence based solely on their enthusiasm for Donald Trump, multiple cabinet secretaries called me to complain about how McEntee had airdropped unwanted and untalented people into their circles.

I didn't have that problem because I had Ulrich. A fearless negotiator, he had the ability to say no to the White House, which is not the same thing as saying no to the president. He also knew he was backstopped by my own loyalty to the president.

In January 2021, I received a call from President Trump. He said, "My Mike, have you seen the *Washington Post* this morning?"

"I don't read it. My cardiologist told me it was bad for my health."

He chuckled and said, "There's an article that says you are my most loyal cabinet member. They're right, you've been great."

"Mr. President, you realize they didn't mean that as a compliment to me or you?"

"You know, you're right." We had a good laugh and he hung up.

I tried every day to be loyal and competent. I expected others to carry themselves the same way and set the tone as pipehitters.

THE NATIONAL SECURITY REVOLVING DOOR

The revolving door of leaders in the top national security jobs was not helpful. Four secretaries of defense, four national security advisors, and four chiefs of staff meant that we were always working with new colleagues. The turnover suggested instability and disorganization to our adversaries as well as our friends. For the only core member of the national security team who stayed all four years, my work meant constantly bringing new team members up to speed. If it takes a year to settle into a big job, most of these leaders never hit cruising speed.

The reasons for the turnover were many and varied. Trump's first national security advisor, Michael Flynn, was disqualified from service for lying to the vice president and the FBI. But more problematically, the president selected many people for service who either didn't share his foreign policy instincts or were unwilling to accept them, especially in the first two years. Case in point: before the highly competent and adaptable Robert O'Brien filled the post, the national security advisor was first H. R. McMaster for a year and change and then John Bolton for a year and a half. Rex Tillerson, similarly out of sync, was another short-timer. It wasn't that certain people weren't capable and talented. The challenge—as in every administration—is to be part of a team executing on the president's objectives, not your own. President Trump got 270-plus electoral votes; they got none. And the duty of all senior leaders is to adapt their style to their president's, not the other way around. Some of my colleagues either couldn't or chose not to do so. Our America First foreign policy happened despite this turnover, although there is no doubt that the churn prevented us from finishing some of the business that still needs to be completed, especially regarding China, the Middle East, Cuba, and Venezuela. All of it reinforced to me that leaders who build winning teams surround themselves with those who can challenge their ideas when necessary but execute their directives always.

The secretary of defense job was perhaps most emblematic of the problem. General Mattis is an unquestioned patriot and a brilliant man and was a great partner of the CIA. He was also deeply and very personally invested in the "forever war" view of Afghanistan, and he enjoyed the backing of a DC public-relations machine that churned day and night to praise him as the adult in the Trump administration room. Despite not being in full alignment on how to achieve American victories, he and I got along well. But why President Trump ever chose him to be secretary of defense remains a mystery to me. The two of them were as different as any two people on our team.

Among other things, Mattis never trusted the president. In June 2017, Mattis prevailed in his attempt to convince the president to increase combat strength in Afghanistan by three thousand service members—a decision that completely contradicted President Trump's instincts. Yet even after receiving authorization, Mattis refused to send the soldiers for an extended period because, he said, "I don't believe the president won't pull the rug out from under them." The president told me on October 5, 2018, "I made Mattis a star and now I'm going to have to fire him," after Mattis continued to say he believed, contrary to policy, that the JCPOA was in our national interest. He was gone in December.

On the day Mattis went to the White House to resign—or get fired, depending on whom you ask—he came by the State Department to see me. "Michael, you have to stay. You're the last man standing and without you the risk to America is too great. You are the only one on the national security team that he listens to, and you can speak to him in ways no one else can. I'm sorry I can't hang in there, but I've lost any ability to get the old man to listen to me. I've worn out my usefulness." I told him that his service to America had been noble and that he had saved countless American lives during his career.

But I also believed that his resignation was months too late. He didn't buy into America First, and he fought so much of what President Trump was seeking to accomplish. The story he told in his resignation letter—that US policy in Syria was the reason for his departure—was, at best, only part of the conflict between him and the president. In my opinion, Mattis held deeply establishment foreign policy views on an America First team. In the end, he quit believing in the hard work and acceptance of risk that comes with a disruptive effort to defend America.

Once, when I was calling for a direct response against Iran after it had attacked Americans, Mattis said, "Michael, the place to fight Iran is in Iraq." I disagreed. Killing some Shia-militia chump who worked for 550 rials a month has zero deterrence value. But Mattis didn't even follow his own strategy. He opposed serious operations in Iraq, too. He just didn't want to confront Iran anywhere, at least with this president. When he told me that Iran should not be the focus of our work because of China, I'd accept the hypothesis. But when we began to push back against the CCP, he wanted no part of that confrontation either. The fact that he was fired by both President Obama (who ended Mattis's term as the commander of CENTCOM, or Central Command, early) and President Trump is a most unfortunate ending to a glorious life of public service. I still admire Mattis's leadership of the US Marines, but he was not a sound fit for our team—and fault for his short tenure lies with both him and Trump.

The revolving door at the Pentagon didn't stop spinning with Mattis's departure. Patrick Shanahan lasted only a few months before my West Point classmate, Mark Esper, took over. Mark is a friend, a good man, and a tirelessly hard worker, but as he points out in his book, he bristled at defending the president's plans. He said that he'd resign if he was ever ordered to do anything unlawful, but then says he was not ordered to do so. I know I was never ordered to do so either. Did the president ever propose a knowingly unlawful action? I don't remember it happening in my presence, but floating an idea when you're unfamiliar with the law is different from issuing an order that you know to be illegal. Heck, I had lawyers pushing back on my ideas at State and CIA all the time. "Mr. Secretary, you can't do what you've proposed," they would say—and I suppose one could claim that I had suggested doing something illegal. (The lawyers sometimes were wrong, by the way.) Other times, I was unaware of a legal barrier, and we'd find another way to accomplish the mission lawfully. That was my experience with the White House, too. Lawyers were everywhere, making sure we all did it right. Isn't that how American government and a team of get-it-done pipehitters is supposed to work?

In any event, the turnover at Defense continued. On July 19, 2020, as I was on a flight back to DC, White House chief of staff Mark Meadows called me. "Mike, Esper is not going to make it," he said. He added that the president told him that he wanted me to "dual-hat" and take on leading the Department of Defense as an additional duty. I told Meadows that I thought that was a nutty idea. I had plenty to do running the State Department and couldn't possibly command Defense at the same time. But the evident loss of confidence in Esper meant that I began to assume a bigger role in political-military deliberations. This wasn't the first time the president had suggested I take on more than one role. Upon Bolton's imminent departure, someone had reminded the president that Henry Kissinger had been both national security advisor and secretary of state. President Trump pitched the idea to me—I think he was half kidding. I told him that I didn't think it worked the first time, and it wouldn't work the second time either. His national security advisor needed to be a neutral arbiter between the various cabinet leaders, not one of them. This idea faded, all for the good.

HALEY AND BOLTON: NOT TEAM PLAYERS

Sometimes the revolving door kept turning because of resignations, not firings. On March 18, 2018, with my nomination for secretary pending, Nikki Haley called me and said, "This place [the United Nations] is turning cartwheels." America's UN team was happy in the moment because

Haley and her team hated Tillerson, but I thought later about how the United Nations came to despise me because I had little time for the organization's uselessness and deep-seated anti-Semitism. A little more than nine months after that phone call, she was gone. While she spun her exit well in the press, Haley flat-out threw in the towel after two years as the US ambassador to the United Nations—a job that is far less important than people think, despite its sometimes being a cabinet-level position. She did an excellent job helping Tillerson put in place UN sanctions on North Korea and she gave fine remarks supporting Israel, but didn't do much else. In quitting, she forced President Trump to pick a replacement when turnover was already high, which was the last thing the national security team needed at that time. She has described her role as going toe to toe with tyrants. If true, then why would she quit such an important job at such an important time, with at least two years to go? That is, she abandoned the governorship of the great people of South Carolina for this "important" role and quit it after just months on the job. Was it simply to join Boeing's board of directors, or did she leave to protect her reputation from the inevitable so-called Trump taint the media inevitably slaps on people? Whatever the reason, her decision to quit after such a short time did not evince a commitment to team over self.

Nor did I love how in at least one instance she undermined our teamwork. As an operational matter, ambassadors were supposed to report to me. I had no problem with ambassadors who had preexisting relationships with Trump checking in with their old friend, but Chief of Staff Kelly and I had made sure that when ambassadors sought to see the president, they would clear it with me first. This was for my own situational awareness, and I nearly always said yes. In fact, this happened frequently. Indeed, sometimes President Trump would call ambassadors directly. No problem. My only ask is that to the extent that there was an action required or a policy impacted, our team needed to know so we could support it. This is a basic organizational imperative for any high-performing team.

I received a call one evening from Kelly, who apologized for allowing Ambassador Haley to go to the Oval Office. He had initially told her to follow the protocol and check with me. She insisted that she needed to see the president about a personal matter and that it had nothing to do with her work at the United Nations or for State. He acceded to the request and did not flag it for me. Now he was pissed. It turns out she had not gone in for a personal matter, but rather had entered the Oval Office with the president's daughter Ivanka and her husband, Jared, who were both senior advisors. As best Kelly could tell, they were presenting a possible "Haley for vice president" option. I can't confirm this, but he was certain he had been played, and he was not happy about it. Clearly, this visit did not reflect a team effort but undermined our work for America.

But no national security team member was less of a pipehitter than John Bolton. No matter the subject, Bolton was constantly scheming to win for himself and no one else. He cared far more about taking credit and nurturing his ego than he did for executing the president's directives, the very thing that is expected of him under the American constitutional order. If everyone had behaved as selfishly as Bolton had, very little would ever have gotten accomplished.

This was too bad. I'd known John a bit before he joined the team, and I respected his commitment to defending America. I also knew *of* him— his reputation for being tough to work with, and his inability to adapt his views. He and the president had very different instincts on policy. President Trump knew this, too. Still, he chose Bolton.

Perhaps the best example of Bolton working against Trump's plans involved North Korea. In April 2018, just weeks before the planned sum- mit between President Trump and Chairman Kim, Bolton went on TV and said regarding denuclearization, "I think we're looking at the Libya model of 2003, 2004." This suggested to the North Koreans that the United States would trade sanctions relief for denuclearization, just as we had done with Libya. But Bolton knew the North Koreans would also interpret "the Libya model" as suggesting a US-backed effort at eventual regime change, just as we had also done in Libya in 2011. Chairman Kim didn't want to go out like Muammar Gaddhafi, whose last moments of life were spent hiding inside some drainage pipes before being sodom- ized with a bayonet and riddled with bullets, with his lifeless body later displayed in an empty freezer on the streets of Misrata, Libya. It seemed to me that what appeared to be a throwaway line by Bolton was in fact designed to spook Kim to the point he would refuse to engage with the

Trump administration. When Trump heard Bolton's comments, he blew a gasket, and immediately shut Bolton out of the North Korea process entirely. I was untroubled, because the president already despised John within months of him taking the National Security Agency job, and this simply removed an obstacle to a successful execution of our plan.

I still wish things had been different with Bolton because we agreed on so many things. But we diverged wildly on process. We both thought Kim Jong Un and the Taliban should receive zero unconditional gifts, but I was willing to talk to them; he wasn't. We both sought to establish deterrence against Iran. When he advocated for a strike on an Iranian missile facility that we knew would fail, I recommended less overt options. Like Mattis, Bolton made clear to me as he was walking the plank that I should stay to the bloody end to save the world from President Trump.

On the day President Trump fired Bolton, I was having lunch with reporters. A staffer passed me a note: "POTUS needs to speak with you immediately." I excused myself. As I did, the journalists' phones lit up. They knew I was not coming back to lunch. I went to the White House, where Secretary Mnuchin and I were previously scheduled to give a briefing on Iran in the White House press room. We decided to check in with the president before we took questions, which we knew would be 100 percent about Bolton's firing.

"Should we cancel the briefing?" I asked him.

"Hell no! Don't cancel. Bolton is a scumbag loser, tell them that."

"Well, we'll take a different approach, but we get your point, Mr. President."

Steve and I went out, spoke about important Iran matters, and then took questions. The pictures of him and me grinning ear to ear as reporters lobbed questions went viral. We weren't all smiles simply because Bolton was fired (although neither of us missed him). We were smiling primarily because the situation was a bit comical: Bolton claimed that he quit, but the president said he had fired Bolton. Moreover, we laughed about the predictability of the Washington press corps, always eager to report a story of palace intrigue. Nonetheless, Steve and I have a bit of regret about displaying so much levity at that moment. It was a serious thing to have a national security advisor depart, and it created turmoil.

I stopped thinking about John the day he left the White House. But on the day I learned he was writing a book—while we were still serving—I thought about him a good deal. My mind turned to Edward Snowden, who exposed Americans to great harm back in 2013 when he illegally leaked classified information. At least Snowden had the decency not to lie about his motive. Bolton spun his book as an act of public service to save America from Donald Trump, but he could not even be honest that he just wanted to make a buck. His self-serving stories contained classified information and deeply sensitive details about conversations involving a sitting commander in chief. That's the very definition of treason. To Judge Royce Lamberth, the federal judge who presided over the White House's suit against Bolton to stop him from publishing classified information: "Defendant Bolton has gambled with the national security of the United States. He has exposed his country to harm and himself to civil (and potentially criminal) liability."

John Bolton should be in jail for spilling classified information. I hope I can one day testify at a criminal trial as a witness for the prosecution. To permit such behavior to become normal and lawful—for a personal staff member of the president of the United States to take notes and get paid to publish them while his former boss is still the commander in chief—is dangerous beyond imagination.

This is also a good moment to raise something that consistently grinds my gears. Senior leaders who leak to the press are often lauded as truth-tellers. Wrong. They are just commonplace, dishonorable leakers.

Early in my time as secretary of state, David Sanger, a longtime foreign policy reporter for the New York Times, came by my office. He wanted to meet and introduce himself. After a short, cordial chat, he told me that previous secretaries of state had given him substantial time—often two or three hours per month or more—to "tell their side of the story."

"I don't have that much time for even some of my most senior team members."

"Well, Colin Powell always had time, and so did others. Mike, if you don't tell your story, someone else will."

"Who would tell my story?"

"Look, I have been at this for decades. I have sources all over this building—some of them I've known for years and years from family and school functions."

"So, do you think it's okay for someone working for me on behalf of America to share with you proprietary information about what's going on inside the State Department? Do you think it's ethical? Legal?"

He smiled as if I were playing him, or an idiot, or perhaps both. Without answering my question, he replied, "It happens all day, every day. It's how this place works."

I understood that Sanger was, in this conversation, doing two things. First, it felt as if he were threatening me. Not that it fazed me, as I've been threatened—and indeed still am threatened—by people who can do me far more serious harm than some jackass at the *New York Times*. Second, he was also welcoming me to his elite club of insider influence, power sharing, and information peddling. Think of dozens and dozens of reporters transacting in this way with hundreds and hundreds of government employees over days and weeks and years, and you can begin to truly feel the swamp.

I spent very little time shaping the news, and while I did seek to respond to attacks, I can count on zero fingers the number of reporters that I cultivated to be my "go-to" mouthpiece to whom I could leak to protect me from the president or a colleague, or to preserve my reputation. I spoke with reporters from the State Department podium. I conducted one-on-one interviews on the record. On a case-by-case basis, and always with the knowledge of my team and in pursuit of a national objective, I would provide off-the-record answers to a reporter who was headed down the wrong track or had an important fact wrong in a way that undermined the president's agenda.

The brutal irony is that people like Sanger—and he is simply the tip of the iceberg—make the case that they are saving democracy with their work while encouraging behavior that I believe is illicit and, at a minimum, corrosive to important democratic norms. The outrageousness—combined with the demonstrated hubris—of a reporter inviting senior US officials to join his little club that knows best for the American people infuriates me to this day.

I likewise chafe at the double standard for senior leaders who mishandle classified information. If they spill secrets, they don't have to worry about it. If ordinary soldiers, engineers, and junior personnel do it, however, they get thrown in jail. Take Jake Sullivan, President Biden's national security advisor. I'm sure he's a bright and capable guy. During his first tour at State, however, he and his boss, Secretary Hillary Clinton, knowingly and repeatedly exchanged multiple emails containing highly classified information over an unclassified email system. If Jake Sullivan were an E-5 in the Navy or GS-12 at the Department of Energy, he would have lost his security clearance. Today he wakes up every morning viewing the world's most sensitive classified information.

★ ★ ★

In the end, I was the only member of the president's core national security team who made it through four years without resigning or getting fired. I may also have just been lucky. And I know it was with His help. Yet I face the same question all the time: "How'd you do it?" In other words, how did I survive not only Trump himself but the onslaught from my own party, Democrats, and the media? Sometimes the question comes with a wry smile: "I know you'll never tell, because you'll never admit just how crazy it was." Sometimes it comes with a look of stern judgment: "Just admit you sold your soul for fame and power." Sometimes folks ask in a spirit of amazement: "Okay, how the hell did you do that?" Or, from friends: "You da man!"

The answer isn't quite as much fun as the question, but here it is: I survived all four years because I worked my tail off, always counted public service as a privilege, and executed the commander's intent. No president ever had more people volunteer for missions they had no plans to carry out. I came into the Trump administration with no illusions about how Trump saw the world and our place in it. I was convinced, and continue to believe, that I helped him deepen and execute on the central thesis of American strength at home delivering security around the world. I also survived because I stacked my teams with pipehitters determined to deliver for America.

CHAPTER 5

DRAW LINES, AND DEFEND THEM RELENTLESSLY

I didn't need this.

I'd just flown 5,500 miles to meet this wolf. Already I'd been waiting twenty minutes for him to receive me—a long time in a diplomatic world obsessed with cordiality and an eternity for this former military officer.

Then I reminded myself that this is just how Vladimir Putin rolls.

I was in Sochi, Russia—the town most famous as the host of the 2014 Olympic Games, as well as a playground for the Russian elite. President Trump had asked me to meet with President Putin to see if we could improve a bad US-Russia relationship.

Russia was the last place I wanted to go. In the past week, I had made stops in Finland, Iraq, the United Kingdom, and California, taking the State Department red-eye back from Los Angeles through the night of Saturday, May 11. I was skeptical that a trip to Russia was worth it, but President Trump was the boss. On the evening of Sunday, May 12, I was back on the plane and heading toward Putin.

I continued to wait for the Russian leader. At the half-hour mark, my irritation turned into aggravation. It was taking every ounce of concentration and patience not to come unglued. Of course, throwing me off my game was exactly what Putin wanted. His KGB career and subsequent ascent through the Russian mafia state were built on a keen understanding of human psychology. German chancellor Angela Merkel, for instance, was known to fear dogs. In one meeting, Putin greeted her with his pet Labrador in tow.

I decided I wasn't going to play his game any longer, diplomatic niceties be damned. At that moment, I didn't care that he was Vladimir Putin.

"Call them," I ordered Morgan Ortagus, our spokeswoman. "Tell
them I'm about to get back on the plane and go home." Morgan saw the
look on my face. She didn't have to ask if I meant it.

Morgan dialed up her Russian counterpart and broke the news. "The
secretary isn't bluffing. This could be bad for all of us. This guy *will* leave."

I have no idea if that call mattered, but Putin arrived a few minutes
later. At one level, his behavior was petty and even childish. At another
level—one that Putin surely understands—personal dominance can drive
important outcomes. We've watched him force French president Emmanuel Macron and others to sit twenty feet away from him, at the far end
of a long table. He was sending a message in those meetings: this is my
rodeo. I wanted him to know that engagements with the United States
were America's rodeo. Whether it was a minuscule line such as this one
or all-encompassing strategic markers, we weren't afraid to draw lines for
our adversaries—and defend them relentlessly.

THE TRUMP ADMINISTRATION STOOD
FOR PEACE THROUGH STRENGTH

The Trump administration built its foreign policy on a simple principle:
peace through strength. While many other foreign ministers would have
put up with ill treatment at Putin's hands, I refused to wait like a student outside a principal's office. I wasn't going to let this madman think
that he could establish some kind of psychological superiority through
sheer rudeness. Had I accepted his affront, this Russian shark would have
smelled blood in the water and felt empowered to try to take advantage of
a tired and agitated secretary of state. Not today, Vlad. Not ever.

Strength is an indispensable pillar of foreign policy. It comes in many
forms. Superior military and economic power are important tools, but
so is pure willpower. Our first president knew this. In his Fifth Annual
Address, delivered in December 1793, George Washington observed,
"There is a rank due to the United States among nations which will be
withheld, if not absolutely lost, by the reputation of weakness."

When enemies see weakness, they are emboldened to strike. If we lack the right tools (or the will to use them), our adversaries will calculate that American retaliation against bad behavior will be minimal or even nonexistent. I believe that President Obama's refusal to enforce his own "redline" in Syria in 2013 helped convince Putin that annexing Crimea in 2014 would come with relatively little cost. He was right. In the same way, Putin likely sensed a posture of weakness from the Biden administration before he invaded Ukraine in 2022. His appetite to devour a neighboring country was always present. The Biden presidency persuaded him that it was time to eat.

This is not to say we should exercise our capabilities—military and otherwise—irresponsibly. The best way to keep America safe isn't by getting into unnecessary confrontations that could cost American lives. The best strategy is to be so strong and so willing to use force over a handful of no-BS imperatives as to stop adversaries from inflicting harm. Deterrence requires convincing your rivals not to take certain courses of action because of the intolerable consequences they will suffer in response. Drawing clear lines of deterrence and defending them relentlessly stops bad actors. Weakness provokes them.

There is precedent in American history for this idea. President Teddy Roosevelt's approach to foreign policy encompassed something of a deterrence principle when he famously said he preferred to "speak softly and carry a big stick." Before rising to the presidency, Roosevelt was an assistant secretary of the Navy, and he was heavily influenced by the book *The Influence of Sea Power upon History*, by Alfred Thayer Mahan, a Naval War College professor who argued that control of the seas was the key to geopolitical power. Later, Roosevelt built a fleet of modern and powerful battleships—"The Great White Fleet"—and showed off this armada to the world. This waterborne big stick signaled to other world powers not to screw with America. During the Cold War, America's nuclear arsenal served as the ultimate deterrent against the Soviet Union and any other enemy contemplating a dramatic attack against the United States or our allies. When you wield the threat of unspeakable destruction against your adversaries, it causes them to think carefully about their actions.

Like President Reagan before him, President Trump was willing to talk to enemies such as Kim and Putin, but they always knew that we would bring out the hammer if we had to. Whether by words (threatening North Korea with "fire and fury"), kinetic action (the Soleimani strike), or economic warfare (vigorous sanctions against Iran and Russia), our enemies knew we would punish bad behavior. In addition to wringing greater amounts of defense spending out of NATO allies, we also set up America's future deterrence capabilities by funding our military to the tune of $700 billion at the end of 2017. We needed to revamp a military that risked losing its edge to China—and there is still much more work to do there, especially in bolstering our naval- and cyber-warfare capabilities. And judging by the situation in Ukraine that rages as I write, the United States must remain prepared to meet the menace of Vladimir Putin's Russia—and all bad actors—with strength. I'm proud to say that the world can learn from the Trump administration's example of drawing clear lines of deterrence and then defending them relentlessly.

UNDERSTANDING THE PUTIN REGIME

Establishing deterrence is most important when it comes to dealing with the actors that can harm America most. Today, that's the CCP, first and foremost. But Russia is a threat, too. While the Soviet Union that I confronted as a young lieutenant is no more, there are still important reasons to maintain deterrence against Russia and its efforts to undermine the West. The country is led by a regime—not just one man—that is not afraid to use hard power. It maintains a global footprint, with partners in China, Iran, Venezuela, Cuba, and Syria. Russia is striving to control the Arctic territory adjacent to the United States, and has developed powerful space and hypersonic capabilities to deliver nuclear warheads, of which it has about 4,500. Russia continues to flood the world's screens and smartphones with fake news. The wily man in the Kremlin still runs the world's eleventh largest economy as of 2020—one with an ability to shape energy and commodities markets. Even if that ranking has dropped since the invasion of Ukraine, Putin still wields quite a bit of leverage.

To understand the Putin regime's enmity toward the United States, you must understand the man himself, as well as those around him. Ever since becoming the president of Russia in 2000, Putin has been on a messianic quest to restore Russia's lost Soviet-era power. A former KGB agent, Putin regards the downfall of the Soviet Union as "the greatest geopolitical catastrophe of the century," and he wants a revived Russian empire. Putin sees the West as an obstacle to this goal, and he is committed to undercutting the United States and our allies everywhere. His aggression is also a reaction to shortsighted Western strategies of regime change or open-ended military campaigns. American interventions in Iraq, Libya, and Syria in this century have heightened Putin's paranoia—an enduring characteristic of Russian leaders. He fears that he could be the West's next target for removal.

Of course, Putin's project of returning Russia to glory has completely backfired with the humiliating performance of the Russian military in Ukraine, and the coalescing of the West against his deranged effort. A true resurrection of the USSR is impossible, he must know. But the Finlandization of the former Warsaw Pact nations—limiting their choices of allyship with the threat of force—is a project worthy of Putin's effort. It might well succeed if the West fails to protect the sovereignty of NATO's eastern flank allies. We must draw lines of deterrence and defend them relentlessly.

Further from Europe, Russia wants to be a power broker in the Middle East and has in the last few years solidified relationships with Iran, Syria, and Saudi Arabia. Russian mercenaries unofficially under Kremlin control, such as the Wagner Group, have fanned out across poorly governed countries such as Libya, Sudan, Syria, and Mali. Hiring private contractors helps the Putin regime avoid official casualty counts and gives the Kremlin plausible deniability for abuses such as looting, torture, executions, and forced disappearances. Closer to the United States, Russia has successfully cultivated relationships with atrocious regimes in Cuba and Venezuela as part of a plan to gain military footholds in the Western hemisphere, close to America's borders.

Most troubling for the United States is the bond between Russia and China. Vladimir Putin and Xi Jinping share the goal of weakening the United States and the Western alliance. In early 2022 the bear and the dragon gave each other a sloppy wet kiss, when Putin and Xi formalized what they are calling a "no limits" partnership between their nations just prior to the Beijing Olympics and Russia's invasion of Ukraine—and I suspect the Chinese are lying that they didn't know Putin's invasion was imminent. Those who suggest that the United States try to forge a partnership with Russia as a hedge against China are untethered from the reality of Putin's unyielding hostility toward the United States and his complete untrustworthiness. An American partnership with Russia is a fool's errand so long as Putin and his thugs are in power. We must therefore deter Putin from pursuing his dreams of a revived empire, as well as limit Russia's ability to operate as part of a powerful bloc that includes China and Iran.

THE RUSSIA HOAX'S DAMAGE TO AMERICAN DIPLOMACY

From our first meeting in November 2016, President Trump and I were both seeking to build our policy around these twin objectives. Getting to a better place with the Russians was a worthy goal but difficult to achieve.

Between Russia's invasion of Georgia in 2008, its seizure of Ukraine's Crimean Peninsula in 2014, and its support for pro-Russian separatists in eastern Ukraine, the US-Russia relationship was already badly strained even before 2016. Then things got even worse because of Russia's feeble but real efforts to sow chaos around the 2016 presidential election. I often reminded the "Russia, Russia, Russia" crazies that Ted Kennedy believed the Russians were messing with US elections as far back as the 1980s. Call it more than four decades now that Russia has been trying to foment strife in the United States. There is nothing new under the sun.

This brings me to January 6. No, not *that* January 6, the one the Left wants to exploit for political advantage. I'm speaking of January 6, 2017—two weeks before we came into power. On that day, the Office of the Director of National Intelligence released a report, the *Russia Intelligence Community Assessment,* or the *Russia ICA.* It alleged, among other things, that Putin sought to influence the presidential election and that he and the Russian government preferred a Trump victory. On that same day, FBI director Jim Comey presented President-Elect Trump with the classified version of that same document.

It was a setup.

I first learned of this meeting from Steve Bannon. I was still a member of Congress when Bannon asked me to come to Trump Tower for an intelligence briefing with Comey, Director of National Intelligence James Clapper, CIA director John Brennan, and Admiral Mike Rogers, then the head of the National Security Agency. The CIA opposed my attendance—after all, I was but a mere congressman, and they assertedly were worried that this would impact my confirmation. Ultimately, because I had a top-secret security clearance already in place, they relented. I was one of the few people that attended that gathering that had a clearance sufficient to read the most highly compartmentalized version of the report.

This gang presented a rather dry summary of the *Russia ICA*. When the meeting ended, Director Comey asked President-Elect Trump if he could have a few minutes alone. We all left. Being the only participant in the meeting with a preexisting clearance, I headed down the hall to a secure facility where the top-secret, compartmentalized version of the *ICA* was in a safe. As I read it, I instantly came to two conclusions. First, this issue was going to be part of my life for my entire time at CIA. Second, this product was different from all the other intelligence products I had previously read during my time on the House Intelligence Committee. The intelligence regarding Russia's effort was real, but the *ICA's* narrative was something else. It seemed to me that the *ICA* was a political document designed by political leaders—which is to say, Comey, Clapper, and Brennan—to provide a foundational myth that Trump and his team were tainted by Russian ties.

How was this like no intelligence estimate I'd encountered in my years of reading these documents?

First, it is only on the rarest of occasions that a president would direct his intelligence community to prepare an intelligence estimate on a foreign adversary's clandestine activities for the *express purpose* of publishing it in a few weeks. The speed suggested a rush to damage Donald Trump before he took office.

Second, the fact that the director of national intelligence, the national security advisor, the FBI, and the CIA all created specially focused teams to perform this miracle was highly unusual.

Third, it struck me as irregular that the intelligence community had produced three separate versions: an unclassified version for the public, a secret-level version for congressional oversight committees, and a top-secret-level, highly compartmentalized version, which was the one that I read that day. This top-secret version had been shared with only a handful of folks inside the intelligence community, plus the Gang of Eight group of top leaders in the House and Senate.

Fourth, President Obama had demanded the document itself be prepared on a timeline that was uncharacteristically short for a deep and important assessment. It should have taken months. This came together in weeks.

All of it added up to one thing: this was a political document.

Of course, I didn't know much of this on January 6, 2017. I learned many of these details after I became the director. But even then, a simple reading of the document, combined with the bizarre briefing, suggested something was wrong.

As for the end of the January 6, 2017, meeting, I did not know what had transpired when Comey asked to be alone with the president after the larger group briefing. I thought it might be that Comey was offering to tender his resignation. Trump was a new president, so perhaps Comey thought it useful to let the president have his choice for FBI director. It also crossed my mind that the president would provide Comey with a vote of confidence by rejecting a tendered resignation, thus giving Comey valuable approval from the new administration. While I do not know exactly what happened between the two of them, I know it wasn't Comey offering to resign. Imagine you're a brand-new president, with zero experience, receiving complex, arcane intelligence briefings, sitting alone with an FBI director you don't know. Then you're told there is information proving that you did what the dirty Steele dossier alleged? You'd come to be leery of the intelligence community, too.

The release of the *Russia ICA* turned the volume up to eleven on the amount of noise surrounding Russia and the Trump campaign. Talking heads on TV intensified their speculation that President Trump was a Russian asset. The president, in turn, was constantly lamenting how President Obama had spied on him and his friends. One day, I was briefing the president in the Oval Office on a remarkable new American espionage gadget. Director of National Intelligence Dan Coats suggested we call it "the Trump." The president, without skipping a beat, offered, "No, it should be called the Obama, because its purpose is to spy on people." On another occasion, he insisted, "My Mike, the only interactions I've had with Russia involve pageants."

Overall, the Russia Hoax created twin challenges. A president wrongly accused of being an asset of a foreign country had nearly zero space to befriend that nation, in any way. Secondly, it drove an unproductive wedge between the FBI and the president as well as, to a lesser degree, the president and the entire intelligence community.

A few weeks later, shortly after becoming CIA director, I launched my own effort to get to the bottom of the *ICA* business. It was like chasing a ghost. The CIA team that worked on the project was loathe to share all that they knew. They answered my questions, but I could tell early on that it would take near-waterboarding to get them to volunteer a single fact. I don't think it was because they were partisans. I think they were doing their best to protect the institution that they knew had been subject to inappropriate political influence. Most of what I learned about the *ICA* came from those who had been kept away from its drafting. I discovered that senior analysts who had been working on Russia for nearly their entire careers were made bystanders. Indeed, the head of the analysis unit, a man with forty years of experience, along with his deputy, were almost entirely shut out of developing the *ICA*'s conclusions.

In February 2017, a senior career analyst and his colleague approached me to say that they had formally and vigorously objected in writing to two of the central features of the *ICA*. Their objections were twofold. First, it was their judgment that there was no basis for the claim that Putin had sought to undermine Hillary Clinton and support Donald Trump. Second, they believed that the *ICA*'s mere mention of the unvetted, lie-ridden document known as the Steele dossier—which instigated a raft of unlawful FBI spying on the Trump campaign—was analytic malpractice. They told me that Brennan believed this second point, too, but Comey didn't. So, Brennan and Comey struck a compromise in the drafting process and referred to the Steele dossier in a footnote. These two analysts were enraged even at that outcome and protested to Brennan in emails that I have read. They were essentially told to pound sand. The politics of burning Donald Trump mattered more than anything else. These two officers had known Brennan for decades. They were not surprised at how he had navigated this one.

I consider it darkly humorous that after leaving Langley, Brennan unwittingly advanced Putin's goal of inflaming American civic disunity by stoking the Russia Hoax on TV. Historically, former CIA directors have stayed out of the limelight immediately after leaving office. Brennan did just the opposite: He was a regular on MSNBC and CNN, saying that Trump was a Russian stooge or worse. I sent him a polite message asking him to back off. I reminded him that he had told me how important it was that intelligence leaders never permit themselves to be drawn into political battles. Yet he continued to spin lies. My team described Brennan as a liberal hothead and suggested it was best to leave it alone. But eventually I couldn't take it anymore. The entire process of the *ICA* was a political hit job on President Trump, and it was clear much of it was Brennan's doing. With every TV hit, Brennan damaged American national security by constraining the president's ability to deal with Russia. I called him directly.

"John, you need to get off stage. Your commentary is hurting morale. They know the attacks you're leveling are political, and that's not consistent with the agency's traditions."

"Mike," said Brennan, "Trump is threatening our democracy. It's not just Russia. You all are going to hand the Iranians a nuclear program."

"John, you all had a different approach on Iran. You were idiots for providing a terrorist regime $150 billion."

"Mike, I'm not going to stand for that!"

"Yeah, that and the national anthem!"

Click.

★   ★   ★

Meanwhile, in May, former FBI director Robert Mueller was appointed as a special counsel to investigate the allegation of Russia's interference in the 2016 US election and subsequent Russia-related developments. In June 2017, the Mueller team asked to interview me. Apparently, they wanted to ask about a particular meeting in the Oval Office from the previous March—one that I surely would not remember, given that I briefed the president nearly every single day. Moreover, if President Trump had asked me to do something improper, illegal, or even merely bothersome—Team Mueller's theory—I would absolutely have remembered. So, my first thought was to tell Mueller to take a hike. But the more I thought about it, the more I came to believe it was important to kill their conspiracy theory with the facts on how I had interacted with President Trump over the investigation. I also wanted to tell them what I knew about how the *ICA* had been built.

We set a date for the interview. I didn't tell the president or anyone else. The media didn't report on it. The interview focused on an occasion I was thought to have stayed behind with the president. The investigators wondered if the president had asked me to deny key documents to the oversight committees, including the House Intelligence Committee led by Adam Schiff, a partisan Democrat. The questioning, conducted in my office at Langley, went something like this:

"Mr. Director, did the president ever express to you that he was unhappy or angry about the investigation being conducted by Robert Mueller?"

"Oh, dozens and dozens of times."

"Did he tell you why he was unhappy or angry?"

"No."

"He didn't tell you why?"

"He didn't have to tell me. You and I both know why he was unhappy, if you check his Twitter account."

"Do you recall being asked to stay behind for a private conversation with President Trump, perhaps with Director Coats?"

"Happened all the time."

"Do you recall this happening on March 22, 2017?"

"Don't know."

"Is it true that you have been delaying providing documents to the intelligence oversight committees?"

"No. Although they probably think that I am. I'm trying to protect classified info that Adam Schiff keeps leaking from documents we've already provided."

A long pause.

"Did the president ever talk to you about providing these documents to the committees?"

"Yes."

"He did? What did he tell you?"

"Something like, Mike, stop f——ing around and give them the damn documents so they finish their report and the world can see that the investigation is a total hoax."

By the look on the FBI guy's face, that was *not* the answer Mueller's people were hoping for or expecting.

I went on: "The president was hearing from, I assume, Chairman Devin Nunes, that CIA was slow-rolling the House Intelligence Committee. So, in fact, your question suggesting the president was asking me to hide documents from the committee was exactly the opposite of what he said to me on multiple occasions." He had not wanted me to hide anything. "Get it all out" was his directive.

The interview ended shortly after that. But the hysteria didn't. The Hoax lasted four years, and not just because of allegations against Trump that originated before he took office. In June 2020, an unnamed source stated that Russian security services had offered the Taliban "bounties" to kill Americans in Afghanistan. This was almost certainly fake news. American intelligence had no credible evidence that it was true. But the Left was addicted to the Russia Hoax and there was an election a few months off. "Intelligence reports on Russian bounty operation first reached White House in early 2019," crowed the *Washington Post*.

Liz Cheney, who surely knew the truth, chimed in with a bloviating tweet: "If reporting about Russian bounties on U.S. Forces is true, the White House must explain . . . who did know and when?" Not to be outdone, then-candidate for president Joe Biden lied to the American people, too: "I don't understand why this President is unwilling to take on Putin when he's actually paying bounties to kill American soldiers in Afghanistan." A year later, with Biden in office, the *Politico* headline acknowledged the false narrative: "White House dials down likelihood Russia offered bounties in Afghanistan." None of the journalists who spread the fake news have apologized, although many have tried to blame the errors on bad sources. Representative Cheney? Crickets. And I'll let Joe Biden answer the question of which president has gotten American soldiers killed in Afghanistan.

Just two months later, and days before the 2020 election, the Hoaxers were at it again. When the story about Hunter Biden's laptop emerged, including the revelation of emails potentially implicating the Biden family in dirty Ukraine business, more than fifty self-proclaimed national security pooh-bahs hoodwinked America. They cosigned a letter that described themselves as nonpartisan experts—a coded phrase asserting that they were above criticism. They claimed—based solely on public reporting—that "our experience makes us deeply suspicious that the Russian government played a significant role in this case . . . It is high time that Russia stops interfering in our democracy." Oh, it had self-protecting caveats, such as: "We do not have evidence of Russian involvement" and "We do not know whether these press reports are accurate." But the message to the American people was clear: "Ignore the Hunter Biden laptop, it's Russian disinformation."

Well, we know today that it wasn't—something that was easy to know back then. Despite all their experience, James Clapper, John Brennan, Mike Hayden, and others engaged in a massive disinformation act of their own. None have apologized for their error or for hiding behind the reams of weasel words qualifying an unfounded, nakedly political assertion. People who regarded themselves as serious veterans of the intelligence community continued to perpetrate the Russia Hoax for the Left's political benefit throughout our four years.

TACKLING RUSSIA AT THE CIA—AND
COOPERATING TO SAVE AMERICAN LIVES

My purpose in relaying the Russia Hoax so extensively is to provide context for our administration's Russia policy. Comey, Clapper, and Brennan's witch hunt complicated the execution of a strength-centered foreign policy toward Russia. It became nearly impossible to communicate with Russian leadership and even more difficult for us to make clear the things that were acceptable and those that were not. If you're going to do deterrence, your adversaries must know where the lines you will defend relentlessly are.

The swirl of false allegations coming from Democrats made it difficult to present real data and sound analysis to the president about the need to thwart Putin's continued aggression. The president had come to believe that the intelligence community was trying to screw him on all things Russia. Nevertheless, I knew the Russia-related intelligence pieces I was presenting him were not politically motivated fabrications but real reporting on Russian schemes. Putin was building up his mercenary armies in the Middle East and Africa to wreak havoc wherever he wanted but with plausible deniability for the Russian government. In a well-documented and ghastly incident in March 2018, British intelligence determined Russia tried to murder a former Russian agent, Sergei Skripal, and his daughter with a nerve agent in the United Kingdom. My recommendations to President Trump on how to punch back went down about as smoothly as a double shot of Stolichnaya. It led to his constant refrain: "Russia, Russia, Russia . . . You guys are always worried about Russia."

I nevertheless continued to worry about Russia and tried to find creative ways to confront this adversary. I still do. My understanding of Putin and analysis of our intelligence led me to a few conclusions: First, we had to find places to separate Putin from Xi. This would be an echo of Henry Kissinger's mission in 1971–1972—create divisions between the Soviet Union and China—albeit for different reasons. Second, embarrassing or underestimating Putin could prompt him to lash out. Third, we had to persuade him that we would defend relentlessly the lines we drew. As Winston Churchill once said, "From what I have seen of our Russian friends and allies during the war, I am convinced that there is nothing they admire so much as strength, and there is nothing for which they have less respect than weakness, especially military weakness."

I thought it was important to communicate to the Russians early on that in a crisis, America would mean business. In May 2017, I went deep into the Russian snake pit in Moscow for meetings with the director of the Russian foreign intelligence service (SVR), Sergey Naryshkin, and the head of the Russian federal security service (FSB), Alexander Bortnikov. I had to send the right message to these two Putin confidants, so I presented Naryshkin with a few DVDs, just for fun: *Rocky IV*, *The Hunt for Red October*, and *Miracle on Ice*. He didn't laugh but thought it was ballsy—at least that's what I took away from the translation of the interaction! Naryshkin, like Bortnikov, wasn't especially likable, and he believed he was likely to be Putin's successor. He told me repeatedly over the course of our conversations that "the only way to be an effective leader in Russia is to have been chief of its intelligence service." I knew that he knew that wasn't true. Nor did he and I agree on what an "effective leader" of Russia should actually do.

My lunch with Bortnikov was a classic display of Russian glitz and extravagance. Cocktail waitresses who looked like ladies of the night kept our glasses filled with copious amounts of vodka. And, to be clear, I almost never drank more than a few sips of alcohol in one sitting during my Trump administration years. I always wanted to be prepared in case of an emergency, so my beverage of choice was Diet Coke, which I consumed by the caseload.

This meeting was also a classic Russian-government affair in that Bortnikov rattled off an endless, misinformed litany of grievances against America and the West. Bortnikov went on for so long that John Tefft, the acting US ambassador with me, fell asleep in the middle of his harangue—I was kind of envious of him. I'd heard it all before, from Putin and others. When we left, I thought we'd been treated poorly, but my translator said that we had received by far the most gracious welcome he had seen in more than twenty years of interpreting. Both Naryshkin and Bortnikov thanked us for our counterterrorism help and told us that we should not push Chairman Kim too hard.

The Russians were unpleasant, but Naryshkin and I forged an uncommonly good working relationship—something that would have made liberal heads explode had they known the full extent of it. Our bond ultimately saved American lives in at least one instance. In October 2017, the CIA called our counterparts in Russia to alert them to some intelligence on an imminent attack by ISIS terrorists on St. Petersburg's Kazan Cathedral. A successful strike would likely murder many innocent Russians—and it was likely that American tourists also would have died. We shared our information, and the Russians did the hard work of disrupting the terror plot.

Not long after, I was on the road and received a call from President Trump. "I just got off the phone with Vladimir Putin, and he wanted to thank you for saving the lives of so many Russian people." It took me a second to process. The president went on: "He's going to call you about it, too, and then it sounds like he is going to issue a press release thanking you personally." As my memory recalled details of this joint effort, I shared them with the president. Given that this was during the height of Adam Schiff's Russia charade, my main thought was "Damn, now I'll be accused of being a Russian asset too."

Shortly after that talk with the president, the call from Putin came in. He told me that Bortnikov told him, "Tank Man saved our ass." I was surprised that Putin and his intel chief had a nickname for me. "Tank Man." I actually like that moniker, even if came from an unreconstructed KGB officer. I suspect they usually say far worse about me. Putin eventually put out a press release thanking me personally and the CIA for saving Russian lives. I was glad he did, because my team deserved the recognition.

Despite occasional opportunities to cooperate on life-or-death matters, we maintained our commitment to deterring the Russians. It often involved the spy wars that raged in the shadows between our countries. We were constantly working to build our capabilities against the Russians and—equally important—prevent them from spying on us. In August 2017, Secretary Tillerson ordered the closing of the Russian consulate in San Francisco. At the CIA, we wanted them out fast so that the Russians had little time to destroy files and move assets to their Seattle consulate. The FBI agreed with the need for speed. But the State Department slow-rolled our directives in the name of diplomatic protocol—yet another example of State valuing process and the established order over defending a clear line of what America would tolerate. There would be no such fight in 2020, when, as secretary of state, I directed the closure of the Chinese consulate in Houston. Gina Haspel, FBI director Christopher Wray, and I all agreed to shut their doors quickly.

In general, I was not impressed by the Russians' tradecraft. When the Trump administration, in March 2018, closed the Russian consulate in Seattle and expelled sixty Russian "diplomats," some on my team worried that if the Russians took the reciprocal step of evicting sixty Americans, it would hinder our own capabilities inside Russia. I wasn't concerned. After all, I observed, "It takes sixty of their guys to follow one of ours."

TAKING DOWN TRAITORS AND ENEMIES

That comment reflects a long-held belief that American spies are the best-trained and stealthiest operatives in the business. When they have the right level of support, they are unstoppable. Which is why I was as mad as I have ever been in my life over the exposure of some of the CIA's most sensitive espionage tools. In March 2017, my team discovered the compromise of "Vault 7," a set of CIA cybertools that assisted with surveillance and helped us disrupt adversaries' plans. The breach had occurred about a year earlier, during Brennan's directorship. My reaction was that an insider had raped America. The man ultimately at the helm of this operation was indeed an accused rapist, Julian Assange, the founder of Wikileaks, which I regard as a nonstate hostile intelligence service often abetted by state actors such as Russia.

From time to time, I see people laud villains such as Assange, Wikileaks, Edward Snowden, Chelsea Manning, and similar bad actors as "whistleblowers." Real whistleblowers seek neither fame nor fortune. Nor are they seeking to undermine their nation and its success. They provide information discreetly, through legal mechanisms that are well known, easily followed, and likely to address the very concerns raised. Those who leak classified information on serious matters are nearly always self-aggrandizing know-it-alls who choose to make news rather than changes through approved means.

So who are these people? They certainly aren't journalists. If they are foreigners, they are enemies. If they are Americans, they are traitors. A few Americans on both the Left and the Right condemn efforts to prosecute these foes. They misunderstand what is actually happening. If you believe that there should be zero government secrets—absolutely none—then Assange and Snowden are heroes. But if you, like me, believe that classified information must be protected to keep our nation and the men and women who serve it safe, then they're monsters.

Snowden and Assange's thefts jeopardized American security. They put our soldiers, sailors, airmen, Marines, intelligence officers, and diplomats at greater risk. We lost years of work and handed it to the Russians and the Chinese. The world now knew about the tools we had painstakingly developed to keep America safe. In a different episode from Vault 7, Assange and company caused Americans to shell out billions of dollars to rebuild a compromised Department of Defense system. These activities are neither noble nor protected by the First Amendment. These crooks claim to be honoring human rights and free expression. They are in fact serving the interests of the most evil and repressive regimes with every leak and document dump.

These enemies and traitors must be punished. Because of America's extradition request against him for crimes unrelated to the Vault 7 intrusion, by 2017, Assange had already spent four and a half years hiding out in the Ecuadorian embassy in London. I pursued Assange's extradition hard as CIA director and secretary of state, both because the American people and our CIA officers deserved justice and because I wanted the Russians to know that I was on a mission to crush the nominally independent hacking groups they sponsored and used as their pawns. I lobbied the Ecuadorians to kick Assange out of his pathetic accommodations inside their embassy, and they finally capitulated on April 11, 2019. On that same day, the Department of Justice publicly unsealed an indictment for his dealings with Chelsea Manning in stealing classified information and weeks later piled on seventeen more charges. I was a happier man, and, more importantly, America was just a bit safer. Harsh criminal penalties and extradition proceedings will tell future enemies targeting our state secrets that America will defend the lines we have drawn.

Ultimately, while we weren't able to bring Assange onto US soil during the administration because of legal challenges in the United Kingdom, we laid the groundwork for that ultimate outcome, which I do believe will happen one day. I will be delighted the day he is thrown into an American federal penitentiary. Just one less useful idiot free for Russia to exploit—and a warning to all such scoundrels in the future.

DETERRING RUSSIAN AGGRESSION AS SECRETARY OF STATE

While I was secretary of state, little changed in my mission of trying to find a path to cause Russia to look West for answers, while simultaneously showing that we would not abide Russian aggression in any of its nefarious forms. Other leaders often grumbled to me about what a headache Russia was for them, too. One African leader told me, as I know he has told many others, "When my country's forces train in the US, they come to love the US. And when my country's forces train in Russia, they come to love the US." Hamid Karzai, the former president of Afghanistan, also told me a story that I have little reason to doubt. In the fall of 2017, Putin met with him in Afghanistan. He encouraged Karzai to run for a second term, but Karzai said he couldn't likely win. Putin jokingly shot back that if he could fix elections in America, he could easily fix them in Afghanistan.

My first major Russia-related work as secretary came in July 2018, when President Trump met Putin in Helsinki. This engagement is remembered for the press conference held at the end of their meeting. To be clear, Trump's language there was neither accurate nor helpful. To stand next to Putin and say that he believed Putin's claims that he didn't meddle in the US election was very Trumpian. It was also a mistake. It lacked the depth to address the question that had come from the American reporter: "Do you hold Russia at all accountable for anything in particular?" Trump's answer reflected his inability or refusal to separate the Russia Hoax from the fact that Russia had tried to sow chaos in the 2016 election. For Trump, every question about Russia and the elections was poisoned by the narrative of the Russia Hoax. These horrible lies about him—propagated by Comey and his deputy, Andrew McCabe, plus Mueller and Schiff, aided and abetted by the likes of Rachael Maddow of MSNBC and almost the entire crew at CNN—were connected in Trump's mind to the Russian government's chaos campaign.

Many of us tried to convince the president to separate these two ideas, but we failed. He knew that when reporters said "Russian interference," the world heard "Trump collusion"—and that is in fact what many reporters wanted their listeners to hear. The president wound up fighting the wrong battle for what may have been the right reason. In any event, too much was made of this single moment in Helsinki. For me, what mattered about the meeting was that it signaled that I could try to improve the US's relationship with Russia. A strategic arms treaty was set to expire, the Russia-China nexus loomed, and Russia was making moves in Syria, Libya, and elsewhere. Relitigating the 2016 election was important only insofar as it related to our efforts to prevent Moscow from trying it again. In that effort, I ultimately failed.

Russia's involvement in Syria was yet another mess bequeathed to us by the Obama amateurs and, specifically, National Security Advisor Susan Rice. Few remember that Rice had some responsibility for the Africa file on the National Security Council in 1994, when genocide in Rwanda claimed one million lives. She also has the ignominious distinction of committing what I thought was one of the worst lies I have ever heard told in politics when, as UN ambassador, she appeared on a round of Sunday political talk shows in 2012 to claim that an obscure video on the internet had triggered the attacks on Americans in Benghazi. In fact, the vulnerable security posture of the Benghazi consulate and the madness of radical Islamist ideas sparked the violence. I was part of the Benghazi committee that deposed Rice in hopes of getting answers for our nation and the families of the four Americans who died that night in Libya. She was petulant, snarly, grudging, and completely uninterested in accounting for her role in the massive failure. For this, she was rewarded with a promotion to national security advisor during Obama's second term, and today she runs the Biden White House's Domestic Policy Council—proving that there is no easier place to fail upward than in Washington, DC.

Rice, along with John Brennan, was also at the center of Obama's debacle in Syria. In 2012, Obama warned that the use of chemical weapons would represent the crossing of a "redline." When Syrian president Bashar al-Assad gassed his own people the next year, the administration responded—at Rice's urging—with no action at all. This refusal to follow through on promises of deterrence haunted America for the entirety of Obama's time in office. The Russians and the world watched this strategic failure to live up to a clear commitment. In 2015, Russian forces answered their ally Assad's desperate call for military assistance, and they have never left.

Because of the fight against ISIS, the Trump administration inherited a situation in Syria with American boots on the ground. We tried to find a way to use our small military footprint along the Euphrates River and at a place called Al-Tanf to support Israeli efforts to keep Iranian forces off their border. This meant that we often bumped up against Russian forces operating in Syria as well. Indeed, one night in February 2018, a group of fighters allied with the Assad regime—composed substantially of Russian mercenaries, probably from the Wagner Group—advanced on an American position near Khasham, Syria. The US and Russian militaries have a communications channel in Syria to prevent accidents. In this instance, US military leaders reached out to Russian commanders and asked them to stand down. The Russians claimed that the force was not under command of the Russian military. This was almost certainly false. The Russian mercenaries kept advancing, and our generals in the field had to decide whether to kill or be killed. They made the right choice. The *New York Times* later reported that MQ-9 Reaper drones, F-22 stealth fighter jets, F-15E fighters, B-52 bombers, AC-130 gunships, and AH-64 Apache helicopters unleashed holy hell on the pro-Assad fighters, as did American special-operations ground forces. Dozens, if not hundreds, of Russians were killed.

Regardless of whether those Russians were formally under the command of the Russian military, I'm sure that Russian commanders noticed how America's warriors annihilated members of what is known to be a Kremlin proxy force. I believe our willingness to defend with force the lines we drew in Syria—in this case—actual physical boundaries—caused Russia to fear what America would do to them in a confrontation inside Syria or elsewhere. In the fall of 2019, I made a call to Russian foreign minister Sergey Lavrov, a boorish man but skilled diplomat: "Sergey, we are going to be flying in space you fly in during a specified period. Let us go. Don't so much as scramble a plane." Within a few hours, the United States completed a raid in Syria that killed Abu Bakr al-Baghdadi, an ISIS leader whom we had pursued for three years. The Russians didn't so much as flinch. I don't think it's a coincidence that the Russians acquiesced that night, more than a year and a half after the episode at Khasham. This is the deterrence—in this case tactical deterrence—that follows drawing lines and defending them.

As the months went on, I found that much of my Russia business as secretary of state was in fact Ukraine business, a country on which I had focused quite a bit in Congress. My work then built on the knowledge I had acquired studying the history of Ukraine as a cadet at West Point. In the spring of 2014, as a member of the House Intelligence Committee, I traveled to Kyiv, and visited its Independence Square, known as the Maidan. This was where Ukrainians had spent much of the previous winter encamped in the bitter cold to protest the rule of Russian puppet Viktor Yanukovych. Their brave efforts eventually forced a regime change. I also met with leaders from the Ukrainian Orthodox Church, such as my friend Father Oleg, who had set up hospitals to tend to the injured from the fighting in the Maidan. On another trip to Ukraine, I visited Babi Yar, a site outside Kyiv where the Nazis slaughtered more than thirty-three thousand Ukrainian Jews in just two days in 1941. Thousands more would be killed at Babi Yar during the war. It was a nightmarish reminder of man's inhumanity toward his fellow man—and of how Ukraine has suffered from conflict and mass murder throughout its history.

On both trips to Ukraine during my time in Congress, I met with the deeply troubled Ukrainian intelligence services. I wanted to understand how the United States might work to support them as they left behind the Soviet practice of spying on Ukrainians and pivoted to doing good espionage on behalf of their own people. As CIA director, I went to the front lines of the battlefield in the Donbas region, to learn from Ukraine's intelligence services how we might assist them, and also met with President Petro Poroshenko, the predecessor to Volodymyr Zelensky. I saw the moving memorials to those who fought and fell to escape Putin's iron fist.

The US government was helping to train the Ukrainian special forces, and I'm confident that this effort helped Ukraine defend itself when the Russians attacked in 2022. An even greater nation may arise from the ashes of Putin's war, but only if Ukrainians can conquer the deep-rooted corruption that infests their country. Ukraine is a beautiful place, with beautiful people of warm hearts and kind dispositions. They deserve better than foreign invasion and domestic thievery.

Putin has long lusted to put all of Ukraine under the Russian flag, either by direct annexation or installing a puppet government. I saw this threat and recognized the potential for Ukraine to become the world's next major hotspot, so I set the tone early in my tenure as secretary of state to reinforce the country's sovereignty and independence. In July 2018, the State Department released the Crimea Declaration, which reaffirmed, among other things, that "Crimea Is Ukraine." The declaration was a line of deterrence. It told the Kremlin that any further moves to take Ukraine could mean consequences from the United States. For the rest of my time at State, I kept a formal copy of the Crimea Declaration framed on an easel in one of the rooms outside my office.

Despite the Hoaxers' bad-faith efforts, we deterred Russia relentlessly for four straight years. Our administration championed a concept of "deterrence by denial," an idea supported by Wess Mitchell, assistant secretary of state for Europe and Eurasian Affairs and a brilliant strategist who served nobly at State through February 2019. The traditional concept of deterrence holds that you can dissuade an adversary from taking action because of the threat of counteraction. Deterrence by denial is the idea that hardening a target also can cause an opponent to stand down.

Our administration knew that if we armed Ukraine with enough weapons, ammunition, and other military gear, Putin might calculate that challenging Ukraine was not in his country's interest. While the Obama administration delivered gear such as helmets, night-vision goggles, blankets, and medical supplies, we recognized that Ukrainians needed much more to defend their homeland against a Russian onslaught. The president initially resisted providing defensive weapons to Ukraine, but repeated efforts by Bolton, Esper, and me ultimately convinced him that it was the right thing to do for America. We stepped in and delivered the real goods—weapons that included $47 million worth of Javelin antitank launchers and missiles in 2018 and another shipment worth $39 million in 2019. An additional $400 million worth of aid included tools of war such as sniper rifles and rocket-propelled grenade launchers. This deterrence by denial, plus the shows of strength that President Trump put on in private conversations with Putin, caused the Russian leader to delay his ambitions in Ukraine. I am proud that as I write these words, the ordinary Ukrainians resisting the Russian war machine in the fields and streets of their country are the beneficiaries of American weapons supplied during the Trump administration.

Because of urgent business involving Iran, and the sensitivities surrounding Ukraine in the sham impeachment proceedings, I held off on a personal visit to Kyiv as secretary of state until January 2020. My day there was miserably gray and rainy. But it was made a bit brighter by spending a long time with its now-famous comedian-turned-politician president Zelensky.

Two years before the Russian invasion of 2022, I saw that Zelensky was a serious man. Like President Trump, he had come to power from outside of government. He had a deep understanding that he had only some control of events inside his country, and he was working to determine how he might more firmly grasp all the levers of governance to deliver a better life for the Ukrainian people. He didn't deny the level of corruption inside his borders. He was trying, however unsuccessfully, to mitigate it and make a transition. His slight build belied his fortitude. I certainly did not foresee the leadership he has demonstrated since February 2022, but I was convinced he was trying to fortify an independent and sovereign Ukraine. Kurt Volker, who was working on this agenda for me, had a theory of how we might build a consensus, even among the oligarchs, to transform the Ukrainian government into one where the people had a real say and its leaders were not on the take.

Sadly, because of the partisan hysteria over the phone call between Trump and Zelensky, we never were able to execute that plan. The reality is that media didn't care about Ukrainian sovereignty or the threats posed by Russia. It was dying to know only one thing on my trip to Kyiv: Had Zelensky and I discussed anything related to the impeachment proceedings? The answer was that Zelensky and I had spent the bulk of our time talking about important matters, including how to protect his people from the tyrant on their border. I also made clear that corruption in the senior-leader ranks of his country made our work alongside him infinitely more difficult. I'm troubled by the evil that has befallen his country but also encouraged that this onetime Jerry Seinfeld has turned into a kind of General Patton. Corruption will still exist in Ukraine after the conflict, but I am hopeful Zelensky can lead his country to eradicate it.

I also wanted to show solidarity with the people of Ukraine. Prior to my arrival, I had told my staff that I wanted to visit a military hospital in Kyiv. Pro-Russian Ukrainian separatists had been keeping up a fight in the Donbas region for seven years, leading to some fourteen thousand dead. Meeting the wounded who had served so nobly was important to me. Whether because of a miscommunication or some other error, my team had not set up the trip. I turned into a human howitzer. That got them moving, and they worked all day to set up a tour while I was in meetings with government officials. Arranging such things is complicated because of the diplomatic, security, logistical, and public relations considerations. In the end, they got it done, and I'm grateful that they did.

By late afternoon, I was touring the hospital, a grim and impoverished place filled with wounded heroes. Through a translator, I spoke to a young man who was in substantial pain from an injury sustained in the line of duty. He told me that he was an army captain. I told him that I, too, was once a captain in the military. As I was getting ready to leave, he hoisted himself up on his crutches and struggled onto his feet. Then he shuffled across the room to his wall locker, where he kept his uniform. From its sleeve, he ripped off the patch signifying his unit. He handed it to me and told me to keep it. I still have it.

Why did that soldier give me his treasured emblem? It wasn't because I was Mike, the former Army captain. It's because I was America's secretary of state. I occupied an office endowed with the responsibility of carrying America's torch of freedom. Ukrainians have fought for their lives against a much bigger bully on their border, one whose imperialist yoke weighed heavily on them for decades in the Soviet era. In that dismal hospital room, we weren't just two men or even two soldiers. We were two brothers in the fight for freedom against the regime in Moscow. As President Truman told Congress when he asked it to fund the Marshall Plan: "It must be the policy of the United States to support free peoples who are resisting attempted subjugation by armed minorities or by outside pressures . . . We must assist free peoples to work out their own destinies in their own way." The best way to do that is to adopt a posture of strength and defend the lines you have drawn.

Assisting Ukrainians in charting their destinies also meant supporting their religious freedom. Putin has used the Russian Orthodox Church, which often functions as an arm of the Russian state, to undermine the independence of the Ukrainian Orthodox Church. The Russian church demands ecclesiastical authority over its Ukrainian counterpart, a claim that has nothing to do with spiritual welfare or church doctrine and everything to do with turning the Ukrainian Orthodox Church into another cudgel that Putin can use to crush the Ukrainian people. In January 2019, I issued a statement in support of the independence of the Ukrainian Orthodox Church and the right of its believers to worship as a free people.

STRENGTHENING AMERICA'S NUCLEAR DETERRENT

A foreign policy of peace through strength doesn't matter if you don't actually possess strength. Chief among America's capabilities to deter our adversaries is our mighty nuclear arsenal. The Trump administration's Nuclear Posture Review culminated in a presidential decision to rebuild our nuclear force, a duty our country had neglected for years while the Russians and Chinese made great strides. Given that the United States had reduced our nuclear weapons stockpile by 85 percent from its Cold War high, while Russia continued to beef up its force over the past two decades, it made perfect sense to modernize our nuclear forces. As in all other domains of warfare, having the strongest possible deterrent force is the best guard against aggression.

This philosophy informed our approach to the renegotiation of the New Start Treaty, which was set to expire in February 2021. Russia was demanding—both publicly and privately—that we renew the treaty. Yet an extension of the agreement without any concession from the Russians made no sense for America. In addition, a nuclear weapons agreement designed to reduce the risk of nuclear aggression that had only two parties may well have made sense during the Cold War. But it made zero strategic sense in a new century that included the CCP's burgeoning nuclear, missile, and space programs.

We made a good run at reversing the damage of the Obama administration in our efforts with the Russians to renegotiate the New Start Treaty—and to try to bring China, which is rapidly growing its nuclear arsenal, into the deal as well. Under the terms of the treaty, only 45 percent of Russia's nuclear arsenal is subject to numerical limits. Meanwhile, in yet another instance of stupid diplomacy that no one would define as winning for America, 92 percent of the US arsenal faces numerical limits. Ceding the strategic high ground on nuclear weapons is the definition of a bad deal, exposing the American people to horrible possibilities.

Under the leadership of arms negotiator Marshall Billingslea, we got Putin to agree verbally to a cap on warheads, a key step toward rebalancing the numbers. Unfortunately, I think the Russians were waiting to see the outcome of the US presidential election before they made any further concessions or signed any papers. Their gambit played out well for them because in 2021, President Biden signed America up for another five years of the treaty without demanding any Russian concessions. If he was hoping to gain some goodwill or keep Putin at bay through its renewal, he miscalculated badly. This was probably the first signal from the Biden administration that caused Putin to believe America had no appetite to confront him. Instead of drawing a line and defending it, the Biden administration's weakness in one area has had ripple effects in others.

WE DETERRED RUSSIA. BIDEN'S WEAKNESS
HAS EMBOLDENED PUTIN.

For four years, critics pilloried us for everything having to do with Russia. Well, how'd we do?

We punished more than 365 Russian targets with crushing sanctions for committing human rights abuses, perpetrating cyber intrusions, using a nerve agent to assassinate a dissident in the United Kingdom, and attacking Ukrainian vessels in the Kerch Strait of the Black Sea. Better still, we built up our military. We grew our economy. We freed the American energy sector and not only achieved energy independence but also became more capable than ever of exporting what we produced. This kept energy cheap, which is great for American consumers and devastating for Russia, which relies on other nations to purchase its fossil fuels.

Here's another simple way to answer the question: when we were calling the shots, Putin didn't dare invade Ukraine. Some have argued that the reason that Putin didn't make a move on our watch was that he was getting what he wanted—what they claim was a NATO-skeptic president who didn't care about the Donbas or Crimea.

But what did Putin actually get from America during our four years? A rebuilt American military and more American troops forward-deployed in Europe. Jens Stoltenberg, NATO's general secretary, said NATO became stronger, and he is right. We withdrew from the Intermediate-Range Nuclear Forces Treaty that Putin wanted to continue—more on that later. Energy prices were lower, denying him wealth to bribe his oligarchs. I could go on.

It wasn't American acquiescence to Putin's goals that kept him from invading Ukraine for four years. It was American strength. This is the very essence of deterrence. Putin felt constrained by a strong America with determined leaders who drew clear lines and defended them relentlessly. He wasn't willing to test us. We had indicated that we wouldn't give an inch.

During the 2020 presidential campaign, Joe Biden claimed that President Trump's "entire presidency has been a gift to Putin." Yet on Biden's watch, Putin has not only attacked Ukraine but bolstered its strategic partnership with China. And he re-upped a losing deal for America on nuclear weapons. It turns out that Biden's weakness is the gift to Putin that keeps on giving.

CHAPTER 6

DON'T APPEASE. GO ON OFFENSE.

The terrorist mastermind was never my pen pal, but I once wrote him a letter. I revealed its contents on December 2, 2017, while I was still CIA director.

At the Reagan Defense Forum, in California, a popular conference in the national security world, I revealed to the audience that I had recently sent a letter to Iranian Quds Force terrorist general Qasem Soleimani: "What we were communicating to him in that letter is that we would hold him and Iran accountable for any attacks on American interests in Iraq by forces under his control."

If an official from any previous administration had said this, it likely would have been regarded as a toothless statement of accountability—a ho-hum, box-checking act that is all too common in American diplomacy. But this time was different. I was in fact announcing a massive change in policy. Before the Trump administration, the United States responded to Soleimani's attacks on Americans by killing a few of his mooks. This imposed zero cost on him, and he probably laughed at such weak retaliation. Soleimani was now on notice that those days were now over. I was on a mission to protect America.

Soleimani never wrote me back, and two years later, on December 29, 2019, I was sitting with President Trump at his opulent home in Florida, Mar-a-Lago, now as America's secretary of state. Beside me were the secretary of defense and the chairman of the Joint Chiefs of Staff. We were there on serious business: "Mr. President, we have a recommendation for you—the target is General Qasem Soleimani."

In just a few days, Soleimani and the Iranians would feel the full effect of our refusal to appease their evil. Instead, they would get a taste of American offense.

THE FOLLY OF APPEASEMENT

Appeasement is like too much alcohol. A little bit might not have an immediate impact, but the addiction risk is real. And, in larger quantities, it may feel good in the short term, but you'll feel terrible in the morning. Another metaphor, for those of us old enough to remember, comes from the old commercials for FRAM oil filters: "You can pay me now, or you can pay me later." The price of the cheap filter bought today is nothing compared to suffering an expensive car repair next week.

In foreign policy, nothing is more counterproductive to peace and security than appeasement is. It's the flip side of deterrence. Bad actors see concessions and endless rounds of talks as proof of weakness to be exploited. Only displays of strength—including offense that puts them on defense—stop them from crossing the line. Appeasement is also limited in what it can accomplish against the truly worst actors, who are motivated by ideology. Jihadis in the Middle East, the Communists in Beijing, Putin-style thugs driven by claims of historical grievance, and theocrats in Tehran may from time to time make strategic compromises, but their fervor for their twisted causes sustains them and fuels their aggressive pursuit of long-term geopolitical goals. Goody bags of foreign aid and other concessions only generate more bad behavior. If you want these bad actors to change, they must be *made* to change.

Appeasement, however, is a standard practice in international relations. "Can kickers" who occupy positions of authority are legion. They know that they can defer the pain or the cost of their bad choices and their successors will have to deal with the consequences. The FRAM guy missed something in his equation: sometimes the current leader will not purchase the filter, leaving someone else to buy the new engine. Think of Neville Chamberlain at Munich in 1938 and what he left to Winston Churchill. Think of how the League of Nations did nothing after Japan's invasion of Manchuria in 1931, causing Adolf Hitler to lick his lips in anticipation of his own offensives. In the Bible, think of King Josiah, who was left to clean up the mess of idolatry that started under his grandfather Manasseh and continued with his wicked father, Amon.

President Reagan understood that appeasement was a losing strategy. As a young solider posted along the Iron Curtain, I savored his fine leadership, and I have tried to follow his example in all my public offices. When asked about what his approach to the Soviet Union would be, he responded, "We win and they lose." He saw not just the wickedness of the Soviet Union, but also its weakness. He saw it must and could be defeated. President Reagan resolved to bring the Soviets to their knees by supercharging America's economic engine and overwhelming the USSR in defense spending. But even more importantly, he had an unquestioned faith in the moral superiority of the American system. He did not believe that capitalism and Communism could coexist. Communist doctrine regards capitalism and freedom as permanent enemies. Communism seeks to export revolution. Under those conditions, appeasement is just a fancy word for giving an inch at a time toward defeat.

President Trump installed a bust of Churchill in the Oval Office, and at times we felt the way Churchill must have felt when he became prime minister and inherited Chamberlain's appeasement failures. President Obama had given the ayatollah money, time, and a direct path to a nuclear weapons program. The best that could be said for this approach was that it might delay Iran's development of the bomb. We believed it was far better to confront this problem directly and to do it on our timeline and terms—and not later, when the Iranian kleptocrats were loaded with money and armed with nukes.

Our Iran policy rejected the appeasement of the Obama years. Obama's team dreamed of an improvement in Iranian behavior once the payments started flowing. Yet Obama's appeasement was demonstrably failing by the time we took office, as the full-on Iranian takeover of the Middle East had continued, and the regime had secretly kept up prohibited nuclear work during the deal.

So, soon after pulling out in May 2018, the Trump administration embarked on an unprecedented campaign of maximum economic and diplomatic pressure, alliance building, and military deterrence against

Iran. Behind the scenes, we continued to build a coalition composed of Israel and its Arab neighbors. Our sanctions caused European companies to flee Iran in droves. And as for military deterrence pressure, in addition to shifting American troops to the Middle East, President Trump put it pretty clearly in a 2018 tweet, "To Iranian President Rouhani: NEVER, EVER THREATEN THE UNITED STATES AGAIN OR YOU WILL SUFFER CONSEQUENCES THE LIKES OF WHICH FEW THROUGHOUT HISTORY HAVE EVER SUFFERED BE-FORE." Message sent. We recognized Iranian regime evil for what it is. We refused to appease it. We went on offense instead.

TURNING UP THE PRESSURE ON IRAN

I wish I could say every member of the president's national security team supported this bold stance. But just as they had tried to thwart our pull-out of the JCPOA, Secretary of Defense Mattis and the bureaucracy at the Pentagon were loath to stir what they saw as an Iranian hornet's nest. They would constantly brief the rest of the president's team as if they had grabbed John Kerry's slide deck. Mattis would complain to me: "Michael, if we take on the Iranians, they control the escalation ladder, and we will end up in a very bad place." This disturbing mentality—the belief that we should be more afraid of what America's adversaries can do to us than vice versa—is the default position inside the US national security bureaucracy. More inch giving.

I was confident that we could control the so-called escalation ladder through our massive diplomatic, economic, and military superiorities. I had more confidence in America than most of our senior Pentagon leaders did. So did my team. Twice per week, I huddled in my office with Brian Hook, and later the great Elliott Abrams, to strategize on the campaign. In advance of every meeting, Brian would show progress on lines of effort such as pushing Iranian oil exports toward zero. I'd give positive feedback by sending back his slide decks with hand-drawn smiley faces next to each data point.

By 2019, with the pressure now causing the Iranian rial to plunge toward worthlessness, the Iranians worked to break free of sanctions in every way imaginable. They tried to perform a diplomatic end run around me by lobbying American allies to pressure President Trump. The Iranians would don a cloak of self-pity and pitch to the Europeans and others that if they could get around Pompeo and talk to Trump directly, they could get a deal to lift sanctions. When foreign ministers warned me that their bosses were planning to sidestep me to get to the president, I told each of them the same thing: "I'm not the problem. Ayatollah Khamenei and Qasem Soleimani are the problem, and the president agrees with me."

Some heeded my words, but many had to learn the hard way. None were schooled more harshly than French president Emmanuel Macron. He believed he was the "Trump whisperer" on many topics—Turkey, Lebanon, tariffs and taxes with the European Union, and so much more. But most annoyingly, and with the least likelihood of success, he was relentless in trying to convince President Trump to reenter the nuclear deal. At the G7 meeting of world leaders in August 2019, Macron had pitched a plan to offer vague inspection regimes and enrichment reductions in exchange for nearly full sanctions relief on Iran, including non-nuclear sanctions that covered activities such as terrorism. Macron thought that he would be able to persuade the president to take this "deal." But Bolton and I—with the help of Israeli prime minister Netanyahu—worked to thwart Macron's plot. It was doomed to fail anyway. Trump was deeply aware of the nature of the Iranian regime, and he never once even hinted at taking Macron's inadequate offer. The president and I both understood that sanctions were hard to put back on once taken off. They gave us massive leverage over the Iranians. We couldn't give an inch.

But Macron was undaunted. He spent the weeks leading up to the September 2019 UN General Assembly—the annual Super Bowl of world-leader gatherings—trying to broker a meeting between President Trump and Iranian president Hassan Rouhani. Both Bolton and I believed this was sheer lunacy. Most importantly, no one should ever regard the Iranian president as being on the same level as the president of the United States. Whoever holds the regime office of "supreme leader"— currently Ayatollah Khamenei—is Iran's top dog. Furthermore, Rouhani was in a very weak political position at home, having become the scapegoat for the disaster that had become the Iranian economy. There was no chance that he could deliver what America was demanding.

Nevertheless, Macron phoned the president before the assembly claiming that a meeting with Rouhani could take place but that President Trump first had to honor Rouhani's demand to sign a certain document before a sit-down.

I recall the president saying he would not sign a damn thing.

Macron said that if there was no signing, there would be no meeting.

That didn't bother President Trump, who said that he had plenty of other things to do, and that we had all the cards. He knew we controlled the escalation ladder.

Macron balked. Iran had the cards. That's how we got into this situation.

Then the president crushed him, noting that we just hit 28,000 on the Dow, while the Iranians' GDP was down 25 percent because of our sanctions policy.

Still desperate for a Trump-Rouhani meeting, Macron said he would go back to the Iranians and ask if they would meet without the president's signature on whatever this piece of paper said.

This infuriated the president: "Stop! Stop calling me. Stop calling them and begging—you look like a weak little girl! Run your country or the yellow jackets will." (This was a reference to the populist protestors on the streets of Paris who wore yellow vests.) "Tell them to call me, and you get back to working on the guys with yellow vests."

He hung up. The Iranians never called. France gave up on its mediation effort.

My friend, the now-deceased prime minister Shinzo Abe of Japan, also made a run. As the leader of an island nation that must import vast amounts of oil, Abe was frustrated by our sanctions regime because it crippled Iranian oil exports. Many in the diplomatic world suggested to Abe that his good relationship with the president could break the Iranian impasse. I actually thought Prime Minister Abe had the best chance of any world leader to convince Iran that America was serious about its commitment to maximum pressure. He had demonstrated that Japan was back as a security partner for the West, was trusted to be a faithful interlocutor for everyone he met, and had a deep and strong relationship with our team. I remain saddened by his assassination in 2022, which took a great leader from the world.

When he called me to discuss his plan, I told him I would be happy to see him mediate, but the odds that the president would capitulate to Iranian demands was a zero-probability event. Abe gave it his best shot. In June 2019, he visited Tehran on a friendly mission to present himself as a negotiator. It was the first time a Japanese prime minister had visited Iran since 1978. The Iranians thanked him on that very day by attacking a Japanese-flagged ship in the Gulf of Oman. Abe soon quit trying to broker an agreement and apologized for ignoring my stop sign. He learned that, especially with respect to the ayatollah, appeasement doesn't work.

We spent a fair amount of effort making sure that the Russians and Chinese didn't form an alliance with Iran. Both countries were wary of getting too close to Islamist extremists, but Iran had something they needed: oil, in the case of China, and a launching pad into the Middle East for Russia. The Russians, too, tried to fix "the Pompeo problem" for Iran. Their scheme was to work with White House senior advisor Jared Kushner to draft a proposal to bring to the president. But they failed to understand that unlike my predecessor, Secretary Tillerson, I had a close working relationship with Jared. He informed me about the Russian outreach. We both agreed that it didn't make sense for America, and we jointly shut it down. I knew their hopes were crushed when Russia's foreign minister, Sergey Lavrov, called to admit that our efforts were well played and killed their negotiations with Iran.

The diplomats who went back to their capitals empty-handed failed to understand that Iran wasn't my pet policy item. It was a clear American national security imperative on which President Trump was totally focused. One day he said to me, "Mike, why would I lift sanctions before they stop building weapons?" It was a commonsense statement backed by airtight logic. We wouldn't try to appease anybody. We would be prepared to go on offense.

I took extra-special delight in frustrating the Iranians in areas where they had come to expect deferential treatment from the United States. In each of these microdemonstrations of American resolve, we were telling the world we would not look the other way or appease to avoid minor diplomatic skirmishes, as previous administrations had done.

In 2019, Iranian foreign minister Javad Zarif wanted to come to the United States for what Iran claimed was UN business. The truth is that he loves New York, fine restaurants, and five-star hotels. He also relished the opportunity to spew Iranian propaganda—"Our nuclear program was never intended to produce nuclear weapons"—to solicitous and incompetent mainstream American journalists. He liked to meet with Senator Dianne Feinstein, Senator Rand Paul, and other leaders who refuse to acknowledge the extent of the regime's threat. And he often participated in think-tank meetings with outfits such as the Council on Foreign Relations, where he and so-called elite policy wonks can bemoan Mike Pompeo's radical Christian zealotry. Establishment secularists and Islamist theocrats—it's a true meeting of the minds.

Brian Hook and I directed that Zarif's visa be denied because he had no real UN business—an action that is within America's legal right to take under the 1947 UN Headquarters Agreement. Our team ultimately relented on a complete ban on Zarif from coming to the United States, but we were able to restrict much of what he did and added restrictions on what his permanent UN representative could do in the future. Not only did we restrict Iranian activity in the United States, but we showed globalists at the UN that we were a very different American leadership team. On this tactical matter, I could give an inch in the end because I had initially demanded two.

There would be no such leniency in 2020, when we made known that we were going to deny Zarif a visa entirely as he sought to visit the UN Security Council just days after the Soleimani strike. Before long, the world's greatest appeasers called me. First up was UN secretary general António Guterres—an avuncular, socialist radical from Portugal whom I like very much on a personal level. His pleas reminded me that we were getting two benefits for the price of one visa denial. Minutes later, another call came in from UK foreign secretary Dominic Raab—almost certainly at the request of Guterres—because he was known to have a good relationship with me. He pressed the same matter, albeit with more subtlety. No dice. This time, I didn't give an inch.

These visa episodes also exposed how little the world expects from Iran. Case in point: In 2016, along with Representative Frank LoBiondo of New Jersey and Representative Lee Zeldin of New York, I applied for a visa to travel to Iran. I'm still waiting on an approval. While I understand that the United States must make special accommodations for the world's diplomats because we host the UN headquarters, there is no reason Zarif should be able to travel freely to the United States if America's members of Congress or secretary of state can't visit Iran. Although I'm sure the Iranians would roll out the red carpet for a regime sympathizer such as Ilhan Omar or an appeaser such as John Kerry.

Also critical to the diplomatic effort was keeping in line the international body responsible for nuclear inspections. In 2019, the director of the International Atomic Energy Agency died. The fight for his replacement was, at its core, a fight about Iran getting a nuclear weapon. It should come as no surprise that the Russians and the CCP had a preferred candidate. We wanted a fellow named Rafael Grossi, whom I had met on my trip to Vienna as a member of Congress, when I discovered those secret side deals John Kerry and Wendy Sherman had agreed to. While Grossi wasn't perfect, and he would face enormous pressure from the Iranians, he wasn't in the pocket of the Russians and the Chinese. That was good enough for me, and for Jackie Wolcott, the outstanding American patriot who represented the United States at the IAEA. There is no previous administration that would have expended the effort we did to get a better outcome at the IAEA. Instead, with Jackie leading the offensive, we whipped the votes, crushed the other candidates, and got Grossi elected by a landslide. The Iranians had wanted an appeaser. Now they complained bitterly that Grossi was "the US's guy." We hoped they would be proven right.

IRAN RETALIATES AGAINST THE PRESSURE CAMPAIGN

Rejecting the false promises of appeasement isn't easy. You must be prepared to absorb the retaliatory costs of a tough stance. You often pay for a future benefit that might not come until after you're gone. But buy the best-value oil filter you can get your hands on. You'll avoid a crippling payment later. The West has largely forgotten that freedom and security come at a price. We didn't.

Throughout 2019, as economic sanctions choked Iran's economy, the regime began to thrash against the pain, just as we expected it to do. It planted mines on internationally flagged ships. It began to enrich uranium overtly, to levels beyond what were allowed under the nuclear deal. The regime's leaders acted as the outlaws they really were. Iran had two goals: to cause nations imposing pressure to abandon that pressure; and to keep the Europeans and other democracies that had not joined the campaign on the sidelines.

At the helm of Iranian terrorism was Qasem Soleimani, whom I had studied even before heading the CIA. He was a hero of the 1980s war between Iran and Iraq, and Iranian propagandists had turned him into a household name. Even though he stood only five feet nine, he had a military bearing and a hero's face. He looked like the "Most Interesting Man in the World" from those Dos Equis beer commercials featuring the catchphrase "Stay thirsty, my friends."

Despite Soleimani's diminutive stature, he instilled true fear in the hearts of Middle East leaders. Hardened by spearheading decades' worth of Iranian military action in Iraq, Lebanon, and Syria, Soleimani had since 1998 run the murderous Quds Force unit of Iran's IRGC. This cadre of terrorists sought to spread the "Islamic Revolution" outside Iran's borders, usually with violence. The Quds Force is behind innumerable bombings, assassinations, and destabilizations. Its agents often enjoy diplomatic cover. Their provocations are a major reason why countries such as Iraq, Lebanon, Syria, and Yemen are such a chaotic mess today. But what really focused my attention was how Soleimani's units, by directing Shia proxy militias and terrorists from the shadows, aided the killing of more than six hundred American troops during the Iraq War.

Soleimani exercised complete control over this butchery. And his men loved him. No other figure, not even the ayatollah, has commanded more loyalty from Iran's military and intelligence complex. Though ruthless, he was far from a bloodthirsty oaf. In addition to being a shrewd tactician, he had cultivated a wide political network across the Mideast. In 2017, I met with Iraqi prime minister Haider al-Abadi in his palace and asked him a question: If the United States offered financial support, would Iraq cease importing electricity from Iran? Otherwise, Iraq could be at risk of American sanctions on its power grid. Prime Minister Abadi looked me dead in the eye and said, "Mr. Director, when you leave, Qasem Soleimani will come see me. You may take away my money. He will take away my life." Hard rules to live by.

I wanted Soleimani to know that America wasn't afraid of him. That's why I sent him a letter stating our intent to hold him accountable for any attacks on Americans in Iraq for which he was responsible. I also briefed President Trump about Soleimani, usually about how Shia militias under his command were threatening American interests in the Middle East, including the US Embassy in Baghdad. The president agreed with me that there were no competing factions of "hard-liners" and "moderates," despite press accounts and think-tank papers that suggested as much. In Iranian leadership, there was just the revolution. If Zarif or other Iranian diplomats showed up in a Western suit and spoke crisp English, it was meaningless. The ayatollah and Soleimani drove Iran's place in the world.

Now, at Soleimani's direction, new levels of Iranian aggression were threatening the pressure campaign. In May 2019, I was in the tiny town of Rovaniemi, Finland, at a meeting of the Arctic Council, the group of nations whose territories extend into the Arctic Circle. Although my mission of preventing Chinese and Russian malign activity in the Arctic was critical, I was distracted. Months earlier, I had made the decision to close America's consulate in Basra, Iraq, not too far from the Iranian border. I was concerned for the security of our diplomats after Iran-backed Shia-militia terrorists under Soleimani's command launched rockets at the facility. Upon detailed review, it was clear that the value of the work at that site could be, almost entirely, gained from other places.

I was determined to avoid another Benghazi. But the rocket attacks persisted across Iraq. I couldn't sit back and do nothing. Nor could I tolerate the Iraqi government's complacency in failing to counter these militias. It's a complicated matter, because Shia groups with deep ties to Iran were and are prominent in Iraqi politics, and Iraq had even folded Iranian-backed militias who fought ISIS into its armed forces. We needed to send a forceful message to Iraq's leadership. On the morning of May 7, in my hotel room in Finland, I decided to cancel the next leg of my journey to Germany and make an emergency trip to Iraq instead.

It was a risky decision, one that many officials would have punted on. An official trip to any country is always a challenge for the secretary's staff, especially when it's a last-minute detour to a land filled with people who want to kill Americans. We went anyway. As we prepared to touch down at the American air base on the outskirts of Baghdad, the plane's lights went dark, and the crew ordered us to close our window shades to help escape the notice of those who would love nothing more than to pop off a shoulder-fired missile at a plane whose fuselage says "United States of America." On the ground, we were whisked into a room on base where we prepared for a military-helicopter flight into Baghdad's Green Zone—driving there was too dangerous. It's worth noting that American officials must carefully plan discreet, short visits to Baghdad. Iranian officials wander about at will. That tells you all you need to know about who's in charge.

I suited up with body armor and received a briefing. Then off we went in the chopper to central Baghdad, where I met with Iraqi president Barham Salih and Prime Minister Adel Abdul-Mahdi. Salih is well-known in Western circles. A brilliant leader from Kurdish Iraq, he was cautious but always clear about was possible and what was reckless. Abdul-Mahdi, by contrast, was an Iranian tool, with no appetite for risking any political capital. My time with him was as close as I came to meeting with actual Iranians.

I made clear that we were prepared to escalate if any American was so much as injured by Iranian militias. Not only might the United States be forced to withdraw what remained of its forces from Iraq—something that no Iraqi leader wanted—but we would hold Iran directly accountable. Abdul-Mahdi mouthed platitudes about how America's support to counter terror in Iraq was valued, blah, blah, blah. But he reminded me again of the geographical fact that Iran was his neighbor. As the meetings wrapped up, I knew that we had laid down a marker.

Another tense decision point came the next month, in June 2019, when Iran shot down an American drone operating near its airspace but not in it. This act of aggression provoked a set of discussions between President Trump and his national security team on how to respond. I thought our solution was both appropriate and necessary. The president initially approved the operation but later, as was his prerogative, gave an order to stand down. It turns out that a White House lawyer had walked into the Oval Office—apparently alone—after the president had already issued his military orders and told the president something that caused him to change his mind. This was not the ideal way to do things, but he was the president. I credit him for sticking with the pressure campaign throughout his entire presidency. And even though we did not respond to Iran with military force in this instance, he would show true fortitude in refusing to appease Iranian aggression soon enough.

The consequences of our refusal to appease Iran by backing down on sanctions were again clear on September 14, 2019. Just a couple months after Iran shot down the drone, cruise missiles launched from Iran hit Saudi Arabia. The targets were major oil facilities belonging to the oil company Saudi Aramco, so the strike threatened global energy supplies. In addition, Americans worked within range of the attack. The Saudis immediately called me, and we worked to help bring the facilities back online. Aramco did amazing work—the price of their products briefly spiked, but they made a credible case that they could mitigate the damage and continue to supply the world. And they did.

The Saudis also wanted to know what we were prepared to do at this dangerous time. I recommended to the president that we send air-defense systems to Saudi Arabia. He was on board with providing defensive weapons to them, but he declined the second part of my recommendation— that the United States go on offense with a direct, cost-imposing action against Iran. It was a fluid time in the administration, as John Bolton had just left and his successor, Robert O'Brien, had barely gotten his feet wet. It would have provided more security for America if we had done more to help Saudi Arabia and the United Arab Emirates, and I regret that I could not marshal a more vigorous response to these attacks, but we did the best we could under the constraints. I felt in my gut that we were losing deterrence against Iran. I told the president what I thought. "Patience, my Mike," came his response.

SOLEIMANI TASTES AMERICAN VENGEANCE

New Year's Eve is supposed to be party time. For me and the Trump administration's national security team, it was anything but that as the calendar approached 2020. We were at risk of losing our campaign of deterrence against Iran. Soleimani felt feisty enough to challenge us in part because of a diplomatic development between the United States and Turkey in October 2019. During a phone call, Turkish president Recep Tayyip Erdoğan convinced President Trump to remove US forces from the Turkey-Syria border, lest they become casualties of a Turkish military advance to push away Kurds who were fighting ISIS. Turkey has a minority Kurdish population, and, with some cause, views armed Kurds, even those in other countries, as a threat. The president sent me, Vice President Pence, National Security Advisor O'Brien, and our teams to Istanbul to negotiate the conflict zone. It was a real balancing act. Our goal was to remove US soldiers from danger, but without exposing to Turkish attack the very Kurdish forces who had been the tip of the spear against ISIS. We were accused, on both the Left and the Right, of abandoning the Kurds. This wasn't true, but the Iranians interpreted our actions as a retreat. They were wrong but felt emboldened.

On December 27, a Shia-militia group conducted a rocket attack on an American installation in Kirkuk, Iraq, killing Nawres Hamid, an American contractor, and wounding American soldiers. We decided to retaliate with air strikes in Iraq and Syria, targeting members of the Kata'ib Hezbollah terrorist group, one of the main Iranian proxy groups. We took out twenty-five of them. But the response was inadequate to stem the rising tide of Iranian aggression. The time had come to stay true to what I had said earlier that month: "We must also use this opportunity to remind Iran's leaders that any attacks by them, or their proxies of any identity, that harm Americans, our allies, or our interests will be answered with a decisive US response."

With Iran's intentional killing of an American, it became clear that the time for that decisive response had come. I called Haspel, Esper, and the chairman of the Joint Chiefs of Staff, General Mark Milley. O'Brien also was briefed on what I intended to recommend to the president. All were on board with the plan, some of which was a direct result of work that had been set in motion sometime prior. God's hand was on this, too.

On December 29, Esper, Milley, and I flew to Mar-a-Lago, where the president was spending a few days. I took the lead at the meeting.

"Mr. President," I said, "Soleimani is traveling from Beirut to Damascus to Baghdad. He's flying on commercial flights, and we know his flight path. He is plotting to kill even more Americans. We have the tools needed to stop him from leading these murderous efforts. They shot down two American UAVs, fired ballistic missiles into Saudi Arabia, and now have killed an American—all at the direction of General Soleimani. It's time to stop his murderous reign. This is a legit military target."

Going on offense by killing Soleimani would be a seismic event. Normally, when America has taken out a terrorist leader in the post-9/11 world, the now-leaderless organization follows what American football coaches call a "next man up" mentality—the next best player who is available to play takes the field. In Soleimani's case, another general would come along—but none with his combination of authority, brains, brutality, and public appeal inside Iran. Trying to replace him would be like trying to replace an original Rembrandt. Good luck with that, as there is simply no good substitute.

President Trump understood the big risks. So did we all. But it was time to pull the trigger. We had warned the Iranians publicly. I'd sent Soleimani a letter directly. They thought they could get away with downing an American unmanned aerial vehicle, and they more or less did. The Iranian regime had brazenly fired ballistic missiles from their own soil in hopes of taking down the world's oil supply at a site with many Americans. And they had killed an American. Doing nothing would have shattered American credibility. Deterrence was at an ebb.

Milley and Esper briefed the president on the proposed plan. I added that we were prepared to communicate directly with the Iranians after the strike to make clear that this was not an attempt to decapitate the regime but that we were prepared to escalate if that was their wish. Other leaders would be watching, too, I said. The CCP, the Russians, and Chairman Kim were at that moment scrutinizing America to see if the Trump administration was prepared to deter aggression against its own people.

He gave his answer: Let's go.

As we got up, I said, almost as an afterthought, "Mr. President, one more reminder, we will be commanding a missile from six thousand miles away to strike an international airport. We haven't done this before." I was comfortable with the risk, as we had a plan for controlling the airspace for the most important five minutes. The only civilians potentially in harm's way would be those on Soleimani's commercial aircraft. We would wait for Soleimani to deplane, enter his vehicle, and get as far away as possible from that aircraft before leaving the airport confines. The president looked straight at us and nodded his head. He didn't say a word, but his eyes screamed, "Do not f——this up."

The date was set for January 3. We informed all the required partners, and our teams began to execute the plan.

On December 31, the president's decision looked even more right. Operating at the ultimate direction of Soleimani and the Iranians, dozens, and later hundreds, of Kata'ib Hezbollah forces and other Shia militiamen stormed the American embassy in Baghdad. They massed at the embassy's security checkpoint and smashed through doors and windows, vandalizing the reception area and setting it ablaze, all while chanting "Death to America!" and "Death to Israel!" Thankfully, with the help of verbal warnings and tear gas, our guards dispersed the rioters before they were able to breach the embassy's main wall.

The detachment of US Marines at the embassy and the presence of Apache helicopters had also convinced the mob to back down. Unlike in previous administrations, State and Defense were totally in sync. The embassy was well-armed, and I had given express instructions, at the direction of the president, that no one should come over the walls alive. Esper and Milley, through General Frank McKenzie of CENTCOM, and the military leaders on the ground provided massive support for my diplomatic team. I can't thank them enough. The incident made me think of the attack on the American embassy in Tehran—as Americans saw recreated in the great film *Argo*—in 1979. We were committed to denying the Iranians a similar victory. The Shia militias damaged the facility, but everything was repaired in relatively short order and our demands of the Iraqi government ultimately gave them the wherewithal to restore order around the embassy compound. But we all knew that come January 3, this dangerous episode might look like a mere warmup act.

Back in America, we prepared for the strike. At the appointed moment, I was with Esper and Milley at the Pentagon. The president was in Florida. We went through the final approval process that morning and tracked Soleimani's movements.

Our intelligence folks had done an outstanding job tracking Soleimani as he moved from one Mideast warzone to another, and we had a bead on him. After midnight Baghdad time on January 3, 2020, Soleimani landed at the airport, where he received a hero's welcome from Abu Mahdi al-Muhandis, the founder of Kata'ib Hezbollah and now the head of a powerful group of Shiite militias in Iran. Little did he know that an American MQ-9 Reaper drone was tracking their every move from above. As Soleimani's sedan departed the airport on an access road, Hellfire missiles came screaming down. American power, American technology, and American justice slammed into his vehicle. American deterrence struck, and Soleimani would never hurt anybody ever again.

It took only minutes for social media to erupt with reports of an explosion at Baghdad International Airport. The Iranians soon confirmed that their evil hero was dead. Around the world, we were ready for vengeful attacks on US facilities. The Israelis also were ready, knowing that Iran could choose to retaliate against them. In the same way, we had worked with our Gulf Arab partners, giving them a heads-up without revealing our specific plans.

I also passed on my message to the Iranians. Within a few hours, Iran lobbed ballistic missiles at Al Asad Airbase in Iraq. The missile strike injured US service members, some seriously, but no one was killed. Afterward, I received a note from my Iranian counterpart via the Swiss that this was the totality of the Iranian response. A relief to be sure, as well as more proof that we controlled the escalation ladder.

Yet we could not be sure the Iranians were truly done. The next day, President Trump reinforced our kinetic deterrence with rhetorical deterrence on Twitter: "We have targeted 52 Iranian sites (representing the 52 American hostages taken by Iran many years ago), some at a very high level & important to Iran & the Iranian culture, and those targets, and

Iran itself, WILL BE HIT VERY FAST AND VERY HARD. The USA wants no more threats!"

For good measure, I sent a letter to the ayatollah on behalf of the United States, informing him that we were closely monitoring the activities of the Shia militias in Iraq and Syria. I said that any attack on American forces would be directly attributed to him and Iran, and that the American response would come down against all those to whom the attacks could be attributed. Soon we could see that the Shia militias in Iraq had been ordered to stand down.

Another blowup followed days later—this time in Washington. In the days and weeks after the strike, many Democrats and the media retreated for their fainting couches. Joe Biden said it was "hugely escalatory." Senator Chris Murphy wondered if America had just set off "a potential massive regional war." The screaming Ben Rhodeses of the world could not imagine using such precision and power to slow down an evil enemy.

On January 8, Esper, Haspel, Milley, and I briefed an all-member gathering of the US Congress in a secure setting. Of course, within minutes of our briefing ending, Democrats were publicly claiming that we had risked American lives for nothing and that our basis for having taken the strike was nonexistent. In the hallway outside the hearing, Speaker Pelosi began to scream at Haspel, saying that she had gone from being an intelligence professional to a Trump toady. All Gina had done, in fact, was to lay out what we knew and why we were determined to stop Soleimani from killing again. That someone whose greatest problem in life is getting Alexandria Ocasio-Cortez to behave would challenge the integrity of a woman who had risked her own life for years at the CIA made me want to retch. So, I walked over and got right back in Pelosi's face. Gina didn't need my help, but I felt duty bound to go on offense myself.

Let's review the tape, as they say, on the consequences of the Soleimani strike. Did our deterrence work? Would it have been better to appease the Iranians?

The skeptics couldn't have been more wrong. Instead of igniting a new war, our bold actions had in fact *de-escalated* the situation. We protected American lives from a terrorist who was orchestrating further harm in the days and hours before his death. Iran got the message that if its aggression continued, there would be even more hell to pay. And in the context of our Iran strategy, it made perfect sense to cut off the head of the octopus that had wrapped its tentacles around nearly every Middle Eastern nation. It would make subsequent efforts to dismember the remaining parts easier. We can also look at the behavior of Kim, Putin, and Xi after this strike—and add Venezuela's Nicolás Maduro to the list. We not only punished Iran, but all these leaders understood our deterrent power much better on January 4 than they did on January 3. It was a collateral benefit of going on offense.

As an addendum to this whole episode, it's worth remembering that as tensions flared, the Iranian military shot down Ukraine International Airlines Flight 752 seconds after it lifted off from Tehran bound for Kyiv. The Iranian surface-to-air missile—and the regime's evil and incompetence—killed 176 innocent civilians, most of them Iranian. The regime initially lied and tried to cover up its deadly mistake. Bulldozers razed the site where the plane came down. Agents of the government delayed handing over the black boxes for investigation. That kind of cover-up, that absence of valuing human lives, is par for the course for Iran and all despotic authoritarian regimes.

To this day, the Iranian regime is still hungry for revenge over the killing of their revered warlord. The very president of Iran, Ebrahim Raisi, has proclaimed, "If Trump and Pompeo are not tried in a fair court for the criminal act of assassinating General Soleimani, Muslims will take our martyr's revenge." Likewise, the head of the IRGC navy has stated: "The supreme leader has emphasized revenge, and the IRGC's overall commander has said that revenge is inevitable, and we will determine when and where revenge takes place . . . All the perpetrators of the assassination of martyr Soleimani will surely be punished in this world for their dirty deed."

We know Iran has the capabilities to operate inside the United States, so a year and a half after leaving public service, I still retain a security detail. Trip to the grocery store? Diplomatic security will shadow me while I evaluate which eggplant looks the ripest. Susan's going to get her hair done? Let's hope Hezbollah sleeper agents aren't casing the salon. Son's getting married? Agents will need to send an advance team to the church. Every day, everything my family and I do is preplanned and coordinated with the people in suits and sunglasses (and we are profoundly thankful to those great Americans who protect us). On at least one occasion my son's day has been massively disrupted because of security concerns. I will probably never drive my own car again or enjoy the level of privacy that I once had.

So be it. Beyond these inconveniences, these threats, this fatwa, has not caused me to alter my life one bit. Refusing to appease evil comes at a price for individuals, such as our service members, for families, and for our country. But standing up to a rogue nation and its evil terrorists determined to kill Americans is worth it. I bought the oil filter. And I am confident that we saved American lives.

SUPPORTING THE IRANIAN PEOPLE

Our deterrence effort counted on pressure from within Iran, as well. One of the things I am most proud of in our Iran campaign was our support for the Iranian people. Many of them oppose their despotic rulers—a stance that connects deeply with a policy of nonappeasement. They know more than anyone the brutality of the regime. They also know that the JCPOA gave the regime more resources to keep the Iranian people under the boot of tyranny. Unlike the Obama administration, which gave only token, delayed, mealymouthed support for the "Green Revolution" protestors in 2009, the Trump administration amplified the voices of the Iranian people who were crying out for a brighter future. I was happy to help put them on offense.

One of the millions of fed up Iranians was Pouya Bakhtiari, a young electrical engineer who was sick of what he called criminal and corrupt Iranian leadership. In November 2019, he took to the streets of Mehrshahr to protest the regime's abuses, alongside his mother, Nahid. They promised that they would hold hands to stay together, but when security forces attacked the crowd, they became separated. Then Nahid experienced every parent's worst nightmare—the sight of fellow protestors holding her son's lifeless body. He had been shot in the head by the regime's thugs. Now Nahid grieves with so many other Iranian parents. "Now, Pouya's ideals are mine," she has said. "I want to witness and celebrate the freedom of the people of Iran."

Stories of violent oppression such as these have been common since 1979, when the ayatollah's band of revolutionaries seized power. Indeed, the current president of Iran, Ebrahim Raisi, was responsible for helping slaughter at least five thousand political prisoners while deputy prosecutor of Tehran in 1988. I was proud to help lead a new round of sanctions on him while at State.

The regime's oppression infiltrates every area of personal life. Women who refuse to wear headscarves are beaten and taken to jail. Out of fear of persecution, and even death, Iranians who wish to leave Islam and be baptized into the Christian faith must secretly resort to using hotel swimming pools in foreign countries for such ceremonies. In July 2021, the regime plotted to kidnap a US citizen of Iranian origin in New York. The Department of Justice thwarted that evil deed, in just the latest example of how regime agents have fanned out across the world to capture or kill their enemies. The Trump administration was never afraid to expose the regime's depravity. We even asked Iranians to tell us their stories on a secure messaging channel—and the State Department received thousands of responses. I also met frequently with Iranian Americans who sustain ties to family members inside Iran.

In July 2018, I spoke about our Iran policy at the Ronald Reagan Presidential Library. I delivered the speech in America, but its real audience was the Iranian people, who have ways of eluding their Islamist censors to learn about what's happening outside their borders. "The level of corruption and wealth among Iranian leaders shows that Iran is run by something that resembles the mafia more than a government," I said. I described thieving ayatollahs and women beaten in the streets. The room was packed with Iranian Americans who received almost every line with cheers and applause, if I modestly say so myself. I'd like to think they were channeling the voices of the silenced Iranian people, seven thousand miles away.

Later on, I met with Iranian exiles who knew that the Soleimani strike mattered. Their contacts back in Iran—including people in the streets for his funeral because the regime forced them to be there—knew that we had dealt a blow to their oppressors.

OUR MODEL OF DETERRENCE AND PRESSURE WORKED

Ultimately, our pressure campaign—while not perfect—was a success. A lot of critics claimed sanctions didn't work, but that's crazy talk. By sanctioning more than 1,500 Iranian targets, especially in Iran's oil industry, we deprived the regime of more than $70 billion in revenue that could have bankrolled missile and nuclear programs and terrorist attacks. More than one hundred companies withdrew from Iran or canceled their planned investments, causing the country to lose additional billions. From 2017 to 2020, Iran's GDP sank from $445 billion to $192 billion—it was practically cut in half—and its GDP world ranking plummeted from 31st to 51st. Our sanctions caused the IRGC to reduce its budget by 20 percent from 2018 to 2020. In March 2019, one Iran-backed fighter in Syria who saw his salary slashed by one third confessed to the *New York Times*: "The golden days are gone and will never return . . . Iran doesn't have enough money to give us."

Many of our allies joined our offensive, too. Australia, Albania, Bahrain, Lithuania, Saudi Arabia, the United Arab Emirates, the United Kingdom, and the United States banded together to stop Iranian harassment of shipping in the Strait of Hormuz, and Iranian mine attacks on international ships stopped in August 2019. The United Kingdom, Germany, Kosovo, Estonia, Argentina, Paraguay, Guatemala, Honduras, and Colombia put various new terrorism designations on Hezbollah. Having new South American countries on board—largely thanks to the great work of Nathan Sales, the State Department's top counterterrorism official—let us pour cold water on a hotbed of Hezbollah's financing. And of course, the Abraham Accords peace agreements were an unprecedented step for the forces of stability and peace in the Middle East over the forces of chaos and death.

By the end of the Trump administration, the regime was in full-on panic mode over the collapse of its economy and the anger of the Iranian people. We had an abundance of evidence suggesting that, had President

Trump extended his term of office, the Iranians were ready to come to the negotiating table and beg for mercy. One cannot predict the future with certainty, but I know this: the ayatollah was within months of reaching for that "chalice of poison" once more—as Supreme Leader Ayatollah Khomeini described doing a bitter peace deal with Iraq in 1988.

Unfortunately, the Obama administration's appeasers are back in positions of authority, looking for new ways to make bad deals. Failing to enforce sanctions, allowing Iran to enrich uranium at a 60 percent level and keep enriched uranium in country, and peeling back designations of Iran-backed terrorists such as the Houthis are acts of weakness. Iran is still recovering from what we did, but its hopes of dominating the Middle East are revived. Nuclear weapons are back within its reach. We need to deter Iran once again because we can't afford the folly of more appeasement. Staying on offense is the only way forward.

CHAPTER 7

AMERICAN SOVEREIGNTY MATTERS

The most useless statements in the world are probably diplomatic communiqués. Even the effete-sounding name makes me bristle. Foreign ministries live to draft these pointless documents, which usually represent the lowest common denominator of agreement between the participants at multilateral (more than two parties) meetings. The most difficult issues are set aside for senior leaders to hash out toward the end, which is what makes the meetings occasionally worthwhile. But the communiqués are an extravagant waste of time.

Almost every time a meeting approached, I would get a hair-on-fire call from one of our diplomats negotiating the communiqué. He or she would say something like this: "Mr. Secretary, there are only two items remaining, one on China and one on climate. All twenty-four other countries have signed off on the language, and we are the lone holdout. It may have already leaked to the press that we have refused to join the communiqué. This will truly embarrass America and your visit will be marred by our refusal to sign on with the others." To describe this tactic of trying to force my hand as extortion is too harsh, but only by a bit.

After this happened two or three times, I made clear to my team: "I don't give a rip about a communiqué at any of my meetings. If we don't get the language we want, they are free to sign without us, and I'm happy to take questions at the closing press conference and explain why language such as 'we are working closely with our Chinese partners for a win-win solution on climate change' is dangerous, false, and feeding the communist narrative." This breach of diplomatic protocol did not make me popular.

In May 2019, at a meeting of the Arctic Council, Nordic foreign ministers were trying to browbeat me into putting America's name to a communiqué stuffed with language on the environment and climate change that I knew did not accord with Trump administration policy. They hammered me, but I wouldn't give an inch. I wasn't going to affirm a consensus that did not exist and, more importantly, that wouldn't be good for America if it did. To my great surprise and amusement, Russian foreign minister Sergey Lavrov came to my defense: "Stop bothering him. He's not going to sign it. Let's enjoy our vodka and talk about happier things."

In the end, we all agreed to a short statement about the meeting that did not include the phrase "climate change." America First, yes. Regrets, not one. I knew that a sovereign defense of our national interests mattered to the American people, and I wasn't going to sign America up for multilateral commitments that disregarded their will.

AMERICA FIRST: GOOD FOR AMERICA AND THE WORLD

"America First." We've heard it thousands of times. Count me among those who never get tired of hearing it. When Donald Trump first adopted this mantra on the campaign trail, Democrats, the media, and even many Republicans hyperventilated. Granted, Trump was using a phrase taken from the name of a group that opposed America's entry into World War II before the Pearl Harbor attack. That gang unfortunately included a few anti-Semites. But it was also made up of cautious Americans, such as future presidents Gerald Ford and John F. Kennedy. It made no sense to let the mistakes of people in a previous generation wreck a great phrase that can enjoy a different meaning in a new century. It's amazing what educated people who parse words for a living pretend not to understand. They let their personal dislike of Donald Trump eclipse their common sense.

Trump's vision of America First was a bold and unapologetic reassertion of American sovereignty and national interests in our foreign policy. Such an approach is consistent with our Founders' ideas, normal in the history of US foreign affairs and expected by the American people. Unfortunately, especially in the post–Cold War era, too many of America's leaders had failed to heed the words of Alexander Hamilton: "Under every form of government, rulers are only trustees for the happiness and interest of their nation." They "cannot, consistently with their trust, follow the suggestions of kindness or humanity toward others, to the prejudice of their constituents." Our leaders, alas, showed kindness and humanity toward others to the prejudice of their own constituents. Whether by turning a blind eye to a crisis of illegal immigration that eroded the American foundation of law and order; binding the United States to international trade agreements, such as NAFTA, that eviscerated our manufacturing base; or failing to push back when leftist international organizations overstepped their bounds, many of the so-called brightest minds in Washington decided to set policies that won the praise of corporate titans and Geneva bureaucrats but left people in Wichita and Winston-Salem feeling angry and ignored. Prizing American sovereignty isn't an exercise in eggheaded international relations theory. It directly impacts the welfare of the American people.

Our administration decided to stand up for sovereignty in ways that hadn't been done in many years. We didn't shy away from making America First the principle of our decision-making, even if some allies got upset about it. Nor did we trust "the international community" to advance American interests—America's leaders can never presume others will do their job. As President Trump said in his speech to the UN General Assembly in 2017: "Sovereign and independent nations are the only vehicle where freedom has ever survived, democracy has ever endured, or peace has ever prospered. And so we must protect our sovereignty and our cherished independence above all."

In my 2019 speech to the Claremont Institute, I backed up this statement of commander's intent and recounted how we had lost our way: "We had too much confidence in the international system and not enough confidence in our own nation. And we had too little courage to confront regimes squarely opposed to our interests and to our values."

It was this simple for me: America is an exceptional nation. No nation like ours had ever existed before America's creation, and to this day, no other does. Our exceptionalism is born of an understanding of our nation's founding and carried on through a commitment to ensuring the pursuit of life, liberty, and happiness.

Defending American sovereignty benefits other nations, too. A prosperous, robust, and secure America—both physically secure and confident in its place in the world—improves the lives of people everywhere. An America that is powerful, yet humble and restrained, drives the world forward toward greater prosperity and greater dignity for every human being. I will never apologize for our history, nor will I ever forget that our republic, if we can keep it, is fragile. We guarantee its continuity only by putting our confidence in the words of our founding documents, not globalist pabulum. Prioritizing American sovereignty does not by definition mean forgoing friendships and alliances, but if acting alone is in the best interests of our people, then so be it.

Finally, you cannot put America first without first deciding what America is. Our Constitution and the Declaration of Independence define the essence of the United States. Globalists want to ignore these underpinnings of American sovereignty. Our administration knew that globalism was the path to perdition and, even worse, threatened the republic that we had sworn an oath to defend from enemies foreign and domestic. As America's seventieth secretary of state, I was determined to preserve the American way of life—and that meant putting America first.

STANDING FOR SOVEREIGNTY AT THE SOUTHERN BORDER

During the 2016 campaign, Trump gave a voice to millions of Americans who had been frustrated by years of politicians talking a big game but ultimately doing nothing to crack down on illegal immigration. Building the wall, of course, was the centerpiece of his agenda. The fights to secure funding and raise up that wall are legendary, and its completion remains unfinished business. But our southern border is, of course, an international boundary. Getting it right involves international diplomatic efforts, in addition to barriers and US Border Patrol agents. It is likely that I spent more time working on this issue with our neighbor to the south than any other secretary of state or CIA director in history.

We spent countless hours developing our diplomatic efforts to protect

American sovereignty and stop the flow of those seeking to violate our laws and our border. I had an excellent team working on this for me, starting with Ulrich Brechbühl at the head of State's effort. He teamed up with Stephen Miller at the White House and leaders at the Department of Homeland Security (DHS) and the Department of Justice, as well. Kim Breier did exceptional work as the assistant secretary of state for Western Hemisphere Affairs. And once we were able to get him confirmed, Chris Landau became a talented ambassador in Mexico City. We were candid, frank, obnoxious, brutal—you pick the word—in laying out our expectations and the actions we would take to protect our borders.

Democrats and the media completely missed what we were trying to do by enforcing border security and reforming the asylum process. A sovereign nation must be able to ensure security and regulate the flow of people across its own border. Illegal immigration erodes the law and order that a government owes to its citizens. It often involves the attendant crimes of human trafficking and drug smuggling. It dishonors Americans who have patiently followed the law to come here and join us in citizenship. We felt obligated to honor these simple principles of nationhood by securing the border.

The enthusiasm for this mission that President Trump demonstrated the day he came down the gold escalator in 2015 did not wane a bit in the White House. Between the border and trade issues, we talked about Mexico almost daily. Early on, at one PDB briefing, the president was trying to get a sense of Mexico's capabilities relative to those of the United States.

"Mike," he mused, "How would we do if we went to war with Mexico?"

"Sir," I quipped, "They'd come in second."

It's worth pausing here for a moment, before you jump on Twitter and announce that you've discovered evidence that President Trump wanted to attack our neighbor. This kind of musing was frequent in the White House, and it always panicked a certain kind of official. Some would likely have run out of the Oval Office and written notes in their files to protect themselves. Their answer to the president would have been different from mine, something more earnest, such as, "Sir, it would be illegal go to war with Mexico." Those people mostly became former cabinet members. The president had no intention of invading Mexico. He was simply testing and expanding the range of ideas that might be useful in fulfilling his essential promises to the American people.

In his own Trumpian way, the president sought to understand power relationships, probe the internal dynamics of other nations, and reframe the conversation around, in this case, what was clearly a government encouraging and promoting massive violations of American sovereignty. Like Trump, I often have scattershot conversations, toss out ideas that I know are taboo, and try to expand the discussion beyond traditionally cramped debates. This is how creativity and hard thinking work. It allows us to look at old problems from fresh angles. That's how we can come up with the unique approaches that the American people need.

And, by the way, America would finish first at war with every country today. One of the objectives of putting America first and preserving our sovereignty is to ensure that never changes.

REFORMING A BROKEN ASYLUM SYSTEM

Once I became secretary of state, I proudly got to work on issues with Mexico that mattered a great deal to my boss and my country. Already we were seeing fewer illegal entries, because of stepped-up enforcement and tougher detention policies. With Stephen Miller running point in the White House, the number of apprehensions in fiscal year 2017 was the lowest since the turn of the century. Then-DHS secretary John Kelly referred to what we were seeing as "the Trump effect." People didn't even want to try to enter the United States illegally, hence the low number of apprehensions.

Yet it was an uphill battle to create lasting change. Federal courts routinely blocked sensible reforms. The media was showing "kids in cages"—a practice that started under President Obama but that journalists had only managed to discover now. As accusations of racism flew everywhere, funding for a border wall was difficult to obtain from Congress, even though it was popular with the public. President Trump, who had, rightly, invested an enormous amount of political capital in promising to plug the dam, was constantly unhappy with his team.

By the time I led the State Department, this team included Kirstjen Nielsen as DHS secretary. It also included her chief of staff, Miles Taylor, who proved to be one of the most shameless hypocrites I have ever encountered, which is quite an accomplishment. He wrote an infamous op-ed in the *New York Times* that denounced his boss's boss. Instead of signing his name to it, as a man of integrity would do, Taylor hid behind the cowardly byline of "Anonymous." Nielsen mostly channeled Trump's instincts on border security; her challenge was convincing the president that some of his proposals were unworkable. She couldn't figure out how to tell him that something could not be done and get him to accept it. Several of us tried to provide her with fire support, but she was undermined from within. She couldn't trust her own chief of staff, who had a completely different agenda. I put Taylor up there with Snowden as someone with an ego that far exceeds his competence and a level of self-righteousness that exceeds belief. I don't fault Nielsen.

With various immigration-control efforts stalled, we shifted focus to diplomacy, seeking an agreement with Mexico to stem the flow of people coming across the border. The US government had never tried this before. Asylum seekers posed a special problem. During most of my time as secretary of state, the largest number of claimants entering our country from Mexico were not fleeing Mexico. They were from El Salvador, Honduras, Guatemala, and elsewhere in Central and South America. Many were from other places even further away, such as the Middle East and Africa. They flocked to our southern border because it was an easy entry point. While many who seek asylum are genuinely fleeing war, persecution, or other forms of violence—Ukrainians in 2022, for instance— nearly all who want to enter the United States by invoking asylum do so under false pretenses, gaining entry without so much as a colorable claim of meeting the legal standard for asylum. Then they disappear into the country to begin a new life while their case is being adjudicated, which usually takes years. The federal government can't trace them. They have children who are citizens at birth. In addition to the American people, the real victims of asylum fraud are those with legitimate claims. The US immigration court system gets clogged with dishonest cases while the true victims of political violence and persecution wait in limbo.

It is worth noting, too, that illegal aliens make a mockery of the legal immigration system. Frankly, it is not outrageous to think that a law-abiding person who wants to be an American and files the appropriate paperwork to do so is a sucker. When I was in Congress, my office took calls from constituents who were trying to help someone, often a family member, gain legal residency. We would joke privately that they could spend a decade and money to do it right or just learn to swim the Rio Grande. Our system is a farce, and stopping illegal immigration is the prerequisite for a rational legal immigration policy.

Because the courts and Congress were rejecting our calls for commonsense fixes to border security and immigration, we developed a creative way forward. We prepared to tell the Mexican government that Mexico, not the United States, would host asylum seekers while the United States processed their claims. Our plans were complicated by the fact that Mexico was in a presidential transition from the administration of President Enrique Peña Nieto to the left-wing administration of President Andrés Manuel López Obrador, popularly known as AMLO. Neither one accepted the idea that Mexico should enter into an agreement to house all asylum seekers coming to the United States via our shared border. Additionally, the Trump administration had not yet identified what basis existed in US law to force Mexico to take asylum seekers while the United States adjudicated their claims. But in November 2018, officials grew comfortable with using a provision in US law—Section 235(b)(2)(C) of the Immigration and Nationality Act—that had previously been used to justify returning asylum seekers to Mexico after filing a claim in the United States.

The plan for asylum seekers to wait in Mexico had two benefits: First, it complied with US and international law, as it put the asylum seekers outside of our nation pending resolution of their claims. Second, it turned off the spigot by flipping the incentives. Go ahead and file your claim, but live in Mexico while it's processed. No sneaking off to Chicago or Denver in the meantime. We were confident that the scammers would view living in a camp in the north of Mexico as a deterrent. The key to stopping migration is to impose hard controls and change the incentives. This idea did both.

I also knew this America First imperative—soon to be known as the "Remain in Mexico" policy—had a very high chance of success because of the team implementing it. Jared Kushner had developed strong relationships with Mexican officials, and Stephen Miller, along with Ulrich, was quarterbacking the internal responsibilities for asylum policy shared by DHS and the State Department.

I was the first to share our plan formally with the incoming Mexican government. In Houston on November 15, 2018, I described it to Marcelo Ebrard, who was about to become Mexico's foreign secretary in the AMLO administration. The former mayor of Mexico City, Marcelo is very bright and very Marxist. He's also affable and capable, and he may well be Mexico's next president. Having run one of the biggest cities in the world, he was a pragmatist. He understood power and risk. He was also determined to put Mexico first—just exactly as he should do. He and I had already established a good relationship, so when I asked to see him, he agreed to meet me halfway between our two capitals. I loved working with him.

Beginning in two weeks, I told Marcelo, we would accept asylum seekers at US border crossing points and then return them to Mexico.

Marcelo was visibly shaken. He insisted that his government could not accept these terms, pointing out the obvious fact that his people would be very unhappy to have thousands of illegal aliens staying in their country.

"Can you hear yourself? That's exactly why we're establishing this policy. It's unacceptable to have not just thousands but hundreds of thousands of illegal entrants to our country staying in the US forever."

Marcello emphasized that he understood my goal. But he was skeptical it could be done, both as a logistical matter and as an action consistent with Mexican law. Most of all, he was clearly concerned that we wanted it all to happen in only fourteen days.

"Marcelo, here's the deal. If in fourteen days State and DHS can't return nearly every single asylum claimant to Mexico, we are going to completely shut down the Mexican border."

Marcelo thought I was pulling his leg, bringing up the fact that hundreds of millions of dollars flow across the border every week.

"Completely. Nothing will move. No doubt this will impact the US, but so does massive illegal immigration. You are welcome to have your boss call the president—he knows I'm delivering this message to you today—but he was very clear. Fourteen days or bust."

Marcelo did what every good diplomat does in such a situation. He promised to take it back to his boss but warned that it would not work.

I went into friend mode. This is why relationships matter. "Marcelo, you and I have to make this work. We know all of the turmoil, all of the chaos, all of the bad blood between our two countries that will follow if we fail. We will do what we can to help you at your own southern border, where this is mostly coming from. We will help you find ways to take care of these people who will now be in Northern Mexico illegally. We are also engaging diplomatically and through DHS to tell the Central American countries that we are going to return people to them as part of this plan. We hope this will reduce the size of your camps and detention facilities."

Then, my closing: "Marcelo, we don't need your permission to do this. We want it to be cooperative, but it's not a requirement. These migrants will not be remaining in the US in fourteen days. We have done the work on our side to ensure that. I am happy to fly down to meet with your president to discuss, but our teams should begin to work these issues immediately."

Marcelo had one final question. He asked whether we had to publicly tout Mexico's agreement to our terms, or whether his government could say it was opposed to it, without acknowledging any agreement.

"I don't give a rip. Whatever helps you domestically, that's on you." We parted, amicably, knowing that we both had a lot of work to do.

Marcelo's last comment turned out to contain the seeds of the answer to how we would manage the politics of this decision. I think that as Marcelo thought this through, he realized that if we could turn off the magnet that attracted hundreds of thousands of migrants to move through his country, it would be good not only for Mexico but also for AMLO and for him.

Nonetheless, Foreign Secretary Ebrard had several challenges. The first was related to domestic politics: He had to protect his boss from looking as if he had caved to El Norte. Second, he couldn't work with his own new ambassador to the United States because she was radically opposed to even thinking about a concept such as this. We did everything we could during our discussions to keep her in the dark. We kept others in the dark, too, knowing that the likelihood of leaks grows exponentially according to the number of persons in the know.

How our respective publics would react was also a sensitive subject. President Trump wanted Americans to know that he had achieved this major change in US asylum policy. But AMLO would not be able to admit that America had pushed him around. Thus, as we began to draft the outlines of the operational plan, we spent a great deal of time deciding what could be publicly announced. It became clear that AMLO took seriously President Trump's threat to close the border. Each time we hit a hard stop in drafting an agreement, I would simply remind everyone that "our days are numbered."

Two days before the deadline, I asked Marcelo if he would like to speak with President Trump to update him alongside me. We had done this before, and his initial response was positive. Less than an hour later, however, he called back and said that there would be no need for a meeting. He believed we had a solution. Ebrard's plan was simple: Mexico would agree privately to allow the United States to return nearly all migrants who transited from Mexico to the United States and requested asylum. His major ask was this: he would not sign anything, and there would be no public announcement of this plan. Of course, we had to announce something. We needed to articulate what we were doing as a matter of policy, and the public deserved to know, too.

So we bargained and reached a deal, drafting a document for public release that described how Mexico would enforce the plan. We pledged to them American help and support. Another document made clear that Mexico would "not object" to the United States' returning asylum seekers to Mexico.

The man who held the drafting pen was my critical partner and *paisan* Pat Cipollone, the brilliant White House counsel. He had what may have been the most difficult and least appreciated job in our administration. From managing impeachment, to addressing complex claims about the election, to helping the secretary of state, Pat delivered excellence all around him. His two deputies, Patrick Philbin and Michael Purpura, did yeoman's work for President Trump, as well. That team—along with my dear friend Emmet Flood—served America nobly and with excellence.

When we reported the outcome of our "Remain in Mexico" negotiations to the president, he wasn't as happy as I'd hoped. "My Mike, this is a great deal, but we need a press conference."

I told him the truth: "We can have a press conference announcing the Mexican government's commitments on enforcement and that the US is going to return asylees, but we cannot—*cannot*—convey an understanding between our two governments to move down this path together."

The president relented, and we arrived at a good solution. Remain in Mexico, formally known as the Migrant Protection Protocols, worked magnificently. We sent a strong message of deterrence. The simple fact that people around the world learned that coming to the United States illegally with a bogus asylum claim no longer led to automatic entry stopped many crossings before they started. It took a few months to implement effectively, but combined with amazing work by Immigration and Customs Enforcement officers and the building of barriers along the border, we changed the calculus for illegal immigration and didn't have to shut down the border. The Mexican government saved face, too. It was free to complain about our policy and to pretend that it had not signed onto it.

This deal had what every good deal needs: something for everyone. Marcelo knew that for Mexico, the politics were tough in the short run. But he also knew he was helping his country. Having hundreds of thousands of people transiting through his country to make their way to the United States was not only bad for America but bad for the Mexican people, as well. Marcelo knew that if we could deter would-be illegal immigrants, it would reduce costs and risks for his country. His diplomatic skills on behalf of his own nation were truly magnificent.

★ ★ ★

Even as we cut the flow of questionable asylum seekers, the Trump administration, paradoxically, was also a victim of its own economic success. The domestic economy under President Trump roared, producing massive gains for people in every income strata. This prosperity drew people seeking a piece of the action from all over Latin America. When the numbers from May 2019 reflected the highest number of illegal border crossings in thirteen years, the president became furious. He threatened tariffs on Mexico if its government didn't do more to control the surge. He proposed an escalating system that started with a tariff of 5 percent on all goods crossing the border and increased to 25 percent if the problem persisted.

The National Security Council convened meetings in the first week of June on how to find a way forward with Mexico. Kim Breier came back from one meeting and told me, "I have just two words for you on tariffs: Michigan. Ohio." As it turns out, the president's proposal would have decimated the US auto industry. In many cases, individual automotive parts and pieces cross the US-Mexico border multiple times during a vehicle assembly. Each one would have been subject to a tariff at every instance of entry.

This threat to the American automotive sector, combined with the president's pressure, led to creative diplomacy. On June 7, 2019, the United States and Mexico jointly announced reforms that better protected national sovereignty and local communities. Mexico agreed to deploy its National Guard near its own southern border to deter illegal migrant flows from Central America. And we expanded the Remain in Mexico policy beyond the initial pilot programs at certain checkpoints. If Mexico didn't enforce these deals, the United States would require it to absorb all asylum seekers before they even reached the United States. Mexico hated this idea, so it served as our main point of leverage, which had to be kept secret, save for a handful of trusted souls inside the US government.

When we briefed the president on the final deal, he asked Cipollone for a copy of the final document that would not be made public. President Trump was thrilled that we had gotten this done, congratulated us for the work, and then placed the paper in his suit-coat pocket. Days later, on a walk across the White House lawn to Marine One, he held it up and proclaimed that Mexico would have to honor the agreement. I immediately called Ebrard and apologized. Nonetheless, implementation of the plan continued.

Getting this agreement over the finish line involved a bunch of difficult, ticking-time-bomb negotiations between the Mexican delegation on one side and Breier, Cipollone, and me on the other. Kim's strong rapport with the Mexicans helped smooth over various rough patches, and she was a major asset for our Western Hemisphere diplomacy all around. I was sorry to see her depart public service soon after, but I understood how senior-level jobs at the State Department took a brutal toll on folks with young children. I also missed her because she was an uncompromising fighter against the socialist regimes in Cuba and Venezuela—a rarity at State.

Over the course of 2019, we signed similar agreements with El Salvador, Guatemala, and Honduras. Chad Wolf and his team at Customs and Border Patrol were extraordinary in working to make this happen, and it would not have happened without them. These agreements were a big deal, as more than 71 percent of apprehensions at the US southern border during fiscal year 2019 involved migrants from those three countries. Ultimately, our border-security policies defended American sovereignty and stemmed the tide of irregular migration. In the year after our deal-making, the number of apprehensions at the southern border dropped 53 percent. Our administration had not just the more effective policies but the more humane ones. We freed up resources to help legitimate asylum seekers, and we cut into a major source of income for the Mexican cartels that prey on people trying to get to the border.

Under President Biden's lax policies, however, Customs and Border Patrol recorded an all-time high number of detentions at the US-Mexico border in 2021. Mexican coyotes and cartels are exploiting vulnerable people and getting rich doing it, because President Biden has given the green light for people to come via lax enforcement policies. The fact is that the Biden administration believes these newcomers are future Democratic voters and thus is willing to compromise national security, the rule of law, and the essence of nationhood to bring them here. Americans must never cede the moral high ground to the Left on immigration—or any other issue.

LOOMING THREATS FROM UNGOVERNED SPACES

Now that I'm out of office, I frequently get asked things such as "What would you do if China invaded Taiwan? Or "Should the Biden administration bomb Moscow?" What these questions miss is that the hard work of deterrence must happen *before* a crisis. You can't fix that failure to prepare after the crisis has begun. A sure tell for failed preparation is whenever a White House press release at the onset of a dire situation reads, "In response to this crisis, we have convened a Deputies Committee meeting of the National Security Council." I love that agency deputies meet, but in the moment, such meetings—if not accompanied by a real-time response of deeds executed without delay—are proof of inadequate preparation. The bad guys love it when a cumbersome interagency planning process is the response to real challenges.

That's why America must begin thinking now about the challenge of undergoverned spaces—something I tackled during my four years. Early on in my time at the CIA, an intelligence professional told me something that I had already suspected but was disturbed to hear confirmed. For the first time in perhaps over a century, our country was confronting what a junior analyst called "ungoverned spaces on our border." The problem of ungoverned spaces (or more accurately, territory not controlled by any nation-state government) is not new. Throughout history, security threats metastasize when malign actors can exploit a geographic location without interference from a legitimate national government. An "ungoverned space" may become a breeding ground for evil if a government doesn't have the resources and capabilities to police it. Al-Qaeda in Somalia, also known as al-Shabaab, thrives in ungoverned spaces. In Colombia, the Marxist-Leninist FARC and ELN terrorist groups have built their power bases in rural areas of the country. In remote areas of Nigeria, terrorists routinely slaughter churchgoers. Our enemies love the vacuum of ungoverned spaces.

Yet asserting control over these lawless zones is not just a matter of having enough resources such as bodies, guns, and surveillance assets. In some cases, ungoverned spaces also reflect political decisions. The 9/11 attacks were successful in large part because the Taliban had given al-Qaeda safe haven to gain strength and plot external operations from the remote caves of Tora Bora. Every American should know that today, the United States faces significant ungoverned spaces close to places such as El Paso, Phoenix, and San Diego. Significant parts of Mexico are no longer policed by the central government; the *Washington Post* has reported comments from several current and former US officials concluding that drug-trafficking groups now control a significant portion of Mexican territory. There are entire well-armed militia forces—the private armies of Mexican criminal syndicates—that impose their gangland rule without government interference. Just as ISIS could resemble a civil government inside its own terror state, the drug cartels act as the civil authority in cities and towns under their control. Of course, they use their power to protect their ill-gotten wealth and to prevent the apprehension and prosecution of their murdering leaders.

Attorney General Bill Barr and I took ungoverned spaces very seriously, for two main reasons: First, while drugs have flowed into the United States across our southern border for decades, the smuggling of chemicals from China for the manufacture of fentanyl has increased a massive drug-related threat to the American people. Second, ungoverned spaces, in addition to destabilizing Mexico, could provide safe havens for terrorists seeking to strike Mexico or the western United States. The cartels are known to have contacts with jihadist groups and Hezbollah through the international arms and drugs trade. Mexican drug lords could invite their terrorist friends to crash at their houses if counterterrorism pressure in Afghanistan, Syria, or Yemen becomes too much. One group of foes worships Allah, and the other worships power, but they are coreligionists in their devotion to money and banditry.

The media reported in May 2022 that President Trump had at one point considered flying drones into Mexico to take out the cartels with missiles. Attorney General Barr had begun to think about this issue seriously. The leftists at CNN and MSNBC prattled on about how this would violate Mexican sovereignty, which they seemed to care about far more than our own. Go ahead and call me crazy for considering how to take out groups that are—functionally speaking—terrorist organizations.

On the diplomatic front, the Trump administration asked Mexico to partner with the United States to regain control of its ungoverned spaces. We sketched out ideas on resources, protection for local officials, rules of engagement, and more. Mexican leaders didn't want to hear it.

I told Foreign Secretary Ebrard that what looks like the mafia today would look like jihad tomorrow. Still nothing. To the Mexicans, allowing a greater US presence on Mexican soil was an admission of failure. Letting the Yankees operate on Mexican soil also presented an intolerable domestic political cost. The depressing irony, of course, is that Mexico has already ceded sovereignty to the Mexican cartels in allowing them to run rogue governments inside their own borders. Our concern was never to cede ours. There will come a day when the way the United States addresses this risk of ungoverned spaces will have to change. Whether with the Mexican government's permission or otherwise, the United States must ensure that these spaces do not expand or become breeding grounds for terrorist activities. My assessment is that Mexico as a safe haven and launching point for terror operations inside the United States is a serious possibility within the next ten years. If we refuse to put America first, we may have to wait until we have a *Nueve-Once* event—and then it will be on the backs of those who failed us.

MULTILATERAL BODIES: BATTLEGROUNDS FOR AMERICAN SOVEREIGNTY AND INTERESTS

Over our nearly 250 years, America has signed up for many international commitments, from NATO and the United Nations to recent trade deals. One of my missions under President Trump was to make sure these international arrangements, understandings, and organizations enhanced our security and prosperity. Foreign policy elites, many of whom crafted these relationships, joined media partisans in condemning our efforts as blasphemy. The media was constantly snarking and complaining during our four years that we were upending American commitments left and right, including breaking "treaties." They bleated sensationalist drivel about America's retrenching, withdrawing from the global stage, and becoming an international pariah.

What hogwash. We were simply and importantly conducting a performance review of our international commitments and asking the reasonable questions: Does staying with this arrangement or being part of this international organization honor our sovereignty? Is it good for the

American people? And if not, what would be better? One option was to stay in it because the cost of leaving would damage American credibility in the world. A second option was to try to fix and reform it. Finally, if we couldn't solve a problem, and if leaving an arrangement was lawful and not too costly to our interests, we had a duty to walk away.

The claim that we were breaking treaties was a product of ignorance. For many, a "treaty" connotes any kind of international commitment. But in the United States, a treaty is a specific kind of commitment, one that requires a majority vote in the Senate. When a president makes a deal with another country but refuses or fails to gain consent from the Senate, we have not a treaty but a press release. For the historical record, the Trump administration did not unlawfully break or withdraw from a single treaty during our entire four years.

The initial America First departure from a bad international arrangement happened early on. Almost immediately, the Trump administration stood up for America's economic well-being by pulling out of the Paris Agreement, or climate accords, the 2015 pact that imposed limits on US greenhouse-gas emissions. One study found that the deal would have cost the US economy $3 trillion and 6.5 million industrial sector jobs by 2040. Obama had also put a down payment of $1 billion into a Green Climate Fund to help developing countries, with billions more to come. At the same time, the climate alarmists allowed China—the world's largest greenhouse-gas emitter, and never a country to uphold its promises—to increase its emissions until 2030. This bad deal for America—which Secretary Kerry no doubt obtained at the cost of spending gobs of taxpayer dollars on fuel for his many flights to France—was poised to slow our growth and hurt our competitiveness. President Trump saw this and announced a pullout from the accords in June 2017.

We had no compunction about pulling out on procedural grounds, because the Paris Agreement is a nonbinding international agreement. It isn't even close to a treaty, and the Senate never would have ratified it if the Obama administration had put it forward. This agreement wasn't even necessary to help or force America to reduce carbon emissions. From 2005 to 2020, with virtually no domineering restrictions on carbon emissions in place, America's emissions fell by 10 percent, even as our economy grew by 25 percent. Those sounds you hear are liberal heads exploding over the fact that the free market is the secret weapon for reducing emissions! Unfortunately, climate change has become the Left's religion, and they want to impose all regulations necessary to achieve net-zero carbon emissions, which is the Left's idea of global salvation. Joe Biden got right back in the Paris accords on his first day in office.

My role in pulling America out in 2017 was limited, but I made clear to the president, Tillerson, and Mattis that we had no intelligence showing that the CCP had any intention of complying with its commitments under the Paris accords. Indeed, to the contrary, it was to be expected that they would not comply even with the generous terms we gave away to them. The CCP was in the deal because it raised costs on America and gave them political cover. The first rule of international agreements is not to evaluate what a deal pledges, but to identify your no-BS enforcement mechanisms to punish violations. Without enforcement provisions—and these accords had none—there's a near-zero chance that authoritarian regimes will comply with any element that doesn't suit their needs.

The Iran deal, too, was just a press release, not a treaty. As with the Paris Agreement, President Obama didn't submit it to the Senate because he knew it would never pass. As secretary of state, I encountered enormous resistance from Europeans who refused to back away from the deal and join our pressure campaign. Many of them told me behind closed doors that they agreed with our concerns, but they couldn't ultimately break from the deal. I'm glad we had the flexibility and resolve to quit.

European anger over our decision to say adieu to the Paris accords and Iran deal reflected a curious feature of Europe's geopolitical psyche. Many Europeans believe that multilateralism—multiple nations working together—isn't just a good way of doing things but a great end unto itself. They live in the historical shadow of two continent-destroying world wars, so they see multilateralism as an ethical imperative. This in part explains their anger over the Trump administration's decisions to back out of bad international deals.

We believed multilateralism has its uses, such as when we reinvigorated the Quad—a partnership of Australia, India, Japan, and the United States—to strategize on defending our people from China. When we worked with more than seventy partners to take down ISIS, multilateralism again made sense. So did the international effort to defend ships transiting the Persian Gulf from Iranian assaults. Our multilateral work was important. But we also knew that American sovereignty and interests must come first. Sticking with a deal just because it's already in place is foolhardy.

Multilateral bodies didn't usually much care for us. One that actively opposed American interests was the UN Human Rights Council. It was a complete sham, and I authorized the United States to withdraw from it early in my tenure as secretary of state. An international body dedicated to human rights shouldn't permit notorious revilers of humanity—such as the governments of China, Cuba, and Venezuela—to sit in its membership. Their involvement ruined the council's credibility, and America needed no part of that. Moreover, the council was a hotbed of anti-Israel vitriol that often became outright anti-Semitism. From 2006 to 2021, it hosted more special sessions to criticize Israel (nine) than it did to condemn the Assad regime for butchering its own people (five) or the murderous regime running Burma (three).

Multilateralism also has the tendency of allowing aggressive bad actors to set policy while meeker, well-intentioned nations fail to speak up simply because they are reluctant to break from the herd, fight battles, or jeopardize other interests. The United Nations in general fails to honor one of its stated purposes—"To maintain international peace and security"—because of both structural and political defects. I can't think of a better example of the multilateral system, first built by American visionaries after World War II, failing to uphold its own values than that of the hypocritical Human Rights Council. Or maybe I can: in June 2022, North Korea became the chair of the UN Disarmament Forum, which, among other things, focuses on stopping the spread of nuclear weapons. This is multilateral madness.

As long as I was secretary of state, we would never support lazy or counterproductive multilateralism. I said as much in a speech at one of multilateralism's most sacred sites: Brussels, Belgium, home of the European Union and NATO. I flew there in December 2018 for my second meeting with NATO foreign ministers. At a German Marshall Fund event, in remarks delivered before the icy stares of Europe's foreign policy elites, I challenged them to consider whether multilateral arrangements were truly serving the purposes for which they were established:

> After the Cold War ended, we allowed this liberal order to begin to corrode. It failed us in some places, and sometimes it failed you and the rest of the world. Multilateralism has too often become viewed as an end unto itself. The more treaties we sign, the safer we supposedly are. The more bureaucrats we have, the better the job gets done.
>
> Was that ever really true? The central question that we face . . . is the question of whether the system as currently configured, as it exists today, and as the world exists today [works]? Does it work for all the people of the world?

I had a fresh example of whether international arrangements were serving national interests in hand that very day. Since 1987, the United States had been party to the Intermediate-Range Nuclear Forces Treaty with Russia. For years, Russia had been violating the treaty by developing an intermediate-range, ground-launched cruise missile. Both the Obama and Trump administrations had told the Russians to stop. We also gave them opportunities to come back into compliance. Alas, our efforts failed. The agreement wasn't worth the paper it was printed on—and the Founding Fathers had warned us about the ineffectiveness of "parchment barriers" to stop "the encroaching spirit of power." To me, the logic of a pullout was unassailable: the American people and their allies should not expose themselves to a strategic disadvantage on nukes against a rival that cheats.

Behind the scenes, our NATO allies were horrified that the United States was poised to take a wrecking ball to a precious agreement. But thanks in great part to the diplomatic jujitsu of Assistant Secretary Wess Mitchell and NATO ambassador Kay Bailey Hutchison, we generated unanimous NATO support for our withdrawal from the INF treaty—a decision I announced on that Brussels visit. Our departure from the treaty lifted constraints on America's ability to position ground-based, intermediate-range missile forces where we wanted to. Given that China is not party to the treaty and has spent years building up its own intermediate-range nuclear forces, we will, one day, need capabilities of our own installed within reach of the Chinese periphery in order to maintain strategic nuclear balance with our chief rival. Preserving our sovereign ability to defend Americans matters.

DEFENDING AMERICAN SOVEREIGNTY FROM THE INTERNATIONAL CRIMINAL COURT

I also spent a great deal of time punching back at a so-called judicial body named the International Criminal Court. On paper, the ICC sounds like a good thing. Built to mirror the Nuremberg tribunals that prosecuted the genocidal criminals of World War II, the ICC bills itself as a permanent, judicially independent forum for prosecuting killers and human rights abusers. By its own definition, the ICC "investigates and, where warranted, tries individuals charged with the gravest crimes of concern to the international community: genocide, war crimes, crimes against humanity and the crime of aggression." Who can disagree with that mission? In some ways, such a judicial body is in fact necessary. The court can only assert its authority when national judicial systems cannot or will not do their job of holding accountable those who have committed vicious acts of violence and repression. There are no shortages of dark places where dictators, warlords, corrupt generals, and other evildoers escape punishment for trampling human dignity.

The United States, of course, is not one of those places. Our judicial system works. This is the main reason why our county has not joined 123 other nations as a party to the ICC. In fact, every presidential administration going back to the Clinton administration has refused to submit America to the ICC's jurisdiction. As with the UN Human Rights Council, the court is rife with potential for bad actors to hijack the proceedings and target law-abiding nations. Israel, which also refuses to join the ICC, is consistently in the court's crosshairs. Yet our opposition to the court wasn't only about supporting our best ally in the Middle East. The ICC's America-hating Eurocrat lawyers love to target Americans.

This is exactly what happened in November 2017, when Chief Prosecutor Fatou Bensouda opened an investigation into US personnel who had served in Afghanistan. This all-out assault on our sovereignty made a mockery of the rule of law the court claims to uphold. Not only is the United States not subject to the court's authority, but our military's court-martial system swiftly and thoroughly addresses alleged abuses by men and women in uniform. Our intelligence community has its own mechanisms for adjudicating abuses, too.

At first, we tried to convince Bensouda and the court to stand down. But they continued to pursue an investigation against US service members. This wasn't going to happen on my watch—not without a counterpunch. We fired a warning shot in March 2019, with visa bans on officials involved in the investigation. I issued more warnings the next year that if the court continued to proceed, we would exact consequences. Nothing changed. So, in June 2020, we authorized asset freezes and visa bans on court officials and employees who were party to this needless investigation. If they wanted to come after America, they sure as hell weren't going to be allowed to travel here or spend American dollars. Foreign ministers excoriated me for playing hardball, but I wasn't planning on giving an inch. The sanctions worked. By the summer of 2020, ICC staff were "politely declining," as I was told, to work on the Afghanistan file because they were afraid their families might be sanctioned. Turmoil reigned inside the prosecutor's office. The deputy head of the investigative division reportedly refused to allocate money to continue the prosecution.

Still, the ICC did not shut down its inquiry. So, in September 2020, we piled on more financial sanctions—this time on Bensouda herself, and another court official, Phakiso Mochochoko. These sanctions were a fit punishment for these now-sanctioned actors who had no authority to pursue an unjust, lawless prosecution against Americans. Again, European foreign ministers and so-called human rights watchdogs complained. But to me and President Trump, we were proudly doing our job of putting America first.

Unfortunately, the Biden administration lifted these sanctions in April 2021. Secretary of State Antony Blinken claimed, "We believe . . . that our concerns about these cases would be better addressed through engagement with all stakeholders in the ICC process rather than through the imposition of sanctions." This was typical progressive foreign policy—worship at the altar of European opinion and expect that more dialogue will solve the problem, even when it's already proven futile or other methods are starting to work. I hope that Bensouda and her team, which I became convinced was corrupt, never return to power. They'd like nothing more than to grab a young GI on vacation and prosecute him, simply to satisfy a political agenda with hatred of America at its very core.

PROTECTING SOVEREIGNTY BY PROTECTING LIFE

A final word on multilateralism: The Trump administration worked constantly with various coalitions to get things done—we just weren't always doing it in the areas that the leftist media and the Democrats cared about. One special case in point is something Secretary of Health and Human Services Alex Azar and I worked on with the help of two Trump administration pro-life warriors: Valerie Huber, who served at the Department of Health and Human Services, and Pam Pryor at the State Department.

For years, pro-abortion radicals have dominated the United Nations and other multilateral institutions. These bureaucrats don't represent the views of most Americans, even though our taxpayers in 2020 funded about one-fifth of the UN's total budget, donating about $11 billion, which was more than any other country. Even though we pay a lot of the UN's tab, UN apparatchiks in New York and Geneva are always working against Americans—and pro-lifers in particular—by trying to sneak terms such as "reproductive rights" into UN documents. It's a backdoor means to chip away at our sovereign right to believe what we want on issues of human life and pass national laws accordingly.

We decided to rally every nation that was sick and tired of abortion-rights radicalism. In 2019, Secretary Azar and I assembled a coalition of nineteen other nations and delivered a letter to the United Nations condemning pro-abortion language in UN documents. Many of these nations were developing countries who hold traditional values about human life and the family—the Democratic Republic of the Congo, Haiti, and Nigeria among them. They were tired of Western secularist progressives imposing a new colonialism by telling them to build their societies in anti-life, anti-family ways. After we released this letter, one of our colleagues received an email from a friend active in the pro-life movement in Africa. She wrote, "Never did I think that America would use its great power to speak for the protection of the unborn in the most unambiguous and unapologetic terms." The world saw American leadership in our defense of both sovereignty and human rights—in this case, the right to life.

Our letter was only the first step. In October 2020, more than thirty nations—representing about 1.6 billion people—united to set forth some simple principles in a document called the Geneva Consensus Declaration. Among other truths we avowed was the fact that "there is no international right to an abortion" and that "each nation has the sovereign right to implement programs and activities consistent with their laws and policies." The declaration aimed to protect the unborn, promote women's health, and recognize the importance of the family as the foundation of society. Nearly all of the original signatory nations are still part of it today. Sadly, but predictably, the United States isn't one of them. The Biden administration withdrew America from the Geneva Consensus Declaration on the very first day it took office, rebuking both multilateralism and the laws of God. You didn't hear the media calling the Biden administration isolationists or enemies of the global community.

Ultimately, the America First foreign policy was tethered to three central ideas: realism, restraint, and respect. I elaborated on these concepts in my speech to the Claremont Institute in 2019, one that I think was the definitive statement of the America First foreign policy.

First, seeing the world with clear eyes matters. As I said in my remarks, "The Founders . . . saw that conflict is the normative experience for nations. Hamilton said, 'To judge from the history of mankind, we shall be compelled to conclude that the fiery and destructive passions of war reign in the human breast with much more powerful sway than the mild and [beneficial] sentiments of peace.'" Our Founders knew that the world is a mean, nasty place.

I also commented on the importance of restraint: "The Founders sought to protect our interests but avoid adventurism. The Barbary War, fought so soon after independence, was an effort of last resort to protect our vital commercial interests. The Monroe Doctrine—relevant even today—was a message of deterrence, not a license to grab land."

And I reiterated how the Founders knew the power of the American example to produce transformation in other nations: "As the first nation of its kind, the world would see America as a model for self-government and liberty." Today we must respect our founding principles first and foremost to guarantee security and prosperity in our own nation. Respecting them also provides a model for other nations to emulate.

The Trump administration saw that twenty-first century American foreign policy had drifted from these ideals. We had not realistically evaluated Russia and China, instead hoping that these regimes would become kinder and gentler as they were enfolded into the world order. We'd not exercised restraint in commitments of American power overseas. And as I told the audience that night in California: "We had lost sight of respect—not for other nations, but for our own people and for our ideals . . . Many of our leaders were more eager to delight the Davos crowd than champion the principles that have made us the greatest nation that civilization has ever known."

No more. We in the Trump administration saw our enemies with clear eyes. We didn't rush headlong into new wars without a clear sense of mission. And we restored a high respect for America's first principles and national sovereignty—as well as the sovereignty of other nations—in our foreign policy. As I look back on it, I'll add another r-word to characterize our foreign policy: recovery. We recovered the spirit of what makes America great, and Americans are safer and more prosperous for it.

CHAPTER 8

NO BAD DEALS

Chairman Kim Jong Un had just accepted the idea of an in-person meeting with President Trump.

I was on my second visit to Pyongyang, about a month after the first. This time, on May 9, 2018, I was the newly minted secretary of state. Before a summit could happen, however, the North Koreans had to meet a key American demand. Chairman Kim already knew about it, but I wanted to remind him: it was time for the three Americans who were then languishing somewhere inside the North Korean prison state to come home.

To emphasize the point, I asked Kim to speak alone, away from the entourage of unsmiling functionaries that often surrounded him. He agreed. With only our interpreters present and the "secret" recording devices to monitor us, I put it plainly: "The president fully expects that the three Americans you're holding hostage will return with me on my plane to the United States."

It couldn't have surprised him, because my team had already said as much to his people.

Kim dodged my demand, and simply said that he looked forward to seeing me with the president soon.

We stared each other down for what seemed like several forevers.

I finally broke the awkward silence. "I also look forward to introducing you to the only president you can actually make a deal with." He smiled, and I headed on my way.

Back at the airport, I climbed out of the car and hurried up the steps of the plane. As I settled into my cabin, I was hopeful of getting what we asked for. Prior to my return to the plane, North Korean vehicles had pulled up, and their occupants asked for a couple of my team members to come with them. We had suspected that such a contingency might develop, so I had brought along two senior officers to execute this hoped-for leg of the mission. Within fifteen minutes, I watched from the door of the plane as two vans pulled onto the tarmac. We were all on pins and needles in hopes that the three Americans would be inside those vehicles. But we didn't let our spirits rise too high. Even if the three Americans were there, we had no idea of their physical condition or mental health. The horrific death of Otto Warmbier a year earlier was front of mind. God hears even the quietest prayers, and I said one quickly under my breath.

Then three men, one by one, climbed out of the vehicles. Through the tears in my eyes, I could see that they looked to be in good health. Kim Dong-chul, Kim Hak-song, and Tony Kim (Kim Sang-duk) walked briskly, nearly running the last few yards, as they approached the airplane staircase. As they ascended the steps, they looked like the happiest men alive. I hugged each of them as they climbed aboard an aircraft marked "United States of America."

Then I looked at the plane crew and gave them the order: "Get us the hell out of here."

We sequestered the three newly free men so that they could receive any medical attention they might need, and as our plane cleared North Korean airspace, the entire plane broke into cheers. As I prepared to call President Trump—the Air Force powered down our communications systems until the plane hit a certain altitude—I thanked my team for its amazing work and then went to my cabin to thank the Lord in solitude for what He had done. It was one of the most moving and important experiences during my entire career in public service. The sight of freedom had never been so raw and personal.

I reached the president as soon as our communications systems were back up.

"Mr. President, I'm on my way back. We had a nice meeting. Not only have we secured the summit, I also have three Americans who were held hostage sitting on my airplane."

"Great news, Mike! Does the press know?"

"We have press on the plane, but we believe they will honor the embargo we have asked for and won't report it. We've not yet been able to reach the hostages' families, and we're working to do that."

"I'll see you in a few hours. I'll be at the airport to greet you when you land. Well done."

We stopped in Japan to put our new guests on a specially equipped medical plane that we had forward-deployed in anticipation of their release. Then the two American planes headed for Andrews Air Force Base, outside DC, where my three Christian brothers would be welcomed with open arms by the president himself.

My plane landed first, in the darkness of an early morning. Even though I was exhausted, the sight through my window gave me a powerful shot of adrenaline. Hundreds of patriotic Americans had gathered amid huge lights and dozens of TV cameras.

As I walked into the airbase waiting lounge, nearly every Trump administration senior official was present. Everyone cheered—not for me but for freedom. When it quieted down, First Lady Melania Trump said loud enough for all to hear, "So, Mr. Secretary, what are you going to do that tops this?" Everyone cracked up except me. I realized she might be right—I had peaked only two weeks into the new job!

A few minutes later, the second plane landed, and we all went out to greet it. President Trump and the First Lady climbed the stairs at about two thirty in the morning. Millions of Americans would be uplifted hours later at the sight of their fellow Americans returning to home soil. When the freed hostages came to the bottom of the stairs, one of them handed me an index card. I tucked it into my coat pocket and hugged him. I had no idea precisely what they had been through, but I was sure it was the stuff of nightmares.

When I finally got home a couple hours later, I hugged Susan and read the index card with her. On it were words from Psalm 126:

When the Lord brought back the captives to Zion, we were like men who dreamed. Our mouths were filled with laughter, our tongues with songs of joy. Then it was said among the nations, 'The Lord has done great things for them.' The Lord has done great things for us, and we are filled with joy.

I soon thereafter had that index card put in a frame alongside a photo of me celebrating with those men as their feet hit the tarmac. I kept it in the formal meeting room in my office at the State Department for the duration of my tenure as secretary of state, in part to remind me—and visitors—of the American lives at stake in our diplomacy. It also served to tell me—every day—that hard-fought negotiations could produce good outcomes; America didn't have to strike a bad deal to get things we wanted. And we didn't.

BAD DEALS HURT AMERICA

No word is more closely associated with President Trump than *deal*. He wanted good deals for America, and our dealmaking to gain the release of hostages from North Korea showed that they could be had.

For decades, however, American leaders had made bad deals. Allowing China's entry into the World Trade Organization (WTO) and refusing to hold China accountable for cheating undercut our middle class. The Paris climate accords under President Obama threatened the same. We'd also gotten hustled in arms-control agreements—our treaties with Russia had put America at a dangerous nuclear disadvantage. And the senseless giveaway of the JCPOA would have handed the world's most dangerous weapons to its most terroristic regime. And it wasn't just arms control in which America took a loss on the Iran deal: in 2016, the Obama administration paid Iran a $400 million ransom to release four hostages—a number that would later swell to $1.7 billion. While I am overjoyed that those Americans came home, it would have been a terrible signal to send to the world that America could be extorted had we done the same with North Korea. We didn't pay a penny to get captives back from the DPRK.

The best dealmakers—in business, law, and politics—have a few things in common: They map out a strategy. They defend their interests. And—critically—they aren't afraid to push for what they want, even if that means looking like a jerk. I think for too long American leaders didn't want to take any risk that they might be seen as jerks, even as they negotiated against the likes of Putin and the ayatollahs. They wanted America to be a submissive and compliant nation in the "global community." Too often they came from the Rodney King school of dealmaking: "Can't we all just get along?"

We took a different approach. We developed our deal strategy around the central idea of power dynamics: Who has it, and who is prepared to use the power they have? We were willing to lose popularity contests in Beijing and Berlin as long as we were winning great deals for America.

When it came to North Korea, the United States had a history of bad deals. In previous rounds of talks, the United States granted concessions in exchange for promises North Korea was destined to break. As I prepared to meet Chairman Kim, I studied the old files. The classified accounts of negotiations largely tracked the public accounts of what President Clinton had naively entered into, such as an unverifiable "Agreed Framework" that the North Koreans blew before the ink was even dry. While executed to great huzzahs in 1994, and surviving until the Bush administration, it never constrained North Korea's program in any material way. President Clinton knew that it would not work, but he approved it anyway. The George W. Bush administration tried the series of Six-Party Talks but accomplished nothing. President Obama's team wobbled back and forth between diplomacy and ignoring the North Koreans' growing nuclear and missile capabilities under a do-nothing policy of "strategic patience."

The North Koreans probably counted on us to continue the mistakes of the past, but we weren't going to make a bad deal. Nor were we going to make a deal for the sake of saying we made one. This, I believe, was counter to what the North Koreans expected us to do. They were betting that the president would be so desperate for a deal of any kind that he would give away the store to Pyongyang. Moreover, the Trump team was determined to avoid the cardinal sin of arms-control deals: the presumption of compliance. The president and I never wavered on insisting that in any pact, the North Koreans would have to abide by strict and immediate verification measures. They would have to put up or shut up in showing they were serious about denuclearization before we granted any major concessions. There would be no bad deal on our watch.

NORTH KOREA NEGOTIATIONS CONTINUE

When I returned to the United States after my initial visit with Chairman Kim on Easter weekend 2018, I made a beeline for the White House. I had two items on my agenda. The critical one was to brief President Trump, Vice President Pence, and National Security Advisor John Bolton on what I had seen and learned. Meanwhile, Nick and Susan were on the South Lawn for the White House Easter Egg Roll, reading a classic Kansas-themed story to children, *The Wizard of Oz*. My mind was still racing from everything I had seen and heard inside North Korea—I felt as if I had just taken a trip to the land of Oz myself. After the egg roll, Nick, Susan, and I slipped away for a few minutes to pray together, as we always do. There was much to pray for.

My next stop was Langley to discuss what we had seen and heard and what we should do next. Andy Kim and I agreed that Chairman Kim, then age thirty-five, was no accidental leader. He had the brains, savvy, and ruthlessness you'd expect from someone who had clawed through a lot of capable people who preferred he be dead. Beneath his accomplishments and gargantuan ego, however, I detected insecurity. Although he'd spent a bit of time outside North Korea as a child, Kim was running the Hermit Kingdom as a hermit himself. He was locked away from the rest of the world and constantly being viewed as evil by the West and his own countrymen. While with me, he was constantly asking questions to learn more about the world, of which he did know a few things. He loved basketball and Kobe Bryant in particular. His knowledge of NBA basketball appears to have been rivaled only by his knowledge of Western liquor brands.

Andy and I knew that final, fully verified denuclearization was unlikely. Even less likely, though, was achieving our goals through the conventional negotiations that had frustrated Americans in the past, so the talks were worth it. Our diplomacy had subsidiary goals, as well. We knew our meetings would present opportunities to gather intelligence on the state of North Korea's weapons program, and getting inside this hard target would provide us some opportunities to do so. We also wanted to meet with North Korea's other leaders, including Kim's sister, Kim Yo Jong. This would give us a fuller picture of the regime's thinking.

My confirmation as secretary of state on April 26 freed me up to build out a diplomatic team. To lead it, I chose Sung Kim, then the ambassador to the Philippines. He was a career Foreign Service officer who had been part of the Six-Party Talks. In addition to having experience with the North Koreans, he supported our unique approach to the problem set. And he knew what he was in for: negotiating with the North Koreans is about as pleasant as licking the floor of a New York City subway car. They stall, insult, talk in circles, lecture, and change plans at the last minute. They want to make the experience so miserable that you capitulate, agreeing to their proposals just to end the ordeal. I caught a glimpse of this after several conversations with Chairman Kim's right-hand man, Kim Yong Chol. I also determined that he had exactly zero authority to talk with me about anything substantive. I concluded the only way forward was to meet with Chairman Kim again.

So, in May 2018, I made my second trip to Pyongyang—the one in which I was able to bring home the three Americans. Winning release of the hostages was only one of our goals, however. I also wanted to set the table for a summit between the two heads of state. As I was winging my way there, I received a welcome boost when President Trump announced that we were quitting the Iranian nuclear deal. This sent a powerful message to Chairman Kim: The United States will not accept crappy deals that permit an adversary to enrich uranium, process pluto-nium, and threaten the world.

Upon arrival, we were again warmly welcomed, but this time Kim seemed far more tense. His agitation revealed itself in a list of requests. He was desperate for the meeting with the president. He wanted us to declare the end to the war between North Korea and South Korea, which had signed an armistice in 1953 but never agreed to an actual peace treaty. And he wanted the United States to stop conducting military exercises with the South Koreans.

My objectives included picking the location of the summit and laying out for Kim what we meant by total denuclearization—the permanent, verifiable end of all weapons development, enrichment, and plutonium-processing capabilities. I told him I wanted to back up a truck and take away his whole stash. Kim was unhappy with this definition of denuclearization and immediately began to backpedal, saying that these demands were excessive. I told him that we could move forward in steps, rather than all at once, but that only a massive first step on his end that guaranteed total denuclearization could possibly lead to the lifting of sanctions. While he did commit to a summit, he refused to pick a location. Of the choices we had offered (Hanoi, Geneva, Singapore, Vienna), he clearly believed only Singapore was possible.

I also told Chairman Kim that it would be difficult for President Trump to meet with him while he still prevented the remains of American servicemen who had died in the Korean War from returning to the United States. He agreed to permit repatriation, which was a major relief. For the families of the fallen, even grandchildren and great-grandchildren, a proper burial of their loved ones on American soil provides enormous comfort. For this American, it was important because I've told my men in the Army and my diplomats serving around the world that we will never leave them behind. I wanted to honor a previous generation of warriors, too. Because of this demand, the remains of at least thirty-five Americans came home.

After our arrival back in the United States—and after the fanfare surrounding the return of American hostages had died down—we began to work with the North Koreans on the summit. First came the substance: What was our objective? Second: How would we keep America's allies, South Korea and Japan in particular, apprised of our plans without exposing information that would scuttle the summit? Third: How would the logistics of the summit itself work, and where would it be held? Chairman Kim had made a pitch for Pyongyang. "You came to Pyongyang, Mike, why can't your boss come? It will be great!" he told me. There were zero votes for that on our team. While President Trump was intrigued, he, too, understood why the sight of an American president venturing into the heart of darkness at that time was impossible.

We countered with Coronado, the city on a peninsula near San Diego, and an easily securable location with beautiful vistas. The North Koreans insisted that Kim could not travel to America. Kim had an additional constraint: he had no airplane that he believed could be trusted to fly beyond his own borders, and our offer to provide US transport didn't appeal to him. My first choice for a summit was a US aircraft carrier anchored somewhere off the coast of the Korean Peninsula. This had the advantage of easy travel for Kim as well as the all-important flashy visual for us, with President Trump welcoming his guest aboard a carrier that could take down North Korea from the place it was parked. Secretary Mattis was not amused at this idea, to put it mildly. In the end, we mutually chose Singapore, and Chairman Kim bummed a ride on a Chinese plane.

There was one more item to address. The North Koreans needed to come to America because President Trump wanted to finalize the agenda for the summit with them in person. On May 30, General Kim Yong Chol arrived in New York City. He was like a zoo animal released into the wild for the first time, seeing this otherworldly Mecca of chaos and capitalism in person. He couldn't quite admit it, but he knew just from appearances that American civilization had beaten the North Koreans already; their key regime decision points were now reduced to how best to keep their own people from learning about freedom and prosperity.

I greeted Chol at the UN ambassador's residence. Though the entire world was focused on the summit, it was something far more trivial that captured reporters' attention. I had worn a pair of black socks patterned with green toy army soldiers that day—my standard issue footwear whenever I met with bad guys. Some astute observers saw them in a picture, and it caught fire on social media. I'm convinced it will be the only time in my life when my fashion will be the talk of the town—especially in trendy Manhattan! The next day, Chol asked to see my socks. I told him that I wasn't about to show them to him. But I did say they were black, and patterned with pictures of a free, non-nuclear Korean Peninsula and him in jail. I clearly articulated it poorly, because he just looked at me confused. I still think it's funny.

Chol informed me that he had a letter from Chairman Kim for President Trump, which he would deliver the next day on a visit to the White House. That meeting attracted enormous criticism—rarely has such a troglodyte ever set foot inside the Oval Office. In the very first moments, it became clear that something was amiss, and one of Chol's staff sprinted out of the West Wing to where the North Koreans' vehicles were parked. John Kelly and I couldn't figure out what the hell was going on as we sat with Chol and the president. A few minutes later, sweating profusely, Chol's staffer returned with the letter from Kim to the president. He had accidentally left it in their vehicle! That young man had a look on his face for the entire meeting that suggested he did not know if he would live to see the next day. I almost wanted to offer him political asylum. It turns out this young man was the personal interpreter for Chairman Kim who sat next to him when I met Kim the first time. I later found out this young man apparently disappeared, and the chairman did not bring him to Singapore. I felt a lot of pressure because of those negotiations, but it wasn't anything like what those on the North Korean side faced.

THE SINGAPORE SUMMIT PRODUCES PROGRESS

Ten days later, the president and his entourage made the long trip to Singapore for the historic summit on June 12, 2018. I have never seen such a media horde. Nobody on planet Earth knew what to expect when the leader of the Hermit Kingdom would stand alongside the leader of the free world for the first time in history. Cameras clicked like a swarm of crickets as the two leaders approached each other. I watched from the meeting room and noticed immediately that my North Korean friend wore platform shoes that left him about a foot shorter than President Trump. At somewhere around five feet five, Chairman Kim could not afford to give an inch—literally.

A lot of people expected that Kim and the president would execute a formal agreement. As with so many of these meetings, we were not obsessed with documents and communiqués. Still, I had arrived in Singapore ahead of the president and negotiated with the North Koreans to get Kim to make a written commitment to denuclearize. His team wanted a formal declaration of the end of the war—something that did not materialize. We negotiated all night, with Ambassador Kim getting as little sleep as I did. I kept the president apprised of our progress, or lack of it. John Bolton simply fumed. He hated that we were there and hated even more that we might actually sign a piece of paper. But we had to break the model of empty promises, and getting Kim to commit to something real on paper was a good start. The only man who could make that commitment and then deliver on it was Chairman Kim, and even if the chances were near zero, there was absolutely no downside to getting him on record.

At about seven thirty in the morning, before the two leaders first met, we had the document done. While I was checking with the president on changes and proposals, my counterpart Kim Yong Chol was checking not only with Chairman Kim but also with a higher authority: the Chinese. The CCP gave Chairman Kim almost zero leeway to cut a deal. Each time he met with me or the president, he had a long discussion with Xi Jinping within days, usually in person. The North Korea problem should always be thought about as a proxy battle with the CCP. While China's control of the country is not total, it's close.

The meetings in Singapore were serious and cordial. Kim reiterated his commitment to denuclearize, even though he never had the authority to do that from his Chinese handlers. Our pitch—that we could improve the lives of every North Korean—meant little to Chairman Kim and even less to his boss in Beijing.

In the first meeting, Kim and the president agreed that North Korea would cease all nuclear and long-range missile testing. In exchange, we would not conduct major joint exercises with the South Korean military. We had debated this extensively before we arrived. President Trump hated the exercises, believing that they were too provocative and expensive. The Pentagon saw them as necessary preparation to "Fight Tonight," which is the watchword for US forces stationed in South Korea. My view was that they weren't provocative or expensive but that many of them were inessential for staying at high levels of readiness. I was fine with what President Trump agreed to, knowing that we could make sensible adjustments. Over the coming months, the exercises would prove to be an irritant between the Department of Defense (DOD) and the president. In the end, we did the training that was most needed, and we kept Kim from further developing his capability to strike America. Not a home run, but a worthwhile trade. At a minimum, it wasn't a bad deal.

The day's program included a lunch attended by both delegations' expanded teams. The president broke the ice by introducing John Bolton to Chairman Kim, saying something to the effect of "John is the problem." John took great pride in that. He still seemed nervous, always fretting that the president would give away the store. The lunch included a moment of humor when Trump asked Kim, "Do you know who Elton John is?" Kim replied, "No." Trump explained that John's famous song was his source for "Little Rocket Man," the nickname he gave Kim. Trump said it was a great song, and he intended the reference as a compliment. Kim's response was classic and we all laughed: "'Rocket Man,' okay. 'Little' not okay." I thought back to "Low-Energy Jeb" and "Lyin' Ted"—those were the days.

The signing ceremony the next day revealed the totalitarian nature of the North Korean regime. I was to be the clerk who placed the document in front of the president for his signature. Kim Yo Jong was to perform the same duty for her brother. As she and I waited backstage, she completely refused to engage with me. I didn't even rate a courtesy hello. We had met on my trips to Pyongyang, but now she might as well have been a mute.

Preparations for the signing also gave Kelly and I a chuckle. The North Korean protocol team appeared to be in a frenzy: running, sweating, passing papers, leaving and then coming back into the building, and otherwise looking nervous and confused. As Kelly and I watched this unfold, we learned that their side had become worried about the possibility of a minor translation error. (We also came to find out that the North Koreans used translation issues as an excuse so that Chairman Kim would have plenty of time for his smoking breaks.) The expressions on the faces of these young North Koreans suggested that their lives were at stake—a more than plausible theory, based on the absence of the young interpreter who had left the letter in the vehicle days prior. Chairman Kim's interpreters are uniquely vulnerable because they are among the very few people who know what Chairman Kim has ever actually said.

My advice for life-insurance agents who offer policies to North Korean interpreters is to seek a high premium.

Ultimately, the summit reaffirmed my suspicions that North Korean denuclearization remained a longshot. But there was some cause for hope. The notable outcome of the summit was a joint declaration that included a North Korean commitment to "work toward the complete denuclearization of the Korean Peninsula." Almost immediately after the summit ended, we got back on our horses to convince the North Koreans to live up to that goal. By this time, voices in the foreign policy world, especially those of the Chinese and Russians, were urging us to entertain a phased, "step for step" model of denuclearization, in which we would trade appropriate economic relief for every corresponding step North Korea took to denuclearize. But we held firm on the message in public and private that no sanctions relief would occur until Kim Jong Un completed the final, fully verified denuclearization of his country, and did it fast.

Unsurprisingly, we didn't see much progress from the North Koreans. So, in July, I went back to North Korea. I think Kim was expecting a more generous secretary of state to show up, but I had reiterated the same unwavering message of what the United States was expecting in exchange for sanctions relief. As a result, Chairman Kim was a no-show. The North Korean press, such as it is, reported that he was "visiting potato fields." At least he didn't say he had to wash his hair.

Not long after I left, the Kim regime blasted me with a statement trashing my "gangster-like" attitude—a clear ploy to appeal to President Trump to take the North Korea file away from me. They suggested at one point that they would have preferred a family member of Trump to meet with them. I thought it was rich that the North Koreans were accusing me of being a gangster.

The next month, I was preparing to go to North Korea again, as we had made some modest progress on a framework for denuclearization thanks to the leadership of Steve Biegun, our new special representative for North Korea. It may be the case that Steve had the worst job in the US government. He was the lead negotiator with a nasty North Korean team led by Che Son Hui, but he did a solid job with the hand he was dealt. Just before the trip, however, I received a letter containing quite undiplomatic language from my counterpart, Kim Yong Chol. I showed it to the president, and we agreed the trip made no sense. As we sat together, he tweeted: "I have asked Secretary of State Mike Pompeo not to go to North Korea, at this time, because I feel we are not making sufficient progress with respect to the denuclearization of the Korean Peninsula. In the meantime, I would like to send my warmest regards and respect to Chairman Kim. I look forward to seeing him soon!"

Nevertheless, we were committed to seeing this difficult process through, thinking that maybe, just maybe, North Korea would become serious about denuclearizing. After all, Chairman Kim had told me that he was a father and didn't want the specter of nuclear weapons hanging over his children's heads. President Trump seemed to believe that one-on-one diplomacy was the way to crack Kim on his nukes. And so, after some more diplomacy with the North Koreans to assure them of my ungangsterly intentions, I departed for North Korea yet again in October, this time with President Trump's directives in hand to plan a second summit. At this meeting, the North Koreans hinted that they might be prepared to shutter a significant facility. We agreed we would continue to work, and Chairman Kim indicated he wanted to meet with Trump again in person.

STANDING FIRM IN HANOI

The second Trump-Kim summit took place in February 2019 in Hanoi, Vietnam. The site was the Metropole, a French-colonial-style hotel that first opened in 1901. I was pleased that the North Koreans had agreed to Vietnam. I wanted them to see in person how a former American enemy could be transformed into an economically flourishing society at peace with the United States. As secretary of state, I made three trips to Vietnam, and it was remarkable to see the energy and entrepreneurial spirit of the Vietnamese people each time. Engagement with the United States and the world since the 1990s has transformed the country. Swarms of buzzing motorbikes and block after block of shops showed that an Asian nation that had fought a war with the United States could recover and flourish. Vietnam's government is still too repressive, but we must continue to strengthen our relationship with this nation as we compete with China.

The Vietnamese were happy to have us, and on the road from the airport I was treated to the strange and somewhat disturbing sight of intertwined miniature American and North Korean flags. On the drive over to meet Chairman Kim, inside the presidential limousine known as The Beast, President Trump caught me off guard by saying, "Mike, what are you going to do next?" I thought I might be getting fired or asked to leave.

Before I could respond, he said: "Look out these windows. I can't go back and try to save a nickel apiece on kitchen sinks for some crappy New York building—how can any of that compare to what we're doing today?"

He was right. There is not much that compares to serving America as a senior leader and grinding every day to put America first.

As with the first summit, this one had plenty of pageantry, as well as public cordiality. Behind closed doors, however, it was more businesslike, and the talk turned tough. Going in, we had believed that the North Koreans had agreed to the complete and verifiable dismantling of the Yongbyon complex, which was their main nuclear facility. We had many other objectives, but we believed that achieving this reduction in exchange for green-lighting a few small South Korean investment projects was a worthy trade. We would have given up almost nothing and would have gotten the largest absolute reduction in North Korean enrichment capabilities ever achieved and verified. We thought the North Koreans were ready to make a deal on these terms.

We were wrong. The North Koreans were not willing to go this far. In the first Hanoi meeting, attended only by Kim, Trump, Chol, and me, Chairman Kim said that he would be willing to undertake an American-verified dismantling of the Yongbyon complex in exchange for a complete lifting of sanctions. Contrary to what has been previously reported, the president needed no coaching to know that this was totally unacceptable. He told Kim that straight up. The look on Kim's face suggested that he had expected a different response. He stared at Kim Yong Chol with an expression that required no translation: "WTF?" The moment revealed a huge disconnect between Kim and his negotiators. For all practical purposes, the summit was over.

When we got back to our holding room, a disappointed President Trump snarled at me: "Do we have to stay for lunch?" I was pissed off—not at the president but at the North Koreans and their apparent misunderstandings. The team agreed that we could cut the afternoon short.

Although we failed to reach agreement, the window of diplomacy remained open, and we made plans to keep talking. Chairman Kim assured us that while we continued to negotiate, North Korea would refrain from nuclear and long-range missile testing. North Korea can't be trusted on much, but Kim's word held true through the end of the Trump administration's time in office. This was an important achievement for keeping Americans safe.

More than anything, I was confident that we did the right thing that day. We made no bad concessions, no bad compromises, and no bad deals. Even as we went back to the drawing board with some frustration and uncertainty on how to pry nuclear weapons out of a dictator's hands, I was satisfied that the Trump administration didn't give an inch.

RESCUING AMERICAN HOSTAGES

You can't say you're putting America first if you aren't striving to protect the unalienable rights of "life, liberty, and the pursuit of happiness"—and sometimes that means getting Americans who want to exercise those rights out of unjust captivity. Of all the issues I worked on as secretary of state and CIA director, bringing home Americans was perhaps the most satisfying. We regarded violations of their freedom and dignity as tantamount to violations of America's independence and sovereignty. Securing their release was the ultimate demonstration of the America First mindset in action. I'm proud to say that over the course of the Trump administration, we were able to bring home more than fifty Americans from at least twenty-two countries—places such as North Korea, Iran, and Turkey. I am likewise proud that we never paid any ransom or made an unethical compromise. In other words, we didn't take bad deals.

One of my greatest tests as director of the CIA was helping to coordinate the rescue of Caitlan Coleman and her family from the Haqqani terrorist network in Pakistan. Seized along with her Canadian husband, who inexplicably took his pregnant wife to Afghanistan in 2012, she had been held for years and had given birth to three children in captivity.

One day, my team came in to brief me. The intelligence community had detected what looked like a small child who would have been about the age of one of Caitlan's children. I told them to, literally, keep everyone's eyes on the child. Over the next few days, my team and our intelligence-community partners became increasingly convinced that we had located at least some of the members of the Coleman family. The intelligence community and DOD began to consider options in conjunction with David Hale, who at the time was the ambassador to Pakistan (and later would become my undersecretary of state for political affairs). One option was to tell the Pakistani military to go get them. But they were unreliable and prone to tipping off the Haqqani network, an Islamist terror group operating in Afghanistan and Pakistan. Involving them might lose the operation before it even started. An American-led rescue was possible but fraught with complexity. We were not sure we knew what we had, and hazardous operations can have casualties. It was easy to imagine worst-case scenarios of death and failure.

The family was moved after a few days, but we tracked them to an area near the border with Afghanistan. We were now certain that we were seeing at least some of the Coleman family. Before we could take action, I took a call in the middle of the night. The family was being moved again, possibly out of range for a rescue. Immediately, US officials reached out to Pakistan's military leadership, told them where the Colemans were, and made clear that Washington was watching. If the Colemans were killed or if they disappeared, the US government would hold the Pakistanis accountable. That motivated them. Soon, Pakistani military forces descended on the caravan and took the Colemans, and my team helped to get them transported out of the country. Amazing work by CIA patriots caused all of Caitlan Coleman's American children to be freed from captivity.

Sometimes we had to free Americans from our supposed allies. Our

NATO ally Turkey had wrongfully detained a remarkable Christian pastor named Andrew Brunson in October 2016. An evangelical Presbyterian, he belonged to the same denomination that Susan and I had been part of at our church in Wichita. Many faith leaders here in the United States had begun to lead a very public campaign to gain the return of Pastor Brunson. We pressured President Erdoğan to let him go, and several times we thought we had succeeded. But Erdoğan always wanted to make a deal, demanding that we send him a Turkish individual living lawfully inside the United States. But we wouldn't budge. Ultimately, in a classic America First action, President Trump warned Erdoğan that he would place economic sanctions on Turkey and then actually made good on his threat by sanctioning Turkish cabinet members. After a phony trial, the Turks released Pastor Brunson. His return to the United States came later than it should have, but it was glorious in the moment.

We also worked to get Americans out of Iran. Even after President Obama's deal with Iran, the regime kept taking more hostages. One American, Xiyue Wang, a PhD student from Princeton University with a wife and young son, was detained by Iran when he traveled to the country in 2016 for academic research. At one point, he was held in solitary confinement for eighteen days. Because we refused to do bad deals by paying bribes to Iran, contrary to what the previous US administration had done, negotiating these releases was an arduous undertaking. Adding urgency to our efforts was the knowledge that Americans were being held in deplorable conditions inside the notorious Evin Prison in Tehran. Through it all, we never stopped wearing down the Iranians, and our Swiss interlocutors were remarkable allies. In December 2019, we were able to bring Xiyue home, and I was delighted to see the pictures of him smiling as he held his son for the first time in more than three years. We also brought home Michael White, a wrongfully imprisoned Navy veteran. Patient work by Brian Hook, our ambassador in Switzerland, Ed McMullen, and many unsung heroes delivered these Americans back to their families. Sadly, other American hostages remain trapped in Iran, and Tehran continues to use them as tools of diplomacy.

Some release efforts lack this same gravity. Consider the case of A$AP Rocky, an American rapper whose name I'd never heard before President

Trump called me and said, "Hey, you need to get this guy A$AP Rocky home from Sweden." My first task was to figure out what the president was talking about. My second task was to work with National Security Advisor Robert O'Brien, who previously had been my lead hostage negotiator at State. A$AP wasn't a hostage in any normal sense. He had been accused of committing a crime in Sweden and was facing a trial. But he had become a cause célèbre, and Jared Kushner called for action from inside the White House. O'Brien headed to Stockholm and liberated our man. O'Brien told me later that he had threatened the Swedish government, asserting that we would "sanction them down to the last Volvo." It was a funny story—and maybe it even worked.

Lamentably, not every effort to rescue hostages was successful.

I still pray for Bob Levinson and his family, folks for whom I have much love and admiration. Bob was connected to the US government, captured by Iranian intelligence services in 2007, and held hostage for years. The Iranians used him as a bargaining chip, or maybe they just wanted to practice the cruelty that defines their regime. For some years, the US government was not certain as to whether he was still alive. Alas, the Obama administration did not demand Bob, or even his body or other proof of death, as part of the $400 million handover of American hostages that greased the skids for the JCPOA's completion. They didn't even get answers as to his whereabouts. It was a horrible deal that was a prelude to an even worse one.

In 2020, we were forced to conclude that Bob was almost certainly dead, contradicting more than a decade's worth of Iranian lies about his status. I met Bob's family many times over the years. These remarkable patriots were determined and decent people—and at times frustrated, naturally. With their permission, I spoke of Bob on many occasions. If you want a clear example of a Middle Eastern nation that assigns no value to human life, look no further than the Islamic Republic and its utterly inhumane treatment of Bob Levinson.

The Iranians and their Syrian tools were equally sinister in their treatment of Austin Tice, an American journalist and former Marine who was abducted inside Syria in 2012, most likely by the Assad government. I worked his file ceaselessly. Indeed, within minutes of becoming

CIA director, I spoke with a senior Syrian official to see what we could do to get Austin back. It was the first of many fruitless conversations with Tice's captors. But we stayed at it, and we did our best to keep his family informed about what we knew. Few moments were as personally hurtful for me as the one in 2020 when Austin's mother suggested to the press that I was opposing the administration's efforts to secure her son's release. Her misunderstanding was the result of an administration official's scheming to damage me in the public eye. Privately, I couldn't believe what I was hearing. I had spent an enormous amount of political, economic, and diplomatic capital on this mission. I did my best. But the effort failed, and it saddens me to this day. I also refused to face off against a grieving mother. She has every right to be sad and angry.

It is easy to say that the United States should just pay the asking price every time one of our people is taken hostage. After all, defending American lives is the paramount goal of foreign policy. But doing that would likely trigger an explosion in hostage taking, making the problem worse. As our leaders work to negotiate the release of those detained abroad, we should pray every day for the innocents held hostage by terrorist regimes. The misery they suffer and the anguish that their families endure are often unspeakable. I regret that we couldn't deliver on mission for them all, but I am grateful we brought many home without taking bad deals.

CHAPTER 9

KEEP YOUR FAITH

Six words on the invitation caught my eye: "Cookies and Soda Will Be Served." It was Plebe Summer—essentially boot camp for West Point cadets—and I never missed an opportunity for food and drink. What I missed on the invitation was that it was for a Bible study. The Lord works in mysterious ways.

Or maybe they aren't so mysterious. At any rate, I showed up, and it changed my life. Or maybe I should say that it *saved* my life.

Growing up, I was only loosely involved in church. My parents took me to Sunday school, but I didn't really engage with it. I'd memorize my Bible verse quickly, demonstrate proficiency, and then begin to think about shooting free throws in my driveway. My mind was focused on trying to become the next star for my hometown LA Lakers. Spoiler alert: I was too short and too slow. At least I was a great fan.

At the Bible study at West Point, we read verses, just like we did in Sunday school, but now they connected with me in a new way. Led by a couple of upper-class cadets, our group discussed how the verses related to our lives as soldiers. I went every week for the rest of the summer.

It was through these meetings that I came to understand Jesus as my savior and to know Christ for the first time. It wasn't long thereafter that by God's grace I gave my life to the Lord and vowed to take up my cross and follow him. Since that time, I've strived to live by that same grace. It's not been a straight line, but the thread of knowing that He is bigger than our earthly challenges and that through His grace we are saved has been at the center of my life since those days four decades ago. I keep my faith because He keeps me.

Susan and I have tried throughout our lives to pass along what those two young men gave to me. I served as a deacon at our home church, East-minster Presbyterian in Wichita, Kansas. Being a deacon taught me that politics in the church is as tough as its Kansas state counterpart! Susan and I also taught fifth-grade Sunday school, along with two other couples. Susan would teach the lesson while I tried to keep the boys in their seats. Getting them to behave was the perfect preparation for a career in international diplomacy.

If my faith in the Lord has served as the most important influence on my worldview, the second most important has been my faith in the political thought of the American Founders—the enlightened logic and reason that undergirds our nation. No American should ever underestimate what they achieved. The Declaration of Independence affirmed the basic unalienable rights and equality of every human being and laid down the mandate for all governments to protect them. As Alexander Hamilton wrote, "The sacred rights of mankind . . . are written, as with a sun beam . . . by the hand of the divinity itself; and can never be erased or obscured by mortal power." Thirteen years after the Declaration, the Constitution came into force, with the Bill of Rights following in 1791, providing a structure of government and the protection of those rights.

To this day, those documents remain the foundation of the nation that has protected the rights of the individual better than any other in history. The fragile American experiment in liberty—a nation specifically born dedicated to the cause of freedom—is a monumental bright spot in the many millennia of human suffering and autocracy. Its survival for nearly 250 years is a marvel. I am confident that it will keep enduring—if we keep our faith in our glorious founding principles to guide us.

PROTECTING RELIGIOUS FREEDOM: AN AMERICAN LEGACY

My appreciation for the American Founders that started with reading *The Federalist Papers* at West Point grew even deeper in the early 1990s. I was now a twenty-seven-year-old former Army captain studying at Harvard Law School. I needed some pocket money, so I answered a bulletin-board ad for a research assistant. It said nothing about cookies or soda, but I looked into it anyway.

The professor who posted it was named Mary Ann Glendon. I didn't know anything about her, but she was offering seven dollars per hour. That wasn't much, even in 1991, but I needed the money. I wound up becoming a much richer man under her tutelage.

Professor Glendon is one of the world's most thoughtful scholars on human rights. Talk of rights dominates our political discourse: the right to life, the right to keep and bear arms, gay rights, transgender rights, and more. These conversations—often heated—have always been at the core of American politics. The women's suffrage movement demanded that women have the right to vote. Abraham Lincoln looked back to the Founders' understandings of natural rights to inform his condemnation of slavery. And Dr. Martin Luther King Jr. took inspiration from the Declaration, which he called a "promissory note" that "guaranteed the unalienable rights of life, liberty, and the pursuit of happiness."

But what is a "right"? Who decides? Are some more important than others? These questions were the essence of Professor Glendon's work. As I researched projects for her, I began to ponder these questions for myself with more intensity. One theme I consistently noticed in the Founders' writings was their reverence for religious freedom, which they regarded as fundamental. Thomas Jefferson wasn't just one of our nation's Founders, he was also our first secretary of state—and therefore a predecessor of mine. Written on the walls of the Jefferson Memorial in Washington, DC, are some words from the Virginia Statute for Religious Freedom, which he helped write: "No man shall be compelled to frequent or support any religious worship or ministry or shall otherwise suffer on account of his religious opinions or belief." Similarly, James Madison, quoting the Virginia Declaration of Rights, wrote, "We hold it for a fundamental and undeniable truth, 'that Religion or the duty which we owe to our Creator and the manner of discharging it, can be directed only by reason and conviction, not by force or violence.'"

Protecting religious freedom is at the core of the American idea.

Protecting it around the world is one of our oldest foreign policy traditions and likely the longest-running international human rights issue.
Throughout the 1800s, Americans and their leaders consistently denounced the persecution of religious minorities across the Middle East
by the Ottoman Empire and other governments. In December 1880, the
Jews of Casablanca conveyed their thanks to the State Department for
pressuring the king of Morocco to honor their rights: "It is to America,
the great pioneer of liberty and equality," they said, "that this unfortunate
people lift up their eye." When the Ottoman Empire began persecuting Armenian Christians in the 1890s, prominent Americans such as
John D. Rockefeller and Clara Barton led nationwide relief efforts on
their behalf. And after the USS *Tennessee* helped evacuate six thousand
Jews from Ottoman-controlled Palestine during World War I, Captain
Benton Decker accepted a silver tablet from his passengers in the name
of the American people, who, he declared, "stood, in this time of great
turmoil and upheaval, for the interests of humanity." During the Trump
years, the press derided our mission of defending international religious
freedom, claiming that it was a quixotic and cynical play for conservative
votes. They didn't know America's great history.

As secretary of state, I decided to reinvigorate this tradition of using
American diplomatic power to protect international religious freedom.
The State Department has had an office devoted to this issue since 1998,
but upholding the right to believe and worship freely was mostly a second-
tier concern in the great buffet of human rights causes. That changed in
the Trump administration. We knew that millions of people all over the
world were suffering harassment, torture, and even death for their faith—
Hindus in Pakistan, Christians in North Korea, Baha'is in Iran, and
many other examples. Our decision to speak up for the persecuted was
yet another example of how the Trump administration restored American leadership.

Defending the right to worship abroad also has massive implications
for American security. Nations that provide more religious freedom are
less likely to have the internal sectarian turmoil that leads to instability.
They make better partners and allies for America, too. Wholly apart
from protecting the human rights to which we are all entitled by being

made in the image of God, American national security is well served by the spread of religious freedom and tolerance for other faiths. We were determined to keep America safe by using every tool available, including by helping others keep their faith.

RESTORING THE DEFENSE OF RELIGIOUS FREEDOM IN AMERICAN DIPLOMACY

I made it a point as CIA director to greet the new officers who came aboard each month. They would have orientation in the entrance hall, their chairs seated over the CIA's famous seal, which you can see in every good spy movie. What the movies don't usually show are the words from John 8:32 chiseled in granite behind the officers: "And Ye Shall Know the Truth and the Truth Shall Make You Free." In front of them was the Memorial Wall, with a single star for each CIA employee who had given his or her life in service. Beneath the stars was the "Book of Honor," which contains the names of the fallen—or at least those that can be disclosed. On the wall by the book is an inscription: "In honor of those members of the Central Intelligence Agency who gave their lives in the service of their country."

The location and imagery were intentional. I wanted these new officers to see on their first day the agency's founding ideas: Honor, Faith, Truth. To sit in that place when the director walked into the hall reminded them of the history and continuity of the team they were now joining. My remarks to them centered on America's founding, reminding them that they were now part of an organization dedicated to preserving the ideals carved into the stone around them. I shared with them, too, that faith mattered. It mattered to their well-being. It mattered that they had faith both in their teammates and in America. And it mattered that not everyone they would encounter in their career would share their faith. The faces that looked back at me—men, women, mostly young, but some also older, many veterans, nearly all of them speaking more languages than I do—were about to embark on incredible acts of duty to country. In time, they would all come to know what it meant to put our nation's Judeo-Christian traditions into service.

Once I became secretary of state, I was grateful to discover that I had a partner in the mission to protect international religious freedom. Sam Brownback, a fellow Kansan, a rock-solid conservative, and an energetic fighter for religious liberty, was already in place as ambassador-at-large for International Religious Freedom. During my confirmation, he came by to see me. He had an idea, but he was going to need, as he put it, "cover from the top." He had a vision for creating forums for faith leaders across the world to come together around the idea of religious freedom. He wanted to hold these gatherings at Foggy Bottom, but he was facing resistance inside the department.

Things changed after I arrived at State. We set up the first-ever Ministerial to Advance Religious Freedom. A *ministerial* is just a fancy diplomatic word for a meeting of foreign ministers, but this was to be more. We wanted faith leaders to join us as well, plus leaders of NGOs (nongovernmental organizations) that were working to protect persecuted religious minorities. Lay leaders, such as those working to build house churches in the most difficult places, were invited, too. Our concept of religious freedom was broad. I remember taking heat for inviting leaders from a country with a poor record on religious freedom. I knew, however, that the foreign minister was working hard to make things better. So, we invited him. That's something I learned from high school basketball: we should reward not only the best but also the most improved players.

And come they did. The 2018 conference had a strong showing, but by 2019 we really had it right. The demand to attend the event that year was so great that we had to procure overflow space outside the State Department's headquarters. When all was said and done, the 2019 Ministerial to Advance Religious Freedom was the largest human rights event the State Department had *ever* hosted—who says the Trump administration didn't lead on multilateralism or human rights? This wasn't just an event for Americans of the Christian faith—it was for people of all faiths from across the world. Orthodox rabbis mixed with Muslim imams and Catholic priests. Baha'is and agnostics joined together for freedom. It wouldn't surprise me if we even had some Wiccans in attendance. All those who wanted to help others keep their faith were welcome. Everyone mingled with what can seem to be the most priestly caste of all: DC policy wonks and diplomats.

That event gave me an opportunity to draw attention to the worst crisis of religious freedom of the twenty-first century, which was just beginning to gain notice in the West. The Uyghur Muslims of the Xinjiang region of western China are a small and peaceful religious-minority group. But to the godless CCP, they are a major threat to power. As far back as 2014, CCP general secretary Xi Jinping was personally giving guidance to the party on what to do in Xinjiang, telling officials that they "must not hesitate or waver in the use of the weapons of the people's democratic dictatorship and focus our energy on executing a crushing blow." By April 2017, under the pretense of national security, the CCP was engaged in a vicious campaign of religious persecution against the Uyghurs. In reality, the party wants to turn all its citizens into perfect little Communists who never embrace their religious or ethnic identity (except if that identity is Han Chinese).

In Xinjiang, the CCP has demolished mosques, forced Uyghur families to quarter Chinese officials, performed forced abortions and sterilizations on Uyghur women, and imprisoned as many as one million Uyghurs in what are, functionally speaking, concentration camps. Perhaps most terrifying of all, the CCP has used powerful surveillance and facial-recognition technologies to create a dystopia ripped straight from the pages of George Orwell's 1984. The atrocities in Xinjiang aren't just horrible for their own sake; they are a microcosm for the CCP's disrespect for human life and a warning about the lengths to which the party will go to crush freedom. It was only right that I used my time at the podium that day to denounce these crimes as the "stain of the century." Coupled with the powerful testimonies that day from Uyghurs whose own family members had been imprisoned, the world was now on notice that shedding light on the plight of the Uyghurs would henceforth be a major American foreign policy priority. In addition to it being the right thing to do, the effort to call out the treatment of the Uyghurs, Tibetans, and Hong Kong dissidents being abused had the incidental benefit of giving the Europeans—strong global human rights advocates but generally weak on China—a China-specific issue where they could join forces with the Trump administration.

I continued the drumbeat on Xinjiang throughout the rest of my tenure as secretary of state, especially as I engaged with foreign leaders. It frustrated me that most Muslim-majority nations and the Organization of Islamic Cooperation were unwilling to push back on China's crimes. Many of them even signed a letter in July 2019 supporting China's false claims that its activities in Xinjiang were focused on ensuring national security and fighting terrorism. Muslim-majority nations have even honored Chinese requests to extradite Uyghur Muslims back to China, where they are no doubt destined for internment camps or a position on a slave-labor assembly line. Just as many Western CEOs bend the knee to China for fear of their companies losing market access, majority-Muslim nations are likewise too enslaved by Chinese money and markets to take a tough stand.

When I told UN general secretary António Guterres in 2019 that the CCP's crimes came close to those of the Third Reich and urged him to use his power to convince countries to speak out, he tried to change the subject to how he supported China's "green" infrastructure programs in developing countries. This was dereliction of duty. Guterres knew of the horrors. Had this been Israel or Sudan or, frankly, the United States, he would have launched a committee, issued a report, and held dialogue sessions. But because it was China, silence. His tenure at the UN will go down in history as a shameful one because of this. To me, China's mal-treatment of the Uyghurs looked like genocide, and I began to talk to my team about what we could do to stop China from oppressing people who were simply trying to keep their faith.

One of the most memorable moments for me in my travels was meet-ing in Kazakhstan in February 2020 with relatives of ethnic Kazakhs imprisoned in Chinese camps. As they showed me pictures of their loved ones, they told me heartrending stories of losing contact. The foreign ministers of Russia and China would never take a meeting such as this. Those regimes see liberty as a threat, not a right. On another occasion, the sister of a persecuted Uyghurs recounted the horrific stories of when her brother was forcibly removed from the family. To this day, she knows only that he is confined in western China. She has seen pictures of men in the camps who look like her brother, but she cannot be sure if any one of them is him or whether he is even alive. She escaped from China with her children, but she declined to have her picture taken with me for fear of reprisals against her brother.

When we think of national leaders, we tend to think about presidents and prime ministers, parliamentarians and finance ministers, and judges and governors. But faith leaders move people and nations forward. The troika of Ronald Reagan, Margaret Thatcher, and Pope John Paul II worked as a team to take down Communists across the world. So, as I traveled, I made it a priority to visit with religious leaders, encouraging them in their own fights against persecution.

A highlight of my travels was meeting with Orthodox Christian leaders in various countries in Europe and the Middle East. In recent decades, Orthodox communities in countries such as Iraq, Syria, and Turkey have been decimated by persecution. In Egypt, I toured a remarkable Coptic cathedral and met with leaders of that ancient Christian sect. And in Lebanon, it was an honor to meet Bishop Audi, who became a dear friend, and to spend time with the grand mufti of Lebanon as well.

In November 2020, I visited Patriarch Bartholomew, the head of the Orthodox Church, who leads about three hundred million members worldwide. The Turkish government threatens his church, so on that trip to Istanbul, I made a point to not meet with any Turkish government officials. It was a simple message: this church must remain independent, separate from the state, and free. President Erdoğan and Foreign Minister Mevlüt Çavuşoğlu were not happy, but the Orthodox world understood that America was supporting their God-given right to keep their faith. Besides honoring human dignity, protecting international religious freedom for Middle Eastern Christians and others redounds to America's benefit by creating populations friendly toward America—and Lord knows America needs as many friends in that part of the world as we can get.

THE HOLY SEE'S HYPOCRISY

On at least one other occasion, I spent considerable time and energy trying to convince one of the world's most influential religious institutions to support international religious freedom. I might as well have been trying to convince Isaac Newton of the laws of gravity or teaching Kareem Abdul-Jabbar how to perform a hook shot. Life shouldn't work that way, but here I was.

Religious freedom in China is in abysmal condition for people of all faiths. Catholics have suffered grievously. The government has desecrated and destroyed their churches and shrines. Authorities order churches to replace pictures of Jesus with those of Chairman Mao and General Secretary Xi Jinping. They have also imprisoned the Catholic bishop Augustine Cui Tai. As I write this, his whereabouts are unknown.

In light of such monstrous abuses, one would think Pope Francis would be quick to live up to his own words from 2013: "Christians must respond to evil with good, taking the Cross upon themselves as Jesus did." Yet he and many of his cardinals have done the opposite. The Vatican's foreign policy has always leaned to the left, but not since Pope John XXIII's support for the liberation theology movement of the 1970s has it gone so fully against freedom as it has today in China.

In 2020, the Vatican's diplomats met with their Chinese counterparts to renew a secret 2018 agreement between the Vatican and the godless CCP, an unholy pact that gives the party improper say over which bishops will oversee the seven dioceses in mainland China. The church believed that appeasing the party would cause Beijing to ease up its campaigns of persecuting Catholics who will not render unto Xi. But "the situation has not improved at all," said one anonymous underground Chinese priest two years into the deal. For the Catholic Church to strike a secret agreement with such a wicked regime is a most massive failure of duty and moral witness.

As a man of faith, I felt compelled to do something about this. But I also saw religious freedom in China as a matter of national interest. Pressuring the CCP and the Catholic Church to allow Catholics to worship freely and choose their own bishops could help make China a more stable and less adversarial country. I stood mostly alone among the world's leaders in seeing things this way. A generation ago, President Reagan was blessed to have the freedom-loving Pope John Paul II and Margaret Thatcher as allies in taking on the God-hating Soviet Union. We were stuck with Pope Francis and Theresa May.

I urged Vatican leaders to walk away from their deal with the devil. One of my great allies in this fight was Joseph Cardinal Zen, a true hero of mine who has battled his church's decision to cede its authority to the CCP. Formerly the bishop of Hong Kong, Cardinal Zen knows that the Catholic Church's acceptance of the seven bishops chosen not by the Church but by atheistic Communists is morally reprehensible. And as a longtime voice in support of freedom for Hong Kong, Cardinal Zen, like fellow Hong Kong Catholics Jimmy Lai and Martin Lee, knows all too well that Beijing will go to any lengths to crush individual freedoms. On protecting Hong Kong's civil liberties, too, the church has been pusillanimous. Cardinal Zen made clear to me in a phone call that the Church's failure is in some ways worse than war, because "the enemy has become the leaders of our own country." If one needed any more evidence of the righteousness of his efforts, Cardinal Zen was arrested and imprisoned by the CCP on false charges in 2022. The Vatican released a tepid statement expressing "concern." Xi must be trembling.

I raised the issue of religious freedom for Chinese Catholics directly with the pope when I had the privilege of an audience with him in 2019. He acknowledged that people across the world were being persecuted. Then he turned the conversation to urging the United States to put its policies at our southern border in alignment with our Christian calling to take care of the least among us. He just didn't get it.

In the fall of 2020, I planned more travel back to the Vatican, where I hoped to see the pope again. I had a great ambassador to the Holy See, Callista Gingrich, who had developed deep and important relationships with the Vatican's foreign ministry and was beloved among Catholics throughout Italy. My objective was to press the pope to use his unique moral authority to call out Chinese human rights violations. I decided that it was best to announce my goal ahead of time, so I published an article in the scholarly religious journal First Things calling for such action. Shortly after publication, the Vatican informed Ambassador Gingrich that the pope would not meet with me because of a policy of not meeting with political leaders during election periods. But the fact is that the pope has met with many leaders who have been part of a government standing for election. It wasn't principle but timing that led to his unavailability.

Case in point: the pope met with French president Macron in November 2021, just five months before the French people went to the polls in April 2022. And in any case, Western politicians are always in an "election period," making the window of time associated with that term totally arbitrary.

I went to Rome anyway to speak at a conference hosted by the Holy See on international religious freedom. The event was perhaps a fig leaf to cover up the fact that the Vatican was at that moment failing a crucial test. I delivered a speech designed to nudge the Vatican to do the right thing, telling the church's leaders, "Religious leaders should understand that being salt and light must often mean exercising a bold moral witness." In a meeting with Archbishop Paul Gallagher, who is essentially the pope's secretary of state, I asked, "Why am I defending religious freedom while you let Xi tell you who should be a bishop in China?" Ultimately the Vatican re-upped its private deal with China. The pope and the Vatican higher-ups know that their deal is morally unjustifiable, because they've never allowed its text to be made public.

My only consolation is that when Rome gave many inches on the religious freedom of Catholics, our America First foreign policy did not.

LETTING MY LIGHT SHINE AS SECRETARY OF STATE

The audience with which I felt most compelled to discuss the importance of international religious freedom was the American people. Giving speeches to domestic audiences is not unusual for a secretary of state. But when the secretary does speak in America, he or she usually preaches to the choir on ivied campuses in the northeast or at DC think tanks. It has rarely occurred to other secretaries to get into the heartland to let their fellow citizens know what their State Department does on their behalf. It was also important to make the case to our people about how American diplomacy benefits them—they needed to keep the faith that we used their tax dollars in ways they could support.

I wanted to do that and also make progress on the secondary goal of broadening the geographic base from which we sourced talent. I hit the road for places such as Detroit, Michigan; College Station, Texas;

Louisville, Kentucky; and even the horse-country town of Bushnell, Florida. On many occasions, I spoke to churches and social-conservative groups, something previous secretaries, even the Republican ones, would never dream of doing. I wanted my fellow Americans of faith—people who could have been my neighbors back in Kansas—to know that America's top diplomat was now standing for their values all over the world. I told them that we were channeling their own faith-based moral convictions in banning funds for abortion from our foreign assistance under the Mexico City Policy, tackling the evil of human trafficking, and defending religious freedom. The Left went nuts, but I kept my faith that I was doing the right thing.

I also used my engagements to speak about how my faith informs my work. This, too, is an old tradition in American history, though in recent years we haven't done it as much. Benjamin Franklin proposed opening meetings of the Constitutional Convention of 1787 with prayer: "How has it happened that we have not hitherto once thought of humbly applying to the Father of Lights to illuminate our Understandings?" He wasn't successful, but it was a good idea. In the hours before the 1944 D-Day invasion, a great Kansan, General Dwight D. Eisenhower, urged his troops, "Let us beseech the blessing of Almighty God upon this great and noble undertaking."

When I first ran for Congress, with all of 1 percent name identification at the time, I was asked how I would separate my faith from my work in public life. I thought about it for a second and said that I wouldn't even try to. My Christian faith is the prism through which I view the entire world. Fortunately, the tenets of my faith dovetail with America's calling as a force for good. As secretary of state, I told a meeting of the American Association of Christian Counselors in Nashville, Tennessee, "I am grateful that my call as a Christian to protect human dignity overlaps with America's centuries-old commitment to the same mission in our foreign policy all across the world."

I also wasn't going to hide my light under a bushel, and I traveled to risky places to talk about religion. In January 2019, as I prepared for a major speech on the Middle East in Cairo, Egypt, I added a few lines, right at the beginning, about my Christian faith. I wanted an overwhelmingly

Muslim audience to know that I'm a man of faith, too, and we have more in common in how we see the world than many people might think. My speechwriting team and Middle East experts advised against it, saying it could alienate the audience and send the wrong message. They sent back a version of the speech with the opening deleted. I ordered them to put it back in, and I have no regrets about telling the people of Cairo: "I keep a Bible open on my desk to remind me of God and His Word, and the Truth." To this day, I get more comments and letters about this one sentence than any other I uttered in my one thousand days of serving as secretary of state. These notes are mostly from Muslims who were encouraged by my candor. It shows how much we have to gain from speaking honestly about faith.

Indeed, my diplomatic counterparts who follow Islam were vital partners on so many missions. While political Islamism is a cancer, we should not assume that all Muslims are terrorists or terrorist sympathizers. The president once asked what I made of Ilhan Omar, the radical Democrat. "It's not that she is Muslim," I said. "I work with Muslims every single day. It's that she is an Islamist fellow traveler." Her personal religious affiliation does not make Omar hardwired to blame America first and despise Israel. It's her anti-Western and anti-Semitic ideologies. Americans must know the difference. Our country will continue to have great strategic need for Muslim leaders overseas to promote peace, resist the ayatollahs, supply energy to the world, and more.

DEMOCRATS, THE MEDIA, AND THE STATE DEPARTMENT WISHED I WOULD SHUT UP

My approach to my faith and my work drew critics. The Left had initially homed in on my outspokenness during my confirmation hearing for secretary of state. Senator Cory Booker, a Democrat from New Jersey, flat-out took the position that no follower of Christ who believes what the Bible teaches on sexuality could be secretary of state:

BOOKER: Is being gay a perversion?
POMPEO: Senator, when I was a politician, I had a very clear view

on whether it was appropriate for two same-sex persons to marry.
I stand by that.

BOOKER: So, you do not believe that it's appropriate for two gay
people to marry?

POMPEO: Senator, I continue to hold that view.

BOOKER: And so, people in the State Department, I've met some
in Africa who are married, under your leadership, you do not
believe that that should be allowed?

POMPEO: I believe it's the case we have married gay couples at the
CIA. You should know, I treated them with the exact same set of
rights . . .

BOOKER: Yes or no—do you believe gay sex is a perversion?

POMPEO: Senator, I'm going to give you the same answer I just gave
you previously. My respect for every individual, regardless of sexual
orientation, is the same.

I believe America's first secretary of state and his founding colleagues would have viewed Senator Booker's views on gay marriage—not
mine—as heretical. Indeed, I'm confident that even as recently as 2008,
America's sixty-seventh secretary of state, Hillary Clinton, would not
have supported what Senator Booker was espousing. But forget all that.
What would have truly troubled the Founders was Booker's attempt to
disqualify me from office based on a view of marriage that flowed from
my religious beliefs. The framers of our Constitution would have seen
that as an inappropriate assault on my religious freedom.

Many others reached that same conclusion. The evangelist Franklin
Graham was one such prominent voice, tweeting, "So does holding a traditional view of marriage now make you inappropriate for public office in the
eyes of some? That's incredibly wrong—and it's dangerous for the future of
this nation." I equally appreciated support from ordinary Americans and
even CIA officers who came up to me and apologized for Booker's effort
to exile from the public square all who did not share his view of sexual
ethics. I have been clear that we should, and I would, treat every person
the same, even if he or she was not a Christian. And I expected that each
person would treat everyone else equally, even if he or she *were* Christian.

As a Christian, I am not surprised that I would be attacked for my biblically rooted view of human sexuality. As an American, I fear for my country that the progressive left is prepared to deny faithful Christians any place in our public discourse or civic institutions on this basis, even if they affirm the fundamental equality of all human beings. If you are a professing Christian who holds to Judeo-Christian beliefs on marriage, family, and gender, the woke mob wants to prevent you from holding public office or even displaying your faith in a private workplace. Keep your faith anyway. Never give an inch.

The secularists in the so-called mainstream press also raked me over the coals, time and again, for speaking about my faith. The *New York Times* later wrote in response to my Cairo speech, "Observers found it remarkable that Mr. Pompeo would open a speech in a majority-Muslim country by highlighting his Christianity." They clearly didn't talk to enough "observers" if they thought talking about your faith was something "remarkable." Doing so is a command from Jesus to all Christians—no matter where you work. As Jesus tells us in the Great Commission, "Therefore go and make disciples of all nations, baptizing them in the name of the Father and of the Son and of the Holy Spirit."

I could sense the agitation in the *New York Times'* words: "No Secretary of State in recent decades has been as open and fervent as Mr. Pompeo about discussing Christianity and foreign policy in the same breath." As my son, Nick, joked, how many breaths am I supposed to take between the two? That same *Times* writer, Ed Wong, claimed my faith talk "increasingly raised questions about the extent to which evangelical beliefs are influencing American diplomacy." Would the *Times* have the gall to insinuate that "Jewish beliefs" were unduly influencing American diplomacy? Someone writing that would properly be fired and escorted out of the building for repeating an old anti-Semitic trope that Jews control US foreign policy. But perhaps my favorite jab was an article with the headline "Mike Pompeo, God's Diplomat." When my team brought it to my attention, they were worried I'd be angry. Indeed, upon reading the contents of the article, I wasn't happy. But that headline? Susan and I hope to this day that we should be so full of grace that such an epitaph would appear on our gravestones!

President Obama's former national security advisor Susan Rice said it was "problematic" that I was "overtly religious," thinking that I was alienating people of other faiths. She just could not see how faith can be an asset in diplomacy. She certainly wasn't in the room when non-Christian leaders and ordinary people I was meeting for the first time expressed appreciation for my faith-based worldview. In places such as Peru and Senegal, I attended church services like any other Christian on a Sunday. That's a statement of the American commitment to religious freedom.

One of my most remarkable engagements was with an Indonesian group called Nahdlatul Ulama, the world's largest independent Muslim organization, with tens of millions of members. I'd forgive you for doubting that a Kansas evangelical and a group of Indonesian Muslims would find a lot of common ground, but that's exactly what happened when I spoke to them. Their leaders and I share a faith-based approach to the world that leavened our conversations. In fact, even though I was of a different religious background than they were, I probably had more in common with them than your typical secretary of state would have. Respect for the unborn, the family, and the preservation of religious traditions aren't just values found in Christian America. These are in fact *the norm* in most non-Western, non-Judeo-Christian societies. The leftist-secularist shapers of American culture, politics, and foreign policy fail to consider that their values place them firmly in a global minority.

Moreover, defending life, preserving the family, and upholding religious traditions are the cultural foundations of healthy and stable societies. Broken families, secularism, cultures that do not celebrate life, and weak ties of community create atomized societies with ever-growing degrees of dependence on government. Such conditions endanger American prosperity and national security.

I expected gripes from the media and Democrats when I spoke about my faith. But what really should worry us all was the fact that the State Department also tried to suppress my mission. I don't think it was just a secret "deep state" mission to thwart the Trump administration. Nor do I think it was entirely anti-Christian bigotry. It's just that many of the State Department's bureaucrats are liberal, timid Washington lawyers who are also badly miseducated on how to understand the legal principle of separation of church and state. Very often, they tried to stop me from speaking to religious organizations and church groups because, they claimed, it created the impression I was preferring one faith over another.

Even worse were their pedantic proposed edits to my speeches. Lawyers petrified that common phrases such as "God bless America" violated the Constitution's Establishment Clause drained their red pens on my remarks. As a former lawyer, I know that attorneys are paid to worry about legal problems. They can tend to discover issues that nobody else can see. But I'm sure that if State Department lawyers were asked to review Lincoln's Second Inaugural Address, they would cut his famous line: "Fondly do we hope, fervently do we pray, that this mighty scourge of war may speedily pass away."

Yet not every federal employee was hostile to my mission of being open about my faith. Many of the political appointees were people of deep faith. And there were career employees on board with the mission, too. As CIA director, I once deboarded an airplane in the middle of the night in one of the world's toughest countries. As I came down the steps, an older gentleman working for the US government who was there to receive me reached out and shook my hand. He also slipped something into it, but I couldn't see exactly what it was. I thanked him and got into my car. Once I examined the gift, I saw it was a well-used, palm-sized Bible, with a note inside: "Mr. Director, you have been a light to me and to the world. Bless you." I later heard that he was a member of the State Department team. I never learned his name, but I'm proud to know that there were people like him supporting American diplomacy.

The first-ever officially recognized Christian employee group at the State Department also organized themselves during my tenure, although I take no credit for this. This headline in the *Washington Post* tried to credit me anyway (or perhaps lay blame at my feet): "State Department's first-ever employee Christian faith group underscores Mike Pompeo's influence." Written by Michelle Boorstein, the story recounted that despite the many affinity groups at the State Department—groups for gays, veterans, women, racial minorities, and others—there had never been a place for Christians. Now there was, and she seemed to think it was newsworthy or even concerning. But the group's incarnation was about as newsworthy as a headline that says, "Christians go to church on Sunday." Guess what? Christians get together in the workplace all the time. Why should the State Department be any different? Our nation was built by people of faith. The First Amendment makes clear that Christians, Jews, and adherents of all other religions should be free to worship. The State Department's Christian affinity group—beautifully named GRACE— sprang up with guidance from above. By that I mean the Lord, not the Secretary's office.

I learned of GRACE's existence from a remarkable young female career officer. She had come by my office at my request. She had pulled off a remarkable feat of public service to America by helping dozens of stranded Americans return home from Peru at the onset of the COVID-19 pandemic. Her presence filled a void of leadership: the ambassador at the time, a career Foreign Service officer, had abandoned his post as the virus descended and declined to tell any superiors in his chain of command. My goal was simply to congratulate her and thank her. I noticed a cross around her neck but thought little of it. As she was leaving, she thanked me for providing space for GRACE and for giving courage to Christians to come out of the closet, so to speak, joking that they were a persecuted class. I told her to keep her faith and to encourage more to join her in being outspoken. It struck me later how many Christians in America's foreign ministry feared expressing their commitment to the Lord openly. How much work there remains at home is clear.

BRINGING SANITY TO HUMAN RIGHTS POLICY

My faith also informed our overall approach to human rights policy. As a Christian, I know every human being is created in the image of God and therefore has an inherent dignity that deserves protection. We are the greatest nation in the history of civilization in part because we use our unmatched power to defend human dignity. If we as Americans believe that the proper purpose of government is to protect every person's unalienable, God-granted rights, then surely some of our diplomatic influence must be devoted to protecting the weak from tyrants. In fact, it is essential to America's international standing that we lead on the issue of human rights. It gives us a moral credibility that no other powerful nation can match. That moral credibility is good unto itself. But it also serves as a seedbed for partnerships in all other areas of geostrategic interest. It strengthens our case in the competition with China, Russia, and other authoritarian powers over the shape of world order. It convinces other nations and people that America seeks to engage with them in a spirit of friendship and freedom, not intimidation and domination.

Balancing human rights concerns with the tough choices necessary to advance American security and economic interests is always hard. Making the right call means making the right decisions about when to pound the table and when to hold fire. Knowing when to act was often a prudential matter involving how much leverage America had over a particular country. On one trip to North Korea, my aide Lisa Kenna informed me that the North Koreans were in a huff because the State Department had issued a report that concluded, to the surprise of absolutely no one, that the human rights situation inside the Hermit Kingdom was abysmal. The timing wasn't optimal, but sometimes the truth can't wait. When I landed, Kim Yong Chol, who helped kill forty-six South Korean sailors in 2010, let me know that Chairman Kim was upset about the report having come out just as I was traveling to talk with them. Maybe I should have just been glad they read it, but I fired back: "We don't set our clocks based on you. Stop killing innocents by sinking ships and disappearing people, and the report might disappear, too." I didn't hear another word about it after that, and our negotiations continued.

When America-haters denigrate our nation as the prime source of chaos and strife in the world, I cannot help but shake my head at their ignorance. We're not perfect, but are we not better than the Russians who barrel-bomb civilians in Syria and mutilate and massacre scores of Ukrainians? Are we not better than the Chinese, who have raped Hong Kong, Tibet, and Xinjiang? Don't our sacrifices of blood and treasure reflect a determination to create a better world? Take the case of Afghanistan. In hindsight, it was unrealistic to expect that the United States could transform what is essentially still a premodern, tribal society into a pluralistic, rights-respecting, Western democracy. But it was a uniquely American ambition to lead in lifting the veil of Islamist darkness from a nation of forty million people. Only one country has such a humanitarian ambition and capacity to attempt such a mission.

Moreover, if America is so terrible, why do people risk everything to come here? The world's elites do not scramble to send their children to school in Russia, Iran, or Venezuela. The CCP doesn't need to build a wall to prevent overwhelming illegal immigration. My friend Bill Bennett, President Reagan's secretary of education, has something he calls the "gates test." When a country opens its gates, do the people run in or out? Few natural-born citizens choose to leave here, while millions of foreigners crave the chance to come to America.

Coming into Foggy Bottom, I knew that the State Department cared about human rights, but that its moral and operational compass required a reorientation. Each day at State, I examined a series of hand-selected cables from around the world on the most pressing security issues. I also asked for cables on our human rights agenda. When the team couldn't even agree on which cables were about "human rights," I knew we had a problem.

State's human rights policy had in large part adopted the progressive cultural leitmotif of what some have called "expressive individualism," which roughly means the need to affirm every individual's self-constructed "identity," especially racial, sexual, and gender identities. Issues that had the weakest connections to the protection of human rights, such as climate change, creeped into discussions. At least one matter—abortion, which sometimes goes by the vile euphemism of "reproductive freedom"—was at odds with human rights as I understand them. I feared that the Bureau of Democracy, Human Rights, and Labor was transforming into a permanent cadre of diversity, equity, and inclusion commissars, trying to graft progressive views onto a world that neither wanted nor needed to adopt them. The State Department needed a human rights policy based on American founding principles and constitutional traditions. If America was going to urge countries to honor human rights, we needed clear rationales and priorities that reflected our unique civilizational beliefs and moral and political commitments. We had to keep our faith in our founding ideals and to translate them unapologetically into our diplomacy.

Out of this necessity, I created the State Department's Commission on Unalienable Rights, an independent panel of lawyers, scholars, and practitioners from across the political spectrum who would delve into America's human rights traditions and issue a report. I instructed them to supply advice on human rights grounded in our nation's founding ideals, the best traditions in American constitutional government, and the principles of the 1948 Universal Declaration of Human Rights. My goal was to spark a debate and help us escape from the endless array of "rights" invented by the international NGO-industrial complex. I also sought to provide guidance for the State Department, inform American citizens, and help friends and partners around the world understand better what the United States stands for.

Well, we had a debate—if accusing me of hatred and slapping me with a lawsuit counts as joining issue. Our critics savaged the commission as a vehicle to attack gay marriage and transgenderism. Four human rights organizations even sued me, saying I "deliberately stacked the Commission on Unalienable Rights with members with known hostility to LGBTQ+ and reproductive rights and without any known human rights practitioners." The charges were demonstrably false. A few thoroughgoing social liberals sat on the commission, and it was chaired by my old mentor, Harvard Law School professor Mary Ann Glendon. As an accomplished scholar, a former US ambassador to the Vatican, and a former member of President George W. Bush's Council on Bioethics, she was a leading authority on human rights.

Similarly, the State Department's Policy Planning staff director, Peter Berkowitz, who served as the commission's executive secretary, brought expertise in America's political ideas and institutions. He is one of the most remarkable scholars of faith, philosophy, and the American tradition. He can rip out your heart with logic and convince you that it was your idea all along. He and Professor Glendon built an excellent panel of thoughtful commissioners. Yet it wasn't enough for leftists. The irony that the first secretary of state in at least fifty years to order a serious and scholarly review of the American human rights tradition was sued by the so-called Human Rights Watch organization reinforced my instinct that I was onto something. Nevertheless, even a few folks at the department who agreed with the mission thought that the whole thing was a futile distraction from meat-and-potatoes foreign policy issues. I disagreed. Getting America's human rights policy right was too important for me to give an inch.

I released the commission's final report at the National Constitution Center in Philadelphia, with Independence Hall gleaming in the background. The event's date of July 16, 2020, couldn't have been better. The murder of George Floyd the previous May had ignited a debate about justice and rights. The CCP tried to butt into the conversation with a claim that Floyd's death proved that their authoritarianism is superior to our system of freedom and democracy. Meanwhile, the proliferation of COVID-related restrictions and growing big tech censorship of online speech reignited questions about basic freedoms. Furthermore, leftist revisions of American history, driven by the *New York Times*' 1619 Project, were gaining traction with their claims that the American experiment was permanently corrupted because of slavery in early America. In my speech that day, I reminded the audience that "America is fundamentally good and has much to offer the world, because our founders recognized the existence of God-given, unalienable rights and designed a durable system to protect them." I went on: "I am confident that the American star will shine across the heavens, so long as we keep a proper understanding of unalienable rights at the center of our unending quest to secure freedom for our own people and all of mankind."

I concede that the commission failed to leave a major mark on the State Department. But it did produce an outstanding report with valuable meditations on what it means to protect unalienable rights in an international context. And we did have a significant impact abroad. For example, the report was endorsed by Centrist Democrat International, the primary international group of Christian democratic parties. And it was the report that proved to be the impetus for the representatives of the aforementioned Nahdlatul Ulama to invite me to speak in Jakarta in October 2020. They found that the report gave powerful expression to their understanding of human rights and the place of fundamental rights and basic freedoms in a responsible foreign policy. I happily traveled there to present the report and engage in conversations about cross-cultural understandings of human rights.

The report itself is worth reading for anyone serious about understanding the key issues and gaining a better appreciation of how America's human rights efforts are grounded in our nation's best traditions and highest principles. One of the lines from the conclusion strikes me as particularly pertinent: "One of the most important ways in which the United States promotes human rights abroad is by serving as an example of a rights-respecting society where citizens live together under law amid the nation's great religious, ethnic, and cultural heterogeneity." We cannot give an inch to the leftist mobs that threaten to cancel the right to free speech because they do not agree with what some people say. Their victory would unmoor our democracy from the freedom that allows discussion and debate over how to move forward as a nation. I shudder to think how that will translate into our diplomacy. Will we avoid hard conversations that can advance American interests? I pray it never comes to that.

MY DEPENDENCE ON GRACE

Finally, on a more personal note, each day I looked to my faith to sustain me through the rigors of serving America at such a high level. Leading the CIA and the State Department was exhausting, and at no time did I ever feel as if my time was truly my own. On December 23, 2017, I was sitting with Susan and Nick. We had gone to a site where it was easy for my CIA team to provide protection and still be home with their families for Christmas. I was reading an unclassified summary of the US government's rules and guidelines on extrajudicial killings—not exactly a merry tale of Christmas cheer. In the background, I could hear Susan playing a video to Nick on her phone. The video was of a beautiful boy, Gabriel Cotton, the son of our close friends Tom and Anna Cotton, opening a musical snow globe that we had given him as a gift. The scene was a microcosm for my constant, difficult jumping back and forth between two worlds—one filled with innocence and joy and another rent by darkness and evil.

At other times, I felt—almost literally, being secretary of state—the overwhelming weight of the world on my shoulders. Usually my mornings started before dawn, after four or five hours of sleep. I'd be up early, reading the latest assessments of our missions and about threats to our most vulnerable diplomatic outposts. Many times, I took late-night calls from the president or from world leaders who were just getting their day started when I was winding down. As for multitasking, I wrote myself a note on October 19, 2018: "I'm in Mexico City today, and feel like there are a lot of plates to keep spinning—DPRK, KSA (Saudi Arabia) complexity, deal with United Arab Emirates, Brexit, Iran sanctions, Afghanistan, Syria, Turkey, immigration, Russia and cyber and of course the make or break for the country, China." Susan often jokes that most of the time, when I open my mouth publicly, the topics are dismally dark and complicated: "Mike, you're the best Xanax salesman in the world!"

But for as many times as I felt crushed with stress, I was also sustained by His grace. I held on as best I could to my daily routine of praying and reading the Bible. And I tried to take little moments to slow down and ask the Lord for help. By about six forty-five every morning, my security detail was driving me to the office from my home on the Fort Myer military base next to Arlington National Cemetery. After arriving in the State Department garage, they hustled me into the secretary's personal elevator. Standing in silence in "the box," as it was called, I used that tiny slice of unstructured time on the ride up—perhaps twenty seconds—to ask the Lord to come to my aid. I also took heart from notes that poured into my office from ordinary Americans, many of whom told me they were praying for me.

The many frustrations and crises that attended my work were rooted in the Lord's purposes, which aren't always obvious. In the fall of 2021, I traveled to Southern California for a public event. I had the chance to reunite with one of the American hostages—a missionary—whom I had helped bring home from North Korea more than three years prior. We hadn't been in touch since then, so I was grateful for a chance to reconnect with him in a more pleasant environment than a tarmac in Pyongyang.

He told me the story of his final hours in captivity. In the early afternoon on the day he was set free, the guards came to tell him that he had been deemed "uncorrectable" and that he was going to be executed. An hour or so later, the guards put a hood on his head and led him out of his cell. He told me he was terrified, aching from not being able to see his family again. But he kept praying for his captors to come to know the Lord, even as they shoved him into a waiting vehicle for what he thought would be his final ride anywhere. As I listened to his story, I wondered if I would have showed that same strength and mercy toward my tormentors.

Only when the vehicle door opened and the hood was removed from his head did this man begin to understand what was taking place. It took him a few seconds to process that sitting in front of him was a massive white and blue American airplane—his chariot out of North Korea. In this moment, he told me, "I prayed—and then moved as fast as I could to the plane!" I realized that I had been part of the earthly manifestation of God's will to bring this believer home to spread the gospel.

For me, faithfulness meant late nights, early mornings, long trips, endless meetings, and constant criticism. The biblical notion of stewardship calls on Christians to perform well the duties that God has given us, including the workaday challenges of ordinary life. For me, it meant honoring the will of the earthly authorities placed over me—the president and the voters. It meant pushing my team hard, asking tough questions, and showing up to places I didn't always want to go. It meant skipping fancy dinners in glamorous cities so that I could catch up on briefing papers over a cheeseburger in a hotel room.

For all the glory that supposedly surrounds a secretary of state, the job was very often a weird combination of the stressful and the mundane. By God's grace, I managed to keep my faith through it all.

TELL THE HARD TRUTH

I first met the most dangerous man in the world on June 14, 2018, following the Singapore summit with Chairman Kim. My purpose was to update CCP general secretary Xi Jinping on the denuclearization of North Korea. I also wanted to tell him how an America First foreign policy could be good for China if the CCP changed direction. It was a tough assignment.

But it was a necessary one, being at the core of our China efforts at the time. By the time I had become secretary of state, President Trump had already begun to see that an economic confrontation with the CCP was essential. I knew that fixing the massively unfair trade relationship had to be done, probably with the blunt weapon of tariffs. I also knew that restoring reciprocity on trade—the president's narrow focus—would have to be the beginning of America's effort to address China's dangerous ambitions, not the end. Tariffs were only one weapon to be deployed against the CCP's economic predations targeting America and the world. Indeed, time has shown that a new trade deal wasn't enough to stop China's economic warfare.

Nor did the trade war address the core driver of CCP behavior: its intent to dominate the world. The scale of the party's ambition, capacity, and intent is breathtaking. For decades, neither Republican nor Democratic leaders told this hard truth to the American people. Either they didn't know it or they were afraid to say it. Finally, the time had come for Americans and everybody else in the world to hear it.

So, I got to work.

I'd been briefed that Xi, like most all CCP officials, loved to go on long diatribes. As soon as we were alone, the ranting began.

Taiwan? An internal Chinese matter.

American tariffs? Unfair, because China was still a developing nation.

The Pacific? The nine-dash line—an artificial, Chinese-drawn boundary—was a good way to start mapping it.

I listened. When he paused in his diatribe, I thanked him for seeing me. I briefed him on my meeting with Chairman Kim. Then, in response to his lies, I spoke the truth: the CCP could never match American greatness. A superpower's staying power required creative destruction, not centralized planning. It required building friendships around the world, not coercing others to pay tribute to the great hegemon. It required rewarding excellence, not creating cronies with bribes.

This was the high point of my relationship with General Secretary Xi.

Softly and kindly, I had told him the hard truth.

TELLING THE HARD TRUTH: THE CORE OF STATESMANSHIP

Telling hard truths is foundational to the greatest acts of statesmanship. In the late 1850s, a lawyer from Illinois had something to say about the crisis of slavery. Abraham Lincoln believed that involuntary bondage was a grotesque violation of the Founders' belief that all men are created equal. On June 26, 1857, in Springfield, Illinois, Lincoln looked back to the Founders' own truth-telling. He stated that the Founders "defined with tolerable distinctness in what respects they did consider all men created equal—equal in 'certain inalienable rights, among which are life, liberty, and the pursuit of happiness.' This they said, and this they meant." Lincoln told the nation the hard truth: slavery was intolerable in a nation founded on respect for equality and human dignity.

Through his veracious speeches, Lincoln's national profile grew, and two years later he spoke at the Cooper Union Institute in New York City, giving a bold antislavery speech that helped propel him to the White House in 1860. Lincoln's law partner at the time, William Herndon, said that the speech "was constructed with a view to accuracy of statement, simplicity of language, and unity of thought . . . It was logical, temperate in tone, powerful—irresistibly driving conviction home to men's reasons and their souls." Lincoln's articulation of the truth of the American experiment—and its fundamental regard for human dignity—marked him as the man millions of Americans could trust to guide the nation as the storm clouds of a civil war loomed on the horizon.

More than a century later, another truth-teller emerged to steer America out of a difficult period. In the 1970s, America suffered a crisis of confidence following the Watergate scandal, a defeat in Vietnam, an economic slump, and the disastrous presidency of Jimmy Carter. Many thought the country was in a state of permanent decline (a sentiment that is as pervasive today as it is wrong). Then a great man from the West rode into Washington. President Reagan came with a message that America needed to hear: "We're not, as some would have us believe, doomed to an inevitable decline . . . So, with all the creative energy at our command, let us begin an era of national renewal."

Reagan's truth-telling extended into foreign policy. When he sized up the Soviet Union, he saw a global menace whose Communist ways were diametrically opposed to the Founders' concepts of liberty and human flourishing. And he wasn't afraid to tell the world the hard truth, remarking to the National Association of Evangelicals in 1983 that the Soviet Union was an "evil empire." His rhetoric and personal example offered a good model to emulate.

AMERICA MUST KNOW THE HARD TRUTH ABOUT THE CCP

Today we must follow in that American tradition and tell a hard truth that many Americans would prefer to ignore: the CCP presents by far the greatest external threat to our way of life in America today. The CCP is inside the gates here at home and is determined to become a hegemon—first in its immediate neighborhood, then in the greater Indo-Pacific region, and finally everywhere.

The Trump administration began—and I emphasize we only *began*—to do the heavy lifting against the CCP that America had long neglected. Measured on a curve against recent presidencies, our confrontation of China gets an A+. On an absolute scale of evaluating our success, I'd give us a B for effort and a D for obtaining the outcomes we wanted.

Nevertheless, I'm confident that America will prevail in this confrontation. The first step in every twelve-step program is to recognize a problem. This is why telling the hard truth matters. It lays the factual foundation for action, pointing to the decades of hard work that lie ahead. This is what the Trump administration did.

Americans and the world must first understand that Marxist-Leninist ideology inspires everything the CCP does. Even though a vast majority of the Chinese people no longer have faith in Beijing's bankrupt totalitarianism, the ruling elites who have monopolized all political power in China since 1949 still cling to it. Unlike many members of the *nomenklatura* in the waning days of the USSR, China's leaders—from the murderous Mao Zedong to his successors, Deng Xiaoping, Jiang Zemin, and Hu Jintao—are true believers in Communism. Even as the CCP has integrated elements of capitalism into the Chinese economy in recent decades, it regards itself as the vanguard agent of international Communism. Its mission is to take down or co-opt what it believes are capitalist oppressor states, such as America and her allies.

Leading the charge since 2012 is CCP general secretary Xi Jinping. In the years before becoming China's strongman, he headed the CCP's Central Party School, which is the brainwashing factory for party apparatchiks. With a doctorate in Marxist-Leninist theory from China's Tsinghua University, Xi is a true believer in Communism. To spin the CCP's commitment to Marxist-Leninist fundamentalism as an expression of Chinese nationalism, the CCP also nurses, and often fabricates, historical grievances from a period of internal weakness and foreign subjugation, lasting from 1840 to 1949, the year the Communist Party came to rule the country. The party believes that China—"The Middle Kingdom"—is the true center of world civilization, and that we live in an age in which, according to Xi, "the East is rising and the West is declining."

Xi has therefore acted aggressively to create a new world order led by the CCP, beginning with the Indo-Pacific region. China is trying to dominate the South China Sea, through which about a third of the world's maritime trade flows. In 2020, China killed twenty Indian soldiers in a skirmish over the two countries' shared border—that's just one of the seventeen long-running land and sea border disputes involving China and its neighbors. The Chinese People's Liberation Army, the world's largest military force, whose only loyalty is to the CCP's supreme leader, is preparing for an invasion of Taiwan and has morphed into a formidable power capable of successfully conducting operations in the space, cyber, conventional, nuclear, and maritime domains. In the realm of international economics, the Belt and Road Initiative traps nations with unsustainable debt in exchange for highways, railroads, and pipelines, while Chinese bagmen trot the globe bribing corrupt elites to seal the deals. Yet for all its military might, the CCP, like all totalitarian regimes, is fearful of its own people. China's domestic security apparatus has a bigger budget than its military's—an indication that the paranoid overlords in Beijing are terrified of their own citizens, a weakness shared by so many authoritarian regimes.

Just as concerning is China's attempt to build an empire in the digital world. By subsidizing companies such as Huawei, ZTE, and YMTC and racing to lead the world in 5G, artificial intelligence, blockchain, semiconductors, and quantum computing technology, China is positioning itself to dominate markets, control the world's information flows, harvest user data for surveillance and invasions of privacy, and develop world-leading weapons. In the same way medieval serfs were subjects of their local lords, the CCP wants to make every nation bend the knee to Beijing. Any foreign power that tries to bully China, Xi stated at the hundredth-anniversary celebration of the CCP in 2021, "will be met with a Great Wall of Steel"—meaning bullets.

Those are China's growing capabilities. But as I was taught in my first military history class at West Point, trouble is measured as a combination of capabilities and *intent*. And the CCP's intent is just as worrisome.

For many years, America and the West failed to realize the party's true intentions. Or, perhaps, we didn't want to recognize a hard truth. In the 1970s, China saw that it had fallen behind the rest of the world in almost every way and began to open itself to global investment and markets. Spurred on by President Nixon's visit to China in 1972 and the inauguration of a new era of Sino-American relations, American companies began to trickle in. Dollars flowed across the Pacific. When the Communist governments in Eastern Europe and the Soviet Union fell in the late 1980s and early 1990s, many thinkers in the West saw the potential for history to repeat itself in China. They theorized that an economic liberalization of China would produce a political liberalization. The Germans even have a phrase for this concept: "Wandel durch Handel," or "change through trade."

It was a great and hopeful theory. But it didn't work. China's leaders watched what had happened in the Soviet Union closely. They saw modest free expression under *glasnost* and economic reforms under perestroika lead to the collapse of an empire. In their view, the collapse of the Soviet Union was not an end of history but a betrayal of true Marxist-Leninist ideals by "revisionist" and impure European Communists such as Mikhail Gorbachev and Boris Yeltsin. The party believes it can correct the course of the international Communist movement and lead the world to the final triumph of what it calls "socialism with Chinese characteristics" over democratic capitalism.

Goaded by Wall Street and foreign policy elites, the West spent the better part of five decades setting up shop in China and supporting China's integration into global political and economic institutions such as the WTO. Washington believed that eventually China would evolve into a "responsible stakeholder," with respect for basic human dignity, fair dealings, and sovereign borders. Along the way, the West failed to see the regime's fanatical commitment to its ideology—on display most flamboyantly in the bloody massacre of students and others in Tiananmen Square in 1989. Because China is a closed society, we don't know how many of its own people the CCP slaughtered in Beijing's major city square, but it probably numbered in the thousands. That massacre underscored how democracy advocates and their ideas of freedom pose a mortal threat to one-party, Communist rule.

Throughout the 1980s and 1990s, and the early twenty-first century, China obeyed CCP leader Deng Xiaoping's famous maxim, "Hide your strength; bide your time," quietly building up military power, economic leverage, and foreign influence in anticipation of someday leveraging it against America and the West. The CCP cheated at the WTO and siphoned off American factories. It stole vast quantities of intellectual property—by some estimates, the largest wealth transfer in history. It demanded silence on human rights issues from corporate America as the price of admission to the Chinese market. It launched influence campaigns targeting American universities, media outlets, and state and local government officials. And it conditioned influential American financial and political leaders on both the Left and Right to believe and espouse the view that China's rise was good for the world. The amount of power China has today is thus considerable. The imperialist nature of both Russia and China are on great display today in Ukraine and Taiwan, but only China can mount a realistic bid for empire and make life worse for every American. The naive project to make China a Western-style partner through commerce and integration into the so-called liberal international order was about as successful as the launch of New Coke and CNN+.

But at least one American businessman didn't go along with all the panda hugging. One of the great distinguishing features of President Trump's 2016 campaign was his willingness to tell the truth about China's cheating on trade agreements, harm to American manufacturing by dumping mass quantities of steel and other goods into the United States, and theft of American intellectual property. He called China's entry into the WTO an act that "enabled the greatest job theft in history." It was the most prominent criticism of China the American public had heard in decades. His truth-telling about China's economic practices that started in the campaign carried over into one of the most consequential foreign policy shifts in American history.

Once the administration got underway, an important first step in telling the hard truth about China came in the form of the 2017 *National Security Strategy*. This document went further than previous administrations ever had in describing China as one of the world's "revisionist powers" that wishes to "shape a world antithetical to US values and interests." That language could have been even tougher in capturing Xi's true aims. But credit goes to General McMaster and his talented strategic advisor—Nadia Schadlow—who put pen to the truth in that document. They, for the first time, ripped the Band-Aid off, ditched the "more trinkets from China" model, and issued calls to put America first. The CCP is an adversary. It is in fact our most dangerous adversary. To say this is to speak the truth.

SPOOKS FOR TRUTH

Prior to starting in the administration, I'd begun to watch China with growing concern. As a member of the House Intelligence Committee, I became a close observer of the CCP's Politburo Standing Committee. It was humorous to see the backstabbing inside the CCP bureaucracies but also frightening to see the ruthlessness of its members. When they turned their aggression outward, they perceived that America was a dying civilization. And they believed they were in position to put a stake through its heart.

At the CIA, I knew we had much work to do to improve both our analysis and operational capabilities against the CCP. Much has been written about major setbacks in the CIA's China program from a decade ago. Rebuilding is hard. It is also necessary.

We also needed a broader focus. The primary field of confrontation with the CCP in the early days of the Trump administration was economic. We had to deliver policymakers relevant information on Chinese industry, its key players, and its points of vulnerability. I'm often asked whether I'm willing to go to war with China. Here's a hard truth: the CCP has engaged in economic war against the United States for decades. For too long, we averted our eyes to the facts and said, "Please sir, may I have another?" The result is staggering: billions in property stolen, plus tens of millions of valuable jobs gone. No country in history has, in essence, paid its rival to become stronger, as the United States of America has done for decades. The real question is, "Will *we* fight?"

I also beefed up the China team and am heartened that my successor, Gina Haspel, continued this effort. Her successor, Director Bill Burns, has expanded on this even more. We sought to expose our officers to private-sector leaders, too. One tool was the CIA Advisory Board. This group of personnel from outside the Agency meets about once a quarter, learns about hard problems at the Agency, and helps develop creative solutions. Brennan's Advisory Board was made up of fine people, but nearly all of them were former military leaders, former political leaders, and former intelligence leaders. That composition defeated the goal of having diverse and competing perspectives. Thousands of intelligence officers already worked for me. I had political leaders providing more oversight and input than I wanted. And on my side of the Potomac, there were people in uniform everywhere.

I thanked Brennan's group for their service and brought in America's smartest business leaders from both small companies and commercial behemoths. Each had expertise in a technology, a financial tool, or a resource that mattered to our work. If we were going to confront China, I needed to know what the battlefield looked like. These private-sector giants helped me do that. We paid them nothing, and they served America in the most important ways. Their names will not be disclosed here, but they are all patriots. The intelligence products our leaders read today tell the truth better than ever.

MY EARLY DIPLOMATIC EFFORTS ON CHINA

In that first meeting with Xi Jinping, as I sized him up and told him what I thought, it was clear that he sought to take the measure of me and the Trump team, too. He had already met with Trump at Mar-a-Lago in April 2017. On that occasion, Trump disclosed that he had ordered a strike against Syria and other targets just a few minutes earlier. Undoubtedly, Xi knew this was not Team Obama. My message in Beijing reinforced it.

Personally, I thought Xi was dour. While Putin can be funny and mirthful, even while being evil, Xi was not so much serious as "dead-eyed." I never once saw an unforced smile. The stories he told—and boy, did he tell stories—were about Chinese victimhood and his demands to avenge grievances from long before any of us were born. I also found Xi a quintessential Communist apparatchik: heavy in the abstract, light on the issues under discussion, and always eager to impose his views, even while he pretends to be listening to you. He fit the psychological profile of an East German or Soviet Communist I came to study during my Army days. Xi talked in hollow tones, always in search of words, phrases, and archaic Chinese proverbs of questionable clarity. My China policy advisor at the State Department, Miles Yu, later told me that CCP leaders in general, and General Secretary Xi in particular, deploy overwrought erudition to play gullible American leaders. Of the dozens of world leaders I met, he was among the most unpleasant. How's that for telling the hard truth?

Having now seen the regime personified at the highest level, I was gripped by just how different its leaders were from the Chinese people. When I ran a small business in Kansas, we had a small operation in Shanghai that employed fewer than fifteen people. I traveled there several times in the early 2000s. I had come to love the Chinese people, and I still do. It saddened me that the American model of engagement with China had emboldened a regime with such utter disdain for basic human dignity and that viewed its own people as cogs in the Marxist system of power.

On the heels of this meeting with Xi, and another parley in October, I went into overdrive to work China into nearly all my conversations with my foreign counterparts. Inside the administration, both Bolton and O'Brien shared my understanding of the threat. White House advisor Peter Navarro was a consistent ally, though he also could function as a partially unguided missile. (It is often an advantage to be in the presence of an unguided missile, as the closer you are to the launch point, the lower the risk that the projectile's flight will strike you.) Attorney General Bill Barr and FBI director Christopher Wray, too, were focused on this critical mission. Matt Pottinger was fluent in Mandarin, had lived in China, and was a force for good as a powerful idea machine, first as an NSC director and then as the deputy national security advisor.

In October 2018, not long after my second trip to China, I paid a visit to Panama, a longtime friend of the United States. Two thirds of the cargo traffic crossing the Panama Canal begins or ends its journey at a US port, making the canal a hugely important strategic waterway. The Chinese were trying to buy land at the entrance of the canal, where they intended to build a new embassy. The thought of a Communist flag flapping at the mouth of one of the world's most essential transit points was intolerable. So, I headed down there and delivered a clear message to the Panamanians: Don't let it happen. They relented, but the Chinese didn't. Our work in Panama and the rest of Latin America to undo rapid Chinese encroachment is ongoing.

In another part of the world, the Indo-Pacific, I traveled to the Philippines in February 2019 to meet with President Rodrigo Duterte, the country's mercurial leader. The relationship had deteriorated badly during the Obama administration, largely because Duterte saw America doing next to nothing to stop China's military buildup in the Pacific, even as he sometimes played both sides of the US-China competition. The relationship was also tricky because of accusations of human rights abuses against Duterte's government. Duterte's foreign secretary, Teddy Locsin, was trying to help get things back on track. Americans and Filipinos have strong ties, and the Philippines have been a great partner for the United States in a troubled part of the Pacific Ocean. Additionally, an old US naval facility—Subic Bay—is strategically located close to the Philippines' main port. The Chinese were circling like vultures, waiting to descend and take it over.

I told President Duterte that we understood why he had felt slighted and that the United States was committed to supporting him. He appreciated that and my willingness to clear up some ambiguity over whether the 1951 US-Philippine Mutual Defense Treaty also applied to an attack in the South China Sea. I put this to bed in Manila by stating, "As the South China Sea is part of the Pacific, any armed attack on Philippine forces, aircraft, or public vessels in the South China Sea will trigger mutual defense obligations under Article 4 of our Mutual Defense Treaty." Within weeks, we renewed our treaty obligations and made progress on the Subic Bay issue. By putting America first and our egos last, and taking heed of President Duterte's concerns, we obtained the diplomatic outcome we desired.

Another important trip came later that year to Australia. The Australians were ahead of the United States in recognizing the China challenge and trying to meet it. Dogged scholars and reporters in their country had exposed China's malign influence in their parliament and universities. In August 2019, I spoke at the State Library of New South Wales in Sydney—roughly the equivalent of the Library of Congress in its stateliness and grandeur. I delivered a stark message in an ornate setting: "You can sell your soul for a pile of soybeans, or you can protect your people."

The United States and Australia are also close treaty allies, and I knew I could have frank conversations with Foreign Minister Marise Payne about the need to start working more closely together on China. I also relished getting to know Australia's prime minister, Scott Morrison, who is a conservative in politics and a Christian in faith. After Morrison won a surprise reelection in 2019, I was genuinely happy for him, and I believed his strong leadership and message in embracing the China challenge helped him win. He and his wife even welcomed Susan and me into their home for dinner on my trip to Sydney. When he visited Washington the next month, I held a State Department lunch for this solid leader. Later on, he proved his mettle further by asking hard questions about the origins of the coronavirus, holding firm even when China retaliated by banning the import of Australian wine and coal.

The backdrop to our China activities in 2018 and 2019 was the president's desire to revise our trade relationship with China. Many times when I briefed President Trump, I would bring him a story about a development regarding a country's military or government. He was more inclined to view power through a financial lens. The question was constantly applied to international power dynamics: "My Mike, who's got the money?"

Thus, he directed US Trade Representative Bob Lighthizer and Secretary of the Treasury Steve Mnuchin to negotiate a new trade agreement. While the trade talks were a necessary step to fix imbalances and outright thievery, it limited our ability to pursue other items on our agenda. At various junctures, President Trump was concerned that some idea of mine would kill the talks. This was a fair consideration, but the talks put a dent in our ability to tell hard truths about the party.

The trade talks did serve an important public purpose: They got people thinking and talking about the concept of fairness and reciprocity in our relationship with China. Can a Chinese company invest in American farmland? Sure. But can an American company invest in Chinese farmland? No way. Can a Chinese company go public on an

American exchange? Yep. What if an American company wants to list on the Shanghai exchange? Only under very strict conditions. Are those arrangements reciprocal?

Today, the Chinese walk all over us. A Chinese firm can buy 100 percent of nearly any American company, aside from those connected to the national security sector—and even those reviews are too weak. Yet, with a few exceptions, Americans can't own 100 percent of a Chinese company, and the Chinese government's list of sectors prohibited for foreign investment is vast. What's more, state public-pension funds invest in Chinese technology, which means we've used the retirement dollars of American workers to create China's surveillance tools. Meanwhile, Chinese pension funds are closely controlled and monitored by the CCP. If we fail to demand that trade and commerce with other nations happen on fair terms, American power will be diminished. The hard truth is that it's already happened.

EXPOSING CHINA'S ECONOMIC WARFARE

Warding off Chinese hegemony means winning the economic competition. When China creates business ties with countries, it gives the CCP leverage to impose its will in other areas. Chinese companies—many of them running on funds from Chinese government coffers—prowl the world looking for opportunities to build infrastructure and deliver other goodies for countries. One of China's national champions is Huawei—a huge telecommunications company behind much of the proliferation of 5G technology. If Huawei can dominate 5G, it will give the CCP access to massive quantities of personal, commercial, and national security data. Beijing will use that data to coerce, blackmail, defraud, and propagandize. I knew that I had to help America get serious about winning the global tech race against China. Even if America wasn't yet completely wise to the stakes, the Chinese were. Indeed, Xi Jinping has said, "Technological innovation has become the main battleground of the global playing field, and competition for tech dominance will grow unprecedentedly fierce." I read that less as a prediction and more as a statement of intent.

Fortunately, I had an outstanding ally at the State Department to help win the fight against the CCP's control of technology. Keith Krach is the opposite of the typical understated, buttoned-up diplomat. He's got a big mind and a big personality. His visionary thinking and persuasive abilities have helped him lead heavyweight technology companies, such as Ariba and DocuSign, to great success. After Keith was confirmed by the Senate in June 2019, I sat him down and said I had a big job for him: stop the Chinese from taking over the digital world. He was honored to take on the task and assembled an amazing team of business and technology minds the likes of which the State Department has never seen. When I had lunch with them, I counted at least two billionaires and seven other folks that may well have been, too. All those in this crew had lived the American dream, had taken risks with their own capital, and were now itching to win for America. Especially impressive was Mung Chiang, now the president of Purdue University, a sheer prodigy of electrical engineering who could explain the technological elements of the danger to our partners. Keith, Mung, and their team launched the Clean Network initiative to convince countries and private-sector companies to keep out treacherous tech companies such as Huawei.

By 2021, Keith and his team had convinced sixty countries and dozens of telecommunications firms not to wire Huawei into their networks. This work was so successful because Keith spoke the hard truth lots of people didn't want to hear: the CCP and its companies just can't be trusted. The Department of Commerce also banned American companies from selling certain sensitive technologies to Huawei. As a result, the Trump administration crushed Huawei's global telecom business. The company's overall revenues dropped 29 percent from 2020 to 2021, and the number of Huawei handsets shipped in 2021 plummeted 81 percent from 2020. Such is the power of the American economy to force favorable outcomes—something that was always wind at my back during any diplomatic negotiation.

Keith was also a great asset in his connections to Silicon Valley. This was another critical audience to whom we needed to tell the truth about China, because few industries in America have been more complicit in strengthening the Chinese military and police state than our world-class high-tech companies. Hewlett Packard has profited from investments in a company propping up the CCP's Orwellian surveillance state. Intel has apologized to China for abiding by American laws banning goods made with Xinjiang slave labor from coming to our shores. Apple has built vast data centers inside China at the CCP's request—aiding the party's quest to grab as much information on its own citizens as possible.

A Chinese national policy overseen by Xi Jinping called military-civil fusion demands that nonmilitary institutions in China such as schools and businesses turn over to the Chinese People's Liberation Army any technological knowledge with potential military application. For years, American companies and research institutions operating in China have been forced to set up joint ventures and hand over their sensitive technology as a requirement for market entry—and that knowledge has now been weaponized against the American people. This is to say nothing of the heist of intellectual property from American companies that Chinese hackers have pulled off. FBI director Christopher Wray has said, "The scale of their hacking program, and the amount of personal and corporate data that their hackers have stolen, is greater than [that of] every other country combined."

CEOs often expressed alarm to me about the CCP's damage to their business and to American national security—but their profit motives prevented them from speaking up publicly. This all-too-common experience is the product of China's masterful strategy of influence and coercion. LinkedIn, to name one company, has blocked the profiles of Western reporters inside China, almost certainly at the CCP's insistence. Amazon agreed to delete all ratings of Xi Jinping's biography on Amazon's sites accessed within China (apparently he was getting a lot of one-star reviews). This self-censorship allows Beijing to tell lies about itself and inflict many evils on humanity. Yet many of the same tech companies that keep silent on the CCP's abuses strike a pose as social justice warriors in support of causes such as Black Lives Matter, LGBTQ rights, and other woke campaigns.

The case of Daryl Morey, the former general manager of the Houston Rockets, is but another example. In 2019, Morey tweeted an image that read "Fight for Freedom. Stand with Hong Kong." Small potatoes, right? Not for the CCP. When it threatened NBA revenue streams by removing games from Chinese TV, it took just hours for the NBA—which prides itself on leading the Black Lives Matter charge—to fall to its knees and apologize because one of its executives spoke the truth on a human rights issue. Everyone threw Morey under the bus, from the owner of the Rockets to LeBron James. Joe Tsai, the number two man at Chinese e-commerce giant Alibaba and owner of the Brooklyn Nets, also demanded Morey's firing (not surprising for someone who has made billions in China, with much to lose if the CCP feels like coming after him). China most assuredly saw the deletion of Morey's social media post and those epic, cowardly apologies as vindication of its strong-arm tactics. Every American business leader who depends on China for access or revenue saw this, too. Many avoid defending American interests lest they lose out on Chinese money. Instead, they are content to become part of the CCP's communications team. This posture of appeasement must change. We should think about the whole problem differently: if hundreds of millions of Chinese citizens love the NBA, then let the regime face their scorn for banning games on TV.

USING MY PLATFORM TO WAKE UP THE WORLD

A few months into the secretary of state job, I knew that there was one important public voice missing from the world conversation on China—mine. Part of this was by design. I couldn't slam China and get crosswise with President Trump's agenda as he tried to fix our trade relationship with them. But with the clock ticking on what might be the one and only term of the Trump administration, I couldn't waste a platform as big as that of the secretary of state's office to tell the truth to the world about the CCP. Americans needed to know what they didn't want to hear: confrontation entails costs. Those costs aren't always easy to bear. Businesses lose trade opportunities. Farmers suffer from market shifts. Schools lose massive amounts of tuition money from CCP spies studying and conducting research on behalf of the party. But failing to confront CCP aggression now will only make future confrontation harder. And the long-term gains for America from confrontation will far exceed the short-term costs.

My China team understood this, and they were killer good. One fighter was a brilliant woman named Mary Kissel, whom I had hired as my senior advisor in the summer of 2018. Mary had lived in Hong Kong for many years, running the *Wall Street Journal* editorial page's coverage of Asia. She understood just how evil the CCP was, and she constantly made sure that the timid State Department's words and actions reflected this truth to the greatest extent possible. I was also grateful for her excellent work with the Unalienable Rights Commission and in many other areas.

Another powerful asset was a patriot named Miles Yu. Born in China during the Mao years, he grew up seeing firsthand the brutality of party rule. As a young man, Miles was intrigued by the words of President Reagan, and came to the United States to study. He fell in love with the American ideals of liberty and got involved with the Chinese dissident community. He eventually became a US citizen and a professor of Chinese studies and military history at the US Naval Academy in Annapolis, Maryland. In 2018, as a supporter of the Trump administration, he accepted a temporary assignment to work on China policy at the State Department. He was invaluable to me time and again by providing historical context on China policy, insights into the CCP's thought process, and bold policy recommendations. Miles also held the all-important China portfolio in the Office of Policy Planning. This made him in many respects a guard dog: if Miles didn't sign off on a policy recommendation, it wouldn't move ahead for my approval.

The team also consisted of two other very capable leaders. Peter Berkowitz took the lead in drafting a detailed outline of our counter-CCP diplomatic efforts. David Stilwell, a retired Air Force general, had the burden of leading the Bureau of East Asian and Pacific Affairs as its assistant secretary. He was a serious China scholar and one who had enormous experience in the region from his time in uniform. He often had to tell the permanent career officials working the China file that their boss was about to break some glass.

With Mary, Miles, David, and Peter now teaming up with David Wilezol and the rest of my speechwriters, we unleashed the strongest China speeches a secretary of state had ever given. The first of these major addresses came in October 2019 at Hudson Institute's annual gala in New York City. My mission was to expose the regime's evil Communist ideology to the world and explain hard truths about the party's motives and intentions. I didn't want to repeat the mistake of the post-9/11 years, when Americans were often led to believe that the terrorists were just stateless anti-American thugs, not Islamist fanatics whose ideology motivated their bloodletting. Every American and every foreign government had to know that the CCP was committed to an ideology hostile to democracy, free enterprise, and American values.

Many in the audience were New York millionaires, and most of them were connected to China. I told them, "We have to think anew, and unconventionally, about the People's Republic of China." I said that the CCP is "a Marxist-Leninist party focused on struggle and international domination." My most important point made that night—one that infuriated Beijing—was a statement that no US government official had uttered about China since the 1970s. I spoke the truth that "the Communist government in China today is not the same as the people of China."

As it turned out, this became the single most hated and feared sentence uttered by any US secretary of state concerning China in decades, producing overwhelming vitriol from the CCP's propaganda organs. The exposure of this simple, basic truth that the party and the people are not the same thing is the CCP's biggest nightmare because it plants a seed to challenge the regime in the mind of the Chinese people. Time and again, Beijing attacked me on this particular point. Countless Chinese and Chinese Americans, including dissidents in the Chinese diaspora, former Tiananmen protestors, the Uyghur survivors of Chinese concentration camps, Falun Gong practitioners, Hong Kong human rights defenders, and ordinary immigrants have thanked me for pointing out this fundamental reality.

While many folks in the room applauded my remarks, I also suspect that my words made a lot of them uncomfortable. I also said in that speech, "Beijing's intransigence creates a permanent class of China lobbyists in the United States. Their primary job is to sell access to Chinese leaders and connect business partners." This Marriot ballroom was packed with New York business and finance types. I have no doubt they are patriotic Americans, but it's just the truth that America's business community often kisses up to Beijing. It advocates against the kind of necessary confrontation with China that will protect American national security and the human rights of the Chinese people. But I had to seize the once-in-a-lifetime opportunity to tell them and the rest of America what they had to know—the regnant doctrines of American engagement with China since 1972 had to come to an end.

Some weeks later, it came to my attention that the nation's governors had received invitations to an event called the US-China Governors Collaboration Summit. The summit was cohosted by the National Governors Association and an outfit called the Chinese People's Association for Friendship with Foreign Countries. Sounds nice. But what the CPAFFC doesn't advertise is that it's a full-on subsidiary of the CCP's United Front Work Department—its overseas foreign-influence arm. American governors hosted by the CCP. What could go wrong?

When I noticed that the National Governors Association was also having one of its semiannual confabs in Washington, DC, I called Governor Larry Hogan of Maryland and asked for thirty minutes to address the gathering. He seemed a bit confused about why the secretary of state would want to meet with fifty state leaders but said it was fine with him as long as his cochair, Governor Andrew Cuomo of New York, did not object. One of my State Department veterans knew the governor, and he agreed to let me speak.

They gave me twenty minutes on a sleepy Saturday afternoon in February. Clearly my remarks were not on the top of any governor's list. It certainly felt a little listless in that convention center's ballroom. So, I decided to wake them up with some hard truth. I had just gotten my hands on a Chinese document published by a CCP-backed think tank that listed every governor by name. It put each governor in one of three categories regarding his or her approach to China: "friendly," "hardline," or "ambiguous" (which really meant, "we are working on them"). I shared this information with the governors and told them, "I'll let you decide where you think you belong. Someone in China already has." That got their attention. They all wanted to know how they rated with Beijing. Here's what we know for sure: the CCP is working on every governor, every city councilperson, every state representative, every state senator. To echo the title of Dale Carnegie's famous book, the CCP's United Front Work Department is working to "win friends and influence people." When a fun-sounding Chinese friendship organization shows up at a PTA meeting with the "gift" of a new jungle gym or swing set, their goal is not better health or a fun playtime for your child. And yes, the CCP has targeted American PTA meetings.

We needed every tool and every voice on the Trump team to make the case to the American people. Sometime in the spring or early summer of 2020, I gathered in my office National Security Advisor O'Brien, Attorney General Barr, and Director Wray. Mary Kissel joined us. I proposed that we each give major addresses on the topic of the CCP threat. Between the four of us, we would lay down a model for all the world—including Washington, DC—to see. Everyone was in. I thought there might be reluctance—the headwind of "not screwing up the Phase One trade deal," to quote the president, was ever-present—but you could sense that we all knew what needed to be done. In the four speeches, we sequentially laid down a comprehensive explanation of the threat and described a set of actions that we intended to take. This series of speeches and the commitments we all made were a watershed moment in building a detailed counter-China execution matrix. O'Brien spoke on the CCP's ideological bearings and China's global ambition; Wray gave a brilliant speech on China's massive intellectual property theft, espionage, and other illicit activities in the United States; and Barr delivered remarks at the Gerald R. Ford Presidential Library and Museum on China's relentless efforts to exploit free and open societies in the West.

In July 2020, I delivered the capstone speech, titled "Communist China and the Free World's Future," at the Richard Nixon Presidential Library and Museum. I said that "securing our freedom from the CCP is the mission of our time, and America is perfectly positioned to lead it because our founding principles give us that opportunity." I also quoted President Nixon's 1967 *Foreign Affairs* article in which he predicted that "the world cannot be safe until China changes." The fact that China under the CCP has remained not only an unchanged dictatorship, but also a much stronger and more capable one, marks the abject failure of five decades of China policy. I concluded by pointing out that "today, the danger is clear; and today the awakening is happening, and today the free world must respond. We can never go back to the past." My words made some China-policy old guards uncomfortable. We were, after all, dismantling decades of policy architecture. They had built it, and it had failed.

Reliable sources told me that the speech circulated far and wide in the Chinese underground. This was one of several indications that the Chinese people—both those living in China and around the world—were paying attention and rejoicing at our truth-telling. No one knows the evils of the CCP better than they do.

On June 4, 2019, on the anniversary of the massacre in Tiananmen, I met with a group of survivors from that assault on humanity. The stories were harrowing and a reminder of the work ahead. But there was a moment of levity as well. An older gentlemen said I was very famous and popular among the Chinese diaspora because I had tweeted a picture of me doing dishes while my wife was relaxing at our kitchen table. He said, "Chinese women all across the world have been showing that picture to their husbands, saying that if America's secretary of state can help around the house, so can they!"

The next year, another light moment happened on Twitter—and no, it wasn't a tweet from the president. I posted on my personal account a completely innocent photo of my golden retriever Mercer cuddling up with her favorite stuffed toys. One of those toys happens to be a Winnie the Pooh doll. This would be unremarkable but for the fact that many comparisons have been made between the facial resemblance of everyone's favorite bear and everyone's least favorite Chinese dictator, Xi Jinping. Twitter went wild with speculation that I was throwing a coded jab at General Secretary Xi. I later came to find out that no quarter of the world was more engaged with the tweet than Chinese Americans and Chinese throughout the world. To me, it was a reminder that the world is always watching America's leaders, and not just during TV interviews and press conferences.

And yeah, they do kind of look alike.

HONG KONG: THE STATE DEPARTMENT FIGHTS BACK

These speeches—and subsequent ones like them—told the world that the United States was embracing an unprecedented new strategic direction. They also let the State Department bureaucracy know that there would be no more business as usual with China.

Unfortunately, many at the department wanted things to stay as they were. Although Stilwell agreed with me on the threat of the CCP and did very good work, many career staffers in the depths of his bureau and elsewhere were frustrated at the formulation and implementation of our policies. They were stuck in the failed mindset of maintaining engagement with China and hoping for change without disruption. America's diplomats are conditioned to do all they can to keep relationships running smoothly through docile words, friendly gestures, and benign actions. That's great, but when defending American interests demands a dismemberment of the status quo, they often lose their spine.

Foreign Service officers also depend on favorable performance reviews to obtain their promotions—and coming off as confrontational doesn't endear them to many of their superiors. I recall one conversation with a senior-level officer. We'd gone back and forth on how to approach the conflicts inside Syria. I asked her why the department fought me so hard on what I wanted to do. She laughed: "Mr. Secretary, this is the first time in my seventeen years at the State Department that State has actually had power. We've watched the White House and DOD drive policy the entire time. You've outlasted everyone, and now we have a say. It makes them nervous that they may have an impact and be held accountable for decisions, instead of just bitching and leaking."

I could not comprehend this mentality, which David Hale also confirmed to me existed. You'd think that people who'd been sidelined for so long, who were now working under an administration with a secretary who felt unbound by failed conventions, would be eager to grab the wheel, take risks, and suggest new ideas. Instead, they backed down from asserting their influence. I couldn't understand it.

This apathy and internal resistance to the Trump administration was evident in our policy on Hong Kong. According to the 1992 Hong Kong Policy Act, the State Department must present an annual assessment of Hong Kong's "high degree of autonomy." This freedom is what the CCP promised in 1984 to the people of Hong Kong, the UK government, and the entire world when the United Kingdom agreed to give up control of its former colony. The State Department's report is important because it provides the basis on which the US government decides whether Hong Kong deserves special political and economic treatment by the United

States across multiple areas, including export controls, law enforcement, travel and immigration, and sanctions.

Despite its solemn promise to uphold the so-called One Country, Two Systems framework, the CCP mounted an increasingly aggressive bid to control Hong Kong. The party had been emboldened in part because of the State Department's weak and toothless assessments. I ordered our Hong Kong team to get real and account for the drastic erosion of the promised "high degree of autonomy." But an Obama administration holdover led the office in charge of the report, and I felt that this individual fought my efforts. I sent Miles to sort out the mess. It took several days to fix the problem and get the wording right. When I presented my first annual *Hong Kong Policy Act Report* to Congress in March 2019, I fired a warning shot at the CCP and its puppet government: "The tempo of mainland central government intervention in Hong Kong affairs—and actions by the Hong Kong government consistent with mainland direction—increased, accelerating negative trends seen in previous periods." This was the honest truth, pure and simple.

But my words were not strong enough to prevent Carrie Lam, the Hong Kong chief executive, and a lackey of the CCP, from pushing a bill that would allow the extradition of Hong Kong citizens to the Communist Chinese mainland. Obviously, the CCP intended to use its authority to cripple Hong Kong's pro-democracy movement and silence its critics. In June, Hong Kong exploded in response to Lam's perfidy. Millions of Hong Kongers took to the streets and demanded the withdrawal of the bill. The CCP viewed these mass protests as a challenge to its iron fist. Beijing cracked down, often with the aid of pro-CCP street gangs. They beat and arrested thousands of peaceful protestors. Independent newspapers, TV stations, truth-telling journalists, freedom-loving students, and public intellectuals were harassed, censored, and punished by the increasingly fascistic Hong Kong police force, which was undoubtedly given lessons by the CCP secret police. The eyes of the world were on Hong Kong as never before. I issued statement after statement condemning the arbitrary and brutal treatment of Hong Kong's citizens and met with prominent pro-democracy and freedom-loving Hong Kong citizens such as Jimmy Lai, Nathan Law, and Martin Lee.

China eventually imposed its draconian "National Security Law" on Hong Kong, expanding the CCP's powers to crush civil liberties in the name of national security. Amid suppressions of freedoms, massive manhunts, and rampant arrests of protesters, the independent voices of seven million people fell silent.

I decided that I wouldn't give an inch in my upcoming *2020 Hong Kong Policy Act Report*. I resolved to let the truth speak for itself. I decertified Hong Kong's "high degree of autonomy," transforming the way the United States related to Hong Kong diplomatically and economically. Given the torrent of abuses, I figured that I would have broad support from the State Department's public servants. I was wrong. I faced unprecedented, coordinated resistance from within the department, particularly from the lawyers. I knew that my refusal to certify would complicate business with Hong Kong. But we had to tell the truth to the American people, and build policies rooted in facts. And again, what good does it serve to implement standards if they aren't upheld?

The bombshell report came out on May 28, 2020. I stated up front that "in last year's report, I asserted that Hong Kong maintained 'a sufficient—although diminished—degree of autonomy' . . . After careful consideration, as required by section 301 of the Hong Kong Policy Act, I can no longer certify that Hong Kong continues to warrant such treatment." This was the most consequential statement I made while at the State Department regarding the CCP and Hong Kong. By law, the entire US government now had to act accordingly and revoke all the special treatments for Hong Kong, codified by a dozen or so bilateral agreements and treaties. My Hong Kong decertification received instant, overwhelming support from all parts of the American political landscape. President Trump also embraced my decertification. On May 29, we stood side by side in the Rose Garden, where the president announced the formal end of US special treatment. We told the world the hard truth: under the CCP, Hong Kong had gone from being a gemstone of freedom and the rule of law to just another Chinese city blighted by Communism.

I also tried hard to cut off the CCP's money laundering in Hong Kong. The London-based bank HSBC, which has operated in China since 1865, handles most of the transactions denominated in US dollars flowing through Hong Kong. As a member of a CCP political advisory body, the Chinese People's Political Consultative Conference, HSBC's former Asia-Pacific CEO, Peter Wong, has been a complete tool of Xi Jinping. In 2020, for example, he supported the National Security Law that Beijing invoked to crush freedom in Hong Kong. Working with the National Security Council, I made the case that we should shut down HSBC's ability to move dollars through Hong Kong because it was no longer independent. It was clear to me and others on my team that the bank had become just another subsidiary of the CCP. This move would have put Beijing under enormous stress and raised its cost of capital significantly. I was making headway, but hell hath no fury like a Wall Street banker scorned. I got calls from nearly all the big banks about what this would do to "the US economy," by which they meant their bonuses. My proposal made its way to the president with support from all other agencies except the Department of the Treasury. In the end, in July 2020, President Trump declined to move forward, believing that even if we were right to staunch the flows of dollars into Hong Kong, the risk of harm that could befall the US economy during the confusion of a pandemic was simply too great.

Hong Kong remains yet another area of unfinished business. The failure to do more to protect freedom for the people of Hong Kong remains among my most bitter memories.

OUR TAIWAN POLICY BREAKS THE STATUS QUO

Another policy area I wanted to shake up was Taiwan, a redoubt of independence on the doorstep of an imperialist bully, and the home of freedom fighters who fled from the Communist mainland in 1949. Its status as a literal island of democracy has made it a dear friend of the United States. Xi longs to crush Taiwan because it disproves the lie that the Chinese people can flourish only under a Marxist-Leninist dictatorship and "socialism with Chinese characteristics." Taiwan's economy and its democracy—aided by a rambunctious group of faith leaders—are models to the world. Xi cannot sustain his power narrative so long as Taiwan exists apart from the People's Republic of China.

Taiwan had been a major focus of President Nixon, and it dominated one of his debates with John F. Kennedy during the presidential race of 1960. The two candidates debated, quite articulately, the status of two small Taiwanese islands, Quemoy and Matsu. But our Taiwan policy went awry not long after the 1972 reopening with China, when Secretary of State Henry Kissinger made the fateful decision to adopt the "One China Policy." It said that the United States would honor the People's Republic of China's claim as the only nation that could be known as "China." This left Taiwan in an agonizing limbo. It increased the threat of the CCP's subjugation of the Taiwanese people.

President Trump began our relationship with the Taiwanese by taking a phone call from Taiwanese president Tsai Ing-wen during the transition and then tweeting about it. This was so far out of bounds from foreign policy orthodoxy that not only was the CCP upset but so was every career East Asia diplomat and lefty think tank in town. Ian Bremmer, considered a dean of the foreign policy talking heads, tweeted, "It's almost as if Trump was looking to kick off China relations as badly as possible." The president didn't care what people like Bremmer thought, and tweeted later, "Interesting how the U.S. sells Taiwan billions of dollars of military equipment but I should not accept a congratulatory call." That engagement set a foundation upon which our diplomacy to confront China over Taiwan could be built.

Soon after I came to the State Department, I realized that the diplomatic establishment's reflexive response to that episode was pretty characteristic of its response to most of our China policies. America's engagement with China had previously been predicated on not angering the CCP. The slightest deviation from what the CCP wanted was bound to produce a reaction that resembled that of a toddler who didn't get his juice and nap that afternoon. Taiwan especially gave them the vapors. There was not a single meeting or phone call with CCP officials that didn't begin with a near-tirade regarding Taiwan as an "internal matter for the Chinese people." Threatening, blustering, and massively overreacting to the slightest support for Taiwan became both annoying and telling about the level of CCP paranoia.

This infuriated me, because the United States should set policy based on the merits, not based on how it will make some stodgy tyrants feel.

I directed my team to reevaluate our Taiwan policy and think creatively about how to engage the people and government of Taiwan within the existing policy frameworks. Among other things, given the importance of Taiwan's semiconductor sector and the rest of its tech industry, I endeavored to develop our economic relationship. I dispatched Keith Krach to Taiwan in September 2020 to attend the memorial service of the father of Taiwan's democracy, Lee Teng-hui. With that trip, Keith became the highest-ranking State Department official ever to visit Taiwan while in office. The Chinese flew an armada of warplanes into the Taiwan Strait to welcome him. But we weren't afraid. Keith went back again in November.

One of the silliest things we had at State was the so-called Taiwan Contact Guidelines, which regulate everything from which doors Taiwanese officials could use to enter federal buildings, to which Taiwanese officials we should shake hands with at events, to which rank of officials could or could not visit Taiwan, and more. I asked the bureaucrats why we still needed these guidelines. They said we had to maintain a smooth relationship with China. I said we already had a law—the 1979 Taiwan Relations Act—stating that all our relationships with Taiwan are unofficial. Why do we need an official contact guideline regulating our unofficial behaviors?

The lawyers could not come up with a good answer, so I decided to scrub the Taiwan Contact Guidelines altogether, to the chagrin of many career staffers. I made the cancellation announcement on January 9, 2021, just days before the change of administrations. I even approved an official statement that said, "The U.S.-Taiwan relationship need not, and should not, be shackled by self-imposed restrictions of our permanent bureaucracy." It made a lot of our diplomats uncomfortable—or even mad—but I wanted to send a message about the danger of letting bureaucratic inertia sustain meaningless policies. It was also time to right a historic wrong. Minutes after my announcement, Taiwan's top representative to the United States, Bi-khim Hsiao, tweeted: "Decades of discrimination, removed. A huge day in our bilateral relationship. I will cherish every opportunity." What I didn't know that day was something Miles Yu told me after I left office. He remembered that when he informed a senior Taiwanese official in Washington of my decision minutes before my announcement went live, the gentleman on the other end of the phone call immediately burst into sobbing cries of joy, relief, and hope. Much like our recognition of the basic rights of Israeli Jews living in Judea and Samaria, ending the second-class-citizen status of Taiwanese diplomats was deeply personal, wonderfully emotional, and wholly beneficial to America.

Other China-focused actions likewise continued to push the envelope. State and DOD carefully planned and coordinated overflight and naval missions in the region to demonstrate we would protect international boundaries. Over the course of just the last three years of our administration, we provided $15 billion worth of arms to Taiwan, dwarfing the Obama administration's $14 billion worth in eight years. Much of this included the weapons Taiwan would desperately need in the event of a Chinese invasion of Taiwan. The 2020 sale of 66 F-16s was very likely the largest arms sale the United States had made to Taiwan in a generation. In October 2020, we concluded a $1.8 billion arms sale that included 11 mobile artillery rockets and 135 Standoff Land Attack Missile–Expanded Response missiles. We also developed plans to sell MQ-9 Reaper drones and Harpoon missiles—the latter weapon a critical tool for thwarting Chinese ships.

The Trump administration gave the Taiwanese people what they needed to protect their freedom. When the CCP assault on Taiwan comes—and it will come—history will reveal that we equipped our friend. These days, I am on record saying that the United States should grant full diplomatic recognition to Taiwan. The free people of that island deserve it.

The CCP's seizure of Hong Kong and its lust to conquer Taiwan is definitive proof that the party seeks to turn free nations into vassals. This will not happen, in part because of the work we began in the Trump administration. But even more so, it will not happen because, as an old quote ascribed to Winston Churchill goes, "America will always do the right thing after all other possibilities have been exhausted."

The democratic world tried to treat China with welcoming acceptance. China reciprocated with nothing but aggression, chauvinism, and disrespect. Now that we've exhausted the possibilities of a China made peaceful through engagement, we must keep telling hard truths about the CCP and take the right actions to stop it.

CHAPTER II

LEADERS ALWAYS TAKE
INCOMING—DEAL WITH IT

L IFE IS'NT FAIR."
    That's according to a block-letter crayon drawing that hung on
my office wall at the State Department, complete with the apostrophe in
the wrong place. I made the three-color picture when I was seven, which
means either that I was wise beyond my years or that my parents had just
grounded me.

I often stared at that old drawing inside my State Department working office when the reality of the world as it was smashed into my ideas
of how it should be. That drawing also reminded me how to deal with
the haters. Although criticism of public officials ranges from the rash
and ridiculous to the fair and useful, I've learned that there are right and
wrong ways to handle all of it. The incoming fire will come, whether fairly
deserved or not. Learn to deal with it.

I try to draw on my faith whenever the knives come out. The book of
Isaiah teaches: "'No weapon forged against you will prevail, and you will
refute every tongue that accuses you. This is the heritage of the servants
of the Lord and this is their vindication from me,' declares the Lord."
In other words, persevere. Deal with it. Another inspirational verse is
2 Timothy 2:24–25: "And the Lord's servant must not be quarrelsome;
but must be kind to everyone, able to teach, not resentful. Opponents
must be gently instructed, in the hope that God will grant them repen-
tance leading them to a knowledge of the truth." I didn't always succeed,
but I did try to "be kind."

A good example: Each year since 1978, the Kennedy Center Honors has celebrated American artists who have achieved legendary status. As part of this tradition, the State Department hosts a dinner for the honorees the night before the program. The use of federal properties (i.e., your tax dollars) reduces costs significantly for the Kennedy Center (not that this temple of American arts is on a soup kitchen's budget, but I digress). The awards usually go to God-gifted artists of incredible talent who have brought value to the lives of people all around the world. My wife and I love and have supported the arts throughout our lives. Susan, who has a background in musical theater, worked on a project called Arts in Schools to give every child in Wichita a chance to be enriched through art.

Most of the attendees at the Honors Night dinner are bigwigs in the entertainment industry—the heart of the progressive beast. It should come as no surprise that many of them hate conservative Republicans. Consequently, people on the right can be forgiven for declining to participate in this high-society, virtue-signaling affair. That decision is especially justifiable due to the special animus that the Left had for the Trump administration. I skipped the dinner my first year as secretary, and President Trump wisely chose not to attend the performance at the Kennedy Center, which is part of the weekend's festivities. The night we attended the gala in 2019, I reminded Susan of a great line from *Charlie Wilson's War*, which is one of our favorite films. When the Speaker of the House asks Congressman Wilson to serve on the Ethics Committee, Wilson tells a young aide, "You know I'm on the other side of that issue." The aide says that the Speaker will give Congressman Wilson whatever he wants. Wilson replies, "I'd like to be on the Board of the Kennedy Center. It's a great place to take a date, and I can never afford the tickets." That scene pretty much sums up Honors Night.

The Kennedy Center's leadership wanted to stick to tradition and hold the 2019 dinner at the State Department. I was considering just the opposite: preventing the awards from being held on federal property. But there is bipartisan commitment to this project, and I had priorities much higher than picking this fight. Besides, David Rubenstein lobbied me hard. He's a most decent and learned man and a true philanthropic human being. Deborah Rutter, president of the Kennedy Center, also appealed to me. After some marital debate, Susan and I decided we would do the right thing, walk into the belly of the beast, and host the dinner. In retrospect, it is a fight worth having until such time as the program honors talent without all the rainbow flag preening.

That December evening, with my tuxedo on, we stood for a receiving line to greet everyone who came to the State Department's magisterial eighth floor. Celebrities came out in droves to honor the talented artists being recognized that night, including the actress Sally Field and the musical group Earth, Wind & Fire. Although I shook the hands of very few Trump voters, our guests were generally pleasant, thanking Susan and me for our service. My only other duty that night was to give brief remarks. My role was simple: thank people for coming and keep the rest of my remarks light and funny. My idea was to borrow a lyric or tagline from every artist being honored. For Earth, Wind & Fire, for example, I quoted the line "Do you remember, the twenty-first night of September." I'll admit that I'm not a professional comedian, but it was good enough for my dinner-hosting responsibilities.

For Linda Ronstadt, one of the evening's honorees, I referenced her song "When Will I Be Loved?" I said that I've traveled around the world, and I'm still wondering when I'll be loved. It brought modest laughter. My audience was being polite.

Ronstadt took my lame joke as her cue to come to the podium and say something to the effect of, "You'll be loved when you stop enabling Trump." It got a few cheers, but it mostly generated pained expressions and silence. After the dinner, Rutter and Rubenstein apologized profusely. Susan and I said that they weren't responsible for Ronstadt's boorish behavior. As we headed downstairs, Susan preempted my thinking by saying, "Taking the high road can be a real b——."

By Monday morning, the media, always on the lookout to stoke pointless controversy, was running headlines like "Linda Ronstadt's Delicious Takedown of Mike Pompeo." But I wasn't going to let her or her silly musings knock me off course. If I had let the haters get to me, I never could have served Trump or the America First agenda. Leaders always take incoming. I just had to deal with it.

Linda, I still love your music and appreciate your input!

TAKING INCOMING FIRE COMES WITH
ANY LEADERSHIP ROLE

One of the most crucial tests of leadership is how you respond to criticism. There are two kinds of criticism. The first is well-intentioned correction from people who have your back. By surrounding myself with people such as Ulrich Brechbühl, Brian Bulatao, David Hale, Lisa Kenna, and Mary Kissel, I had trusted advisors who helped me see our errors and how to correct course. It's never easy to admit blunders or failures, whether in government, an organization, a marriage, or any other endeavor. But you are a fool and unfit for leadership if you refuse to let new facts change your thinking. Often, a subordinate's necessary but unpleasant duty is to tell a boss about a mistake. As we have done for forty years now, Brian, Ulrich, and I would shout at each other in my office over a decision point. I may not have liked what they said, but if they had the gumption to challenge me, I knew I had to consider their views. As the book of Proverbs says, "Plans fail for lack of counsel, but with many advisers they succeed."

But much of the criticism public figures receive stems from a less noble objective. Sometimes it involves purported friends or allies looking to make themselves more important or more powerful at your expense. More often, the haters simply don't share your values. They'll say anything, sometimes in hopes of getting a political scalp. We dealt all the time in the administration with nasty reporters who trampled on facts. The correct response to this kind of harassment is to grow thicker skin, step up your game, and keep winning for America.

If you can't endure the criticism that comes with any leadership position, then you shouldn't be leading. That's especially true in America, where we have freedom of speech and a habit of using it. I expected criticism from fellow citizens who didn't vote for President Trump. And it didn't bother me that a free press would try to hold us accountable for our decisions. What did bother me was the extent to which our words and deeds were maligned and twisted. This type of journalism may generate hits on a webpage, but it is completely irresponsible. I almost feel bad for modern journalists. More than ever, the pressure to produce more clicks than the next reporter causes journalists to adopt the tongue-in-cheek adage "Never let the truth get in the way of a good story."

It was great for me and for America that I had a boss who could not have been less prepared to bend to what the media thought. Was President Trump always hungry for good publicity? Of course. Did he carry out American foreign policy according to what the media wanted? Absolutely not. One of the reasons he and I worked together so well was that we were almost totally insensitive to the demands of disingenuous Democrats and the legacy media. Our America First foreign policy would not have existed had we capitulated to criticism from reporters, foreign policy writers, and even many fellow Republicans. Had we bowed to what the "intellectuals" wanted, for example, America would have terminated its vital relationship with Saudi Arabia in the wake of the Khashoggi murder. America would have remained on a course to become a junior partner to the CCP. Our NATO allies would have kept skating by without paying their fair share. Iran would have been free to kill and maim without repercussion. And even if we had deferred to our critics, we still would not have enjoyed one shred of goodwill in the press from them. Serving the American people meant running the gauntlet of tweets and talking heads. We took a few hits. But we never let the incoming fire knock us down.

THEY TRIED TO DRIVE WEDGES. I NEVER TOOK THE BAIT.

My beefs with how the media conducted itself in the Trump administration are many, but let's start with how the foreign policy press tried to drive a wedge between President Trump and me. I don't think that they cared about analyzing how we might be thinking differently about one issue or another. They wanted a catfight between the president and his secretary of state or the White House and the State Department. Not only do such fights sell ads and subscriptions but they make it harder to execute the president's mission. Former secretary of state James Baker warned me about public dissonance between a president and the secretary of state in our meeting shortly before I assumed his old job: "If world leaders so much as sniff a gap between you and your boss, you're nothing more than a man on vacation."

My dad, Wayne Pompeo, died on April 30, 2020, in the middle of the COVID-19 pandemic. As thousands of Americans have sadly experienced, I was unable to attend his funeral due to lockdowns. As I wrote at the time, my dad taught me about hard work, how to throw a curveball, and to compete in everything I did.
(Courtesy of the Pompeo family)

President Trump surprised and entertained the crowd at Osan Air Force Base, outside of Seoul, South Korea, on June 30, 2019, by calling to the podium "Beauty and the Beast" (Ivanka and me). It's up to you to guess which of us is which.
(Official White House Photo by Shealah Craighead)

The friends we pray for and don't deserve. Brian Bulatao, Ulrich Brech-bühl, and I have been best friends for forty years. Having met during our first days at West Point, we served shoulder to shoulder in the Army, and founded and ran businesses together. When I was director of the CIA, Brian served the organization as COO; he later led the State Department in the same role. We were joined at State by Ulrich, who served as counselor. Class of '86, Courage Never Quits.

(Courtesy of the Pompeo family)

I had no better partner in the world than Yossi Cohen, the director of the Mossad. Here's my good friend and me at the White House on September 15, 2020, following the signing of the Abraham Accords. This photo is the Iranian regime's worst nightmare.

(Courtesy of the White House)

A familiar walk, but one I never took for granted. *(Official White House Photo by Shealah Craighead)*

Prime Minister Kyriakos Mitsotakis of Greece and me reviewing a US Navy combat craft medium special operations boat in Crete. We were building a strategic relationship between our two nations—before enjoying some baklava. *(Official State Department Photo by Ronny Przysucha)*

His All-Holiness Bartholomew I of Constantinople is the spiritual leader of Eastern Orthodox Christians worldwide. A man of great faith, he demonstrated moral courage under enormous pressure from the Turkish and Russian governments. On my travels, I endeavored to meet with leaders of all faiths, as history shows us the peace and good things that their spiritual leadership produces for humanity.
(Official State Department Photo by Ronny Przysucha)

We did so much good work with the Poles, who celebrated the 100th anniversary of regaining their independence in 2018. It was at a conference on Middle East peace and security in Warsaw that we realized that something like the Abraham Accords could be possible. On this trip in 2020, I met with Prime Minister Morawiecki. I also signed an enhanced defense cooperation agreement.
(Official State Department Photo by Ronny Przysucha)

Although time constraints often did not permit it, I loved any chance to meet with ordinary citizens of the countries we visited. Here I am greeting Czech friends at the memorial to American soldiers who liberated the town of Pilsen in World War II. My presence often surprised local populations; their comments often surprised us all.

(Official State Department Photo by Ronny Przysucha)

We wrestled with national security threats as a team in the White House Situation Room. Never for a minute did I forget the history of that place and the duty that accompanied the privilege to serve.

(Official White House Photo by Shealah Craighead)

Having a personal security detail meant agents were around for everything, from meetings at the White House to trips to the DMV and the grocery store. Here, on a sunny Saturday in May 2020, my detail shows off the Pompeo family's new golden retriever puppy, General Hugh Mercer, "Mercy." She used to wait in the doorway when her favorite agents came on shift.
(*Courtesy of the Pompeo family*)

I was responsible for the opening prayer of our Cabinet meeting on August 16, 2018, and chose to read the Cadet Prayer from my well-worn US Military Academy Bugle Notes.
(*Courtesy of Oliver Contreras/UPI*)

Metropolitan Epiphanius of Kyiv and All Ukraine, the primate of the Orthodox Church of Ukraine; Ukrainian foreign minister Vadym Prystaiko; and I honored the memories of those lives lost in the Donbas region due to Russian aggression.

(Official State Department Photo by Ronny Przysucha)

President Trump was kind enough to invite the Wichita State University men's basketball team, coaches, and staff into the Oval Office to meet him. A memory for these young men that will last a lifetime.

(Courtesy of the White House)

It was a high honor for me as I served as director of the Central Intelligence Agency to meet the namesake of the Agency's headquarters, George H. W. Bush. Here we are on September 15, 2017, in Kennebunkport, Maine. (*Courtesy of the Pompeo family*)

Here Dr. Walters and the Operational Medicine Team are Wuhan-bound to help repatriate American citizens. Besides assisting in the heroic repatriation effort, the State Department medical team was indefatigable in equipping US embassy medical units around the world during COVID-19, all while handling business as usual. (*Courtesy of Dr. Will Walters/the Pompeo family*)

As a congressman, CIA director, and secretary of state, I wanted formal and informal channels to hear from staff. I took any question on any topic at "Meet with Mike" events at CIA and State. (*Official State Department Photo by Michael Gross*)

I loved every chance I got to thank those wearing the uniform. Here I am saying hello to American warfighters in Grafenwöhr, Germany, the same base where I was once posted as a young second lieutenant.
(*Official State Department Photo by Ronny Przysucha*)

Susan and I loved hosting the annual Unaccompanied Families Holiday Party for children who had a parent serving overseas unaccompanied. The afternoons were always full of activity, food stations, and fun. Here we are with all the kids who could stand still long enough for a quick photo!
(*Official State Department Photo by Freddie Everett*)

It broke my heart to see how the Maduro regime had led the Venezuelan people into total misery. In April 2019, Colombia's president Ivan Duque and I visited a reception center for refugees. The simple act of showing up was always a powerful statement from America's top diplomat. *(Courtesy of Kim Breier)*

Nick took the podium to say a few words to the team during Family Day at the CIA. Behind him are Susan and me, Gina Haspel, and Brian Bulatao. With them, we did great things for America.
(Courtesy of the CIA)

Susan and I attended both state dinners hosted by President Trump and the First Lady. The first dinner, on April 24, 2018, honored French president Emmanuel Macron and first lady Brigitte Macron. Here we are attending the second state dinner, on September 20, 2019, honoring Australian prime minister Scott Morrison and his wife, Jenny. Susan is looking her usual gorgeous self (and I guess I cleaned up OK, too).

(Courtesy of the Pompeo family)

I've always called Susan my "force multiplier," and it was never more evident than when she traveled with me. Her work on the ground included meetings with our embassy staff family members, the medical unit, the security team, and the CLO (community liaison officer), plus tours of housing and schools.

(Official State Department Photo by Ronny Przysucha)

On a visit to France to commemorate the 100th anniversary of the end of World War I, I also had the chance to pay respects to living heroes—soldiers and sailors who changed the world as liberators during World War II. Suresnes American Cemetery, France.
(Official State Department Photo by Ronny Przysucha)

The supreme leader of North Korea, Kim Jong Un, and I walk into a meeting, October 7, 2018. Kim was deeply curious about the world outside the Hermit Kingdom.
(Official State Department Photo by Ronny Przysucha)

Joining President Trump and Vietnamese prime minister Nguyen Xuan Phuc for a working lunch in Hanoi. As with every movement I made (and still make), I'm flanked by Diplomatic Security agents. Not pictured is the team of advance agents who inspect every site for potential threats. Diplomatic Security personnel also guard embassies and diplomatic families around the world, working closely with Marines assigned to our embassies and local law enforcement and security teams. DS is tasked to operate in a nonpartisan, 100 percent confidential manner. They perform in such a way as to minimize inconvenience to the protectees, all while keeping their safety paramount. At both the CIA and State Department, I have had incredible detail leads and agents that my family and I will never forget. Hats off to Matt Baker, Lon Fairchild, Roy Stillman, Nick Masonis, and many more.
(*Official State Department Photo by Ronny Przysucha*)

Whenever time allowed even a few minutes, I wanted to meet with our embassy staff and families to thank them, take questions, and snap photos. Visiting with our embassy kids was always the most fun part.
(*Official State Department Photo by Ronny Przysucha*)

My mom, Dorothy Mercer Pompeo, was one of ten children born to Earl and Grace Mercer. Earl and Grace were hardworking, community-minded Kansans. Earl was the sheriff and owned Mercer's Pool Hall, a joint known for its chili and cold beer. Grace was a Republican precinct chairwoman. She volunteered and worked, even while mothering her brood. My mother reflected the hard work, commitment to parenthood, and family values that she lived by growing up, and raised me and my siblings the same way. Whether planning our next trip to see family in Kansas, packing us in the car to a political event, making sure we read books throughout our summer vacation, or attending one of our school programs, she was a huge influence on why I hold dear all that I do. The values I live by, the importance I place on family and education, and the pull I feel toward service stem so much from her. My mom also made the world's best fudge, hands down.

(Courtesy of the Pompeo family)

I became the first secretary of state ever to pray with an Israeli prime minister at the Western Wall in Jerusalem. Here I am with Prime Minister Benjamin Netanyahu. (*Official State Department Photo by Ronny Przysucha*)

A beautiful nighttime shot from the cockpit of our helicopter as we approach Baghdad, Iraq (it was too dangerous to drive in from the airport). I made an emergency trip there on May 7, 2019, to meet with Iraqi president Barham Salih and Iraqi prime minister Adel Abdul-Mahdi and express my displeasure at how Iraq had become a permissive environment for Iran's malign activity targeting Americans. (*Official State Department Photo by Ronny Przysucha*)

US ambassador to Vietnam Dan Kritenbrink and I walk the bustling streets of Hanoi, July 8, 2018.
(*Official State Department Photo by Ronny Przysucha*)

I made several trips to Afghanistan as CIA director and as secretary of state, always meeting with our men and women in uniform. At the top of my priority list on the Afghanistan file was ensuring that we would honor two decades of American sacrifices in that war-torn land, and we did.
(*Official State Department Photo by Ronny Przysucha*)

The media poured massive effort into trying to create division between the president and me.

In January 2018, as CIA director, I went on *Fox News Sunday* with Chris Wallace. He spent the first half of the interview questioning the president's mental fitness. He was trying to get me to trash President Trump:

> WALLACE: The CIA does psychological profiles of world leaders routinely. What would you say about a world leader who refers to himself as a very stable genius?"
>
> POMPEO: Chris, I'm not going to dignify that question with a response.

Another case in point was Andrea Mitchell of MSNBC. In the days after the Soleimani strike, President Trump had said that in response to Iran's retaliatory strike, the United States could attack Iranian cultural sites. I had gone on TV the previous Sunday and said that anything we did would be completely lawful. Nevertheless, that provided an opportunity for Andrea to ignore the substance of the issue and bait me to criticize my boss:

> MITCHELL: Mr. Secretary, thank you very much. A question about the issue of cultural sites, because the president said on Air Force One coming back, after you had been on the Sunday talk shows, that "they're allowed to kill our people. They're allowed to torture and maim our people. They're allowed to use roadside bombs and blow up our people. And we're not allowed to touch their cultural sites. It doesn't work that way."
>
> Defense Secretary Esper has made it clear that he would not follow an order to hit a cultural site [because that] would be a war crime. I'm wondering whether you would also push back in your advice or in your role. And secondly—
>
> POMPEO: You're not really wondering, Andrea. You're not really wondering.
>
> MITCHELL: Well, the president is saying this repeatedly—

POMPEO: I was unambiguous on Sunday. It is completely
consistent with what the president has said.

MITCHELL: No, but the president has—

POMPEO: We will take—every action we take will be consistent
with the international rule of law. And you—the American people
can rest assured that that's the case.

MITCHELL: But are cultural sites ruled out, sir?

POMPEO: Let me tell you who's done damage to the Persian culture.
It's not the United States of America; it's the ayatollah. If you want
to look at who has denied religious freedom, if you want to know
who has denied—the Persian culture is rich and steeped in history
and intellect, and they've denied the capacity for that culture to
continue. If you go back and look at the holidays around Cyrus and
Nowruz, they've not permitted people to celebrate. They've not
allowed people that they've killed—that Qasem Soleimani killed—
they've not allowed them to go mourn their family members. The
real risk to Persian culture does not come from the United States of
America.

See what's going on here? She wanted me to do what Secretary Esper
had done: contradict the president. Her question was childish and petulant. Most importantly, it demonstrated that she wasn't really interested
in the welfare of Iranian cultural sites. She was simply playing the DC
progressive game so that she could go to cocktail parties and croak with
her peers in the media elite that she had tried to embarrass the president
and me. I refused to give an inch, even in the face of incoming fire.

Another thing that drove me up a wall and was deeply unfair to all
involved was the prevalence of stories built on anonymous leaks. Many
of the stories targeting me and Susan came from information illegally
divulged by career staff in the State Department's Office of Protocol.
State Department staffers with detailed knowledge of social gatherings,
diplomatic choreography, and gifts were working against their boss, and
reporters were happy to indulge this anti-American behavior in the name
of "the truth." That's why the world was treated to so many anonymously
sourced stories on things such as holiday parties, Susan's travel abroad,

and even, after I left office, the whereabouts of a bottle of Japanese whiskey that I had been gifted but never saw in my life.

That reporters would indulge the petty gossipers in Protocol—who clearly need more work to do—with stories that harmed American diplomacy and my family is beyond shameful. The fact that the media runs with so many stories built on anonymous sources has undoubtedly injected tons of lies into the American information ecosystem. It is totally lost on the media that relying on anonymous sourcing completely undermines their purported mission of getting the story right. The condition of anonymity allows bad actors to publicize false information with no prospect of repercussions. At this point, the Fourth Estate's claim to being defenders of democracy is just a cover for generating clickbait and advancing a political agenda.

Knowing the press's dishonesty, I also knew not to invite the wolves into my house if I could help it, even the "most respected" names. One day, I was handed a note while in the White House Situation Room. The president wanted to speak with me immediately. I walked out and got on the phone.

"Mr. President, I'm in the building and can be upstairs in two minutes to see you."

"No need to come up. Call Bob Woodward. He wants to speak with you."

"Mr. President, I have no reason to speak with Bob Woodward. I've never met him."

"No, call him right now! He's writing a book and he needs to speak with you. Here is his cell phone number."

Following orders, I dialed the number provided. Woodward answered. I said that the president had asked me to call him and meet with him. I told him I was very busy but could meet him very early the next morning. I offered the ungodly early start time in hopes of decreasing the chances he would say yes. To his credit, he accepted the invitation and was live and in person in my office early the next day.

He led off by asking to record the interview, as he was "getting older" and his note-taking skills weren't so good.

"No."

"How long do I have with you?"

"You have fifteen minutes and we've already used two of them."

"The president gave me a couple of hours and you're only the secretary of state."

"You now have twelve minutes."

Some twelve or so minutes later he departed. I did my best comply with the president's direction, but I didn't provide anything of value to a reporter who was writing a book with the singular purpose of destroying all that I was working to achieve. Moreover, he used the risk that someone would have dished on me to try and coerce me to dish on others. Sick. I am confident that most days Woodward finds many folks more willing to cooperate than I was.

DENYING THE PRESS MY SCALP

The media also loves to speculate on resignations. Usually this is little more than rumormongering. I can't tell you how many times the public affairs offices at CIA or State got inquiries to the effect of "We understand the Director is considering resigning . . ." or "We are hearing that the secretary has plans to leave the administration . . ." Sometimes they upped the ante, with a question that demonstrated their anti-Trump biases. After some flareup involving the Russia Hoax or President Trump's professing his "love" for Kim Jong Un, for example, reporters would hound every national security official with a version of the same question: "How can you stay with this president?"

I tried to separate the signal from the noise. If the noise was the president saying that he wrote "love letters" to Chairman Kim, the signal was the toughest sanctions ever placed on North Korea. If the noise was "Trump is a Russian asset," the signal was establishing deterrence against Vladimir Putin's designs on Ukraine and the rest of Europe. If the noise was mocking the Middle East peace efforts as a quest for the "deal of the century," the signal was building trust with Middle East leaders sufficient to create the Abraham Accords. The list is longer, but as I dealt with or simply ignored the noise, I worked the signal and was humbled to be part of an administration that was avoiding war and creating peace by putting America first.

Some people on the president's team weren't up for this. They were worried that working for Trump would cause their exile from the clubby world of the foreign policy establishment. Their response was to put themselves ahead of the country. Some resigned to protect their ability to join lucrative boards. Others made a living out of leaking to the press about how much they disagreed with the president. (Memo to John Bolton: I'm talking about you.) They knew nothing about leadership in the face of criticism.

To this day, multiple outlets still have stories posted that claim Secretary Mnuchin and I discussed using the Twenty-Fifth Amendment to remove President Trump from office following the mayhem at the Capitol on January 6, 2021. They of course relied entirely on anonymous sources—always a sign of deceit and misinformation. The only thing true about these stories is that Secretary Mnuchin and I talked after January 6, but it was about how to finish strong in the two weeks we had left. By this time, I was a veteran of wild speculation in the press about invocations of the Twenty-Fifth Amendment. Nikki Haley and I had to mow down such claims from the irresponsible Jim Acosta of CNN at the UN General Assembly in 2018. Bolton claims in his book that he and I had a secret pact stipulating that if President Trump met with Iranian foreign minister Zarif, we would resign together. There is also reporting that John Kelly, Mnuchin, and I had a similar arrangement that if one of us got fired, the others would leave, too. I often read much of the press in utter awe of its recklessness, but these statements take the cake. I can't speak for other cabinet members, but I never had any such discussions.

Even people who should have been friendly to the Trump administration got in on the act. A good example is Bill Kristol, a once rational and thoughtful man who literally lost his mind during the Trump years. In 2019, he tweeted, "On Air Force Two on the way to Turkey, did Pence discuss the 25th amendment with Pompeo?" Sorry, Bill, I never seriously discussed the Twenty-Fifth Amendment with him or any other official. I never even joked about it. Now that you've beclowned yourself within the conservative movement, maybe there's still a place for you with your friends at the Lincoln Project. And take Jennifer Rubin with you.

My only regret about the time I put in over four years is that I didn't have long enough in either role. Shortly after becoming prime minister, Winston Churchill remarked, "I felt as if I were walking with destiny, and that all my past life had been but a preparation for this hour and for this trial." I wouldn't put my own life in such grandiose terms, but I believed the same thing about my own experience. My whole life had prepared me for what I did in the administration. It was a grueling test of endurance, but I loved every second of it.

The only talk I ever had with the president about leaving came in 2019—but not because I was really thinking about it. Senator Mitch McConnell had asked me to run for the Senate following the retirement of my friend, Senator Pat Roberts of Kansas. I heard him out: "Only you can win without spending $15 million," he said. "You have 80 percent approval back home, and I know you love the people of Kansas." I was flattered to be asked, but Susan and I knew the Lord had us in the right place at that time. I let him down with a joke: "Mitch, you and I both know that the 'Kansas boy done good with Trump' act ends the second I enter the race. The voters will call me 'the guy who screwed up my kid's passport application.'"

But there was a wrinkle. We both remembered what had happened in 2018, when Kris Kobach won a crowded primary and then let a Democrat become Kansas's governor. At the time Mitch asked me to run, Kansas hadn't elected a Democrat to the Senate since 1932, so it would be a major debacle were one to win. While I had no intention of resigning or running, I agreed that I would "not deny" I was considering running for Senate. This was a favor to McConnell, giving him time to find another candidate capable of winning.

Sometime after that, the president saw me on TV demurring in response to a question about running for the Senate. "Mike," said President Trump, "are you really thinking about taking that shitty job? You'll be junior to Mitt Romney and Rand Paul. You have the best job in the world, you're fourth in line for the presidency, and you work for me!"

I assured the president that I had no intention of leaving and that I was being careful in my public statements to help McConnell and Senate Republicans. He said, "OK, fine, but you're going to have to kill the story before too long." I agreed and later told McConnell that I had to go public, which I did on the *Today Show* on February 21, 2019. Nevertheless, the speculation didn't end until the next year at the candidate filing deadline. In the end, everything turned out well—I stuck around, and the good people of Kansas sent Roger Marshall, a Republican, to the Senate. As much as Susan and I would have loved to represent the people of Kansas, leaving my role as secretary of state was never an option I considered.

FIGHTING THE FAKE NEWS

The Trump-induced media hostility also produced quite a bit of collateral damage for "civilians." At some point during the administration, I was asked to accept an award from the mother of Daniel Pearl, the *Wall Street Journal* reporter who was beheaded in Pakistan by Islamists in 2002. She wanted to thank me and our team at a dinner with an award for the remarkable work our administration had done in getting American hostages released.

About two days before the event, I was informed that the award had been withdrawn. I came to understand that the evening's emcee, a famous journalist named Christiane Amanpour, whom I have still never met and now hope that I never do, said that she would refuse to participate if I was being honored. Her reasoning, in a word, was "Trump." I was deeply hurt for Pearl's mother, who had obviously been put in a bad position. In the moment, I chose not to make a stink. But I also asked my team to draft a letter to Amanpour saying that I had done more for the cause of press freedom in just two years as secretary of state than she had in her entire career and that her effort to silence me that night confirmed she was no more than a hack.

The letter was correct, but in the end, I didn't send it. Escalating the situation would have created an even bigger headache for the Pearl family and tarnished the effort to support serious journalists who risk their lives to bring important stories to the world. Leaders who deal with incoming

fire sometimes must simply take it quietly, to protect innocent bystanders, such as the brave and honorable Pearl family.

Even reporters who were on the US government's payroll couldn't
suppress their anti-Trump venom. One of the most broken institutions
in the entire federal government is the US Agency for Global Media,
the organization that oversees Voice of America (VOA), Radio Free Europe, and other messaging agencies. They were created to help the United
States tell the world that our country is a force for good, one made great
because of respect for freedom and democratic norms. That's what they
used to do. Sadly, they have become captives of the Left. Rather than
promote America, their reports too often denigrate our country, which
means they simply repeat so much of the bile that the rest of the media
spews. When I gave a speech at VOA in the last days of my tenure, several
of the staff protested my talk. Think about that: people who collect a
check from Uncle Sam didn't want the voice of American diplomacy to be
broadcast on VOA. My decision to speak there exposed this internal con-
tradiction, and I regard it as an act of leadership in support of the Trump
administration's efforts to bring sanity to the agency. We tried to right
the ship with Michael Pack, an accomplished documentary filmmaker,
but the Senate took two years to confirm him, so he had only about seven
months on the job before the Biden administration fired him on its first
day. Two days later, they also fired the heads of the various international
broadcasting agencies—highly qualified people such as Steve Yates and
Victoria Coates. I assume that VOA has gone back to sliding into irrel-
evance and leftism at a time when the global battle against Chinese and
Russian disinformation is at a fever pitch.

In my own personal experience, the media's disdain for the Trump
administration reached a crescendo on November 10, 2020—just days
after the election. The hyenas who cover the State Department asked
me if we were "currently preparing to engage with the Biden transition
team." So much important work was still going on, and their entire focus
was on whether I had held a perfunctory twenty-minute meeting with
someone not yet confirmed to anything. I decided to have a bit of fun
and said, "There will be a smooth transition to a second Trump administration." I said it with a smile and more than a touch of "screw you" in

my voice—more than anything, because I wasn't going to play the media's game of trying to drive a wedge between the president and me, even at the end. Moreover, my ensuing words made clear that I was not declaring that President Trump had won: "The world should have every confidence that the transition necessary to make sure that the State Department is functional today, successful today, and successful with the president who's in office on January 20th, a minute after noon, will also be successful." I didn't think much of it until I returned to my office and saw that all the clown shows had made my words the top story. CNN's anchor Brianna Keilar insisted that I was "peddling baseless claims of election fraud." The reality was that there was still ongoing litigation, and the president had every right to ensure that the election had been conducted in a fair and lawful manner.

The other pet peeve question I heard in those last days was something to the effect of "Why, Mr. Secretary, have you not helped Tony Blinken transition?" The truth is that to speak of a true transition is risible, as the Biden team never really left the State Department. The Obama-era Tony Blinken–Wendy Sherman–Victoria Nuland–John Kerry team is once again back running the State Department, and the career staffers who cozied up to Democratic officials during the Obama years had just burrowed in deeper during the Trump administration. As proof of this, ideological fellow travelers had well-prepared memos loaded in the chamber to fire off within hours of our departure. A great example was the *Ethos* statement that hung in the main lobby. You can't get something like that removed on day one without the directives for formal action being prepared ahead of time, including having a piece of crane-like equipment prepositioned to remove the *Ethos* placard from its hanging point below the ceiling.

And just for the record: I ultimately did brief Tony Blinken before he came in. It was a cordial and professional meeting. I told him to keep his eye on the prize: continuing our critical work on China. In keeping with that, I conveyed that the "Quad" arrangement between Australia, India, Japan, and the United States had real buy-in from all parties; it wasn't just America driving the bus. I also encouraged him to build on another successful multilateral initiative—the Abraham Accords. I didn't care, ultimately, if he had to change the name, but there was outstanding opportunity to sustain a major momentum shift in the Middle East. I filled him in on Venezuela, Cuba, and Mexico, as well as, of course, North Korea. He received all this information appreciatively, but for his part, he was most focused on Russia and Afghanistan. Little did he know how crucial those two issue sets would become during his tenure. During the days that followed our initial meeting, I offered to meet again with Secretary Blinken, but he declined. To this day, I work to try to help Secretary Blinken be successful, and he has, in turn, been most respectful of me. He and I share several views on foreign policy and sharply disagree on many others. He and I have worked for two very different presidents.

A major source of the media's ire at the Trump administration came simply from its inability to fathom how the Trump team delivered such good outcomes. So many of their words and attacks were simply noise on the global stage meant for retweets and clicks. The signal—the hard work of defending American freedom and prosperity at home—was for leaders.

TAKING FIRE OVER UKRAINE

But perhaps no saga demanded that we keep leading through the fire like that of the impeachment circus over President Trump's "perfect" phone call with President Volodymyr Zelensky of Ukraine. We know how the story ends: It turns out that Hillary Clinton personally approved of disseminating false information about Trump's connections to Russia to the media and then that made-up information went to the FBI. Efforts at impeachment ensue. The president is dogged by Congress in connection with withholding security assistance to Ukraine unless Zelensky agrees to investigate. It turns out he provided security assistance without an investigation or a promise to investigate. More efforts to impeach ensue. To bring Russia-Ukraine matters forward to today, when we leave office, Vladimir Putin begins the slaughter of innocent Ukrainians on a scale of warfare in Europe we have not seen since World War II.

I've been accused of being an ultrahawk and a warmonger, by members of both parties. But on my watch, no new wars erupted, and peace spread because deterrence works and we led without fear. Our success in war and peace occurred in part because of our ability to ignore the haters and absorb fire from the media-industrial complex. From January 6, 2017, to the day we left, the narrative of an administration kowtowing to Russia persisted, taking the form of criminal investigations, impeachments, and all-out lies flooding American homes. We soldiered on anyway.

Ukraine these days is showing itself to be a model of courage. But it is sadly beset by a culture of corruption in its institutions and businesses, and I worked to tackle this problem with both President Petro Poroshenko and his successor, President Zelensky. Contrast our work on this file with that of the current president. As is now well known, while Joe Biden was vice president, his son Hunter Biden drew a lavish salary from Burisma, a Ukrainian energy company, in exchange for bringing exactly zero energy-industry expertise to the table. What he did have, though, were connections to his father, known among Hunter's associates as "the Big Guy." Reports indicate that Hunter raked in as much as $1 million per year. Maybe, just maybe, he was getting paid to lobby his father on American policy toward Ukraine.

Of course, the "perfect phone call" in part included President Trump wanting to get to the bottom of this potential instance of corruption. The call was, of course, not perfect, but addressing what we all knew was real Ukrainian corruption and asking the Ukrainians to assist in ferreting out what the former vice president and his family might have been up to is well within basic norms of international cooperation.

President Trump, my team, and I were also hearing accusations from various sources that our ambassador to Ukraine, Marie Yovanovitch, was engaged in illicit activities such as personally benefitting from Ukrainian corruption. My team investigated these allegations and found much smoke but no fire, and so could not corroborate these serious claims. We had also heard Yovanovitch was working to undermine various Trump administration policy efforts, and we had only secondhand evidence of her efforts in this regard.

What we did become convinced of was that she was she not working vigorously to deliver on the sitting American president's mission. Not a chance. There was an enormous amount of smoke suggesting fire: As she has now bragged about in her book, she hated Donald Trump. Her team in Ukraine knew it and acted in accordance with their boss's outlook. This we knew. It's worth remembering, of course, that no evidence of any misconduct is required to terminate an ambassador. These important diplomats serve at the pleasure of the president and can be removed from their post for any reason or none at all. This happens all the time. We had plenty of rationale for replacing Yovanovitch with an ambassador in Kyiv who would work for our mission.

As a matter of both professionalism and honoring the American principle of due process, I wanted to give Yovanovitch every opportunity to demonstrate that she was not part of the anti-Trump resistance. Even with allegations of her working against the Trump administration mounting publicly in the spring of 2019, we sought to provide her with both the benefit of the doubt and a chance to demonstrate her willingness to do her duty.

Curiously, Yovanovitch had not publicly defended herself against charges of undermining the administration. My senior team tried to save Yovanovitch by proposing that she issue a simple statement saying that she was proud to be America's ambassador to Ukraine, and that she was dedicated to doing her job as a professional diplomat on behalf of the duly elected president of the United States. This was later reported as demanding a "loyalty test." That's true, insofar as loyalty is defined as loyalty to the American constitutional order, loyalty to your duty as an American ambassador, and a commitment to executing the policies set forth by the president and secretary, as your job always demands. Otherwise, you're on your own mission or working for someone outside your chain of command, as Yovanovitch was clearly doing.

Yovanovitch refused to put out that simple statement. I suspect that she was afraid of losing face with her Foreign Service colleagues after making her antipathy to the administration known behind closed doors. Seeing that Yovanovitch was unwilling to defend herself, and with the president perfectly within his rights to terminate her assignment, it became easy to send her packing from her post.

The media, of course, gave Yovanovitch what she seemed to want: status as a helpless victim of political persecution. Every American should know the truth: She rejected her duty for the sake of media-driven martyrdom and led her team in Ukraine on a mission to resist my leadership as secretary of state. One can call her part of the "deep state" or the "Resistance." Either way, Yovanovitch was the quintessential example of a leftist, progressive, activist Foreign Service officer who behaved in ways that would have made our Founders cry.

In her memoir, she questions whether the State Department would "survive the betrayals of the Pompeo years." I have a question for Yovanovitch and people like her in positions of authority at the State Department: Do you understand who you work for? You serve at the pleasure of the duly elected president of the United States. You are free to resign for whatever reason, including opposition to what the administration stands for, but you are not free to work against your superiors. I have no doubt that the Department of State will survive the "the betrayals of the Pompeo years." The real concern is whether it can survive the resistance inside the institution that undermines our constitutional order. I recall one time, late in the evening, when Brian Bulatao came to see me. He sat down in front of my desk in my back office and asked, "Do you know what's outside that door?" pointing to a door that led to a main hallway. I said, "Yeah, a hallway and an elevator shaft."

"No, that's Fort Apache out there. These people are trying to destroy us," he said, referring the senior Foreign Service management. It was true; the department's so-called leaders acted in wily ways to undermine us.

With the external fire burning hot regarding Russia and the "perfect phone call," our Ukraine challenges did not end with the change of ambassadors. President Trump replaced Yovanovitch with Bill Taylor, a former Army officer and previous ambassador to Ukraine. Bill had two conditions for serving: First, he wanted to continue the Trump administration's policy of providing weapons to Ukraine to deter Putin—a view he knew I shared. He also made clear that he would take the role only so long as American policy continued to strongly support Ukraine. The second was that he told us, I assume with total sincerity, that if we ever abandoned this policy, he would have to resign. In his testimony at the impeachment hearings, he asserted that security assistance to Ukraine was being withheld until Zelensky agreed to investigate the Biden-Burisma connections. If he believed that to be true, why did he stay? Why did he violate his pledge to resign? I think it's because, contrary to what he said in his testimony, he knew we weren't withholding assistance. He knew that the decision about releasing security assistance was a complex matter— one that President Obama had struggled with when he withheld security assistance to Ukraine—and we treaded carefully in making our decisions about it, too. When called to testify, Taylor omitted explaining why he stayed on, even though he believed we were violating one of his conditions for service. Taylor was trying to do good work for America. Unfortunately, he became trapped inside a tale in which he tried to make himself the hero. Representing the president in a foreign country as an ambassador is not a "Choose Your Own Adventure" story.

The Russia-Ukraine mania just would not go away. Two months after Yovanovitch's departure, President Trump was still hot on the case of uprooting corruption in Ukraine when he spoke to President Zelensky on July 25, 2019. For weeks, the media's "Pompeo was on the call" mantra made me chuckle. Yes, I was on the call, just as I was for nearly every call that the president had with his counterparts around the world. This one caused me little heartburn. We knew that the Bidens—both President Biden and Hunter—were knee deep in the mess. Indeed, the witnesses during the impeachment that the media loved, such as George Kent, had been and were very worried about the Biden family's sordid ties to Ukraine. The irony should escape none of us: the Biden family took money from Ukraine under suspicious circumstances and then pushed a false story that our administration was playing foul.

The drama over Ukraine even melted the brains of talented, smart State Department career officers. Mike McKinley was a fine diplomat, having served as America's ambassador to Peru, Colombia, Afghanistan, and Brazil. I brought him on to serve as a senior advisor when I first became secretary, and he proved useful in doing a great deal of blocking and tackling on Afghanistan, Mexico, and Venezuela and on rebuilding morale at the department. But once the Ukraine business started to heat up, McKinley thought that I hadn't done enough to protect Yovanovitch. He and I had several discussions on this matter, some of them intense. He took incoming fire from current and former colleagues who demanded that he resign. He was angry that I didn't issue a public statement of support for Yovanovitch. Such a statement would have been unfair to decent, committed professionals at State who did not share her insubordinate attitude and her resistance to the president's direction. McKinley wasn't living in the real world if he thought that I was going to get crosswise with the president over, ultimately, a single diplomat's reassignment—in the same way that I wasn't going to tear the relationship with Saudi Arabia to shreds over a single unjust murder. Nor did he understand how Yovanovitch's behavior had caused her to achieve what was, I think, her goal: becoming a saint in the cult of victimhood. He didn't appreciate my mission of leading American diplomacy and resigned. Contrary to what he had promised me, he spoke with the press about it. Perhaps, ironically, he is now working for the Cohen Group, an international consulting firm with way too many former Chinese-government personnel on the payroll. Feeding the beast in Beijing is an action worth getting upset about. My refusal to defend a recalcitrant diplomat who failed to do her duty is not.

The fireworks-filled finale of the Ukraine episode came in January 2020, just days before the end of the wasteful impeachment scam in Congress. It involved my fraught relationship with National Public Radio, a media organization subsidized by taxpayers. As a member of Congress, I voted multiple times to defund the Corporation for Public Broadcasting, the parent group of National Public Radio (NPR). I see no reason for the public to fund a left-wing media outlet, especially when there are so many others. I had also helped force NPR to admit they failed to properly disclose taking money from the Ploughshares Fund—a peacenik organization that lobbied hard in support of the Iran deal. I exposed this journalistic conflict of interest surrounding their Iran coverage—and excoriated them further for refusing to allow me on to rebut Representative Adam Schiff's false claims about the Iran deal.

With this tumultuous history as a backdrop, I reluctantly agreed to an interview with NPR's Mary Louise Kelly. She had promised that our conversation would be limited to Iran. Her interview request said, effectively, "This will give you a chance to say your piece, even if it is years later." Yet she performed what I saw as a bait and switch, as her unstated intention was to focus on the Yovanovitch story. From its first minutes, her interview dripped with hate for me. I didn't say anything provocative—the interview generated no real news—but I was furious at her seeming deception.

I departed the set and asked my communications team to have Kelly come to my office. I told her very directly what I thought, using language that my mother would have called inappropriate. She had wasted a chance to inform the American people of our effort to save the lives of Americans, Iranians, and Israelis. She defended her interview by saying that the "Ukraine story" was the most important news facing the American people. I said that very few people in the world could place Ukraine on the map. She kept on, so I had a map of the world brought in that displayed international borders but not the names of countries. I asked her to identify Ukraine. She put a pen mark on Bangladesh. As they used to say on *Get Smart*, "Missed it by *that* much."

NPR decided to put her on its taxpayer-funded airwaves to say that I was a jerk who had mistreated her. It's true that I probably should not have confronted her over the seemingly false pretenses of her hack-job interview, but I couldn't help myself (or at least I didn't) on that day. I should not have given her an inch to let her pretend to be a hero of press freedom. That was a mistake, as was my use of rough language. Sometimes in responding to the incoming, you need to avoid hitting yourself with friendly fire.

CORRECTING THE RECORD ON THE INSPECTOR GENERAL'S FIRING

The media also chased me for phantom ethics violations. It always boggled my mind that ethics lawyers inside government were determined to "major in minors." This observation was reinforced on one of my first days as secretary of state. The "ethics" team—a group of career State Department lawyers—were in my office to get me to sign a required set of ethics pledges. They were nearly identical to statements I had signed at the CIA. We joked that the rules said that if I so much as accepted a free cup of burned coffee from a lady at my church, I was bound to declare the value of the coffee and whether this "gift" complied with federal rules. I understood the intent of these strictures but also saw them as infantile. They too often prohibited important work while permitting actions that clearly were not in America's interest.

The code of ethics also left glaring holes for a leader determined to behave badly. To prove this point, I asked State's ethics lawyers to consider a scenario: I told them that my wife flies to foreign countries to give speeches for a fee of $500,000 each, all of it paid for by foreign governments, with the proceeds going to the "Pompeo Foundation." Some of the people working for the "Pompeo Foundation" might well be current department employees. I needed to know if this whole setup caused any ethical problems for me or the department. In deadpan style, I told them I needed a memorandum from them confirming that this activity was lawful.

The ethics team didn't get it. What I had described was exactly what Secretary Clinton and her husband had done when she sat on the seventh floor. It's hard to imagine a more significant conflict of interest or ethical risk than a secretary of state's spouse sticking a tin cup in front of world leaders while his wife was still in office. When I let them in on my jest, they didn't think it was funny. I told them I didn't think it was funny either. I asked them to produce for me the document that allowed Bill Clinton to take that money for the Clinton Foundation, with which the Clintons paid (or paid off) certain persons to do their bidding. It was from that moment forward that the "ethics" team and the inspector general (IG) declared war on me.

The good news is they were defeated, even with the media in an uproar. I understand and accept why inspectors general exist. As a soldier, I participated in unit inspections conducted by Army and Defense Department IGs. These audit-like inspections aimed to generate constructive feedback for unit commanders and to make sure operations addressing inventory, maintenance, record keeping, and so on were conducted properly and honestly.

Within the federal government, there is now an IG-industrial complex: seventy-four IG offices across all federal agencies. There are so many IGs that there even exists a Council of the Inspectors General on Integrity and Efficiency. (I wonder if CIGIE has its own IG.) For the most part, IGs don't believe they work for the executive branch; they think they exist in a mystical (and unconstitutional) ether between the legislative and executive branches. Our Founders created only three branches of government for a reason. IGs have to work in one of them, and no one believes they are employees of the legislative or judicial branches. In other words, the IG at the department worked for me. An IG can do a lot of good, but we must recognize the office's limits. If a cabinet member breaks the law, the government should prosecute. It makes no sense to have one of the cabinet member's employees conduct a sham investigation and issue a pointless report.

At the CIA, I kept tabs on the IG who was there when I arrived, and he did a wonderful job. He made us better by telling us where to improve. He viewed himself as serving the agency, the president, and America. He often told us about matters we needed to fix. When he needed to speak to me, I made time for him. I responded to his concerns professionally and completely.

It was a different story with Steve Linick, the IG at the Department of State when I arrived. Although he had been put in that position by President Obama in 2013, my intention was to work with him in the same way I had with his counterpart at the CIA. Almost immediately, details of investigations began to leak to the press on matters such as perfectly legal arms deals, my private travel, and the selection of an International Women of Courage Award honoree. Ulrich, Brian, and I sought to train, educate, and inspire Linick, but apparently failed to do so, because my observations made clear to me he used the IG office to coerce State employees into providing documents and testimony. This was all politically motivated, in my view.

Linick also had a pitiful track record in leading his own office. Every year the department surveys its workforce about their experiences. Year after year his team made clear that the IG's office was not a good place to work. Most bureaus that have low ratings see demonstrated improvement over time. Not Linick's—in fact, his bureau was the only one of thirty-eight to see a decline in all three major index categories in 2019:

the Employee Engagement Index; the Global Satisfaction Index; and the Diversity and Inclusion Index.

Beyond his poor leadership skills, Linick's IG Department suffered a series of other failures. From 2019 to 2020, pre-COVID, the number of IG inspections of our overseas facilities—designed to make sure operations are happening effectively and efficiently—declined by 10 percent. Linick was wasting his time on things other than the essential mission of the IG office, which is to identify waste, fraud, and abuse. Additionally, one of the core functions of an IG is to perform the department's annual financial audit. Linick failed to complete the audit of our fiscal year 2019 in a timely manner, for no good reason.

Furthermore, thanks to decisions Linick had ultimately signed off on, the organization experienced a critical and deeply concerning failure that endangered the security of our personnel around the globe. The investigative report into this failing—the details of which are classified—noted that "oversight by the Office of the Inspector General was demonstrably ineffective . . . ultimately placing the Department's information as well as its reputation, human capital, and operations at considerable unnecessary risk." Trust me when I tell you that this was an enormous error that could have had catastrophic consequences for America. As Brian Bulatao told me at the time, "If this happened under my leadership, I would have resigned."

But the straw that really broke the camel's back was Linick's unprincipled behavior surrounding an investigation into leaks from his own office. Instead of following Deputy Secretary John Sullivan's instructions to have CIGIE—a neutral third party—investigate this matter, Linick asked another agency's inspector general—with whom I imagine Linick was chummy—to investigate. As Brian testified to Congress, "Mr. Linick failed to inform the department that he had handpicked a different entity to investigate potential misconduct by his own office and that he had deviated from the clear course agreed upon with department leadership. . . . After consulting with Deputy Secretary Biegun and former Deputy Secretary Sullivan, I can state clearly that we have no recollection at all of Mr. Linick ever having told us that he was going to abandon the agreed referral to CIGIE and instead to handpick his own investigator." The story gets longer and more complicated from here, but suffice it to say that over the course of this investigation Linick engaged in a series of ethical lapses that tainted the investigation and were completely inexcusable for an inspector general.

And so, I recommended to the president that this bad actor be fired. His response was classic: "You're the first guy with balls. I'll do it."

I knew hell would rain down, but I also knew it was the right thing for the State Department and America and would put other IGs on notice that they simply needed to do their jobs. Once the news popped, the media kept screeching that I fired Linick because he was investigating me for some impropriety or another. This was nonsense, and it's worth noting for the record that neither he nor anyone else informed me about his investigations, which, by the way, never found evidence of ethical violations. Indeed, the secretary's and deputy secretary's offices both issued letters making clear that I was never briefed by the deputy secretary, former deputy secretary, executive secretary, or undersecretary for management on any investigation involving allegations of misuse of government resources by me or my wife. Linick—invested with a responsibility and title that demand the highest standards of probity and nonpartisanship— had, in my opinion, failed in his mission and was responsible for leaks that adversely affected my team and our country. I'll take incoming fire for giving him the ax any day.

ETHICS INQUISITIONS

Democrats in Congress and so-called watchdog groups were also determined to discover massive ethics violations by me, my team, and my family.

At one point, the Washington press corps was hot on the trail of a rumor that a government employee had been directed to walk our dog, Sherman. Reporters who may have imagined themselves as the Woodwards and Bernsteins of their generation skipped covering Iranian malfeasance and instead looked into my family's canine practices. Anyone who has dealt with our dog, Sherman, knows we have not trained him well. Walking him requires enormous strength and skill, so I wasn't going to assign a random office worker from the State Department to do it. Second, it never happened. Not once. I have no idea who proffered this story, but this was "investigated" to no effect. Thankfully, Sherman never faced a congressional subpoena.

Another classic was "Uber Eats with Guns"—the words some anonymous and self-pitying Diplomatic Security agent used to characterize my security detail. One weeknight I was getting ready to pick up Chinese food from my favorite place, City Lights. I ordered the food and paid for it by phone. Then I was delayed by business at my office for about ninety minutes. The security team was on the ground in advance at City Lights. The security team's senior leader made the decision to have an officer grab the food and take it to my house rather than have me run by and pick it up. Right decision or not, I didn't direct it. Today I applaud it, as it saved the detail from the expense associated with having to drive me there. The decision doubtlessly saved the taxpayer money and did no harm. In any event, the food was cold but still good. And that Diplomatic Security officer is a great American.

Yet a third "ethics" story is the great chronicle of the Madison Dinner Series, named after Dolly Madison, who regularly convened diplomatic dinners with her husband, Secretary of State James Madison. My goal was to bring together foreign diplomats, business leaders, academics, scholars, and other interesting thought leaders for a two-hour dinner at the State Department a few times per year. You'd have thought I took the Left's last penny, but nobody in the mainstream media ever cried over John Kerry's taxpayer-funded dinners in Paris. To borrow a line from *Pulp Fiction*, I guarantee he wasn't eating "Royales with cheese" (the French version of a McDonald's Quarter Pounder). My dinners were apolitical—ask David Ignatius—and designed to exchange ideas in a casual setting with no audience and no agenda beyond the general purpose of building relationships, improving communications, and bouncing around ideas that might improve our mission. The IG investigated this, too, and found that it was all wholly lawful. I shook my head at so much time and money wasted looking into a practice common throughout American diplomatic history. While the details can't be told here, I can assure you that the Madison Dinners were worthwhile.

In 2016, having just been nominated to be CIA director, I received an email from a former classmate whom I had not seen for thirty years. Pat was in my squad during that first challenging summer at the US Military Academy, when the Army breaks in new cadets with a series of grueling physical challenges at Camp Buckner. They include long marches with an M60 machine gun that weighs more than twenty pounds but feels like two hundred at the end.

My old classmate wrote: "I brag to people I know you but most importantly every time I see you in the news I remember you volunteering to carry the M60 on the finish march/run at the very end of infantry week at Buckner. Your determination to hang in there when we were all exhausted doing those last few miles stuck with me."

I didn't love getting beat up in the press during the Trump administration. I grew a touch weary of fighting off unfounded accusations of corruption, politicization, and bullying, and I was saddened when I had to divert attention time from the mission to respond to the falsehoods. But I soldiered on, just as I had been taught to do years before at West Point. I wasn't going to quit on America. I took the incoming fire, as leaders always must.

CHAPTER 12

DEMAND ACCOUNTABILITY

In the climactic scene of one of my favorite movies, *The Sting*, Paul Newman's character, Henry Gondorff, plots to extract justice on corrupt crime boss Doyle Lonnegan, played by Robert Shaw. Gondorff tells one of his men that they will "give him the shutout." The scheme works, and the look in Lonnegan's eyes at the exact second he realizes he had been "shut out" tells you that he knew he was in major trouble. It's a great bit of acting—and an example of what can happen when people realize that they will be held accountable for their actions.

Like many Americans, I had followed the trickle of news that began near the end of 2019 about a wave of new illnesses in China. But the whole matter really began to come into focus on January 2, 2020. This was already quite an eventful day, as the president had made his decision to strike Qasem Soleimani days before and preparations were being made for the attack.

Amid the blur of phone calls in the run-up to that operation, I received a call from Dr. Robert Redfield, the director of the Centers for Disease Control and Prevention (CDC) and, in my view, the shining star of the COVID-19 response team. I'd not met Redfield, but the word from my team was that his call was urgent, so I left a meeting to take it. He told me that he had been working with his Chinese counterpart to try to understand what appeared to be a highly contagious virus. He said that the two of them had been collaborating well until the last twenty-four hours, when his counterpart went totally dark. Redfield viewed this development ominously: "Mr. Secretary, I need you to try to reopen the channel of communication with China."

I called China's top diplomat, Yang Jiechi, early on the morning of January 3. "We know about your virus problem," I told him, "We want to send a team to help you understand it better." He said that he would "take this under consideration."

He never called back with an update—and neither did Dr. Redfield's counterpart.

The result was devastating: One million Americans dead (as of the summer of 2022), and millions more in other countries. Hundreds of billions of dollars of economic activity went down the drain. The lock-downs decimated our kids' educational progress. Many of them lost a year or more of learning, and that deficit will adversely impact them and the world for decades.

President Xi and his Communist crew denied the world access to any information about a virus that started in his country and became a global pandemic. The crime boss Xi shut out the forces for good who were struggling to deal with a virus that his regime had failed to stop. We must make sure that he and the Chinese Communist Party ultimately face accountability for the grossly reckless spreading of a lethal virus. Without accountability, this will happen again.

ACCOUNTABILITY UNDERPINS FREE SOCIETIES

"I believe a healthy society should not just have one voice."

These were some of the last words of Dr. Li Wenliang, a thirty-three-year doctor at China's Central Hospital of Wuhan. On December 30, 2019, Li first reported to some of his medical school classmates that a new pathogen that looked like the 2002–2004 SARS virus was spreading. He urged them to take precautions and protect their families. By January 12, Dr. Li was in the hospital, his body succumbing to what we now know for certain was COVID-19. By February 7, he was dead.

When China's internet users found out about Li's death, they turned apoplectic, and for good reason. After Dr. Li had sent his warning to his colleagues, his message went viral on the Chinese internet and attracted the attention of the local authorities. Instead of pushing to get to the bottom of a dangerous virological episode, they accused him of "making false comments" that "severely disturbed the social order." They forced him to sign a statement of renunciation and told him to stop making his claims or face prosecution. In an act of bravery, Dr. Li shared all this with the world, as his tragically premature date with death grew near.

In the days after his passing, one of the top trending hashtags on Weibo, the Chinese equivalent of Twitter, became, "We want freedom of speech." Users were enraged at how the CCP's suppression of knowledge of the outbreak had killed a young whistleblower. "Do not forget how you feel now. Do not forget this anger," wrote one user to his fellow Chinese. "We must not let this happen again." Another addressed the CCP: "The truth will always be treated as a rumor. How long are you going to lie? Are you still lying? What else do you have to hide?" The day after Li died, dozens of Chinese and American citizens demonstrated outside the Chinese consulate in Los Angeles, California. One of them, James Zheng, vented: "I don't think it's a natural disaster. It's a man-made tragedy."

Man-made tragedy is right. And it's the CCP's fault. The buck stops with Xi Jinping.

Authoritarian regimes look unbreakable, but at their core, they are brittle. Because they use a vice grip to retain power, resentment for the regime smolders in the hearts of their downtrodden subjects. The state keeps a lid on this volcano through one-party rule and the suppression of freedom. Because authoritarian leaders are desperate to hold on to power, they create political systems that smother accountability. When problems do happen, lack of transparency causes things to go from bad to worse. This is just what happened in 1986 during the nuclear reactor meltdown at Chernobyl, which was then in the Soviet Union. The disaster infected thousands with lethal levels of radiation. To this day, parts of Ukraine are uninhabitable. Soviet officials tried to cover it up, juking the stats on hospitalizations and failing to inform the world that something had happened until days after the accident.

The CCP is similarly allergic to accountability. In 2003, a novel coronavirus called severe acute respiratory syndrome (SARS) was starting to consume Beijing. Authorities imposed a total news blackout, even as

Chinese citizens began to grow more concerned about what was happening. Only when Chinese doctor Jiang Yanyong wrote a letter accusing government authorities of underreporting cases did the world learn about the extent of the spread, which, by the time the letter went public, had gotten out of hand. Similarly, in 2011, Chinese internet users erupted in anger after evidence emerged that the CCP had suppressed the details of a train catastrophe that killed forty people and injured nearly two hundred. The party quickly buried the mangled train cars in the ground to hide evidence.

In the United States, freedom of speech, freedom of the press, and democratic elections mean leaders face accountability all the time. A dissatisfied public not only can criticize but can vote officials out of office. Those who commit crimes in political office can be prosecuted. By contrast, China's Communist bosses aren't at all accountable to their citizens. They censor, lie, and cover up the truth. Democratic societies can have messy debates, but we know that in an emergency, it's more important to save lives than to save face.

When we hold ourselves accountable, we have the standing to hold others accountable, too. In the Trump administration, for example, we imposed sanctions on Iran's IRGC for its acts of American-killing terrorism. We didn't think it was right that Russia could brazenly violate the INF treaty, so we pulled out of it. At NATO, I called out Turkey for its attempts to buy a Russian-made missile system and illegally explore for energy in other countries' territorial waters. For all the strategic calculations that go into foreign policy decisions, many choices simply come down to whether the United States will insist on repercussions for bad behavior. Perhaps most importantly, we demanded accountability from the CCP and the World Health Organization (WHO) for the plague they unleashed upon the world.

CHINA'S COVID-19 COVER-UP

Although the first confirmed case of COVID-19 seems to have happened on November 17, 2019, hospitals in the city of Wuhan were surging with patients a month earlier. The first known case outside of China seems to have occurred by December 27, and on December 31, the US CDC learned of twenty-seven cases of pneumonia of unexplained origin in Wuhan.

The first instinct of Chinese authorities was not to protect their country or the world but rather to hide the outbreak and insist that there was "nothing to see here." In addition to Li, other doctors and journalists who warned of the virus and questioned the CCP's lie disappeared, their fates unknown. On December 31, the CCP started scrubbing search terms such as "Wuhan unknown pneumonia," "SARS variation," and "Wuhan Seafood Market" from the Chinese internet. On January 1, the Hubei Provincial Health Commission ordered a genomics company to stop testing samples from Wuhan and to destroy all existing samples. On January 3, China's National Health Commission, the country's top health authority, "ordered institutions not to publish any information related to the unknown disease, and ordered labs to transfer any samples they had to designated testing institutions, or to destroy them," according to the *Straits Times*, a newspaper inside Taiwan. On January 6, the United States offered to send a team of infectious-disease experts to China, but China refused to grant them permission to enter. The CCP didn't share a genome of the virus with the world until January 12, despite its being mapped at the Wuhan Institute of Virology (WIV) on January 2. The WIV, too, was ordered to destroy samples and not share them with the United States. The CCP sought to bury the truth, just as it had buried those train cars.

Once the virological cat was out of the bag, China began crushing dissident voices and spinning conspiracy theories to cover up its mess. The day after the WHO formally declared COVID-19 a pandemic on March 11, China's foreign ministry spokesman posted a tweet suggesting that the virus originated in America and was spread to China by the US military. On March 12, an outspoken Chinese businessman named Ren Zhiqiang disappeared. He later resurfaced in a courtroom and was sentenced to eighteen years in prison after a one-day trial. Officially, the charge was corruption. But his real crime was calling Xi Jinping a "clown" in response to his management of the pandemic. And Chinese propagandists became superspreaders of misinformation online, creating panic among some Americans by claiming President Trump was about to impose a mandatory federal lockdown.

At the beginning of March, America and leaders all across the globe went into full-on Wuhan-virus response mode. The president had closed travel from China two weeks earlier, and his team was trying to ensure that we had adequate personal protective equipment (PPE) for health care providers and others. Concerned with the trade agreement with China, the president repeatedly praised China for its handling of the virus. I winced, but I hoped it was conciliatory diplo-speak more than anything else. I do believe the president wanted to get tougher at the outset in demanding information about the outbreak. But Xi told him that continued calls for accountability would jeopardize America's ability to receive PPE shipped from China. The United States was still in the early stages of understanding what we were up against, and the president made the tough call that putting America first meant not jeopardizing our ability to procure potentially life-saving equipment from China.

At the same time, however, I was determined to impose accountability by telling the truth. I knew that the CCP already was not happy with me. But on March 25, I held a press conference at the State Department and ripped into the party over its decision to hide a looming global disaster: "At the beginning of this, when it was clear that this was an issue, China knew about it, they were the first country to know about the risk to the world from this virus, and they repeatedly delayed sharing that information with the globe."

I suspect that my harsh words influenced President Trump's previously scheduled call with Xi Jinping the next evening, March 26. I joined the call from a secure location, while the president was at 1600 Pennsylvania Avenue. It started off cordially, as Xi offered Eastern medicines that he assured us would stem the symptoms of COVID-19, if Trump needed them. Yet Xi's real mission was to get me fired. He railed against me: Pompeo has defamed the Chinese people. Pompeo is antagonistic and a pugilist without reason. Pompeo is risking the trade deal we signed two months ago. Pompeo is immature and jeopardizes all we've built together. I'm sure that he knew I was on the call, so I admired his directness, if not his objective.

The call ended, and my phone rang a few moments later. "My Mike, that f——ing guy hates you!" The president said we should chat in the morning, as the hour was late in DC, but that I needed to "shut the hell up for a while." We needed that health equipment from China, he said. At his direction, I committed to a temporary rhetorical ceasefire.

There was only one moment when I thought my job might be at risk. I'd watched President Trump aim his ire at many cabinet officials over the previous three years, but had never really worried that I could be on the way out. Now it was my turn. A few days later, a group of us were in the Oval Office. When Trump walked in, seeing me in person for the first time since the Xi call, he said, "You guys need to know Xi hates that guy. Mike, you're putting us all at risk—the PPE, our trade deal. Stop, for God's sake!"

If you review my public remarks in the weeks that followed, you'll see I honored that command. I was not happy that the president had tweeted that the CCP was doing a good job on the virus and praised Xi: "China has been working very hard to contain the Coronavirus. The United States greatly appreciates their efforts and transparency. It will all work out well. In particular, on behalf of the American People, I want to thank President Xi!" But I understood the circumstances—we needed health equipment and were at the CCP's mercy for it. I worked for the president, and I would bide my time.

When I went home that night, I told Susan that my good run might be near its end. I would not praise Xi or the CCP for their death-dealing lies. Quiet for a time? Fine. But I wasn't going to give an inch in the long run. Accountability matters too much—and let's never forget that Xi threatened American lives by withholding potentially life-saving materials simply because I spoke the truth.

HOLDING THE WHO ACCOUNTABLE FOR FAILURE

With the party working overtime to obliterate the truth about the origins of COVID-19, I made it my personal mission to learn as much as possible about the roots of the outbreak. The WHO should have been on top of this, but it failed miserably. Its track record in the early days of the pandemic revealed that it had no real intention of holding China accountable. It refused to publish Taiwan's warnings on December 31 that the virus was spreading via human-to-human transmission. It even praised China for its handling of the virus on January 9, when the CCP likely knew it had a raging pandemic on its hands. Even on January 30, when it was clear that the virus was spreading by human-to-human transmission, the WHO expressed confidence in "China's capacity to control the outbreak." Clearly, even the world's so-called public health experts had learned nothing from China's cover-ups during the SARS episode.

The WHO's lackadaisical, nonconfrontational posture revealed that it was more concerned with appeasing its Chinese masters than pushing for answers and access. This was undoubtedly the result of the influence wielded by the WHO's director, Dr. Tedros Adhanom Ghebreyesus, who had achieved his position with Chinese support and was fearful of offending his Communist patron. While I cannot elaborate more here, he owed his job to a deal that he cut with the CCP. One could argue that that deal was simply the typical horse-trading among nations for votes on who would next govern the WHO. But to get the job, Tedros made a promise that haunts the world to this day. He was foreclosed from putting the WHO to work on confronting the source of the pandemic not only because China was a substantial donor nation to the WHO but also because of "arrangements" he had made. Another CCP shutout.

While the CCP did let the WHO "investigate" the outbreak in February 2020, it was a pointless, Potemkin inquiry. The CCP dictated the terms of the investigation, including the stipulation that the probe could only focus on the natural origins of COVID-19. This meant all other theories, including a lab leak, were off the table. But the sham gets worse. The investigators were forbidden from questioning China's official response to the pandemic and from visiting the site of the now-infamous wet market, a possible source of the outbreak. Initially, the CCP even blocked them from visiting Wuhan. Eventually, the CCP let a handful of doctors into the city, where they visited two hospitals and stayed for a day. The WHO started a second investigation in the fall of 2021, but by that point, the best chance to unravel the true origin of the pandemic was long gone.

Tedros tried to draw lessons from his futile investigation, musing aloud that "leadership in a crisis such as this requires listening, understanding, trust and moving forward together." All those qualities are just empty, globalist happy talk when an entity like the CCP is congenitally opposed to transparency and enslaved to dishonesty. The real leadership test, one that I think Dr. Tedros failed, was whether he would have the courage to demand transparency and answers from China in a time of world crisis—the party's image or his own political fortunes be damned. And if Xi Jinping and his Commie minions didn't want to let a proper investigation in at all, then it was up to Dr. Tedros to highlight this stonewalling and publicly pressure the Chinese government to explain to a world begging for answers why it wasn't cooperating.

The cumulative failures of the WHO in the early stages of the pandemic sparked the conversations between the president and his team, including Andrew Bremberg, the ambassador to the UN agencies in Geneva; Alex Azar, secretary of Health and Human Services, Robert O'Brien, the national security advisor; and me. We knew that the WHO had failed at its most important mission. We also knew that others had tried to reform the WHO and that one more attempt would be futile.

We announced America's withdrawal from the WHO on July 7, 2020. In the wake of the pullout, the media rained down vitriol on the Trump administration merely for exercising accountability over an organization that was raking in about $450 million per year in US taxpayer money. The WHO had put playing nice with China over doing its duty to stop the spread of disease and get to the bottom of the outbreak. Now the United States was the bad guy for demanding accountability from a failing institution? The world truly had been turned upside down.

PURSUING THE LAB LEAK THEORY

Most infuriating about the WHO's unserious investigation was the fact that it paid almost no attention to the theory that the virus could have emerged from the now-infamous WIV laboratory. I do not believe the CCP intentionally unleashed COVID-19 on the world as a bioweapon, though I could be wrong. I remain convinced to this day that the virus was cultivated in the WIV and then escaped. Without accepting the facts, there can be no accountability. Bad things will follow.

The evidence to support the lab leak theory is strong. In 2018, State Department officials who visited the WIV—which claimed to be in the highest tier of biosecurity (BSL-4)—cabled back to Washington that the facility was a ticking time bomb, an opinion shared by the French government and the WIV's then-director Dr. Yuan Zhiming. In the second week of January 2020, as coverage of the outbreak was exploding in Chinese media, Miles Yu found it odd that although Wuhan was the epicenter of the cases, none of the discussion in the media mentioned the WIV. Perhaps this was because the lab had extensive connections to the Chinese military, maybe even as a locus of biowarfare experimentation. Miles requested my permission to investigate the possibility of the WIV's connection to the outbreak, and I agreed. A couple weeks later, he brought me a binder filled with open-source evidence: information about gain-of-function research designed to make viruses stronger, for instance, and documented concerns throughout China and the world that the WIV would be the site of an outbreak. Miles also discovered later on that all cell phone activity on the premises of the WIV suddenly, mysteriously stopped in mid-October 2019. It's as if the place was suddenly abandoned, perhaps during an unreported decontamination and cover-up effort.

Given my knowledge of how the CCP had handled past outbreaks and the evidence procured by Miles and the rest of the State Department, I thought there was enough smoke to suggest a fire. I wanted to get the conversation going so that others could join in and demand answers. On April 15, 2020, I publicly raised on TV the circumstantial evidence that the virus emerged a few miles from China's top virology lab. Indeed, officials at the State Department, members of Congress, intelligence officials inside the US government, and even many medical professionals were beginning to take seriously the hypothesis of a lab leak. Even Dr. George Gao, the director of the Chinese CDC, commented in March 2020 that the virus could have come from "a place where the virus was amplified." But Democrats moved fast to pour cold water on my suggestions. Senator Chris Murphy theorized that my comments were "driven by political considerations." An Obama administration foreign policy hand named

Ilan Goldenberg said my comments amounted to an "American disinformation campaign."

The CCP also tried to discredit the lab leak hypothesis, as well as defame me personally. One CCP mouthpiece accused me of "spewing poison and sophistry." China's ambassador to Israel suggested that my well-founded accusations against China were akin to how Jews had often been made scapegoats for the world's problems. The CCP even called me "the common enemy of mankind," and I was likely more famous on Chinese state TV than I was in my hometown of Wichita. Billboards on Chinese subways showed pictures of me with "Liar" stamped in big letters across my face. Even the *Washington Post* noticed by the spring how the CCP was gunning for me, running this headline: "China Wasn't Wild about Mike Pompeo before the Virus. It's Really Gunning for Him Now."

In June 2020, as the war of words over COVID-19's origins reached a fever pitch, I held what would turn out to be my final in-person meeting with my Chinese counterpart, state councillor Yang Jiechi, in Hawaii. The Chinese were desperate for this meeting—I think they hoped they could convince me to shut up about their cover-up and plenty of other bad behavior. It reflected their fear of accountability. I demanded more transparency over the pandemic, just as I'd been saying. Besides spinning the usual CCP tripe on Xinjiang, Hong Kong, and Taiwan, Yang pretended as if China had been a paragon of truth. He promulgated the same tired calls for a return to US-China "dialogue," which is the CCP's code word for tying up your adversary in negotiations while China keeps doing whatever it wants. A well-known CCP toady, State Councillor Yang remained deeply scripted, never spontaneous. He varied from his prepared remarks only for points of emphasis. He defended the CCP's cover-up with the vehemence of a hardened criminal.

I understood why both the American political Left and the Communists in Beijing wanted to malign me as a nutjob for their own political benefit. Inexplicable, however, was the fact that America's top scientists were themselves prejudiced against any explanation other than the natural origin hypothesis. As far back as January 31, 2020, Dr. Anthony Fauci, director of the National Institute of Allergies and Infectious Diseases, was warned by a group of virologists that had collectively analyzed the COVID-19 genome that the virus may have come from the Wuhan lab. One wrote: "Whether you believe in this series of coincidences, what you know of the lab in Wuhan, how much could be in nature—accidental release or natural event? I am 70:30 or 60:40." One day after researchers spoke up on a conference call about the possibility that the virus was genetically manipulated, Dr. Francis Collins, head of the National Institutes of Health (NIH), cautioned against even expressing such a possibility on February 2, 2020: "The voices of conspiracy will quickly dominate, doing great potential harm to science and international harmony."

In the following weeks, Fauci and Collins applied pressure to stifle lab leak hypotheses, and the publication of scientific articles pushing the natural origin theory discouraged the press from digging deeper. On April 16, the day after my TV appearance, Collins wrote to a group of government scientists regarding the WIV theory: "Wondering if there is something NIH can do to help put down this very destructive conspiracy, with what seems to be growing momentum." Fauci replied to him the next day, writing, "I would not do anything about this right now. It is a shiny object that will go away in times [sic]." These leaders—undoubtedly smart individuals—had a right to believe in the natural origin theory if that's where they thought the facts led. But instead of pursuing a line of scientific inquiry, they tried to shut down alternative ideas.

I wish that Fauci, Collins, and others tried to suppress the lab leak theory because they were purely persuaded that the virus had a natural origin. Sadly, I think they were fearful of being exposed for gargantuan conflicts of interests and activities that sidestepped American laws. For years, the NIH funded grants to an organization called EcoHealth Alliance, which in turn used the money to fund dangerous research on viruses at the WIV. This was a massive failure of accountability in how taxpayer dollars were being used.

It's no wonder that Peter Daszak, the head of EcoHealth Alliance, authored an influential article in the *Lancet* in February 2020 denouncing the lab leak theory, without mentioning his organization's ties to the lab. The scientific community by and large followed Daszak's lead to discredit the lab leak theory. What's most disturbing about the suppression of this hypothesis is that researchers who purport to be neutral, fact-oriented observers chose to put politics and private interests ahead of discovering the truth. Many of them are doing the same thing with climate change, denigrating ideas that don't gel with their politics and ridiculing their critics as crackpots. They didn't care about accountability—and they materially assisted in the deadliest cover-up in history.

GUNNING FOR THE TRUTH AT THE STATE DEPARTMENT

Distressed that neither the WHO nor US public health leaders were properly inquiring into the possibility of a lab leak, a band of State Department patriots convened its own investigation in September 2020. The mission was simply to honor the American people's demands for the truth and accountability over a lethal virus. Leading the charge was Tom DiNanno, head of the Bureau of Arms Control, Verification, and Compliance, assisted by a bulldog investigator, David Asher. I told them just to follow the facts where they led and report the truth. They worked with the intelligence community and scientists from the Lawrence Livermore National Laboratory in New Mexico and studied various theories.

But again, the State Department's bureaucracy reared its ugly head—and this time it was a political appointee throwing sand in the gears. Chris Ford was the acting undersecretary for Arms Control and International Security and therefore DiNanno's immediate boss. It's my contention that Ford had a personal animus against me and President Trump. He worried about becoming associated with what he regarded as a lunatic theory. I was told by my leaders that Ford directed his team to refuse to cooperate with the probe except in the most minimal of ways. He also apparently was interested in protecting the linkages of the US-government-funded gain-of-function research at the WIV. He brought in his own preferred team of scientists to dispute the findings of the Lawrence Livermore scientists, which diminished the team's ability to state any conclusion definitively.

In the end, the panel's biggest challenge was that it simply ran out of time. On January 15, 2021, the department summed up in a statement what we could conclude with confidence: First, several researchers from the WIV were hospitalized with flu-like symptoms in August 2019, before the first documented COVID-19 cases appeared. Second, we declared that COVID-19 was 96.2 percent identical to a strain of coronavirus known as RaTG13, which WIV researchers had studied since at least 2016. Finally, we stated that, although it postured as a civilian facility, the WIV conducted secret research for the Chinese military.

By the spring of 2021, with the Trump administration now out of office, more scientists began to consider the possibility that the virus had escaped from the lab. The three experts Ford had brought in to dispute DiNanno's inquiry—including Dr. Ralph Baric of the University of North Carolina, the closest American collaborator with the WIV's lab—changed their minds. They signed a petition published in the leading American journal *Science* that called for investigation into the lab leak theory. The media began to pay more attention, even though many journalists and talking heads just a year earlier had treated the lab leak theory as nonsensical, politically motivated, and racist. Eventually the Biden administration released a useless report that didn't come to any strong conclusion about where or how the virus started, dashing momentum for any chance of holding China accountable. Whenever people in the media pose as dogged sleuths on a quest for truth and justice, remember how they dismissed the lab leak theory until it was politically safe to do otherwise.

COUNTERING CHINA ON A RUNNING CLOCK

Even as my focus remained on confronting China's malfeasance on the COVID-19 outbreak, the clock was ticking down on President Trump's first term, with no assurance of a second. I had to keep imposing accountability on China for decades of other abuses.

I had loads of conversations on China with senior business leaders—and more specifically, the party's efforts to co-opt them. Some of these captains of industry thought I had lost a screw, I think. In the depths of the pandemic, I received a call from a tech CEO who had been involved in global health issues for decades. He urged greater US participation—that is, more money—for the global vaccine effort known as Gavi. I used the opportunity to ask him, "Why do you think the Chinese like you so much?" He didn't appreciate the question, and I left it alone for the rest of our call. But he knew as well as I did that his access to senior Chinese leaders was not secured by his good looks or brains but from the fact that he was simply their next target.

In private conversations, I repeatedly reminded American titans of a few simple facts about what it means to do business in China. There is no such thing as a Chinese private company. Period. Full stop. The Communist state can legally own or take control of any economic and business entity or force you to operate as directed by state authorities. If you are doing business with an entity owned or controlled by the Chinese government, you are doing business with the CCP. Not only do the Chinese national security laws spell this out but so does common sense. Ask Jack Ma—a high-profile Chinese businessman who mysteriously went missing from public view for months in 2020—what he thinks he actually controls.

It's bad enough that Chinese companies are controlled by the CCP. But to have American companies controlled by China is even worse. Under Chinese laws, *all* companies in China, including US companies, must cooperate with Chinese intelligence and security services. In 2022, the CCP even expanded requirements that Western companies integrate party cells into operations in China. Any firm connected to China is vulnerable.

During the pandemic, I watched the CCP stop US companies from shipping products they had made in China for delivery under a contract with a US company. They also intended to ship it on an American aircraft. All good, right? Well, danged if the Chinese government refused to approve the paperwork permitting the shipment. I've watched the Chinese government threaten family members of US citizens living in China if they didn't cooperate. I've seen two Canadians and countless others detained to satisfy a Chinese political objective. The Chinese legal system, an oxymoron to be sure, protects only the party bosses. American companies don't have title to their property in goods in China. They don't have ownership. They have temporary possession.

The warnings to the business world we began in the Trump administration are starting to have a real effect today, as global corporations are now weighing more heavily the perils of doing business in China. We need corporate America's help to force real accountability on the CCP.

A team of Trump administration leaders also worked to stop the CCP's propaganda artists and spies from running influence campaigns just about everywhere. It wasn't just federal officials such as Congressman Eric Swalwell and Senator Dianne Feinstein against whom the Chinese had successfully run operations. They also targeted our universities, local governments, media, think tanks, and more. And the worst part is, so much of it is legal.

The CCP long ago figured out how to inject its poison into America's open society by using both official agents operating under diplomatic cover and Chinese citizens whom the CCP has coerced to do its bidding. For years, China-run "language and cultural centers" called Confucius Institutes have operated on American campuses, although they are much fewer in number now than before the Trump administration made this an issue. (Sometimes it could be hard to distinguish their America-hating subversion from what is taught in so many college classrooms.) The CCP tried to brainwash American elites by paying for the right to publish commentary or advertising from the state-run *China Daily* in the *New York Times*, the *Washington Post*, and even the *Wall Street Journal*. In 2020, the Department of Justice indicted a Chinese spy who allegedly even infiltrated the ranks of the New York City Police Department to keep tabs on ethnic Tibetans living in New York.

No segment of American society is safe from the CCP's United Front operations, which are run out of the Chinese embassy in DC. Some operations are even directly run out of Beijing, such as the CCP United Front Work Department's Council for the Promotion of the Peaceful Reunification of China, which has more than thirty chapters across the country. I urge every civic, business, and academic leader to be wary of people who claim to represent a China-based organization, especially if they dangle a lucrative offer or propose a new partnership. I have no doubt that pushing some CCP-approved lie or looking the other way on some bad behavior is a condition of doing business.

Crushing Chinese spy networks inside the United States is harder than you may think. Federal bureaucracies battle over how to handle foreign nationals conducting espionage, with some agencies on one side and the State Department and the CIA on the other. Often what happens is that US authorities identify bad actors, usually "diplomats" who have permission to be in the United States. When an agency discovers sketchy behavior and asks to kick them out of the United States, State and CIA groan. They know that if the United States expels a Russian or Chinese diplomat, those nations will reciprocate by expelling one of our people, thus diminishing America's intelligence capabilities. Sadly, because the State Department controls diplomatic facilities operating in the United States, the diplomats nearly always prevail. I took a different approach during my four years at CIA and State. No one should use diplomatic cover to spy against the United States. When we find them, we should bounce them, preferably in public.

This was music to law enforcement's ears, but heresy inside my bureaucracies. The best example of this was my three-year effort to close the Chinese consulate in Houston, a central hub of CCP espionage. While it was no great secret to US government officials that this diplomatic property was a den of spies, closing it came with serious ramifications. "Who knows how the CCP will respond?" my teams would tell me. "They'll close at least one of our consulates, maybe all of them. They might deny visas to all government officials. We can't take the risk."

My view was different. Chinese diplomatic personnel in Houston were stealing some of our most important medical technology and practices from the University of Texas Medical System. It is almost certain that China has also stolen troves of cancer-research data from the elite MD Anderson Cancer Center in Houston, just as we know for a fact China was stealing COVID-19 vaccine research all over the world. In fact, MD Anderson fired three researchers in late 2019, effectively over suspicions that they were handing over research to China. We also knew that the Chinese were stealing information from world-class energy-technology firms in Texas and monitoring port activity in ways we didn't fully understand. And it was not only American intellectual property being stolen but European know-how, too. So, my colleagues and I built the case and a plan. We worked with Ambassador Terry Branstad in China to prepare his team for potential reprisals. And we managed to do this without a single leak.

In what history will see as one of the most amazing roll ups of a foreign espionage operation ever conducted, we began with a set of Justice Department indictments. Next came a démarche, a formal statement of a country's policy position from one diplomat to another, on July 19, 2020. Very seldom does a secretary of state issue a démarche to an ambassador, but I wanted to communicate to Chinese ambassador Cui Tiankai that this was serious. When Cui came to my office, he was totally unprepared for this bad news—a good sign that our operational security on this mission was sound. Cui's first words in response were an odd demand that I stop separating the people of China from the CCP. He hated that I was determined to unpack the lie that the Chinese people are represented by people such as him. Flustered, he said that the CCP would have to close the sixth US Consulate in China: Hong Kong. His next step was to launch an all-out effort inside the government to stop our purge of spies. He reached out to the White House, Capitol Hill, Jared Kushner, the National Security Council, the Department of Defense, and whomever else would listen. He worked all his contacts, trying to isolate me and investigate if this démarche reflected a holistic US government effort or just Mike's.

He soon came to see that this was for real. Our operation continued with the July 22 announcement that the CCP had seventy-two hours to vacate the Houston consulate. In spite of Cui insisting that they had nothing to hide in Houston, Brian Bulatao, running the operation for State, came into my office and flipped on my TV a few hours after the announcement. We watched every cable channel report that the Houston Fire Department was responding to fires and smoke from the Chinese consulate. Nothing to see here, comrade, please disperse.

As Cui had threatened, the CCP retaliated by closing down a US Consulate—not the one in Hong Kong, but in Chengdu. That was unfortunate but still worthwhile. The DOJ's indictments and the closure of the consulate convinced the CCP to withdraw nearly all its undercover officers from the United States. It also had the added benefit of causing other countries to move their spy assets, too. I was hopeful I could convince the president to permit me to close further consulates—not as part of a slap fight but because the imbalance between the CCP's operations here and America's inside of China were, and still are, quite drastic. That imbalance should not be allowed to continue.

More actions followed. To slow down the CCP's asymmetrical information-warfare campaign, we forced fifteen Chinese state-run media organizations to register as state missions, because Americans needed to know that when information comes from the Chinese government, it is far closer to something from *Pravda* than from C-SPAN. We mandated that any think tank wishing to partner with the State Department must first declare its sources of foreign funding, because so many of them were swimming in Chinese yuan. And we imposed new restrictions on what Chinese "diplomats" can do inside the United States, bringing our policy in line with what our diplomats are subjected to inside China. If an American diplomat in China sought to move outside our consulate and attend anything, he needed to provide notice and a reason, obtain permission, and, if allowed to go, subject himself to CCP monitoring every single minute. By contrast, if a Chinese "diplomat" from its consulate in Chicago wanted to attend a PTA meeting in Rockford, Illinois, all he or she had to do was just show up. We changed that.

It's not solely the government's job to guard against the CCP's international campaign to destroy American leadership and establish itself as ruler of the world. I also kept up my information-awareness campaign inside the United States to warn different segments of society about the China threat. Universities are especially vulnerable—and not just because China donated approximately $1 billion to US colleges from 2013 to 2020. In 2019, about 11,000 Americans studied in China. That same year, approximately 370,000 Chinese students studied at American colleges and universities. While the vast majority of those students just want to get a good education and mind their own business, there are some who steal research and extend the reach of the CCP influence machine. They often work through Chinese expatriate organizations such as the Chinese Students and Scholars Association. Most of the CSSAs on American campuses are controlled by the education divisions of the Chinese embassy and consulates in the United States. The charters of some CSSAs on university campuses in the west and southwestern United States even openly state that the Chinese Consulate General in Los Angeles must approve their CSSA officers. Virtually all Chinese students inside the United States have experienced the CCP contacting them or their family to "see how their studies are going." The party carefully monitors their classes, activities, and relationships—Chinese students at Princeton have felt the need to use aliases in academic discussions for fear of the CCP persecuting them for opinions that contradict the party line. Those innocent Chinese students who are not agents of the CCP are very often pressured to inform on their fellow Chinese citizens anyway.

I wanted to drive these points home with a speech on an important campus. My first choice was the Massachusetts Institute of Technology, a critical American institution with a massive technology portfolio, brilliant professors doing cutting-edge work, and engineering and innovation programs nearly unrivaled anywhere on the planet. It's also a focus of the CCP's United Front campaign against America.

MIT has long been awash in Chinese money. According to a US government indictment, between 2013 and 2021, a single MIT researcher in nanotechnology, Dr. Gang Chen, took $19 million in funding from a Chinese public research university, though charges were later dropped. In 2018, MIT hosted its first "MIT-China Summit" in Beijing, sponsored by Chinese tech companies such as SenseTime—now under US sanctions for supplying artificial intelligence technology to crush the Uyghurs—and iFlytek, which has supplied voice data collection systems to the prison wardens in Xinjiang. MIT also permitted iFlytek to fund three research projects at its Computer Science and Artificial Intelligence Laboratory. In 2019, the Department of Education opened an investigation into MIT's alleged acceptance of gifts from Trojan horses such as the Office of Chinese Language Council International, Hanban (the parent organization of Confucius Institutes), Huawei, and the Chinese government itself. According to MIT's own data, in 2021–2022, Chinese students made up more than 25 percent of all international students, with no other country comprising more than 10 percent. Between Chinese-funded research partnerships and huge numbers of Chinese students (probably paying full tuition), MIT, its donors, and its alumni would have to reach deep into their pockets were the CCP to shut off the spigot.

Assuming MIT to be an open, tolerant, pro-America campus, we asked if it would welcome America's secretary of state to speak about matters important to its students and our nation's security. They agreed, and we set a date. Suddenly, however, MIT backtracked. At this point, the school would have known only the general topic of my presentation. Yet we received a call a couple weeks before my scheduled remarks. "We're sorry, but we will be unable to host the secretary on our campus," came the message. In the end, the president of MIT, Rafael Reif, made clear that the risk of offending his Chinese students was too great. To me, that was a bald-faced lie, and he had to have known it. And indeed, complaining about the hurt feelings of the Chinese people is exactly the response the party gives whenever publicly confronted with legitimate criticisms.

So, instead, I went to Georgia Tech, where, incidentally, many Chinese students came up to me afterward to thank me for speaking honestly. As my remarks made clear, members of the academic community who have crossed the CCP have paid a price. An unhappy CCP will pull students and grants and programs not only to get even but to send a message: "We own you." Schools hooked on the CCP's sugar must go into rehab. I cannot think of a less patriotic act by a leader of a major American institution than MIT's president caving to the CCP.

Fortunately for America, there are heroes, even at MIT. In 2021, Michelle Bethel, an alumna of MIT and a businesswoman, resigned from the board of MIT's McGovern Institute for Brain Research. When she raised questions about whether the institute's work could be unwittingly strengthening the CCP's military, one board member told her the concern was "racist." Another said, "Stick to science." She resigned, telling the world, "I'm no longer confident the institute can ethically push the boundaries of science for the good of humanity while working with institutions beholden to the regime in China . . . I believe that MIT doesn't have a firm grasp on events in China or on the risks of partnerships with Chinese institutions in cutting-edge areas of science that are subject to misappropriation or abuse for military modernization or repression." Bethel told the hard truth and did her part to hold both MIT and the CCP accountable.

In the last year of the Trump administration, we continued to cram in all we could to hold the CCP accountable for its many evils. We worked diplomatic channels hard to make sure the Chinese candidate to lead the World Intellectual Property Organization did not win the election. For the first time ever, the US government declared the CCP's territorial claims in the South China Sea "completely unlawful" and sanctioned more than twenty Chinese companies for their role in trying to turn that strategic body of water into a Chinese lake. The United States stepped up joint exercises with our allies throughout the Indo-Pacific. And we protected American investors by threatening to delist Chinese companies from the New York Stock Exchange if they didn't comply with American accounting standards. After years of letting Chinese companies with opaque or crooked books trade their stocks on Wall Street, it was an act of real accountability. So was forcing companies controlled by the Chinese military off the exchange.

There were a few times that I became apprised of risks that were so broad that it was worth getting out in front of the team. In June 2020, India banned the Chinese app TikTok, and Australia was considering doing the same because of the risk of massive quantities of information flowing to Beijing. When I went on Laura Ingraham's show in July 2020, she asked, "Shouldn't we be considering a ban on Chinese social media apps, especially TikTok?" I told her that I didn't want to get ahead of the president, but we were looking at that course of action. "Would you recommend that people download that app on their phones?" she inquired. "Only if you want your private information in the hands of the Chinese Communist Party" was my answer.

I immediately received a call from Peter Navarro, one of the White House's resident China hawks, saying, "God bless you!" Another call soon came from Steve Mnuchin, who believed that we needed an interagency review to figure out what to do about TikTok. But I was totally surprised by the support I received from American moms. I received a flood of messages from across the country saying that they used my clip to convince their kids to quit TikTok. While the Trump administration took the first steps to ban TikTok, we couldn't get it over the finish line in time. I wish we had. Beijing loves having millions of young Americans surrender vast quantities of personal data, which the party will try to exploit both now and in the future. The CCP almost certainly will comb through TikTok data to create dossiers on America's future leaders.

We did deliver a final great blow of accountability against the CCP, on the second to last day of the administration. For two years, I had been speaking out against the litany of human rights abuses the party was perpetrating against Uyghur Muslims and other ethnic minorities in the Xinjiang region. Whether it was demolishing mosques, interning Uyghurs in reeducation camps, imposing forced sterilization procedures on Uyghur women, or torturing them, it was clear that the CCP was trying to stamp out the Uyghur population of western China and eradicate their culture. To me, it sure looked as if the Communists in Beijing were trying to extinguish an entire race of people. We have a word for this: *genocide*.

In the last days of the administration, at the urging of Mary Kissel and another political appointee named Kelley Currie, I ordered the Office of Global Criminal Justice to produce all the evidence it had on the Xinjiang nightmare and its recommendation on whether the United States should make a formal designation of genocide. Its researchers had been working on this for months, and they waged big internal battles over the facts. The recommendation from the team initially was a designation of "crimes against humanity"—a tough label, but one that ultimately came up short. The bureau claimed, in effect, that what was happening in Xinjiang didn't fit the UN's legal definition of genocide, and so they didn't feel comfortable making the designation. But there was another major factor holding them back, as I discovered when I pressed them. I realized that they were worried about politics and disrupting relationships with their Chinese counterparts, which would change forever after this. One official from another bureau urged me to be content that I was getting 90 percent of what I wanted in a "crimes against humanity" designation. It wasn't good enough, I told him. "I want the last 10 percent," I made clear, because such an odious label would increase the chances that the world would hold the CCP to account.

I went ahead and issued a determination of genocide on my second to last day in office. It was the only proper form of accountability. It was not lost on anyone that the realpolitik, conservative guy from Kansas was calling out horrors against humankind—not Secretaries Clinton or Kerry, nor the effete philosophers who claim to extoll human rights at left-wing think tanks, nor the functionaries at Foggy Bottom. The fact that the Biden administration has chosen to keep that designation in place says to me that this issue is no longer a debate.

Within a few hours of that announcement, I was no longer the secretary of state—and on January 20, Inauguration Day, the CCP applied economic sanctions on me and many others who fought its predations, including Robert O'Brien, Peter Navarro, John Bolton, Keith Krach, Alex Azar, Miles Yu, and twenty-three others. (It's also worth noting those from the administration who were not sanctioned.) I was also no longer permitted to travel to China, nor was anyone in my family. Showing that she was going to be a great Pompeo, my son's wife, then-fiancé, Rachael, called me and asked, perhaps not totally tongue-in-cheek, "Mr. Pompeo, am I marrying into the sanction regime?" I told her that was a keen observation and that she should consult her attorney. We both laughed.

The primary objective of these sanctions was not to stop me or any of the other sanctioned officials from anything. They were intended to send a message to those who were coming in after us: Tony Blinken, Jake Sullivan, Wendy Sherman, Susan Rice, and their ilk. This was the CCP saying, "The living you made on January 19, 2020—helping clients thrive in and around China—will not be possible if you follow in the Trump team's footsteps." The CCP knows those leaders well. It knows that much of their livelihood, and the livelihoods of the hundreds of people who work for them on US-China policy, depended on their being part of the Chinese-US commercial-industrial complex. These sanctions were a preemptive blow against a Biden administration foreign policy to hold China accountable. It remains to be seen if the CCP's strategy will influence US decision-makers.

To this day, the thirty of us from the Trump administration remain under those sanctions. But the American people and the world now know better than ever that the regime in Beijing is a duplicitous force for evil. Today I wear my sanctions as a badge of honor. It means we did our job to hold China accountable.

CHAPTER 13

CHOOSE THE RIGHT ALLIES

One of the most spiritually powerful experiences of my life came in Jerusalem on March 21, 2019. I stood that day with US ambassador to Israel David Friedman and Israeli prime minister Benjamin Netanyahu in front of the Western Wall—one of the very last vestiges of the ancient Second Temple in Jerusalem, destroyed by the Romans in AD 70. The Second Temple was the successor to the First Temple, built by King Solomon some one thousand years before Jesus walked the earth. In the late AD 600s, above the wall, and atop what Jews and Christians call the Temple Mount, the Islamic Umayyad Caliphate erected the Dome of the Rock shrine and al-Aqsa Mosque, which still stand today.

For centuries, Jews have come to the base of the Western Wall to pour out their prayers before God, often writing them down on scraps of paper and jamming them into the crevices between the enormous ancient stones. It is the hope of many Jews—and many Christians—that one day the temple can be rebuilt on this site. The tension between Jews and Muslims over which religious group should control the Temple Mount is a major reason for tensions between Israel and the Muslim world, including the Palestinians.

Standing there, with a yarmulke on my head in accordance with Jewish customs, I closed my eyes, bowed my head, and placed my right hand on the Wall, lifting up my own prayers to God. I won't tell you what they were, but in that moment, I felt close to the Lord.

I was proud that the world saw America's secretary of state standing in solidarity with Israel. Solidifying ties with our most important friends

was in many ways what that job was all about. At every turn, we endeavored to choose the right allies to help put America first.

ALLIANCES ADD VALUE

Alliances are essential to American security and prosperity. Some foreign policy theorists disagree, invoking George Washington's Farewell
Address, in which he warned against "permanent alliances." But in that
speech, Washington also praised connections with nations based on
"policy, humanity, and interest." His point was that alliances cannot be
unconditional. Indeed, France played a pivotal role in helping Americans win the Revolutionary War against the British, and Washington
depended upon the skillful leadership of the French general Marquis de
Lafayette. In the aftermath of World War II, when the United States was
by far the most powerful and least war-ravaged country on earth, we used
our unmatched capabilities in order to rebuild a continent and achieve
peace. Great Americans such as George Marshall and Dean Acheson
helped bring Germany and Japan back from total ruin; pulled vulnerable democracies such as Italy, Greece, and Turkey out of the imminent
clutches of Communism; and solidified the defense of Western civilization through the formation of NATO. America's allies have since become
one of our greatest competitive advantages.

Many of our foes have very few allies or no allies at all. Russia might
count Belarus as an ally, but that's only because Vladimir Putin could
crush Alexander Lukashenko's regime if he wanted to. Cuba, Venezuela,
and Syria are more like clients than friends. China has no true allies,
just countries that act friendly because they fear the CCP. Then-foreign
minister Yang Jiechi insinuated that China isn't afraid to push smaller
countries around when he said in 2010, "China is a big country and other
countries are small countries, and that's just a fact."

Even Russia is not a real friend of China's. Putin and Xi may be close,
and their authoritarian governments share a paranoia about and hatred of
the United States, but their relationship is a product of raw interest. Xi
views Putin as leading a "bolt-on" nation, a source for discounted energy,

and a proxy for his malign objectives in the world. The historical hatred between the Chinese and Russian peoples, as well as their 2,600-mile border, portends conflict and fear in the long run, not friendship and cooperation. Nevertheless, we must do what we can to ensure that these growing ties do not become a full-on, permanent military and economic alliance. In the West's favor are the forces of history and culture. For Russia and China to overcome them to form a powerful, enduring alliance will prove challenging, especially when Xi has no intention of treating Putin as a peer.

Additionally, combined Russo-Chinese economic power is meager—something that Xi also knows favors the West. Joined together, Russia and China's economies make up less than 20 percent of global GDP. In contrast, the West accounts for nearly 60 percent of global GDP. America's vast alliance network is a force multiplier for projecting a level of military, economic, and diplomatic power that our adversaries can never hope to match. America First must always be the North Star of our foreign policy, but there is no shortage of opportunities for us to follow it alongside our friends. When America leads, the world is better off.

I used to laugh when commentators slammed the Trump administration for a "go it alone" approach. Fareed Zakaria of CNN tweeted: "Pres. Trump does not have a foreign policy. He has a series of impulses—isolationism, unilateralism, bellicosity—some of them contradictory." A couple of retired generals who shilled for Joe Biden in 2020—he of the subsequent Afghanistan and Ukraine debacles—wrote that "Trump's isolationist moves are progressively weakening America." Richard Haass, chair of the Council on Foreign Relations, whined in a long essay for *The Atlantic* that President Trump presided over America's "abdication" from world leadership. When he gave a talk to the State Department's Policy Planning staff in 2018, he urged American cooperation with China on climate change and cybersecurity. The absolute idiocy of believing that Xi Jinping intends to focus his regime on working with the global community to save the salamander and reduce global carbon emissions boggles my mind. Even worse, to believe that Xi Jinping, who operates a cyber-surveillance regime unequaled in history, would sit with Americans and thoughtfully debate how best to protect privacy and freedom and cooperate on cybersecurity is not simply academic wandering. Such thinking threatens our republic.

Foreign policy observers who thought the sky was falling simply hated our principled withdrawals from failed structures such as the Paris climate accords, the Iran deal, and the WHO. Their anguish speaks to the fervent adherence to multilateralism shared by Foggy Bottom, Whitehall, the Council on Foreign Relations, and other preserves of globalism. In other areas—such as pushing for greater NATO spending commitments and revised trade deals with China, Japan, and the European Union—we simply were asking for fair and reciprocal treatment. Foreign policy types also trashed us because we eschewed many fluffy hallmarks of the diplomatic world: beautiful dinners, lofty rhetoric, and communiqués issued at the end of meaningless summits that accomplished little beyond making countries feel good for showing up. The Trump administration knew real American leadership of our allies was not demonstrated by adherence to the performative choreography of meetings, treaties, and press conferences. I personally despised time-wasting ceremonial gatherings and saccharine statements, because our adversaries saw them as displays of East Egg shallowness. They are prepared to use their power and time to move pieces on the board. We must build our alliances to do the same.

I also chuckle because I know that the critics were never in the Oval Office to hear President Trump's actual directives. In nearly every diplomatic initiative, Trump encouraged me to get as many nations as possible on board with what we were doing. The list of what we accomplished with them while we led from the front is long: unanimous sanctions on North Korea at the United Nations, the Abraham Accords, the maximum-pressure campaign against Iran, sixty countries committing to kick Huawei out of digital networks, sanctions with Western allies on Russia for all kinds of bad behavior, fighting pro-abortion leftists at the UN with more than thirty countries, defeating ISIS with seventy-plus partners, and sixty countries pressuring the regime in Venezuela. We focused on solidifying the strategic partnerships that helped us progress against the most serious threats. If someone wants to complain that I didn't show up to enough perfunctory diplomatic back-patting sessions, so be it. We chose the right allies for the right missions.

THE REAL SPECIAL RELATIONSHIP

I'm most proud of our alliance building with Israel. It matters for the security and prosperity of every American. One of America's crowning foreign policy legacies is to have sustained an ironclad bond with this tiny nation for decades, and I resolved to leave it even stronger than I found it.

It's commonly said that America has a "special relationship" with the United Kingdom—and there's no doubt that it is our closest ally in terms of a shared history and language as well as security and economic ties. But America's real special relationship may be the one we have with Israel. No country in the world has supported this oasis of democracy and prosperity in the world's roughest neighborhood as the United States has. And Israel has been since its founding a bulwark on the important security issues facing our country, too.

Our strong ties date back to the founding of the modern Israeli state itself. After World War II, President Harry Truman was deliberating whether to recognize a national home for the Jewish people. Many of his advisors discouraged him from doing so, believing it would turn the Arab world against America and threaten access to Mideast oil. But President Truman ultimately had the courage to say yes, recognizing Israel eleven minutes after its creation on May 14, 1948. He knew the Jews needed a national home after the Holocaust. No one was more grateful for Truman's brave decision than the Jewish people themselves. In 1949, Israel's chief rabbi came to see President Truman. He told the president, "God put you in your mother's womb so that you could be the instrument to bring about the rebirth of Israel after two thousand years." Recognizing Israel was an outgrowth of American values: respect for religious freedom, friendship with fellow democracies, respect for small nations, protecting human life. Truman chose wisely.

Israel's story has consistently overlapped with my own. As a cadet at West Point with aspirations of leading a tank unit, I was captivated by the heroic maneuvers of Israeli tankers such as Avigdor Lieberman as he battled Syrian tanks in the Golan Heights during the 1973 Yom Kippur War. The Israelis never relented in the face of vastly superior enemy odds, showing the "never say die" attitude that characterizes Israel's will to survive in the Middle East to this day. Among my most treasured memories from my time as secretary of state was sitting atop the Golan Heights, looking out at the Valley of Tears and hearing, in person, from the general who led those troops to save Israel. Israel's courage inspired and reminded me to never give an inch.

I also admired how President Nixon proved himself to be as gutsy as President Truman was when Nixon supported Israel during the 1973 war. As Israel came under attack from all sides, he ordered that the United States supply the country with tanks and artillery. It was a risky move that could have provoked a broader conflict with the Soviet Union, which supported the Arab states. But President Nixon nonetheless told his CIA director, Vernon Walters, "You get the stuff to Israel. Now. Now." Israeli prime minister Golda Meir later said, "For generations to come, all will be told of the miracle of the immense planes from the United States bringing in the matériel that meant life to our people." It was textbook American leadership in action.

As I grew a little older, I was surprised to discover that not everyone shared my admiration for Israel's pluck and determination, as well as my belief in Israel's importance to our country. At Harvard Law School in the 1990s, I got my first real taste of the foaming-at-the-mouth anti-Zionism that pervades American higher education. Students and professors spread disinformation about how "colonialist" Israel was imposing "apartheid" against the Palestinians. Sadly, many of my classmates went on to have high-powered careers in the halls of politics and international affairs, where they have helped to spread this disease of ignorance. Anti-Israel bias has only gotten worse on America's so-called prestige campuses today. One study released in 2021 found that for very liberal young Americans, "Israel is on par with China and Iran." In 2022, the Harvard student newspaper, the *Harvard Crimson*, officially endorsed the anti-Semitic, Israel-focused Boycott, Divest, and Sanction (BDS) movement that is so prevalent on college campuses. A rising generation of hateful

Ilhan Omar clones seeks to rupture one of America's most important alliances.

As I continued to read my Bible and study American history, the connections between our two nations became even more personal. In the early 2000s, long before I entered public life, I took Susan and Nick to Israel for a family trip. I also had business there, as my company, Thayer Aerospace, was a customer of and a supplier to Israeli Aerospace Industries. On that trip, we visited Jewish and Christian sites, traveling to Bethlehem as well as through Galilee to Capernaum and Nazareth. We walked the path Jesus walked to the cross and prayed at Gethsemane and the Western Wall.

I also took Susan and Nick to battle positions in the Golan Heights that I had drawn by hand in my maps as a cadet. Walking in the mud on hills near the Golan was not on their bucket list, but it did leave a real impression on us all. That afternoon, we drove past a tank company on a training exercise. The company had stopped for maintenance, and our guide convinced the young company commander to let Nick climb inside his Merkava. I try to imagine young Captain Pompeo having allowed an Israeli family to climb on my M1. Much to my loss, I probably would not have been as hospitable. The trip reminded me of the deep ties of faith and history that bind our two nations.

My next visit was as a member of Congress in 2011, when I also first met Prime Minister Netanyahu. In his speech on security matters, he quoted the Old Testament and cited the history of the Jewish people. I told him that I was deeply aware that God gave the title deed of the land of Israel to Abraham, Isaac, Jacob, and their descendants forever. I also said that I had been reminded of this at a debate among three very politically active Christians at a high school in Kingman, Kansas. He got a good chuckle out of that—he could only imagine the raucous heartland politicking over support for Israel. For many evangelical Christians, support for Israel matters for many reasons, perhaps best summed up in Genesis 12:3: "I will bless those who bless you and whoever curses you I will curse." Sign me up for the blessings part! I've now visited Israel several dozen times, and to be there—walking where Jesus walked and praying where Jesus prayed—is like nothing else on earth.

I'll never forget sitting in Congress years later when Prime Minister Netanyahu urged President Obama not to go through with the Iranian nuclear deal, as it would put a regime with genocidal aspirations on a smooth path to a nuclear weapon. Afterward, I met Prime Minister Netanyahu for the second time. I had only a few minutes with him. To my amazement, he remembered who I was—and now he knew me as that crazy congressman from Kansas who was working his tail off to kill the JCPOA. For that, he said, he was eternally grateful. Neither of us knew how close our working relationship would become. Indeed, it could not have been prophesied.

REVERSING THE OBAMA ADMINISTRATION'S DISRESPECT

Working at the CIA was in many respects a dream job. One reason was that President Trump had given me wide berth to work with the Israelis on virtually whatever I wanted. This was a welcome change for the Israelis, whom the Obama administration had treated with a degree of disrespect unprecedented for a US presidential administration. Never before had an American commander in chief demonstrated, unequivocally, that he was unwilling to support the Zionist project and our best friend in the Middle East. Obama's UN ambassador, Samantha Power, and final national security advisor, Susan Rice, were also at the center of the administration's loathing of Israel. They neglected to choose the right ally.

Instead, they went all-in on buddying up with Iran. The Iran nuclear deal presented Israel with a terrible set of future choices: suffer under the coercion of a regime willing and able to destroy you, or be forced to take preemptive action that could trigger World War III. On terrorism, the Obama administration was just as bad, creating moral equivalency between the Iran-backed Hamas terrorists and the innocent citizens of Israel—Christian, Jewish, and Muslim alike. As for Hezbollah, Iran's proxy in Lebanon, the Obama team crushed a Drug Enforcement administration probe into its drug-smuggling activities, almost certainly to help seal the nuclear deal. Even an Obama administration Treasury official recalled that "investigations were tamped down for fear of rocking the boat with Iran and jeopardizing the nuclear deal." Hezbollah's illicit drug profiteering has almost certainly helped fund the buildup of some one hundred thousand rockets poised to rain down on Israel at the order of Hezbollah terrorist in chief Hassan Nasrallah.

As if to place a fitting coda on its anti-Israel diplomacy, the Obama administration in its final days refused to veto a UN Security Council Resolution stipulating that all Israeli settlements were illegal. It was the first time in nearly forty years that the Security Council passed a resolution critical of Israeli settlements, because it was the first time the United States had refused to stop such recklessness. The resolution demanded that Israel "immediately and completely cease all settlement activities in the occupied Palestinian territory, including East Jerusalem" and declared that the establishment of settlements by Israel has "no legal validity and constitutes a flagrant violation under international law." Days before the end of the administration, John Kerry capped his time as secretary of state with a rambling, hour-long speech defending the administration's position.

Kerry's swan song also reflected the pride of place he and others had assigned to the Israeli-Palestinian peace process. My predecessors gained elite-flyer status traveling to the Middle East and shuttling between Ramallah and Jerusalem. Special envoys, joint commissions, and policy papers were mainstays of every administration's effort at trying to draw, or redraw, lines on a map. All of this was aimed at convincing some terrorists in Judea and Samaria and a bunch of Iranian-backed jabronis in Gaza to allow Israelis to live in peace. We even funded the terrorists who ran the Palestinian Authority (PA) and so-called refugees with UN and American money. Trying to make progress in this effort was, in my view, a giant waste of time. I didn't want to spend a minute on negotiating with the PA.

The president had handed the "Mideast peace" file to Jared Kushner. As CIA director, I still had to work with PA president Mahmoud Abbas and other leaders with some regularity. In fact, I was the one senior-level American they would talk to in our administration for most of the four years, because I knew what was happening regarding the security situation in Israel and the region from my time as CIA director. I worked with Abbas, a senior leader named Saeb Erekat, the PA intelligence chief

Majed Faraj, and the leaders of the three PA security services. One of my station chiefs was a great American who came to the same conclusion I did about the PA: making peace would deprive its leadership of the power, money, and grifting opportunities that allow them to live lavishly while the rest of the Palestinians scrape by. Peace between the PA and Israel would render them irrelevant, and thus I regarded a monumental peace agreement as a zero-probability event. I reminded Jared of this throughout my time as CIA director and he, while often an optimist, knew that the PA's crooked ways likely limited what could be achieved with them.

Nonetheless, by early 2020, Israel was considering agreeing to a map that made some modest territorial concessions to the Palestinians. Not one Palestinian would lose a home, but the Israelis would have given up parts of Israel-controlled Jerusalem in a way that no Jew or Christian who knows the history of that city could accept. The map also would have provided for two states, with the Palestinian capital in East Jerusalem. It was always a work in progress, but I was worried about this development, because I had heard President Trump say many times, "Bibi doesn't want a deal. The PA wants a deal." As the braying and mocking of Jared's effort to cut the "deal of the century" continued, and Israeli internal politics was demanding "something," I became increasingly concerned that political pressure might push Netanyahu to take a deal based on a map that would create too much risk for Israel and violate sacred space within the City of Peace. My ace in the hole was my understanding of Abbas as the loser he was. I was confident that he would reject the map before even considering it—and he did.

One of the administration's great achievements was to fulfill a promise in 2017 that American politicians had been failing to honor since 1995: moving the American embassy to Jerusalem. In that year, Congress passed a law that recognized Jerusalem as the capital of Israel and appropriated funds to move our embassy from Tel Aviv. But year after year, American presidents of both parties waived that provision of the law on national security grounds. Effectively, they were too afraid that such a move would trigger violence directed at Israel from the Palestinians and Israel's neighbors. We made the commonsense decision to follow what the law called for, especially given that Jerusalem was the actual seat of the Israeli government. Imagine if Israel insisted on keeping its embassy in Chicago, when diplomatic work overwhelmingly takes place in Washington, DC. It just wouldn't make sense, but that was more or less the case with our diplomatic presence in Israel. The Israelis were thrilled at the decision to move the embassy, and I think the American people were, too. Most glorious was the fact that the ceremony to open the embassy coincided with the seventieth anniversary of Israel's founding.

STRENGTHENING THE US-ISRAEL BILATERAL RELATIONSHIP

The point man on moving the embassy, and so many other winning outcomes, was our ambassador to Israel, David Friedman. Nicknamed "Sledgehammer," David was the kind of diplomat who made the Trump administration so effective. He was unconditioned by old norms and didn't mind taking risks to break political logjams caused by timidity and stale thinking. David possessed a deep knowledge of his Jewish faith, maintained a cynicism of appropriate and massive proportions, and was a joy to be around. He is a man who works and works and works, as well as one whose word is golden. He believed the US-Israel alliance benefited every American. David and I worked closely to build on the historic decision to move the embassy to Jerusalem.

Perhaps none of our work was more important than the American recognition of Israeli sovereignty over the Golan Heights. Ever since the 1973 war, Israel has occupied the rugged Golan—thus holding a strategically critical high ground between enemy Syria and the rest of Israel. Fifteen years earlier, on that trip with Susan and Nick, I never imagined how the Golan would figure in my life again, but now it loomed large.

On the same trip to Israel on which I visited the Western Wall, Prime Minister Netanyahu invited Susan and me to have dinner with him and his wife, Sara. Susan and I spent the evening getting gussied up for a fancy night with them—a departure from my normal nights abroad spent digging into room service while catching up on developments in Washington. What the world didn't know is that David and I had spoken to President Trump earlier in the day, and he had decided to announce our new policy of recognizing Israeli sovereignty over the Golan. Susan and I had headed over for the evening and were present when the president spoke with Netanyahu to inform him officially of the decision.

Bibi, of course, wanted to hold a press conference to thank President Trump and America. We decided to make it a joint press conference with me as his cohost, but I had not prepared remarks. The good news was that I knew the history. I spoke of the Golan as both righteous Israeli land that belongs to the Jews and a place of military and strategic significance. To Bibi's amazement, and I think to both David Friedman and Susan's amazement as well, I spoke from the heart about the battles in the Valley of Tears and unimaginable bravery of the Israeli military heroes who saved their nation. It turned out that I'd been preparing for these remarks for my entire adult life.

Oddly, the words of that impromptu speech on the importance of the Golan weren't those that made the most headlines that week. A reporter from a Christian news outlet asked me if President Trump was "raised for such a time as this, just like Queen Esther, to help save the Jewish people from the Iranian menace?" I knew the reference from the Book of Esther. Esther, a young Jewish woman, became queen alongside the ancient Persian king Xerxes after he ordered his first wife either banished or killed. A wicked adviser to the king, Haman, hated Queen Esther's protector and cousin Mordecai, because Mordecai refused to kneel before him. Haman thus deceptively persuaded Xerxes to issue an order to kill all the Jews in Persia (ancient Iran). Queen Esther discovered the plot and prevailed upon the king to stop it, thus saving the Jewish people from certain death.

I rarely faced this kind of question from secular reporters in America, but they occasionally came up on my visits to Israel. I'm no biblical scholar, so I was always careful with my responses. In this instance, I said, "As a Christian, I certainly believe that's possible."

This outlook is not controversial for Christians. We know God places ordinary people—indeed, deeply flawed people—in positions of great power, and often those sinners achieve great things. King David is a perfect example. Even more than that, we know a sovereign God is in control of everything and knows all. So, if someone asks you, "Do you believe that Mr. Smith is mowing his lawn or creating world peace because the Lord chose him for such a time as this?" the answer could be yes. The

Washington Post nevertheless fell into hysterics with an absurd headline: "Holy Moses. Mike Pompeo Thinks Trump Is Queen Esther."

Despite this ridicule, I didn't give an inch in standing by our ally in myriad other ways. At the American Israel Public Affairs Committee in 2019, I explained why "anti-Zionism is anti-Semitism." It was the first time in history that a presidential administration had said so. Later that year, I had to move heaven and earth against the State Department's lawyers to fix a mistake that had gone uncorrected for years: America's stance on the legality of Israeli settlements in the West Bank. Ever since 1978, the State Department had believed that the settlements were a violation of international law. I won't bore you with all their specious reasoning here, but I didn't agree. I rolled back that bad policy by saying that they were not per se illegal under international law.

Equally critical was our decision to define the campus-based BDS movement as anti-Semitic. We even changed an American trade rule to permit imported products made in Israeli settlements in the West Bank to be labeled "Made in Israel." On my sixth and final trip to Israel in 2020, Susan and I visited a winery in an Israeli settlement. A vintner who appreciated our efforts presented me with a bottle of wine with the name "Pompeo" on the label. I hope I age as well as that vintage surely will.

Much of our success was due to having an excellent partner in Prime Minister Netanyahu, who spent substantial time in America as a young man. He understood America and our special love for his homeland, and I always made time for him. I was in London on December 4, 2019, when I learned that Bibi desperately wanted to meet. We made a plan for Lisbon, Portugal, where I was flying that night. He told me he was worried that Jared was too willing to give up Jerusalem and that the ayatollah was planning to use Hezbollah's precision rockets to coerce Israel into accepting Assad as the ruler of Syria. We also discussed Soleimani's activities that we were seeing at that time and how we might work to thwart those plans.

After the meeting, Netanyahu leaked that I had promised American acceptance of a formal US-Israel mutual-defense treaty, which would obligate each country to come to the other's aid if attacked. It was false, but it was a good story for him, and, after correcting the record, our partnership did not diminish in any way. On the contrary, momentum was building at that point in time for one of the greatest diplomatic achievements of the century. To get it done required many hands, bold leaders, and extended relationships, not temporary sets of overlapping interests. Above all, it would entail choosing the right allies.

THE ABRAHAM ACCORDS: NEW ALLIES FOR PEACE

Before I delve into the story of the Abraham Accords, I want to make one thing clear: It isn't at its core a story about Israel, or Arab nations, or even Iran. It's a story of the entire Middle East. And it's a story of alliances predicated on America being a force for good in the region in ways that greatly benefit the American people.

Prior to the Trump administration, stale dogmas dictated American policy toward the region. Establishment figures in both parties believed that Israel could never have peace with its neighbors until it had made peace with the Palestinians. It was an article of faith. Take John Kerry, who insisted in 2016: "I've heard several prominent politicians in Israel sometimes saying, well, the Arab world is in a different place now. We just have to reach out to them, and we can work some things with the Arab world, and we'll deal with the Palestinians. No, no, no and no."

It turns out that Kerry's narrow way of thinking was wrong, wrong, wrong, and wrong.

But believing the Palestinian issue had to be addressed before Israel could make peace with more of its neighbors wasn't the Obama administration's worst idea on Middle Eastern diplomacy. President Obama's speech in Cairo that effectively apologized for American influence in the region after 9/11 signaled to adversaries that we were weak and irresolute. His pullback from his declaration of a "redline" after Assad's chemical attack in Syria in 2013 only confirmed what they already knew. And then came the most imbecilic foreign policy decision of our time: the Obama administration's nuclear deal with Iran. For Barack Obama, Joe Biden, John Kerry, Ben Rhodes, John Brennan, and all the rest, the nuclear deal in 2015 was the entrée into a true friendship with the ayatollahs. They believed that their appeasement would reshape the region, as they anticipated working in unison with a regime that enjoys nothing more than shedding blood in the name of the Islamic Revolution.

As we began our independent engagement with both Israel and Arab nations, we soon saw just how terrified they were by the prospect of Iran dominating the region. Those fears were well-grounded, as Iran grew flush with cash, thanks to Obama's rotten deal. Even before the deal, Iran was the primary source of the region's trouble. It supplied weapons and funding to Hamas, Hezbollah, and Palestinian Islamic Jihad—all sworn enemies of Israel. It crushed the people and economies of Lebanon and Iraq through the influence of Shia terror groups in their politics. Iran's support for Houthi rebels exacerbated a human rights catastrophe in Yemen. In Syria, Bashar al-Assad butchers his own people with help from Hezbollah and fighters under Iranian command. And this is to say nothing of the specter of an Iranian nuclear weapon casting a dark shadow of annihilation.

Our administration came to conceive of the Middle East in an entirely new way. Jared Kushner, Ambassador Friedman, and Special Representative Jason Greenblatt brought fresh thinking to the problems of the region. We didn't see things as Jews versus Arabs, or Israel versus everyone but America. We could see with fresh eyes how the region was poised for a realignment, with the forces of peace and stability (Israel and certain Arab neighbors) opposing the forces of extremism and destruction (the Iranian regime, its proxies, and Sunni jihadists such as ISIS and al-Qaeda).

The effort began before I became secretary of state, and it took until our final year in office to pull off. Lots of people deserve credit, starting with Jared and David and Jason, as well as Secretary Mnuchin. Our ambassador in the United Arab Emirates, John Rakolta, and in Bahrain, Justin Siberell, along with the Emirati ambassador to the United States, Yousef Al Otaiba, and the Israeli ambassador to the United States, Ron Dermer, were likewise instrumental.

The winds of change don't always blow hard. Sometimes you just have to feel the breeze. From the outset of the administration, we saw signs that something big might be possible. President Trump made the first-ever direct flight from Riyadh to Jerusalem in 2017—a minor breakthrough. In 2018, President Netanyahu visited Oman, which is effectively the Switzerland of the Middle East. It was the first visit by an Israeli prime minister to that country since 1996. The United Arab Emirates allowed the playing of the Israeli national anthem at a judo tournament in Abu Dhabi that same year. And in 2019, at a conference on Middle Eastern security in Warsaw, Poland, senior Arab leaders and an Israeli leader both attended the same conference on security matters for the first time since 1991. That gathering in Warsaw did not draw much attention, but the fact that Arab and Israeli leaders could publicly meet without an eruption of the so-called Arab street gave us encouragement.

In keeping with our strategy of building a counter-Iran coalition, we hoped that the time was right to push for normalized relations between Israel and certain Arab neighbors. That feat had happened only twice in Israel's history: with Egypt in 1979 and Jordan in 1994. The diplomatic blocking and tackling was going to be tough, but several factors worked in our favor. Small Arab nations such as Bahrain and the UAE—each a short distance from Iranian territory across the Persian Gulf and Strait of Hormuz, respectively—had a vested interest in protecting their country from the Iranian intelligence operations that had been festering inside their borders for years. Both nations had also wanted to turn their nations into financial and tourism powerhouses and believed that a powerful Iran would destroy their economic gains. We also knew that a new generation of leaders in the Arab world didn't harbor the same hard-line Arab nationalist or anti-Semitic views as their predecessors did, which potentially made them more open to formal ties with Israel.

Visionary leaders, a lot of hard work, and a series of events delivered an outcome that nobody had mapped out on any whiteboard in the world. One of those leaders was Mohamed bin Zayed of the United Arab Emirates, or MBZ, as he is known in the diplomatic world. MBZ was a staunch opponent of Islamism. Under his leadership and that of his now-deceased brother, the UAE has consistently afforded enhanced degrees of freedom to its people and the millions of expatriates living inside its borders. It is a nation wealthy in natural resources, a massive hub of global international business, and a country that for many years has welcomed Western ideas, universities, and thinking—including religious freedom.

MBZ was savvy, well read, and troubled by Iranian power. He deeply loved his family, and he spoke about his children often. He knew that the UAE's economic power was important, but not enough to guarantee success and independence. MBZ frequently reminded me of America's failures in the region as he saw them and offered his thoughts on how to avoid them. He made clear that he was counting on America to use its power to rein in the evil from Iran. I reminded him of this after the Soleimani strike, when all the Gulf States feared that their nations would be targets of Iranian revenge. In any event, we worked hard so that they were not. Over the years our conversations were always to the point. He never asked me to deliver anything he didn't think that I could deliver, and I never made a promise to him that I could not keep. He always put the United Arab Emirates first, which was his responsibility. I admired that, and it helped our teams later navigate the complex waters of making peace.

I first met another important Emirati figure when I was CIA director in 2017. His Highness Sheikh Tahnoon always wore a big smile, but don't be fooled: the sheikh is thinking and testing every minute. Our services did really good work together on a number of issues. We became good partners and friends, always sharing our tools to make our countries more secure. For four years, Sheikh Tahnoon always took my call, and I his, because we were both committed to the same end.

Others have written and will write about the diplomatic nuances of how the Abraham Accords ultimately came together. My overarching thought is this: they don't happen without the pillars of America First, Israel as an ally, and the widespread recognition of Iran as the central destabilizing power in the region. But at a more granular level, two factors shaping the diplomatic process stand out. The first is that we were working on these deals against the backdrop of a fragile political coalition leading Israel. The Israelis held three parliamentary elections—two in 2019 and another in March 2020—and none led to a stable coalition majority. The truth is that domestic politics often bind leaders in a democracy— that's how it supposed to work—but the fact that Israeli leaders had little margin for political error made our efforts to keep our discussions quiet that much more important. News of our diplomacy leaking could have made or ruined many Israeli politicians' days, depending on their circumstances. We succeeded in keeping things under wraps: the announcement of the first normalization agreement with the United Arab Emirates, on August 13, 2020, came as a massive surprise to the world.

Second, the PA worked mightily against our efforts. They knew that if the dam broke—if its ability to be a barrier to peace diminished—it would lose its ability to leverage the threat of launching an intifada and inflaming Arabs across the world. The PA consistently leaked scaremongering stories about the annexation of Palestine and the perfidy of Jew-loving traitors in the Gulf. Their despots stirred trouble at the Organization of Islamic Cooperation and appealed to ancient grievances. But the leaders of these four nations—the United States, Israel, the UAE, and Bahrain—were unmoved. They stayed the course of choosing the right allies and delivered peace.

After the initial announcement of the Emirates, other countries followed. Bahrain, under the powerful leadership of its crown prince, joined up a scant twenty-nine days later, signing a deal to fight anti-Semitism and promote peace. Arab Zionists—who would have believed it? America First helped make it possible.

More dominoes continued to fall after that. Since October 2019, we had been working to take Sudan off the list of state sponsors of terrorism, something I'd been trying to do since I was CIA director. This was the right thing to do because the Sudanese had become solid counterterrorism partners. But the notion of removing them from the list also gave us leverage in convincing Sudan to recognize Israel. Fights between the president of Sudan and its senior military leadership delayed the progress, so I became the first secretary of state in fifteen years to travel to Sudan to solidify the deal. Brian Hook, who was a central part of the Abraham Accords team, was instrumental in securing this achievement, as well.

Then Morocco came aboard in December 2020. I liked working with the Moroccans even in my CIA days. They are focused counterterrorism partners. The asking price to get them to a yes was American recognition of a region of southern Morocco called Western Sahara. It made sense for America, and we helped deliver the formal recognition of Israel from yet another Arab country.

To this day, I am so happy about what we accomplished with the Abraham Accords. Who would have believed that Team Trump's Middle East crew, oft-maligned by the foreign policy establishment, would make it possible to watch Emirati fighter pilots meet Israeli fighter pilots in the skies, not to fight but to fly in formation? It was completely the Lord at work. Only the prejudices of milquetoast Scandinavian globalists prevented President Trump, Bibi Netanyahu, and MBZ from receiving the Nobel Peace Prize. (Not that it was worth all that much—Barack Obama received it his first year in office for no accomplishment whatsoever, and terrorist kingpin Yasar Arafat nabbed one, too.) Our reward was to push aside the boulders of animosity in the Middle East. Such are the achievements when nations recognize their interests and commit to working with the right allies and partners to achieve them. I can best sum up the shocking progress of the Abraham Accords with a comment made by one of my heroes, Vaclav Havel, on the collapse of Communism in Eastern Europe: "The mask fell away so rapidly that, in the flood of work, we have literally no time even to be astonished."

SAUDI ARABIA: THE NEXT MEMBER OF THE ABRAHAM ACCORDS?

We tried hard to bring Saudi Arabia into the accords. We came ever so close, thanks largely to Mohammed bin Salman, the Kingdom's crown prince. At the time of our administration, his father, King Salman, remained the final authority over the kingdom's affairs, but much of the day-to-day administration of the country had been turned over to MBS. Without the tacit approval of MBS, the Abraham Accords never would have come into being. The world owes him a debt of gratitude for what he did. It is not an easy thing for the leader of Saudi Arabia to bless steps toward peace with Israel. Saudi Arabia occupies a special place in Islam, not least because it hosts the great pilgrimage, the hajj, and is home to the first and second most holy sites in Islam in the cities of Mecca and Medina.

Despite his young age—he was thirty-one years old when he became the crown prince—MBS had already shown himself to be a savvy operator in a complex and ruthless political environment. The power struggle to replace his father is the stuff of legend, as MBS made the case, through logic and other, much less diplomatic means, for why he should succeed King Salman. As a leader, MBS had demonstrated more than his ability to work inside the ruling family. He had shown his love of the Saudi people and had shared his vision for bringing modernity to the kingdom, along with prosperity and security. MBS has been the driving force behind Saudi Arabia's Vision 2030, which sets out key economic and social reforms for a country dominated by oil production and hard-line Islamic values. Some say he has moved too slowly with his reforms. But no Saudi leader has ever moved this quickly, and I venture that no other leader could have. Some see his efforts as fantastical, from plans for the futuristic city of Neom to building world-class institutions of learning in Riyadh to his efforts to eliminate Wahhabism from the curriculum in Islamic schools across the world. But his leadership is working.

From America's perspective, the kingdom will continue to matter a great deal. MBS is its head and may well be so, inshallah, for decades to come. Under his leadership, Saudi Arabia is working to secure Iraq's fragile democracy and keep it at least partially tethered to the West. The Kingdom helped our efforts to feed fleeing refugees from Syria. When MBS became the crown prince, one of his first efforts was to assist the United States in rooting out Iran's destabilizing influence from Yemen and assisting in the provision of food to avoid famine there. The Kingdom has also contributed millions of dollars to our fight against ISIS. Saudi oil production during our administration bolstered our ability to sanction Iran without imposing huge fuel costs on the American people. Solidify-ing a strong partnership with a complicated country such as the Kingdom wasn't easy, and hefty credit is due to a great American, Ambassador John Abizaid, the former head of all US forces in the Middle East, who led our diplomatic team in Riyadh.

The praise above will no doubt inspire legion "Pompeo, the Khashoggi Apologist" stories. So be it. But watch the bylines—many will be written by those who supported paying billions to the ayatollah, who has killed more of his own citizens than the number of people who have ever even been to the Saudi Arabian consulate in Istanbul. These critics demand changes in the kingdom at a pace no nation could survive and therefore are naively arguing for instability there, the dangers of which are obvious. The US strategic partnership with the kingdom matters to Americans from New Hampshire to Iowa and from South Carolina to Nevada.

We've now gone from wondering whether the Abraham Accords would be possible to guessing which Arab country will join them next. I welcome the speculation because it assumes the permanency, legacy, and importance of the agreements themselves. I do think Saudi Arabia will be a part of it someday. I can also say we were breathtakingly close to having a major Asian nation sign on before we left office. It may come as a surprise to many Americans that none of the six nations with the largest Muslim populations in the world are Gulf Arab states. Four are in Southeast Asia—Indonesia, Pakistan, India, and Bangladesh. Two—Nigeria and Egypt—are in Africa. Permanent peace with the Jewish homeland is in the interest of each of these nations.

While I don't know who is next, I do know the conditions that will permit the next country to enter. First among them is to acknowledge the right for Israel, in all of its rightful land, to exist as the eternal homeland of the Jewish people. Second, it will take American leadership. Without American support, it is nearly impossible to imagine a Muslim nation's leader making such a decision. Third, the world will have to see that the United States is locked at the hip with Israel. Without that perception, Muslim nations will think that, perhaps, one day, the United States will move closer to them than to Israel. Fourth, America must be prepared to defend a would-be Abraham Accords member from the real threat from the regime in Iran. Those four pillars guided remarkable leaders to make real peace deals with their Jewish brothers and sisters in Israel. The world will long see the fruit of choosing the right allies.

CHAPTER 14

TRY NEW IDEAS

The Louisiana Purchase. "Seward's Folly." The Greenland Gain?
August 2019. As usual, the media was laughing at something
they didn't understand. The *Wall Street Journal* had just reported the
Trump administration's interest in buying Greenland from Denmark.
The president confirmed it not long after, saying, "Strategically, it's inter-
esting. And, we'd be interested. We'll talk to them a little bit."

The Danes immediately shut down the idea in public, with Prime
Minister Mette Frederiksen insisting, "Greenland is not for sale . . .
Greenland is not Danish. Greenland belongs to Greenland." OK, fine.
But, madam Prime Minister, if Greenland belongs to Greenland, how
do you know whether it's for sale? Surely you are right, Greenland is not
Danish. So, why are you opining on its desire to be part of the United
States via an acquisition? Even worse was the derision from the media.
Daniel Lippman of *Politico* called it "a proposal that is as impractical as it
is seductive to a media and political class stuck in the doldrums of August."

In reality, buying Greenland was one of the best ideas the Trump
administration had. The president and his team—including his economic
team—all believed that such a deal made sense. For tiny Denmark, subsidizing this territory some 1,800 miles away is a financial burden. For
Greenlanders—all fifty-seven thousand of them—being part of the
United States might be just what they need as a matter of economic opportunities and better living standards. For America—which already has
a military base there—Greenland holds massive deposits of important
rare earth minerals, useful for building F-35s and other defense systems.

Stare at a map of the globe looking straight down on the North Pole, and you will see that the shortest routes from the United States to reach Russia and China traverse Greenland. There is no dispute: access to Greenland and its waters is a big deal—and the Chinese are active there because of it.

While we ultimately didn't buy Greenland, the diplomacy surrounding this effort accrued to America's benefit. On June 9, 2020, the Trump administration announced that, finally, America would deter Chinese and Russian aggression by building a fleet of icebreakers to assist naval vessels in the Artic region. The next day, a project came to fruition that I had worked on for many months with Ulrich and our outstanding ambassador to Denmark, Carla Sands. For the first time since Dwight Eisenhower was president, the United States would once again operate a consulate in Greenland. It's easy to say, "Who cares about consulates and frozen seas?" Some might even say, "Why are we wasting our time on Greenland?" Opening the consulate was a central part of our effort to make allies, confront the Chinese Communist Party, and build a deterrence model that would last for decades.

The Danes were also pleased at the reopening of the consulate. To quote my Danish counterpart, Foreign Minister Jeppe Kofod: "I welcome the reopening of the American consulate in Nuuk . . . It is a clear priority that the increased American interest in Greenland benefits the Greenlandic society. We have been working actively for this objective and I am glad that we are now beginning to see concrete results."

In July 2020, I traveled to Denmark to maintain the momentum. Denmark's foreign ministry is one of the most beautiful diplomatic headquarters in the world, nestled in Copenhagen harbor. But the happenings inside mattered more. Foreign Minister Kofod and I had our own great bilateral meeting, but we also brought in the foreign ministers of Greenland and the Faroe Islands—an archipelago halfway between the northern tip of Scotland and Iceland. That meeting was very important for developing America's long-term relationships.

In the end, Team Trump made America safer by increasing our presence in Greenland, pushing the Chinese option further back in the minds of Greenlanders, and convincing the Danish government that we wanted a mutually beneficial relationship with Greenland. Contrary to the reporting when we opened the consulate, the move was not "a complete departure from" the effort to buy Greenland but rather a logical product of it.

None of this would have happened had the Trump administration not been willing to try new ideas.

TRYING NEW THINGS GETS RESULTS

Trying new ideas—and defying foreign policy orthodoxies in the process—didn't endear us to the media or the Washington establishment. It rarely does. When one of President Reagan's speechwriters visited West Berlin in 1987, in advance of the president's famous Brandenburg Gate speech, he met with an American diplomat. "He was full of ideas about what Reagan should not say," remembered Peter Robinson. Regarding the Berlin Wall, this diplomat urged that Reagan omit any reference to it in his remarks. "They've gotten used to it by now," Robinson recalls him saying about the East Berliners and the wall that blocked them from freedom. In the days and weeks leading up to the famous speech, the National Security Council and the State Department repeatedly sent new drafts over to the White House with what would become one of Reagan's greatest lines deleted. In the end, President Reagan trusted his instincts and spoke the words that have gone down in history: "Mr. Gorbachev, tear down this wall!"

We tried to have the same open-mindedness, and not permit orthodoxy to be a concrete wall of its own. At the top of our administration was a president who, untethered by traditional ideological categories, kept a very open mind about what policies might work, provided they put America first. The Oval Office sometimes resembled a dorm room bull session. We floated ideas and shot them down all the time. Nothing was off-limits. And the president empowered his team to run with the ball if they thought they were on to something. That's how we locked in the Abraham Accords. It's how we moved the US Embassy to Jerusalem. It's how we stood up the Remain in Mexico policy. Being willing to ignore reflexive dogmas of "this is how we've always done it" or "that won't work" matters. Regrettably, much of Washington is conditioned to function—or rather not function—according to those reflexes.

We ignored them. We tried new ideas.

NEW MANEUVERS IN THE MIDDLE EAST

In the Middle East, we made hard choices at different waypoints and sometimes had great success. Iraq, though, was a constant problem. Winston Churchill once said that operating in Iraq is like "living on an ungrateful volcano." Since the toppling of Saddam Hussein, that volcano has put thousands of American soldiers and diplomats in danger. We wanted to see through our obligations to create stability in that country, and to prevent it from being an Iranian fiefdom. In at least one instance, I tried to get creative.

The success of the CIA runs on ingenuity. In 2017 and 2018, we tried to help "good guys" in Iraq have an opportunity to compete in national elections. Iran was bribing parliamentarians to get its hardcore anti-American guy in office. We could not compete in that way, but my team and I did have an idea on how to address the problem. I presented it to my oversight committee in Congress. It wasn't going to be particularly covert, but it was largely free.

I was shocked at the dustup it created. Senator Kamala Harris said, "Well, Iran won't like that." Well, sure, the ayatollahs would hate it. Adam Schiff—in the middle of perpetrating the Russia Hoax—said, "No way, you cannot do this." Most galling was Senator Richard Durbin of Illinois, who had this exchange with me:

> DURBIN: How do you explain this to the *New York Times?*
> ME: Sir, first, we're not doing anything wrong. We are trying to
> slow down corruption and Iran at the same time. And, by the way,
> we're f——ing America. I wouldn't explain it to the *New York Times*
> because they simply could not understand that we are the good guys.

I did have better partners than certain members of the US Congress in the mission to create a more independent and sovereign Iraq. President Barham Salih of Iraq was one. And the Barzanis in the Kurdish north were fine partners, too. Leading the Kurds inside Iraq is challenging stuff. The Kurds are under constant threat from Iran, but the work they did with us, often quietly, was excellent. There are few finer fighters or better friends to the United States. Of course, nothing in the Middle East is easy. In the end, we continued to lose ground to Iran inside of Iraq, and to this day that battle for the freedom and independence of the Iraqi people continues.

After MBS, the most politically despised Middle Eastern leader on the progressive left is probably President Abdel Fattah el-Sisi of Egypt, who became a critically important partner for the Trump administration. Egypt is critical to peace and stability, with its population of one hundred million Muslims bordering Israel, the Mediterranean, Libya, and the Gaza Strip, and also sitting squarely on a land route for terrorists from Africa. America had already once been exposed to real peril stemming from the country. After the forced resignation of President Hosni Mubarak in 2011 and a chaotic interim period, the Islamist Muslim Brotherhood spent months in power until it, too, was ejected in 2013. In its place came Sisi's government, which, much to America's benefit, was committed to suppressing Islamist terror networks.

I first met Sisi in March 2014, when he was still General Sisi. We gathered with two other members of the intelligence committee: Chairman Mike Rogers, a Republican from Michigan, and Democrat Jim Himes, an intelligent, good guy whose Connecticut district is one of the richest in America. Sisi told us two important things that day. First, he was going to announce a run for president the next day. He also told us that his decision to run meant that if we were to visit him in one year, there were only two circumstances in which we'd find him: A) basking in economic success for Egypt or B) sitting in jail, just like his two predecessors who were that day held in Egyptian prisons.

The second item was a request: "Please tell President Obama to give us access to the Apache helicopters we bought. They won't let us take them out of the shrink-wrap. Tell him the Israelis want us to have them too." I laughed, because even though Sisi's English was imperfect, he knew the exact word for "shrink-wrap." What he didn't understand was that the Obama administration didn't care what Israel wanted. The administration was most likely bowing to Senator Patrick Leahy's pressure to hold the helicopters over human rights concerns. Rogers and I agreed Sisi should get them so his forces could use them to kill terrorists in the Sinai. Egypt was and remains a valuable counterterrorism partner.

Denying that country the tools to help us was incomprehensible. During our administration, we also sought the Egyptians' help with the Abraham Accords, as they already had a peace agreement with Israel and proved that Arab nations could recognize Israel and survive. They had tried new things and come out the better for it.

TANGLING WITH TURKEY

Of course, trying new ideas is bound to disrupt existing political orders and interests. But when American security is at stake, leaders must forge ahead anyway, even if it rubs allies and partners the wrong way. This dynamic played out in our relationship with Turkey, a country at the center of many Middle East decision points.

From the beginning, our administration did not have a strong operating strategy regarding Turkey. It should have been much easier to formulate one. Turkey has every incentive to align firmly with the West, as well as a population that would welcome it and benefit from it. Yet ever since a purported "coup" in 2016, President Erdoğan had gone full Islamist-authoritarian. I spent countless hours with him and his national security advisor, Ibrahim Kalin, and intel chief, Hakan Fidan. Erdoğan called President Trump constantly to complain that we were helping the Kurds too much or refusing to return Fethullah Gülen, a religious figure in exile whom Erdoğan blamed for masterminding the coup. I think he felt emboldened to take advantage of America in response to the weakness the Obama administration had shown in the region—a pullout from Iraq that allowed ISIS to grow, not enforcing the redline in Syria, opening the door for Iranian hegemony, and so on.

In the early days of the administration, the most urgent Mideast matter was confronting ISIS. We had zero intention of putting massive American forces on the ground, but we knew that it was imperative to keep ISIS-linked terrorism from coming to Europe, Israel, and the United States. National Security Advisor H. R. McMaster worked with Secretary Mattis, Chairman of the Joint Chiefs of Staff Joe Dunford, Secretary Tillerson, and me to evaluate two options. The first was to work with the Kurdish forces in Syria, known as the SDF, and to assist them in retaking ISIS-held

Syrian territory from Idlib Province in the northwest, down the Middle Euphrates River Valley, and then over to the Iraqi border.

The second option was to support a fairly traditional proposal the Turks had presented: let them do the work. The Turks, NATO allies, claimed they had huge forces that could clear out ISIS and restore order in Syria. McMaster and I both viewed this skeptically, as their plan looked baldly like the ethnic cleansing of Kurds. Erdoğan would use this opportunity to accomplish his long-standing goal of crushing the Kurdish people throughout Syria, with the added benefit of American acquiescence. Erdoğan and Fidan called me repeatedly to stress how the PKK—a US-designated terrorist organization—was no different from the SDF. They claimed that if the United States supported the SDF, it would rupture our relationship with Turkey.

Mattis and Dunford had a different concern: Turkey's military wasn't capable of defeating ISIS. Dunford went to see the "Turkish invasion force" that was training inside Turkey. After the Turks delayed this visit repeatedly, he was finally permitted to review the troops. What he saw convinced him that the Turks had zero chance of beating ISIS without massive American support. We presented President Trump with a uniform, fairly novel recommendation: work with the SDF. They had a demonstrated ability and a real motivation to fight because ISIS was occupying their homeland. They knew the terrain and how to fight. With American intelligence and American air cover, they represented our best chance to take down ISIS. The president agreed.

Now came the diplomatic piece of breaking the news to the Turks. It was left to McMaster and yours truly to tell them what they didn't want to hear. The meeting went poorly. Sitting in the Roosevelt Room inside the White House, we told them that we would continue to provide them with what they needed to fight the PKK, but that we were going to work with Syrian Kurds to crush ISIS. I've never seen such anger erupt so quickly in a room. Kalin and Fidan exploded and then left quickly. It wasn't great for the relationship, but the United States had made the right decision on whom to partner with to crush the caliphate. This new concept made all the difference. By January 2019, Syria and Iraq were liberated from the black flag of Islamist domination. Rather than take the traditional route of partnering with another national military, we went with the Kurds—and Americans benefited.

THE QUAD COMES TOGETHER

No challenge required the employment of more creative diplomacy—more new ideas—than that of pushing back on China. I knew that many other countries were growing weary of Chinese disinformation, intellectual property theft, military aggression, and more. When I spoke to my ambassadors, I told them that their first priority was to put America first. Their second focus was to counter China. Whether they were in Germany or South Africa, Canada or Malaysia, their focus on the CCP, its embassy, its operatives, and its policies was urgent.

One of the most important new achievements of the Trump administration was convening the Quad for the first time ever at the foreign minister level. The Quad consists of four powerful and democratic Indo-Pacific nations: Australia, India, Japan, and the United States. Collectively, we represent approximately 23 percent of the world's population and 30 percent of global GDP. We have real economies, militaries, and diplomatic influence. The Quad originally started back in 2007, but various disputes had kept us from building momentum in the years since. The Trump team recognized that a reinvigorated Quad would be an important new tool for facing down Xi Jinping and the CCP. We renewed a push to get on the same page as part of a true "pivot to Asia"—not the empty slogan President Obama trotted out, which was a laughingstock to many foreign ministers, but a revitalized strategy.

It helped that the United States already had unbreakable alliances with Japan and Australia. My two Japanese foreign minister counterparts and I spent many hours responding to Chairman Kim's many provocations. Always sensible and meticulous, the Japanese foreign ministry is world-class.

Their boss, Prime Minister Shinzo Abe, was a global leader of extraordinary courage, vision, and smarts. A true friend of America, he always took the time to meet or call me on matters of importance to him and his country and make sure that "America understands." His willingness to do the right thing to transform Japan from its historical and understandable pacifism into a nation capable of providing strategic support to other nations in the region was admirable. He is regarded as the father of the Quad, demonstrating his foresight in viewing the CCP as a threat. He also coined the idea of a "free and open Indo-Pacific"—a concept that has gained lasting currency in diplomatic circles. It's worth repeating: What a loss it was for the world that this outstanding leader was assassinated in 2022.

Our mates down under were perhaps the most like me in their willingness to confront China. Prime Minister Scott Morrison, a faithful Christian leader, was bold when he could have been timid and strong when his predecessors would have bowed to Chinese demands. The Japanese and Australian legs of the Quad were strong and getting stronger with our support.

The wild card was India. As a nation explicitly founded on a socialist ideology, India spent the bulk of the Cold War aligning with neither the United States nor the USSR. The country has always charted its own course without a true alliance system, and that is still mostly the case. But China's actions have caused India to change its strategic posture in the last few years. China forged a close partnership with Pakistan—India's archrival—as one of the first steps in its Belt and Road Initiative. In June 2020, Chinese soldiers clubbed twenty Indian soldiers to death in a border skirmish. That bloody incident caused the Indian public to demand a change in their country's relationship with China. India also banned TikTok and dozens of Chinese apps as part of its response. And a Chinese virus was killing hundreds of thousands of Indian citizens. I was sometimes asked why India had moved away from China, and my answer came straight from what I heard from Indian leadership: "Wouldn't you?" Times were changing—and creating an opportunity for us to try something new and pull the United States and India more closely together than ever.

On the Indian side, my original counterpart was not an important player on the Indian foreign policy team. Instead, I worked much more closely with National Security Advisor Ajit Doval, a close and trusted confidant of Prime Minister Narendra Modi. My second Indian counterpart was Subrahmanyam Jaishankar. In May 2019, we welcomed "J" as India's new foreign minister. I could not have asked for a better counterpart. I love this guy. English is one of the seven languages he speaks, and his is somewhat better than mine. Professional, rational, and a fierce defender of his boss and his country, he had spent almost four decades in his country's foreign service, including a stint as India's ambassador to the United States.

We hit it off immediately. In our first meeting, I was bemoaning, in very diplomatic speak, that his predecessor had not been particularly helpful. He said that he could see why I had trouble with his predecessor, a goofball and a heartland political hack.

"Careful, I'm a heartland political hack!" I replied in jest.

He laughed, noting that if that were true, it would make me the first heartland political hack who had ever been an editor on the *Harvard Law Review*. Well played, J.

American diplomacy usually has put Tokyo at the center of its Asia policy and viewed Seoul as its primary location for geostrategic reach. American neglect of India was a decades-long bipartisan failure. Its population rivals that of China. We are natural allies, as we share a history of democracy, a common language, and ties of people and technology. India is also a market with enormous demand for American intellectual property and products. These factors, plus its strategic location in South Asia, made India the fulcrum of my diplomacy to counteract Chinese aggression. In my mind, a counter-China bloc made up of the United States, India, Japan, Australia, South Korea, the United Kingdom, and the European Union would have an economic weight at least three times that of China. I chose to devote serious quantities of time and effort to help make India the next great American ally.

But deepening US-India ties was no simple matter. Besides avoiding alliances, India also has a deeply protectionist and state-directed economy. India's weaponry has been mostly Russian—cheap and good enough—and its trading relationship and long international border with China limits India's appetite for risk. Indian leaders are also intently focused every minute on their bête noire of Pakistan. As a nuclear power controlled by its military and Islamist-sympathizing intelligence services—not its elected government—Pakistan presents a significant strategic and a terroristic threat to India. Every action I took with respect to Pakistan—a trip or a phone call or a comment—was sure to result in a message saying that Prime Minister Modi or Foreign Minister Jaishankar wanted to speak. They were relentless and appropriately so.

I do not think the world properly knows just how close the India-Pakistan rivalry came to spilling over into a nuclear conflagration in February 2019. The truth is, I don't know precisely the answer either; I just know it was too close. I'll never forget the night I was in Hanoi, Vietnam when—as if negotiating with the North Koreans on nuclear weapons wasn't enough—India and Pakistan started threatening each other in connection with a decades-long dispute over the northern border region of Kashmir. After an Islamist terrorist attack in Kashmir—probably enabled in part by Pakistan's lax counterterror policies—killed forty Indians, India responded with an air strike against terrorists inside Pakistan. The Pakistanis shot down a plane in a subsequent dogfight and kept the Indian pilot prisoner.

In Hanoi, I was awakened to speak with my Indian counterpart. He believed the Pakistanis had begun to prepare their nuclear weapons for a strike. India, he informed me, was contemplating its own escalation. I asked him to do nothing and give us a minute to sort things out. I began to work with Ambassador Bolton, who was with me in the tiny secure communications facility in our hotel. I reached the actual leader of Pakistan, General Bajwa, with whom I had engaged many times. I told him what the Indians had told me. He said it wasn't true. As one might expect, he believed the Indians were preparing their nuclear weapons for deployment. It took us a few hours—and remarkably good work by our teams on the ground in New Delhi and Islamabad—to convince each side that the other was not preparing for nuclear war. No other nation could have done what we did that night to avoid a horrible outcome.

As with all diplomacy, the people working the problem set matter a great deal, at least in the short run. I was fortunate to have great team members in place on India, none more so than Ken Juster, an incredibly capable ambassador. Ken loves India and its people. And, most of all, he loves the American people and worked his tail off for us every day. My most senior diplomat, David Hale, had also been the US ambassador to Pakistan and knew that our relationship with India was a priority. General McMaster and Admiral Philip Davidson, the head of what came to be renamed the US Indo-Pacific Command, understood India's importance, too. Although often frustrated by the Indians, US trade representative Robert Lighthizer—a brilliant trade negotiator and a Bob Dole staff alumnus, making him a near-Kansan—was a great partner working to deepen economic ties. We all shared the view that America had to make a bold strategic effort to tighten our ties with India and break the mold with new ideas.

The cumulative effect of our great American team and strong Indian leaders was a much-needed new level of defense and diplomatic cooperation. The reemergence of the Quad security dialogue proved it. With his boss, Prime Minister Modi, on board, Jaishankar and I joined Toshimitsu Motegi of Japan and Marise Payne of Australia in a room together in New York in September 2019. It was the first time in history that the foreign ministers of the Quad had met. We did it again in Tokyo in October 2020—probably the only time in my life that I'll make what was essentially a one-day trip to Japan. This sojourn occurred during the depths of the pandemic, and it was eerie to see the normally crowded streets of Tokyo deserted. Those meetings were a crucial foundation for coordinated action against China from the world's leading democracies.

EUROPE: STUCK IN THE MUD ON CHINA POLICY

As for America's European allies, my work to energize them to confront China—what would be a new idea for them, certainly—was a mixed bag of results. I greatly appreciated the leadership of NATO secretary general Jens Stoltenberg, a man of true vision who supported our efforts to make China part of NATO's focus. Other true allies in Europe were Denmark and the Czech Republic, a country with a set of die-hard anti-Communists in its parliament. The European Union eventually agreed to hold a first-ever strategic dialogue about China with the United States, and its nations did take some actions over Hong Kong and Xinjiang, but the Europeans showed little zeal to push back on Beijing. At the end of

2020, Chancellor Angela Merkel of Germany and President Emmanuel Macron of France sealed a deal with Xi on a massive trade pact, although its passage is still stalled in the European Parliament.

Dealing with the European Union was among the most unpleasant tasks of my tenure. I worked with two counterparts at the foreign minister level. The first was Federica Mogherini, a former member of the Italian Communist Youth Federation. The other was Josep Borrell, a Spanish socialist. Both despised me. And they liked President Trump even less. They believed us to be boorish and dumb. I believed them to be naive agents of the Left. Perhaps that's enough said. They resisted our efforts to stop Iran's nuclear program, to oppose the CCP's rise, and to put trade between the European Union and America on an equal footing. There is much to be said about the European Union, its configuration, and the autonomy it has sucked out of nations such as Greece, Hungary, Italy, and Poland. Germany and France abuse their power over those countries, and Europe is most often the worse for it.

The sad truth is that most European leaders don't have an instinct to see China as a threat. France and Germany depend on China for sales of Louis Vuitton bags and Volkswagens. British universities and parliamentarians are corrupted by Chinese cash. Italy has gone weak on keeping Huawei out of its networks. Small countries such as Lithuania (with a population of less than three million people), the Czech Republic (eleven million) and Slovenia (two million) are the real moral leaders in Europe on pushing back against Chinese coercion. Not coincidentally, these countries all share the memory of life under Communism, spurring them to acts of leadership that should put Old Europe to shame. A regret of mine is that I did not have enough time to visit the Baltic states of Lithuania, Latvia, and Estonia—outstanding allies for freedom for whom American support against the threat of Russian aggression remains crucial. Elsewhere on the continent, I'm pleased that we could count on Poland as the strongest European supporter of our maximum-pressure campaign against Iran, even if the Poles must do more to stop the Chinese economic incursion into their country.

With Western Europe recalcitrant on China, the JCPOA, and NATO spending, I decided not to sink inordinate amounts of time into mending fences and playing nice with them. Instead, I concentrated on something new: moving the ball forward where America had new opportunities to do so in Europe. I'm particularly proud of how we strengthened ties with Greece, a country that was rabidly anti-American in the 1970s but now looks to us as a favored partner. I had an inside track for a good relationship: Prime Minister Kyriakos Mitsotakis had played basketball with Brian Bulatao at Harvard Business School, and I knew he was a good leader we could trust.

Much of my focus with him was on addressing disputes over unlawful Turkish exploration for energy in the Mediterranean. For the first time ever, in 2019, a US secretary of state showed up to the Israel-Greece-Cyprus trilateral meeting to discuss energy exploration in the region. In November 2020, I also did something that hadn't been done in ages and wrote a letter to the Greek foreign minister that commended Greece as a "pillar of stability" in the region. I urged our NATO ally Turkey to "end its calculated provocations and immediately begin exploratory talks with Greece." The last time an American secretary of state made such a clear statement of American support for Greece was by Henry Kissinger in the 1970s—and the Greeks were thrilled by my words now. Two trips to Greece also reinforced that this relationship mattered for the United States. The second of those visits was a real honor: Susan and I stayed at the family house of Prime Minister Mitsotakis in Crete. Our ties with an ally that will only assume more importance in the vital eastern-Mediterranean region are now stronger than at any time since the Marshall Plan.

I'll close with some thoughts on wise words from an unlikely source. Osama bin Laden was evil, and I am glad he's dead. But he was right about one thing when he said, "When people see a strong horse and a weak horse, by nature they will like the strong horse." This is true not only among Islamists and in the Middle East but also in every quarter of international politics. America is the strong horse of the world, and we're made stronger by healthy alliances. But when we are weak or subservient, we can look like a weak horse. America must always lead as the strong horse. And we must always do so by blazing new trails and pursuing new ideas.

CHAPTER 15

KNOW YOUR LIMITS

I never wanted to shut down an American embassy. But on March 14, 2019, we closed the headquarters for our diplomatic representatives in Venezuela.

Our patriotic ambassador, a career professional named Jimmy Story, wanted to stay at his post. As we prepared a diplomatic charter flight to bring our people home, Ambassador Story asked, for the umpteenth time, if he could stay on by himself at another location. I told him no, but I did promise to return to the embassy with him and raise the American flag alongside him one day.

In January of that year, the United States had embarked on a pressure campaign against the regime of Nicolás Maduro. This put a new target on the backs of American diplomats serving in Venezuela. Yet I didn't close the embassy in Caracas because of Venezuela's government forces themselves—Maduro knew not to mess with us. But the *colectivos*—wild bandits—were a different story. These armed criminal gangs patrolled neighborhoods, regulating entry, controlling access to food, and looking to perpetrate whatever acts of violence Maduro would ask of them. Between the daily chaos in the streets of Venezuela and the *colectivos* roaming the streets, the risk to our people had become too great.

So, we left. But as Jimmy told the locally employed Venezuelan staff at our embassy in a somber goodbye, "We know we will return to this beautiful country soon because the path that you, the Venezuelan people, have taken for yourself, is irreversible." I am confident that one day we will raise the American flag again in Caracas. In the meantime, we had to know our limits.

THE FOUNDERS WISELY URGED LIMITS.
WE LISTENED TO THEM.

The American Founders believed prudence was an essential quality of statesmen. In foreign affairs, this often means acting with restraint. The Founders were promoters of democracy, but only insofar as they desired the example of the United States to spur other nations toward a free and democratic way of life. George Washington hoped that the American experiment in democracy would prove attractive "to the applause, the affection, and the adoption of every nation which is yet a stranger to it." This is exactly what happened in Latin America's nineteenth-century revolutionary period and after World War II, when many newborn nations looked to our Constitution as a model for their own.

The Founders knew that the use of national power to advance the cause of others' liberty would entail many costs. They regarded foreign adventurism as imprudent and, at the time, impractical for a fledgling nation. Washington did write in 1796, "My anxious recollections, my sympathetic feelings, and my best wishes are irresistibly excited, whensoever in any country, I see an oppressed nation unfurl the banners of Freedom." But the Washington administration—reflecting a broad political consensus at the time—refused to pick sides in the French Revolution. And America's first war—a confrontation with the Barbary pirates raiding American ships in the Mediterranean Sea—was a defense of a burgeoning commercial republic's national interests, not a crusade of ideology. The Founders' foreign policy was characterized by realism about the world, respect for liberty and national sovereignty, and—crucially—restraint in undertaking overly ambitious or costly deployments of military power.

In the Trump administration, we resolved to wield American power with a similar realism, respect, and restraint. We were realistic in seeing the world as it was, not as we wished it to be. We grounded our work in respect for our first principles. And we exercised restraint in committing

America to costly military engagements. At times, we took necessary, targeted military action. But we did not incite new wars. Our campaigns against North Korea, Iran, and Venezuela all centered on military deterrence and economic and diplomatic pressure.

The president was especially averse to the idea of armed regime change. As much as one would have liked to see the ayatollah and company gone, it wasn't, in his view, America's place to send in the 82nd Airborne Division to eat that porcupine, except as an option of last resort in the most dire emergency. In many ways, this prudence stemmed from lessons learned in Iraq and Afghanistan. The president rightfully complained that our troops in those places were too often acting like policemen and social workers, not warfighters. We shed blood and spent money, with no clear end in sight. The president believed these conflicts had fallen victim to mission creep, lacking a clear rationale for a continued, "boots on the ground" presence. Even though we only had a small residual force in place in Iraq throughout our administration, the president would often gripe to me, "Mike, what are we even doing there?" Consequently, although we always gamed out regime-change scenarios in our contingency planning, it was never the first or second instinct of the Trump administration to embrace them. (Well, for everyone except John Bolton, as the president also complained.) We used varieties of American power to pressure adversarial regimes, but we also knew our limits.

OPERATING WITH RESTRAINT IN VENEZUELA

Two centuries ago, President James Monroe and Secretary of State John Quincy Adams promulgated the Monroe Doctrine, which warned other world powers that America would "consider any attempt on their part to extend their system to any portion of this hemisphere as dangerous to our peace and safety." The Monroe Doctrine told Europe's colonial empires—namely, Britain, France, and Spain—to stay away from interfering in the political systems of North and South America. Today, the United States doesn't mind when countries seek to build friendly ties with other nations in our region or even compete with us on a level economic playing field. But in the spirit of the Monroe Doctrine, we shouldn't allow China, Russia, and Iran to interfere in the systems of sovereign nations. And America shouldn't tolerate it when hostile Communist and socialist regimes, such as those of Cuba and Venezuela, pimp out their countries as overseas bases for America's adversaries.

We recovered the essence of the Monroe Doctrine under President Trump with respect to Venezuela, a former democratic ally of the United States. For decades, because of its vast energy wealth, Venezuela's GDP per capita was one of the highest in South America, and sometimes the top-ranked. By the time I became secretary of state in 2018, however, Venezuelan parents were burying their infants because of malnutrition, middle-class people were eating out of the garbage, and refugees who streamed into Colombia and Brazil were turning to prostitution out of desperation. The economist Adam Smith once observed that "there is a great deal of ruin in a nation," meaning that it can take a long time for a country to fail. Venezuela shows that socialism can do its damage quickly. This is the rotten legacy of Venezuela's former Marxist president Hugo Chavez, and his successor, Nicolás Maduro.

Besides destroying the Venezuelan economy, the Chavez and Maduro regimes strengthened relationships with America's adversaries. Iran has used Venezuela as a transshipment point for metals and minerals for its nuclear program, and the IRGC has turned the country into its main global hub overseas. China has invested $67 billion in the country—an economic lifeline for the regime—and helped Venezuela win a seat on the UN Human Rights Council. The Russian and Venezuelan militaries have trained together, and Russia is the main source of the Venezuelan military's arms. The regime in Caracas is also happy to rent the country to cartels that use it as a transit point for smuggling narcotics into the United States. Call me out of date in wanting to fight the drug war, but nearly all Americans know a loved one killed or otherwise scarred by illegal (or even legal) narcotics. Keeping drugs out of the United States is absolutely consistent with an America First foreign policy.

In the Trump administration, we couldn't tolerate a nation just 1,400 miles from Florida putting out the welcome mat for Russia, China, Iran, Cuba, and the cartels in a twenty-first-century violation of the Monroe Doctrine. We concluded that if left unaddressed, the Venezuela problem

would fester, with terrible security consequences for the American people and our hemisphere. In spring 2018, with new elections in Venezuela about to occur, we believed we had an opportunity to help the
Venezuelan people take back their country from a dictator. By supporting the opposition and putting economic pressure on Maduro, we hoped
to right the Venezuelan ship and force his exit. We hoped to make life so
miserable for the regime that Maduro and his thugs would have to make a
deal with the opposition. If Maduro wanted to live in a Swiss chateau for
the rest of his life, we were willing to let him, as long as Venezuela could
get back on a normal trajectory. At various points, President Trump, John
Bolton, and I suggested the military option for Venezuela. None of us
wanted to take an important means of pressure off the table publicly.

In May 2018, the people of Venezuela voted in a presidential election
that Maduro had irregularly scheduled. He did everything he could to
rig the results. In the aftermath, the United States, along with eleven
other democracies in our hemisphere, called the Lima Group, pressured
Maduro to step down. When he refused, the United States faced a tough
decision point as to whether we would recognize him as Venezuela's
legitimate ruler at the end of his term on January 5, 2019.

We decided that we could not acknowledge Maduro as Venezuela's
legitimate president. Instead, on January 23, we recognized a relatively
unknown thirty-five-year-old opposition leader named Juan Guaidó, the
president of the Venezuelan National Assembly, as interim president. We
took a risk. In the weeks prior to switching our recognition, about half
of the parties in the National Assembly didn't recognize Guaidó as the
country's legitimate leader. Thankfully, our capable diplomat, Ambassador Jimmy Story, worked magic to help line them up behind Guaidó, and
we made our decision.

I was initially skeptical of backing Guaidó. The United States is always looking to find promising leaders in the "hard" places such as Venezuela, Iraq, Lebanon, and Somalia. I believed that we should search for
people willing and powerful enough to punish fellow elites, capable of
avoiding corruption, and sufficiently street-smart to cut deals with the
lesser devils. The problem is that opposition leaders in any country are
often unknown quantities, and those who promise the greatest reforms

can turn out to be the most corrupt and oppressive bad actors once in power. Innumerable times during my four years, I had Venezuelan exiles insist to me and my team that they, and they alone, had a team that could oust Maduro, if only America would provide them with assistance. In some cases, we were told, "the coup is set to happen within hours." We could not support them all, nor would it have been wise to back unknown quantities. We understood our limits.

After vetting Guaidó, we decided we could run with him. Over the next few months, the United States mounted a pressure campaign on the Maduro regime in concert with our allies. We slapped sanctions on Venezuela's state-run oil company and confiscated diplomatic properties in Washington (at the time illegally occupied by the antiwar protest group Code Pink) to turn them over to the legitimate government headed by Guaidó. In January 2019, and again in January 2020, I spoke at the Organization for American States to rally support against Maduro. Historically an anti-American and leftist organization, but by this time under the fine leadership of Secretary General Luis Almagro, the members of the OAS backed our efforts. I also spoke at the United Nations on January 26, 2019, saying: "Now it is time for every other nation to pick a side. No more delays, no more games. Either you stand with the forces of freedom, or you're in league with Maduro and his mayhem."

Meanwhile, Guaidó and other Venezuelans continued to work within the Venezuelan political system. Around four thirty or five in the morning on April 30, 2019, Kim Breier, assistant secretary of state for Western Hemisphere Affairs, called and explained that Guaidó and company were making a move. Members of the opposition, including several generals, were telling Maduro that it was time to go. We hoped the opposition had enough military muscle to enforce this decree. The timing of this attempted removal came as a great surprise, as it was supposed to happen a few days later. We later learned it had been moved up a few days, likely because the Maduro regime had discovered the plan.

All day we tracked the latest developments. At one point, it looked as if Maduro was preparing to flee the country, with a plane waiting to take him to Havana. I went on TV and urged him to get on it. But the

Russians had swooped in. Our information indicated that they persuaded Maduro to dig in his heels. We held out hope that he could still somehow be forced out.

I was committed to give a speech that night at a formal dinner hosted by the group Business Executives for National Security. As the sun set and I changed into a tuxedo, I waited anxiously for a sensitive phone call regarding the situation. One of my concerns was that I would be on stage when it came. As I got up to speak before a packed ballroom at the Mandarin Oriental, I was totally distracted. I had a fairly long speech loaded into a teleprompter on a crucial topic—urging American business leaders to honor American national security in their transactions with China. The speaker before me, Ross Perot Jr.—one of the finest patriots I've encountered anywhere—had ripped through his remarks at lightspeed, so I was going to look especially long-winded.

I decided to burn through this thing and get off the stage quickly. Instead of reading my prepared remarks, I improvised almost entirely, barely glancing up at the teleprompter glass, as the poor teleprompter operator scrambled to connect my spoken words with the text. In what was otherwise a serious moment, I had to stifle some laughter as I saw a speechwriter's face contorted in sheer terror, probably thinking I was forced to improvise because the equipment had catastrophically malfunctioned. It may have been one of my better speeches—not because of any rhetorical excellence but because I communicated my heartfelt belief that the best things America does happen outside Washington, DC, through the good efforts of people such as those in the room that night.

Ultimately, the Venezuelan opposition failed in its effort to oust Maduro, mostly because not enough officers in the Venezuelan military were willing to join the effort to honor the Venezuelan constitution. Even though the push to eject Maduro came up short, we still put pressure on the regime and supported Venezuelan democracy through the remainder of the term. We crippled the Maduro regime's ability to export its biggest moneymakers—oil and gold—while making sure important assets such as Citgo, owned by Venezuela's state-run oil company, were in the hands of the legitimate government. We sanctioned Maduro himself and even indicted him on drug-trafficking charges because he deliberately flooded the United States with cocaine as a way of striking back at us. And I was proud of how we were able to mobilize allies to support Guaidó and the legitimate Venezuelan government. Thanks to the good work of patriots such as Elliott Abrams, Carrie Filipetti, Mike Kozak, and Jimmy Story, about sixty nations had joined us by the end of the term in recognizing Juan Guaidó as the legitimate president of Venezuela. It was another example of the Trump administration's willingness to build alliances. I was surprised by our success in this area but unsurprised by the media's refusal to cover it.

In June 2020 I received a call from Elliott Abrams, now wearing two hats as the special representative for both Venezuela and Iran, saying that some clever Drug Enforcement Agency folks had a chance to nab Alex Saab, Maduro's accused international bagman, while he was on a mission to arrange a swap of Venezuelan gold for Iranian oil. (How pathetic is it that socialism had caused a nation with one of the world's most abundant reserves of oil to import it?) Saab was under indictment on eight counts of money laundering in the United States when his plane, returning from Iran, needed to refuel in Cape Verde, a small island nation in the Atlantic Ocean. I called Attorney General Bill Barr and arranged for our ambassador in Cape Verde and the Department of Justice to file the paperwork for Saab's extradition to the United States. Suffice it to say that no other nation has the global reach to interrupt an Iranian-Venezuelan plot in real time and convince a small island nation to hold a wanted man. We may never know how much money we kept out of the hands of the Iranians and how much oil we kept away from Maduro—it depends on what Saab, who is now in jail in the United States on money-laundering charges, chooses to share with us.

Nor did we forget about the starving and downtrodden Venezuelan people, who received more than $1 billion in humanitarian aid from the United States during the Trump administration. Money was just one form of our support. In April 2019, I visited the Colombian border town of Cúcuta with Colombian president Iván Duque to see how the United States could improve our efforts to assist Venezuelan refugees who had fled the oppressive Maduro regime. Meeting that day with families who had made the hard choice to flee reinforced the need to confront

Maduro's awful regime. Young mothers with multiple children had no idea what was next, but they knew that they could not feed their families in Venezuela's socialist dystopia.

In September 2020, I made another trip to a Brazilian town called Boa Vista, approximately 150 miles from the Venezuelan border. We were close to the equator, and the heat was sweltering. But even more oppressive than the weather were the heartrending scenes of sheer misery. Men, women, and children who had fled socialist tyranny in Venezuela languished in a refugee reception center. They sought medical care, re-unification with family members who had already fled, or even just basic food and shelter. One father told me his harrowing story of escape, and I joined him in prayer as he kept thanking God for delivering his family from the nightmare that has become Venezuela. That trip reminded me of which nation the world looks to more than any other as a source of hope in desperate times.

CONFRONTING CUBAN COMMUNISTS

The Maduro regime owes much of its longevity to help from other tyran-nical regimes. Few regimes are as simpatico toward Caracas as the one in Havana, and policymakers have applied fewer new ideas to the Cuba op-portunity than almost any other. Not content to destroy its own economy and oppress its own people, the Cuban government has helped supply the hammer for Maduro to smash ordinary Venezuelans. The Venezuelan security forces are loaded with Cuban agents. Maduro himself is almost completely surrounded by Cuban security personnel. He can't trust any Venezuelans to have his back.

Havana has schooled the Maduro regime in the dark arts of subju-gation, which it has perfected ever since a failed baseball player named Fidel Castro seized control of the island nation on New Year's Day 1959. Even though the overlords in Havana have taunted the United States for decades, the Trump administration never considered an operation to force a regime change. I doubt the Cuban military forces would prove a match for the US military, but America's experience in the botched Bay of Pigs invasion in 1961 is a reminder that every military action holds potential for failure.

Nevertheless, Cuba matters to American national security. It is another foothold for America's adversaries, and its regime is one of the cruelest anywhere. We wanted to impose costs on them—the exact opposite of the Obama administration's failed idea of rapprochement. Where the Obama administration lifted sanctions, we reimposed them to stop the regime from getting richer. We supported Lithuania in refusing to ratify the European Union's proposed cooperation agreement with Cuba. We allowed US citizens the opportunity to sue the regime to recover property that was expropriated during the Communist revolution. We also designated Cuba a state sponsor of terrorism—the Cuban regime, for example, has refused to return JoAnne Chesimard, a fugitive on the FBI's "Most Wanted Terrorists" list who now goes by Assata Olugbala Shakur. She was convicted of the 1973 murder of New Jersey state trooper Werner Foerster.

I also played hardball with Major League Baseball over the issue of talented Cuban baseball players who wanted to defect to the United States. Ordinarily, Cubans who want to come to the United States to play must endure dangerous, legally dubious journeys to America and separation from their families. MLB had devised a plan with the Cuban government to bring them here in a more normal way. I was sympathetic to talented athletes who wanted a taste of the American dream, but this scheme wouldn't fly with me because the agreement guaranteed that the regime would collect a ton of money. Nevertheless, the Department of the Treasury was considering a sanctions waiver. It took a long time, and I was pissed about the delay, but eventually we built an airtight, evidence-based argument showing how the Cuban government would profit. The sanctions stayed in place. The mighty regime had struck out.

We also cracked down on one of Cuba's favorite plays for influence and cash—a program of exporting Cuban doctors to countries in the region. Far from running some kind of goodwill medical mission program, Havana forces Cuban doctors to work abroad and then confiscates up to 90 percent of their paltry wages. We decided to try to crush this scheme and succeeded in getting Brazil and Ecuador to expel thousands of doctors between the two of them. We also called out the Pan-American Health Organization (PAHO) for facilitating this form of forced labor through Brazil's Mais Médicos program, through which an estimated ten thousand doctors have allegedly been trafficked. I don't use the term *human trafficking* loosely—this is forced labor. These doctors face abhorrent working conditions. To prevent defections, they must go on assignment without their families. These actions galvanized momentum for more accountability for PAHO's role in this mess, and in March 2022 a US Circuit Court of Appeals ruled that doctors who had participated in the Mais Médicos program had standing to sue PAHO. I hope every nation hosting Cuban doctors will soon see this crooked scheme for what it is and send them packing.

Progressives often praise the corrupt doctors scheme as a form of humanitarianism. Their naivete also applies to the regime's other great propaganda campaign: manipulating liberals everywhere into parroting the line that Cuba has one of the world's great health care systems. The truth is far more ugly. Cuba's much-heralded low infant mortality rate is rigged. The regime often forces women to terminate low-viability pregnancies, and what might be a neonatal death is reclassified as a fetal one. Pharmacies often lack the most basic goods. One American doctor has said of his Cuban colleagues, "The [Cuban] doctors are pretty well trained, but they have nothing to work with. It's like operating with knives and spoons." Foreigners may marvel at Potemkin displays of medicine put on for them when they visit Cuba, but these stage-managed scenes hide the truth of a suffering population often lacking access to basic services and medicine. The regime's barbarism makes me proud of our record of restoring moral clarity to America's Cuba policy and doing what was reasonably within our power to do to punish the regime.

SETTING LIMITS IN SYRIA

In Syria, we refused to overextend in a place that we knew would be nearly impossible to fix. It was a clear but uncomfortable call to make because the people of that land have suffered for so long. Even before Bashar al-Assad's regime started shooting, gassing, and torturing its own citizens in connection with the Arab Spring, Syrians had long lived in fear of their evil leader. The explosion of anti-Assad demonstrations in 2011 eventually morphed into an all-out civil war, leading to approximately half a million deaths and twelve million displacements either internally or as refugees by 2017.

It would have been easier to walk away entirely, but Syria remained critical to American interests. For one thing, ISIS had to be defeated before it overran the entire Middle East and expanded its capacity to create new legions of brainwashed terrorists. But Syria also mattered because of Iran, Assad's ally. By pumping Shia fighters into northern Iraq and Syria, Iran seized a land bridge of territory through which it could move men and weapons across Iraq and into Syria, brutalizing Iraq's non-Shia religious minorities all the while. Consequently, Iran's growing presence in Syria was always a top-of-mind concern for Israel, which shares a border with Syria.

President Trump wanted to get out of Syria from the get-go, calling it "sand and blood and death" in early 2017. It wouldn't be so easy. On April 4, 2017, Assad's forces dropped chemical weapons on the town of Khan Shaykhun. The president rang me up when he saw the news and personally delegated to me one of my most critical tasks to date: "Mike, find out what happened today." A retaliatory response to deter the use of chemical weapons in Syria, potentially against American troops operating there, was on the table. The CIA had to obtain the complete facts about who was responsible. We collected the intelligence that allowed us to point the finger of blame at the regime with full confidence and avoid any accusations of sloppy or unfounded intel. I could not give an inch in demanding airtight analysis.

The president ordered an attack on the airfield that launched the Syrian military planes that had dropped the chemical weapons, and fifty-nine Tomahawk cruise missiles from the USS *Ross* and USS *Porter* came raining down on Shayrat Airbase three days later. It was an act of violence as well as an act of restraint: We made our point that we would punish future chemical attacks. We also deconflicted with Russian forces in the area ahead of time, reducing collateral damage. And as much as we hated Assad and hoped he would lose his hold on power, it wasn't an escalatory strike on him or other regime targets, which could have pulled the United States deeper into a messy conflict.

Later that summer, while I was still running the CIA, the US government began reconsidering support for Syrian rebels who were fighting Assad—an action I recommended to the president. The truth was that ever since Russia and Iran intervened in the conflict to save Assad, the rebels Washington was backing had steadily lost their effectiveness as a fighting force. These programs, with enormous price tags, had become black holes of taxpayer dollars. And American weapons were ending up in the hands of al-Qaeda and other jihadist groups. Of course, like any group of liberals, the previous administration had pushed multiple programs along for years without seeing any meaningful results. I ended it. We had to accept that these efforts didn't work.

Of course, there were some who continued to push the president to engage in Syria in ways that he had no interest in doing. For months, Defense Secretary Mattis refused to accept that the president wanted to get out completely once we defeated ISIS. With the complete destruction of the caliphate looming, the president tweeted without warning on December 19, 2018, that the United States would pull out of Syria. Mattis accused him of betraying our Kurdish allies, which wasn't true, and Mattis was soon gone. Eventually, the president relented and kept two thousand troops in northeast Syria, and with good reason. To this day, small pockets of ISIS fighters remain scattered across northeast Syria. They cannot be allowed to coalesce into a jihadist army once again.

But that wasn't the end. In October 2019, the president tweeted again without warning that the United States was now really leaving Syria for good, and that Turkish forces would soon enter northern Syria. Letting the Turks have free rein had the potential to trigger a humanitarian disaster. Turkey lives in perpetual fear of certain Kurdish terrorist groups, some members of which were intermingled with the Kurdish forces fighting ISIS. Disinclined to draw careful distinctions between Kurds who posed a threat and those who did not, Turkey was set to embark on a wholesale slaughter of Kurds in northern Syria. The president sent Vice President Pence and me to deliver the message to President Erdoğan of Turkey that this would be unacceptable.

The trip was challenging. When we arrived at Erdoğan's palace, he asked for a one-on-one meeting with the vice president for "a few minutes." After about half an hour, I told our hosts that I needed to see the vice president. No dice. Another twenty minutes went by, and now I was determined. Without permission, I walked down the hall and tried to push open the door of the room that Erdoğan and the vice president were meeting in. It was locked. I then told my counterpart that we were going to break through the door—I was worried that Vice President Pence was being subjected to the same three-hour video of the 2016 coup that I had been forced to watch on my first visit to Turkey as CIA director in 2017. The video was so long and so obnoxious that I considered it a mental health issue! We also had to discuss sensitive matters unfolding in real time, which required the entire group to be assembled to discuss.

My actual effort to break down the barrier caused my team to worry that I would have to make it through Turkish guards who would react aggressively. But the guards immediately allowed me and the team in, and eventually we all sat in the room together to negotiate. It was downhill from there. We met for a few hours and struck a deal. Erdoğan agreed to a temporary cease-fire. It allowed American troops and Syrian civilians to pull back from the Turkish border zones. Turkey gained access to much of the border region in Syria that we had controlled. Our Kurdish partners were in constant contact with us throughout the meetings and had reluctantly concluded that they could live with this "cease-fire." It was not our finest moment, especially given that the Russians would likely benefit from an airfield that we recently had improved, but all parties understood where the limits of power were in this situation.

Our negotiations led to a telling moment. At one point, we had spread maps on a table, and we were pointing to locations where Americans were located. Erdoğan questioned us on whether we were sure of our positions. When we confirmed, he glared at his team with the look that says, "You've lied to me." His team asked for a short break. The lesson here is that military leaders who serve under dictators are often hiding the truth from their leaders. I'm sure Putin would concur with my conclusion in light of the ferocity of the Ukrainian resistance.

In spite of our prudence in refusing to sink deeper into the Syrian quagmire, we also never let up on the diplomatic and humanitarian front of trying to force Assad out and help the Syrian people. From 2018 to 2020, I worked closely on Syria with Jim Jeffrey, a salty, seasoned diplomat and Vietnam veteran. He has more knowledge about the Middle East in his pinky finger than most experts do in their whole brains. He was a driving force in the diplomatic world to maintain pressure on the Assad regime, the preponderant cause of the world's worst humanitarian crisis. One of our big accomplishments was the Caesar Syria Civilian Protection Act, a sanctions package named for a Syrian photographer code-named Caesar, who documented the regime's torture of its own people. Because we sanctioned Assad and members of his regime for war crimes, nations have trouble doing business inside Syria. These sanctions are especially intended to make sure Assad cannot profit from the rebuilding of his country, as Iran, China, other Arab nations, and especially Russia are eager to help him do. Syria will continue to be a challenge, but we did our best to protect American interests without exposing American personnel to elevated risks.

As secretary of state, I was confronted time and again with the hard truth that not every problem in this mean, nasty world has an immediate solution. I have few regrets about how we chose to involve ourselves in the world's worst places. Even the most overwhelming application of American power has its limits. It will be for history to judge our choices.

CHAPTER 16

HONOR AMERICAN SACRIFICES

Within two days of me being sworn in as a member of Congress, an American patriot was killed in Afghanistan. Army staff sergeant Eric Nettleton was from my hometown of Wichita, Kansas. As a brand-new member, I didn't know much about protocols or what the Department of Defense would do. I knew only this: I wanted to speak with his family and let them know that Susan and I were praying for them and that their son's service was noble, important, lovely, and performed in the finest tradition of our nation.

The family asked that I speak with Eric's father, Jim. "Sir, this is Mike Pompeo," I said. "I'm calling to tell you that Susan and I are mourning your loss and that of Eric's wife, Ashley, and all of your family." Almost before I could finish that sentence, Mr. Nettleton said, "Congressman, we are praying for you and your family."

I was floored. In this moment of grief, in this moment of devastation so personal, so deep, the Nettleton family's commitment to the Lord and to America permitted Eric's dad to have the strength to continue to give. "You have much work ahead of you, Mike. We've watched your campaign, and we know that you and Eric shared the values of our family. Keep doing the right thing." I had called to serve the Nettletons, and they gave back to me more than was imaginable.

I've never forgotten this moment. In the days that followed, I learned that SSG Nettleton's Army service had been exemplary: as a member of the 82nd Airborne, he was a soldier's soldier. He wanted to get back closer to family and so returned to Fort Riley, Kansas, to marry Ashley. After serving once in Afghanistan and then again in Iraq, he signed a waiver so that he could return to Afghanistan with his unit. Such is the character of the American soldier.

Eric's service and his family's Christian grace inspire me to this day. These extraordinary Americans make our nation exceptional. In my years of service in Congress and the Trump administration, I thought often of SSG Nettleton and spoke about him publicly. As I was working to get our troops out of Afghanistan years later, I thought about Eric's sacrifice and that of his family. Whenever Afghanistan came to my desk, I steeled myself to preserve what men and women such as Eric died for. I'm still pissed about 9/11. I strived to protect America with the élan and courage and commitment that would make the Nettletons proud. We must honor American sacrifices. It is literally our duty.

AMERICA STANDS ON SACRIFICES—WE MUST HONOR THEM

The tradition of service in American history runs deep. George Washington set the tone with his humble and dignified leadership as a general and then as president. In the 1800s, a Frenchman named Alexis de Tocqueville observed how Americans labor on behalf of their fellow man "to found seminaries, to build inns, to raise churches, to distribute books, to send missionaries." Lincoln stated, "I freely acknowledge myself the servant of the people according to the bond of service—the United States Constitution; and that, as such, I am responsible for them."

No institution embodies the American tradition of service as the US military does. With a few wartime exceptions, we have maintained an all-volunteer military. Our forces fight not to conquer but to defend. They fight with ferocity, discipline, and honor. And throughout American history, hundreds of thousands who have fought in foreign wars have sacrificed everything.

President Trump campaigned against starting new wars. As secretary of state, I knew that my work was indispensable for keeping American men and women off the battlefield. If diplomacy fails, the chances that our warfighters must deploy increase. This was on my mind every single day. In the previous two decades, more than seven thousand Americans like Eric Nettleton have given their lives in Iraq, Afghanistan, and elsewhere. Many thousands more have suffered permanent injuries or other lasting traumas. The fruit of the sacrifices they and their families made is a more secure America. As we executed on the commander's intent to get out of Afghanistan responsibly, I resolved not to squander those gains, nor to waste the sacrifices that produced them.

IMPROVING AFGHANISTAN—AN UPHILL BATTLE FOR AN AMERICA FIRST OUTCOME

By January 2017, the model of American military engagement in Afghanistan that had been in place since 9/11 was no longer serving American interests well. Afghanistan was also emblematic of the need to adapt America's post-9/11 foreign policy without returning to a 9/10 footing. Just as I pushed for on China, I also pushed for a massive adaptation of our mission in Afghanistan. This was also what President Trump wanted. As far back as 2013, he tweeted, "We should leave Afghanistan immediately. No more wasted lives. If we have to go back in, we go in hard & quick. Rebuild the US first."

At various points prior to becoming president, Trump conceded that we might need to leave some number of troops there. A significant intelligence and unconventional capability could remain present. But the conditions had to be right. After four years of working on this effort with him, I am extremely confident that his instincts were right about getting every single uniformed soldier, sailor, airman, and marine out of the country. We did not achieve our objectives before January 20, 2021. I would say it's unfinished business, except that President Biden finished it in the worst way imaginable.

What had two decades of involvement in Afghanistan gained us? I'll start with the positives. Above all else, America's efforts to crush al-Qaeda in Afghanistan after 9/11 were successful. From the time I was at CIA until the very end of the administration, I would ask the intelligence community, "How many al-Qaeda fighters remain in Afghanistan?" It was a hard question, and no one wanted to answer with a wrong number. Finally, I got a good estimate: fewer than two hundred. This was down from the tens of thousands who were present when we arrived in 2001. Al-Qaeda's leaders have nearly all fled to Iran, where they remain today.

In August 2020, I got a call informing me of the good news that we had smoked Hamza bin Laden, the son of Osama bin Laden, who had at one point been designated his successor. Al-Qaeda's head honcho since 2011, Ayman al-Zawahiri, was still out there—maybe—but we had once again demonstrated our ability to find and eliminate the worst of the worst. In July 2022, America found and eliminated al-Zawahiri. We went to Afghanistan to defeat al-Qaeda there, and we did. Al-Qaeda now has a much bigger presence in Yemen, Africa, and elsewhere. The fight against them is not over.

Another positive from an American presence was "normalcy" in Kabul. It was an Afghan-form of "normalcy," to be sure, but schools were open, businesses sold their wares, and civil life functioned. This was also the case in a few other urban locations as well, though the Taliban still controlled much of rural Afghanistan. This normalcy in the capital made America more secure.

Finally, and perhaps most importantly, we had stopped Afghanistan from becoming a place where terrorists could launch a mass casualty attack on America or anywhere else in the West. For twenty years, we prevented them from planning, training, and executing their plots. This matters a lot. It's the America First outcome we sought when we went in.

These days, when I speak with veterans of the Afghanistan war, they are very down, if not downright depressed, because of Biden's botched withdrawal. They watched their brothers in arms in the Afghan military and American soldiers die as we fled. They watched military planes with Afghans hanging from the landing gear. They saw an America on its knees, begging the Taliban for relief. They are right to be mad.

I want to tell every warrior who answered the call in Afghanistan who is reading this to strip out the politics and know three things: First, your service in Afghanistan was noble and worthy. Second, your sacrifices—time away from family; injuries; and, for family members of those lost, lives changed forever—were made in the finest tradition of the greatest nation in the history of the world. And, finally, you saved countless American lives. Many of the details remain classified, but make no mistake, your work protected our people, disrupted terror plots, and reduced threats to American interests. America must never forget you, your sacrifices, and the good you did for our country. Honoring your work was always at the forefront of my mind.

★ ★ ★

As for the fight against the Taliban, in 2017, a massive CIA presence was still in-country, alongside approximately fifteen thousand American troops engaged in combat operations on the ground. Sixteen years of war had exhausted pieces of our armed forces, with US Army and Marine Corps veterans retiring with a half dozen deployments or more. The Russians, Iranians, and Chinese all welcomed America continuing to shed its blood and sink its treasure—some $2 trillion when all was said and done—into this backwater. There was a bonus for them: not only did Afghanistan absorb our geopolitical focus but we were doing the dirty work of taking down terror threats on their borders.

The role of our NATO allies reminds me of an old saying about a ham-and-eggs breakfast: the chicken is involved, but the pig is committed. NATO was the chicken in this case—mostly sending auxiliary personnel, who, while useful, were not on the front lines in nearly the same numbers as American troops. There were exceptions: French, Italian, and UK special operators were there in some numbers. Canada made real contributions, too. But the operators kicking in the doors and giving support to Afghanistan's armed forces came from Florida far more than France.

For years, the United States had tried, and failed, to transition away from being the main combatant against the Taliban. A centerpiece of America's strategy was providing support to Afghan forces so they could do the most dangerous heavy lifting—after all, it was their country. The Afghan special forces units were absolute killers, imbued with a valorous fighting spirit. Once, when visiting Jalalabad, my team introduced me to some of the most hardened Afghan warriors. One of my guys quipped, "These Afghan special operators are as tough as Chinese math." They really were. And the Afghan National Defense and Security Forces fought valiantly and sacrificed greatly. But they couldn't defend their nation in full without American and NATO support. As the president often said, "The red circles keep getting bigger!" He was referring to the way we designated Taliban-held territory on our maps.

America made a crucial mistake in conditioning the Afghans to fight with American support, especially air support. Instead of training them to fight with F-16s over their heads, we should have trained them to fight with knives in their mouths and small arms at their side. My Taliban counterparts mocked the idea that we could create an Afghan military replicated on an American model. They knew it required an abundance of high-tech weaponry, command and control capabilities, and an ability to operate at scale. It also required an officer corps, and non-commissioned officers, that couldn't be bribed.

A more full-on professional military might have been possible if Afghanistan's civil government had its act together. Unfortunately, years of American efforts to build up Afghan civil institutions had failed. Afghan governance was an oxymoron. In 2017, the watchdog group Transparency International ranked Afghanistan the third most corrupt country in the world. But eradicating corruption also came with its drawbacks, too, as this crooked system of patronage helped to prop up the entire Afghan political system.

In the Oval Office in 2018, H. R. McMaster said, "Mr. President, we have to stay to root out corruption." It shouldn't come as a great surprise that McMaster held this view. As a soldier, he was once in charge of rooting out corruption in Afghanistan and was even interviewed for an article in the Washington Post as far back as 2012 headlined "McMaster: Afghan Anti-Corruption Drive Is Working." I joked with both the president and McMaster that Afghan corruption was "a feature, not a bug," as it was all that held the government together. More seriously, I assessed that Afghan low-level corruption secured a measure of stability, as it kept the country from completely unraveling, albeit at a staggering cost to the government's credibility with its own people. No matter which of us was right, the fact was that even Afghan's president, Ashraf Ghani, and the country's chief executive, Abdullah Abdullah, both led cartels that stole millions of dollars in aid money from the

United States. That corruption at the highest levels limited our ability to exit successfully.

Ghani first came to see me in August 2017. He wanted to ask, "What is Trump like?" I can understand the curiosity, but it was a wasteful reason for a foreign visit. I found Ghani to be exactly what you would expect from a person trained in liberal academia and later employed as a World Bank bureaucrat. With a quiet voice, sweet disposition, and fine Western manners, he never failed to thank America for our sacrifices for his country and his people. Yet for all his eloquence and charm, he was not the leader a war-torn, deeply divided tribal nation seeking to build political institutions needed. He was a dim bulb in his political instincts and a Brussels-style manager in a cauldron of violence that demanded an Ultimate Fighting Championship mindset. Nor did he have much credibility among Afghan leaders, nearly all of whom had been fighting in one war or another for their entire adult lives. When I met with tribal leaders and the Taliban, they would all, with anger in their voices, remind me that while they had spent the 1980s riding horseback into Soviet helicopter fire to liberate their country, Ghani was ensconced in the salons of Johns Hopkins and Columbia.

Ghani's years in the West had made him masterful at gaming American lawmakers and nonprofit organizations. He also spent extravagantly on lobbyists. I say with no exaggeration that Ghani had more friends inside the District of Columbia than he did in Afghanistan. When I met with him the first time during my CIA days, I told him straight up: "You're squandering your time on K Street and Capitol Hill when you should be hustling for allies in Herat and Mazar-e-Sharif." He had come to see the ability to procure American money and friends as the main factor for staying in power and continuing his grift. It certainly was important: American and other foreign aid composed roughly 80 percent of his government's budget. But what he really needed was the backing of tribal leaders and powerbrokers in Kabul, not plaudits and money from America's foreign policy establishment and the World Bank crowd. This misallocation of time, effort, and money gave me fits. I knew we had to put pressure on him to get real about becoming the kind of leader his country needed.

"GET THE HELL OUT"

I can still hear Donald Trump making his popular campaign promise: "We are going to get the hell out of Afghanistan." He repeated this line in directive form to his national security team constantly. More than anything else, President Trump wasn't confronting a tactical or operational failure, but a strategic one. For sixteen years, we had not adapted our strategy, even as the limits of American power to achieve victory on the battlefield became clear. The president saw our current efforts as a protracted, costly failure. But as much as he wanted to get out, he came to understand it had to be done the right way. "Get the hell out" was his slogan, but he would also add, "But we have to get all of our people out, and our equipment out, every nail." He'd then recount the story of his real estate developer father picking up nails from work sites and repeat the mantra, "I don't want to see anyone or anything left behind."

Whenever the team would remind him that counterterrorism concerns might preclude a total withdrawal from Afghanistan, he'd say: "I got it. Do it like we did early on: CIA and small forces. They can bring in the bombers if the Taliban do something stupid." For four years, we kept in mind his three-pronged objective: get out, leave no one and nothing behind, and, if necessary, maintain a small and quiet force to reduce risk of an attack on Americans.

A few different ideas were proposed for how to deliver on the president's orders without compromising American national security. In June 2017, Steve Bannon came to see me at the CIA. He was—or at least believed he was—charged with driving the administration to make good on President Trump's promises. He told me he had convinced the president that Afghanistan needed to become an entirely CIA-run operation. In pitching a plan that entailed no military forces on the ground, he was asking me, as a practical matter, to become the commander of US forces in Afghanistan. Erik Prince, the former head of the military contractor Blackwater, also pitched a new model of involvement much like the one Bannon had proffered the president. In his vision, contractors would supply military planes and train Afghan forces. He claimed it would reduce costs, save lives, and let the DOD turn its focus away from

Afghanistan. President Trump was intrigued. Yet the DOD and General Joseph Votel, the head of CENTCOM, were not impressed and let me know that. My team and I evaluated what was possible. We concluded that several factors, including the need for significant military support for multiple mission sets, rendered Prince's proposal impossible under current threat conditions. The president was disappointed, but we had to be honest about our limits.

It wasn't the only time being honest about Afghanistan was a challenge. Many of those around the president, including McMaster and Mattis, had tasted warfare in Afghanistan and lost men under their command. Chief of Staff Kelly had lost his own son. These were serious men who had taken personal risks in ways I never had. They spent their whole lives successfully leading men in combat. They consistently urged the president to stay the course. I continue to have tremendous respect for them, but time marches on and situations change. This one was no exception. Over their objections, I and others urged an adaptation of our Afghanistan strategy to align with the three conditions the president had set down.

By the summer of 2017, the debate was coming to a head. At one meeting, the president cracked, "You all keep talking about getting Afghan costs down to $5 billion year from $13 billion per year. I'm just trying to find $900 million to build a wall!" His advisors were not amused. The number of casualties remained too high, as was the toll on our combat-arms warriors. But the costs of the Afghan commitment were large, and not just in dollars. We had other strategic priorities. We needed the military to get serious about devoting resources to confronting China, and we could see a clash with Iran coming once the nuclear deal was dead.

The debate raged through the summer, with President Trump's political team saying, "Get out!" and Mattis, McMaster, and Kelly saying, "We are on the cusp of victory." In August, the president convened his cabinet and military advisors to hash out a final decision. Everyone's positions were well-known by that point. My skin in the game was more than just as the intelligence provider—I had a massive operational role on the ground, wholly apart from that of the DOD. Mattis made his pitch for increasing troops, and the president listened.

On August 21, 2017, President Trump made remarks at Fort Myer, Virginia, that stunned many. Instead of a speech about "getting the hell out," he spoke about a new Afghanistan strategy for victory. He spelled out a commitment to fighting to win by "attacking our enemies, obliterating ISIS, crushing Al-Qaeda, preventing the Taliban from taking over Afghanistan and stopping mass terror attacks against America before they emerge." He made no mention of troop strength or a timeframe for victory, but he did say that conditions on the ground would guide our strategy.

The morning after the speech, he was in a bad mood. He was getting hit from all sides. On the right, there were plenty of news stories about his failure to live up to his promise to withdraw. But he was equally irate at patronizing commentary from the establishment saying, in effect, he was finally "acting like an adult" or had "grown in his presidency." I knew that day that this speech would not be the last word on Afghanistan.

SEEING AFGHANISTAN FOR MYSELF

Delivering on my piece of the new Afghanistan strategy at CIA meant more trips to Afghanistan to assess conditions. I'd first visited the landlocked country in the summer of 2013, as a member of Congress on the Intelligence Committee. That trip was led by Representative Mike Conaway of Texas, a good old boy of classiest proportions, who also took along my friend, Representative Michele Bachmann. Conaway had expected State Department and CIA officials to meet us planeside, but when we arrived via commercial flight at Kabul International Airport, no one was there to greet us. "Oh well," we thought, "let's just keep moving."

After making it through customs and exiting the terminal, we spotted a couple of rough-looking characters who spoke enough English to tell us to get in their white van. As Representative Bachmann was about to get in, Conaway said, "Hang on." He had noticed that the van's windows were blacked out, and inside was an arsenal of weapons that did not look like American-issued arms. As he told me later, "It looked like a scene out of a really bad thriller where a bunch of numbskull Americans climbed into a terrorist vehicle voluntarily." We eventually found our State Department helpers, and they confirmed that we had made it into the right van. As I look back on it, this flurry of dangerous confusion was emblematic of how things worked in Afghanistan, despite more than a decade of American effort. None of us could have known that less than ten years later, that airport would be the scene of one of the worst American retreats in history.

My second trip to Afghanistan came early in my CIA tenure. I now had a massive responsibility to oversee the Agency's largest deployment of its officers in any location in the world, and by far its largest paramilitary commitment. By this time, in early 2017, the CIA had been through a great deal in-country. The first American killed in Afghanistan following 9/11 was a CIA officer named Johnny "Mike" Spann. The CIA had been instrumental in crushing the Taliban and establishing an Afghan government. Under the leadership of Leon Panetta, the CIA had been a central player in the killing of Osama bin Laden. The United States had developed the single best capability to train Afghan forces at outposts from Jalalabad to Khost, and from Kandahar to Kunduz, so that Afghans, not Americans, knocked down most of the doors. Our country, too, had developed a set of lethal capabilities to strike high-value targets from the air. Part of this campaign now fell to me to lead.

My priority was to let the team know I had their back as they conducted the hardest jobs in the world. On my first day, I did "all hands" meetings with men and women posted in-country. I wanted them to see me on the ground and in person and to be reassured that I would provide them with the tools and resources they needed. I wanted them to know that in my willingness to deliver, I also spoke for President Trump. After visiting an arms training range, I spent a good part of the evening shaking hands, pouring beer, exchanging stories, and signing ball caps and T-shirts at the Talibar, the Ariana's cleverly named watering hole.

I will never forget the patriots I met that first day. These were hard people, many on their third, fourth, or fifth tours in Afghanistan. They loved Donald Trump. Some of them could recite his tweets. Like him, none of them considered themselves elites, and many were a bit rough around the edges. These CIA grinders typify the agency's workforce overseas. They work hard and long hours. Some go "outside the wire"—outside the confines of a secured base. Others do their important work from computer terminals. They fly Russian helicopters. They love America. They have beautiful children, some with serious developmental challenges. They fix broken things. They make communications work. They protect their brothers and sisters. They know the benefits and limits of Hellfire missiles. They once worked serving food on a yacht in Florida and now made the best chow in South Asia every night for hundreds of people from kitchens in Afghanistan. They know fear. They work and train mightily to make sure they stack up to all who have gone before them. Their friends have been killed. Many of them supported operations targeting terrorists. To a person, they knew what their mission was and were determined to deliver for their new director. They saw the diplomats in-country as soft and ineffective. Meeting these living legends in person stoked my resolve to make sure all they had done here would not be in vain.

Yet ultimate success was not within their power alone—it was up to the president and his team to execute the strategy correctly. I returned to Afghanistan for a third time in August 2017, after the president's speech. Again, I wanted to make sure that our team had what it needed to deliver on our part of the mission. In addition to taking that inventory, I went to Khost and laid a wreath for the fallen CIA officers who had been killed there, as well as to Bagram Airfield. There I ran across a guy named Pete, who had been one of my finest soldiers when I was a young lieutenant and who now worked for me in a completely different role. I also spent time with a fellow named Dan, a 1994 graduate of the US Military Academy, who was on his thirteenth trip to Afghanistan. I had the privilege of presenting him with an award for heroism. Only future writers will have the honor of telling his story after all the classified files are opened. These visits drove home for me why our work in Afghanistan was so important—our forces were strained by years of muddling along against the Taliban, with no end in sight. Men such as Pete and Dan needed fewer trips here on behalf of their country and more time at home on behalf of their families.

I returned from Afghanistan in time for a national security meeting at Camp David that was held to revisit, again, our Afghan strategy. The president was still unhappy with the reaction to his speech at Fort Myer, and even more unhappy that Secretary Mattis and Secretary Tillerson weren't delivering on it, either on the battlefield or at the negotiating table with the Afghan government and the Taliban. Mattis had delayed the deployment of the additional 3,000 troops that President Trump had authorized. This absence of trust between Mattis and the president came back to haunt us repeatedly.

As I was leaving the meeting, Chief of Staff Kelly and the president asked me to come to Bedminster, New Jersey, later that week to brief the president on how the CIA could deliver what he wanted. I made sure that Mattis knew of this ask, but I also asked him to let me brief the president without any Defense Department leaders around. To his credit, Mattis trusted me to handle this meeting without him. I took with me two senior CIA officers. We provided the president with both a granular plan for correcting a failed strategy and a realistic assessment of what our agency could do with small numbers on the ground. But this meeting was also significant in that my CIA team told President Trump that the Agency's support would allow America to cut its uniformed military force posture down to as few as 2,500 personnel, and still deliver on every objective he had laid out at Fort Myer. This 80 percent reduction in forces was to become the lead objective for the next three years. We just had to execute it in a way that honored the sacrifices of all who had waged war in this place.

DIPLOMACY WITH DEVILS

When I became secretary of state, my focus on Afghanistan changed from national security work on the ground to diplomacy. At lunch in early May 2018, the president told me, "Rex f——ed me by not developing a diplomatic plan and not talking to all of the tribespeople." I promised him that I would develop a strategy for advancing peace talks, even if peace was a thousand-to-one shot. He said, "Mike, you have to talk with these people; they'll be there long after we're gone." He was right about that. In hindsight, my "thousand-to-one" oddsmaking was probably optimistic.

Over the next few months, I searched for the right person to help lead our diplomacy. Everyone said, "You'll choose Zal," and then added, "He'll be a pain in the ass for you, but he is your best choice." They were right on both counts. Zalmay Khalilzad, the former US ambassador to Afghanistan and ambassador to the United Nations, had a reputation for freelancing and secrecy. But he had also grown up in Afghanistan and was an ethnic Pashtun, the dominant ethnic group among members of the Taliban. He could speak with anyone and had a long history with most of them. His skillset was unrivaled and would be most useful during the negotiating process. Just as the foreign policy oracles had foretold, I picked him.

Among the president's national security leaders, the appetite for diplomacy with the Taliban was mixed. Gina Haspel was the most supportive of dialogue, noting that the Taliban have had and will have massive influence in Afghanistan, "so we might as well freaking talk with them." Bolton was completely against any talks. He turned physically red in the face each time President Trump demanded that we start talking. I knew, too, that once we embarked on these discussions, Ghani would be an adversary. Members of the Senate such as Lindsey Graham of South Carolina and Jeanne Shaheen of New Hampshire would try to gum up the works, and every NGO within fifteen minutes of Foggy Bottom would besiege us to protect their in-country contracts that generated money for them. Secretary Esper and Chairman Milley had more mixed feelings, but each concluded that given the commander in chief's mission to reduce our footprint, the conversations were a net plus. When National Security Advisor O'Brien replaced Bolton, he supported our effort but could also sense the risks.

As we shaped our negotiating strategy, we knew that it had to sync with action on the ground. That initially meant working with General John Nicholson. Having taken over in 2016 as commander of Resolute Support—essentially the commander of NATO forces in Afghanistan—Nicholson was the longest-serving head of that mission in history until General Scott Miller surpassed him in 2021. Nicholson knew Afghanistan well, having worked this problem set for nearly his entire time as a senior officer. Like so many, he continued to believe that we were making progress. I never saw it. Nicholson was an amazing patriot, but I think he struggled to understand DC politics and the seriousness with which his commander in chief was focused on "getting the hell out." To the best of my knowledge, Mattis never allowed Nicholson to meet or speak with Trump. That was massively unfair to Nicholson, who was engaged in a military mission with deep geostrategic and political ramifications. Ultimately, Trump came to lose confidence in him.

In September 2018, General Scott Miller became the new Resolute Support commander. He was a senior at West Point when I was a freshman. We both believe we met there, but it was probably only for him to scream at me because of some trivial infraction. I knew that General Miller, Scotty, was the perfect leader for the mission. A former Delta Force commander, a commander of Joint Special Operations Command, and a man who had fought from Mogadishu, Somalia, to Iraq, to Afghanistan, he knew how to lead. I counted on him to help me shape our negotiating plan. He counted on me to provide air cover in the Oval Office as we sought to execute that strategy.

We shared a knowledge that we were going to be on watch when America made the transition out of twenty years of massive involvement in Afghanistan. We laughed that we had been handed a problem that was stickier than a movie-theater floor. We debated whether retiring to Fort Bragg or Fort Knox would yield better living for us. More seriously, we knew that we had to achieve President Trump's objectives, that our window to do so was limited, and that we would have to accept significant risk to do so. We also knew that we couldn't fully exit until conditions were right.

It is unusual that a secretary of state would work directly with a four-star in the field. But if you've made it this far in this book, you'll know our administration was never beholden to the usual way of doing things. We made sure that everyone was tied in at the right level, beginning with Scott's boss, CENTCOM commanding general Frank McKenzie, who was always fully briefed. I will always love Frank for his first words to me when I saw him at his home in Florida: "If you want to do Soleimani, I'd support that." I know his predecessor at CENTCOM, General Joseph Votel, would not have said that. General Miller and I tried to do what

America usually does poorly: fight and negotiate at the same time. Our history has been that once peace negotiations begin, our military efforts on the ground ease up and plans for "heading home" begin to dominate the conversation. At the tactical level, we lose the deterrence that protects our men and women. General Miller and I were determined to achieve President Trump's goals while also crushing the Taliban sufficiently to protect our forces and hold the Afghan political-military structure together. By doing so, we knew we would honor the multiple generations of warfighters who had given their all for our country.

As Zal and I began to formulate a diplomatic effort, I told him that the key objectives in any deal had to honor the sacrifices of nearly two entire decades and protect Americans against terrorism. The strategy ultimately had four primary assumptions, each of which we knew was only partially true: First, some important fraction of the Taliban leadership was selfishly interested in a reconciliation deal. Second, the Afghan state could be preserved, and we could restructure its government to integrate the Taliban into it. Third, Pakistan would not fatally undermine the reconciliation process because American carrots—and American sticks—would make sure its interests (and India's) were addressed in any agreement. Fourth, the United States would publicly emphasize that its military presence in Afghanistan was conditions-based, which meant that we would not pull out troops until we were satisfied that the Taliban was holding up its end of the bargain.

It was a high-wire act. Each time President Trump talked of getting out, the Taliban became emboldened to wait out our departure without firing a shot. President Ghani assumed that any deal would leave him out of power, which was probably true, so he led a massive effort to undermine our negotiations. On one occasion, I met him in Kabul, at a time when he was refusing to negotiate in good faith. I warned him that I would stop the transfer of $1 billion in American assistance if he refused to participate in the reconciliation process. Before the engines were started on my flight out of Kabul, I had no fewer than five US senators calling to say that such a move would destroy the world. I know Senator Graham had been called by Ghani, who was totally addicted to American largesse. I'm also convinced that some of our own State Department officers who didn't support our efforts to pressure Ghani alerted Capitol Hill.

Over the course of the negotiations, we developed two other ideas that proved to work well in moving toward an agreement. The first was using our military capabilities to make sure the Taliban understood that we couldn't accept rampant violence during the talks. General Miller and I knew that if we could—in real time—ratchet pressure up and down in sync with our negotiations, we could accomplish something that the West never does: talk and fight at the same time. Here's an example of how it worked: General Miller would let us know when the Taliban had moved too close to an important location. Zal or I would contact Mullah Baradar, the Taliban's top political leader, and tell him he had two hours to fix it. If he didn't, we rained down fire on his people in the field until he got the message. It took only a couple such conversations and demonstrations to make clear that we were operating in tightly coordinated fashion to coerce the outcomes we sought from the Taliban.

There was a second element to deterring the Taliban, as well. President Trump told the Taliban that if they harmed Americans during the reconciliation process, he would "nuke you back to the stone age." This was a typical exaggeration, but it did signal our seriousness. When a Taliban bomb detonated in Kabul in September 2019, killing an American and eleven Afghans, we walked away from the process for weeks. During those weeks, we ratcheted up our aggressiveness on the ground in Afghanistan. The Taliban came to know that our negotiations with them were directly connected to how they operated and how many of them we would kill. When I consider how the United States successfully drew down from 15,000 to just over 2,500 in a few short months, without any American casualties, and without the Taliban overrunning the places from which we had drawn down, the answer lied in this carefully orchestrated use of diplomacy and military power. We had withdrawn massive amounts of forces and had maintained tactical deterrence at the same time.

In the meantime, we worked on all sides to find a path forward to do what no administration had been able to do: get the Afghan government and the Taliban to have real peace talks. Any rational secretary of state would know that peace accords of this magnitude take years, maybe decades, to fully realize, and that the road forward is never straight. I certainly accepted those two facts. But we knew that if we could at least get an agreement with President Ghani to send negotiators and a commitment from the Taliban to do the same, we would move toward peace and reduce threats to Americans.

As negotiations accelerated, Ghani was always a problem. I met scores of world leaders, and he was my least favorite. That's saying a lot when you have Kim, Xi, and Putin in the mix. Yet Ghani was a total fraud who had wasted American lives and was focused solely on his own desire to stay in power. Never once did I sense that he was prepared to take a risk for his country that might imperil his power. This disgusted me.

So, in spite of objections from Ghani and most of the establishment in Washington, DC, I finally traveled to Doha, Qatar, on February 29, 2020, to witness the signing of the "Agreement for Bringing Peace to Afghanistan between the Islamic Emirate of Afghanistan which is not recognized by the United States as a state and is known as the Taliban and the United States of America." Yes, that's quite a mouthful, and yes, it's the agreement's real title. Secretary Esper executed a similar document, often ignored, but just as important, between the United States and the Afghan government at the same time. These agreements provided less a basis for peace than a formal framework for trying to achieve it.

That day, I had my strangest experience as secretary of state. After a long plane ride from DC, I walked into a Sheraton Hotel that looked like a convention in Tora Bora. Before me were many dozens of members of the Taliban, dressed in their traditional garb. Many of them—all part of a delegation legally in the country under diplomatic protocol—wore white tunics, black vests, and head coverings that, to me, evoked the appearance of Osama bin Laden. I wondered how, after being born and raised in the dusty brick huts of southern Afghanistan, they interpreted the glittering skyline of Doha, a majority-Muslim city made wealthy through the relaxation of Islamic law and gushers of natural gas. I wondered how they reconciled their hatred of all things Western with their use of cell phones and air-conditioned halls with beautiful, polished floors. And I wondered how many of these bearded thugs had killed American men and women.

My security team was worried about letting me enter this environment. The sight was certainly unnerving, but I wasn't concerned for my personal safety. The Taliban were eager to achieve what they came here for: Zalmay Khalilzad's signature on a piece of paper effectively declaring the gradual withdrawal of all foreign forces in Afghanistan after nearly twenty years of sacrifice, assuming the Taliban lived up to their end of the bargain.

Before the ceremony, I had to meet with Mullah Baradar. I'd read about him at great length. I'd spoken to him on the phone. Yet being with him and his team—one of whom I'm convinced was responsible for the death of a friend of mine—was as personally sickening as any moment during my time in government service.

A few hours later, in a pyramid-shaped hotel ballroom covered in wall-to-wall red carpet, with the world's media and a swarm of Taliban underbosses looking on, Zal signed the agreement that put America on a responsible trajectory to end our military presence in Afghanistan.

I supported signing it and still think it was the right path forward. But I'm still angry about 9/11, and part of me blanched at the sight of our State Department diplomatic team giving congratulatory handshakes to their Taliban counterparts. But this pact was critical to saving young American lives. It was an acknowledgment that the war on terror need not be defined by endless war in Afghanistan. And it was an admission of the limits of what our former strategy could produce there. I prayed for peace, knowing it was unlikely, but I was determined to do what I was confident we could do: deliver on President Trump's promise to bring our kids home, and do so under conditions that would cause the Americans who served there to say, "Well done." We could have done it. But we did not get a chance to do so.

In the wake of the ceremony, each side issued press releases claiming victory for themselves and supplication for the other. H. R. McMaster later said that I had signed a "surrender agreement." Read it for yourself: We surrendered no American interests. The truth is McMaster and those who shared his views had surrendered any objectivity on the prospects for progress in Afghanistan, and that failure was killing Americans and causing us to deprioritize the great strategic risks of our time.

On March 3, President Trump made history—and angered many—by speaking by phone with Mullah Baradar to put pressure on him to honor the deal. The two of them did have one thing in common: both of them hated Ghani. Baradar thanked the president for committing to leaving Afghanistan, and the president quickly responded, "You have to live up to your commitments in the deal!" President Trump told Baradar that if they didn't live up to their promises on al-Qaeda and terrorism, we would "make their lives hell." The foreign policy establishment held tightly to the view that even speaking to this killer was tantamount to treason. But forty years of studying how peace is ultimately achieved had taught me that absent total annihilation of the enemy—something no one believed the United States could do to the Taliban given the constraints—sooner or later you will have to negotiate with him. So we did, with eyes wide open and guns fully loaded.

★ ★ ★

It might sound crazy, but getting the United States and the Taliban to strike a peace deal was the easier part of this process. Getting the Afghan government, the Taliban, and various groups inside Afghanistan to create peace was much tougher. It got off to the difficult start we had predicted. For one thing, the Afghan government still could not sort out who won the September 2019 presidential election. According to the final nominal tally, Ghani had defeated the country's chief executive, Abdullah Abdullah. But the truth was that Ghani simply had bribed more voters and vote counters than the other candidates had. Now Ghani and Abdullah were fighting about who would be the next president without regard for whether there would even be a government to lead. At General Miller's request, I hopped a plane to Afghanistan on March 23, 2020, to tell them that they needed to find an accommodation, or I would advise President Trump that we should exit the country immediately, beginning with the elimination of the roughly $5–6 billion per year in foreign assistance that we were providing at the time.

This was a real threat. While the public focus was almost always on how the aid provided security assistance, its larger purpose was to preserve civil order. It funded schools and health care, but it also meant "walking around money" for local leaders. That's a euphemism for bribery, and it's the sad reality of both how American aid and Afghan society worked. My message got their attention. Eventually, we shaved off $1 billion in assistance to show we weren't bluffing. In May, Abdullah essentially gave control to Ghani, and we had, at least, a head of the Afghan government.

By April 2020, consistent with the US-Taliban agreement, General Miller had a clear path to reduce our forces to 8,600 and then down to 7,000. This total was sufficient to let us safely pause to see if the Taliban planned a major spring offensive. We knew the next two drawdown steps, assuming the Taliban lived up to its end of the bargain, could get us down to 4,800 and then 2,500 by the late fall of 2020. With the US presidential election looming, the president wanted to be able to declare that he had delivered on his promise to "get the hell out of Afghanistan." While not yet there entirely, we would be at historically tiny numbers by the end of the year. From my perspective, just as importantly, we had a sustainable model that protected American lives, maintained the Afghan military's cohesion, and allowed a rough political process to emerge. Although the intra-Afghan peace talks were stalled, we had instituted effective deterrence against major attacks. The Taliban had not seriously attacked Americans in more than a year. And we had stopped watching hero-filled caskets arrive at Dover Air Force Base.

But President Trump wanted more. Each time that he demanded new drawdowns from the secretary of defense—by the end, it was Acting Secretary Chris Miller—he would hear about unmet conditions and objectives. We knew that the regime in Kabul could fall quickly, and we raised the specter of "Saigon" to remind the president about what was at stake and the potential speed of collapse.

On the day we left office, we still had more than two thousand service members in Afghanistan. We never fully satisfied the command to "get the hell out." We weren't in a position to tell the president that we could get our last man home and still protect America from an attack emanating from that place, so we never told him we could. I'll take responsibility for that failure. At the same time, we never allowed chaos to descend on

Afghanistan. We never left any Americans or equipment behind. We reduced American cost in lives and money. For this, I credit the men and women who stood by us across this years-long process at the risk of their lives.

TWO DECADES OF LESSONS LEARNED

The Trump administration's handling of Afghanistan provided many lessons. First, we showed that the quantity of "boots on the ground" is not the sole measure of power and influence inside a country. We delivered a net reduction of more than 80 percent of our troop strength, but maintained our capacity to influence events through diplomacy, intelligence, air strikes, and NATO support. Yet—largely through poor messaging on our part—we failed to change the narrative of American "boots on the ground" as the most important variable for shaping events in Afghanistan.

The much more enduring lesson, for me, is that it's hard but necessary to change course after a substantial investment of resources. A story from my own life illustrates what I mean.

When I was meeting senators who would vote on my confirmation as CIA director, Senator Dianne Feinstein told me, "I wanted to not like you, Mike, but Bob Dole called and said I should give you a chance. Why should I vote for your nomination?" Frankly, I couldn't blame her for being predisposed to vote against me. We had clashed before.

Senator Feinstein had a long history of supporting the intelligence community and had been a solid leader of the Senate Intelligence Committee. But in 2014, her committee released a report detailing the CIA's enhanced interrogation program. The CIA's actions were lawful and saved American lives, but one of the senator's leftist staffers, Dan Jones, was determined to undermine the program. The report even named a few CIA patriots who participated in it. While I think Feinstein and Jones are fundamentally wrong to second-guess the Bush-era program that delivered for our nation, what I find completely unacceptable was their seeming harassment of the CIA warriors who were tasked with the difficult task of executing the president's directives. Feinstein and Jones failed to understand that leaders at all levels must make hard decisions. That's why I still love George W. Bush, his toughness, and the people who worked to protect my family—men like Jose Rodriguez—by making the hard, complicated calls as they served a nation at war.

I was serving on the House Intelligence Committee at the time of the report's release, and I was invested in making clear that the senator was wrong about the CIA's enhanced interrogation program. But instead of responding to her action on the merits, I launched an irresponsible ad hominem attack in a press release:

> Senator Feinstein today has put American lives at risk. Our men and women who were tasked to keep us safe in the aftermath of 9/11—our military and our intelligence warriors—are heroes, not pawns in some liberal game being played by the ACLU and Senator Feinstein.
>
> The intelligence collection programs described in the report have been in the news and hot topics for discussion for years.

It continued, when it should not have:

> The sad conclusion left open is that her release of the report is the result of a narcissistic self-cleansing that is quintessentially at odds with her duty to the country.

I was right in that waterboarding worked. And the CIA men and women who were tasked with collecting intelligence from the worst bastards to ever kill Americans on our own soil operate with the highest respect for the law. But I was wrong to attack Senator Feinstein as behaving disingenuously. I had no evidence to support the claim that her decision was anything other than her own best judgment, however misplaced, about how best to preserve our nation.

So, in my meeting with her about my CIA nomination, I fixed it. I told her I was wrong to have essentially accused her of treason, and that I'd be happy to admit it publicly. She found this private admission enough and, in the end, voted for my confirmation. I didn't need her vote, and I didn't apologize to get it. I apologized because good leaders change their minds when facts require it and correct their errors when they screw up. This is exactly what the Trump administration did in Afghanistan. It's never easy, especially when the sunk costs are so monumental, as they were in that country. But it must be done.

Third, the Trump administration showed that good planning counts for everything. This was sadly borne out in the horrifying withdrawal from Afghanistan that occurred under President Biden. When we turned over the keys, the Trump administration had demonstrated an ability to draw down our forces in a conditions-based manner, without allowing the Taliban to take over. We were focused on leaving no one and nothing behind. The Biden administration ditched the conditions-based framework and rushed a complete American withdrawal to meet an idiotic deadline of September 11. It was idiotic to set a date in principle and idiotic to set a date with such potent symbolism. Once the date was made public, the die was cast. President Biden telegraphed to the Taliban that they could begin a violent campaign of coercing Afghan commanders to lay down arms because the Americans had announced their date of departure. It was a recipe for the chaos that engulfed the country, to the misfortune of Afghan citizens and to the shame of the United States.

The misfortune and shame were made worse by the confusion surrounding the Special Immigrant Visas, which were supposed to help brave Afghans in their moment of greatest need. The Biden administration opened a massive power vacuum and then sat on its hands and conducted endless interagency meetings instead of making plans to guarantee the safe departure of our Afghan partners and their families. In the end, the airport at Kabul resembled a riotous variation of *The Price Is Right*, with the luck of the draw deciding which audience members would be pulled from the crowd and become the next lucky contestants. The ensuing confusion allowed an ISIS suicide bomber to kill thirteen young Americans in uniform.

You can be damn sure that if I had been secretary of state in a second term, we would have put in place a system for granting visas and exfiltrating our friends months ahead of time. Instead, in the ignominious last days of the American crusade in Afghanistan, one State Department official remarked, "Bureaucracy is killing more people than the Taliban."

The Biden team has sought to blame the Trump administration for having forced them to leave. President Biden, nobody bound you to anything. The agreement we signed laid down set conditions for our departure. They were never met, and so our national security team never recommended to President Trump that we pull out entirely. Because the Taliban continued to violate the Doha agreement, we continued to rain missiles on their heads and support Afghanistan's military in mowing down their soldiers. You ripped up that plan. You sent a message to the world that America's plan to get out—a plan that was coordinated with every European capital and upon which they depended—was no longer operative. Instead, you were determined to pull the rip cord. You left behind our friends. You left behind Americans. The irony is that the world feared that President Trump would behave rashly and that you, the seasoned former vice president and chair of the Senate Committee on Foreign Relations—would behave responsibly. Planning and deterrence could have prevented the deaths of thirteen American soldiers. You weren't forced to do any of this. You chose to do it.

The Biden administration's botched final months in Afghanistan ended a long chapter in American history in the ugliest of ways. We must separate the lionhearted service and sacrifices of all who served in Afghanistan from the timorous and diffident political leaders who lacked the qualities of leadership and foresight to avert this disaster.

At the CIA and the State Department, I saw how our presence in Afghanistan enabled us to reduce threats emanating from inside that country and other places throughout the world. None of this would have been possible without the service of so many amazing American young men and women, both in uniform and under deep cover. My prayer is that our work honored every ounce of strength and sacrifice they poured into defending the United States.

CHAPTER 17

SHOW UP

Four months after the US–North Korea summit in Hanoi, Vietnam, diplomacy with North Korea remained bogged down. While sanctions were still in place and Special Representative Steve Biegun was doing yeoman's work trying to get the North Koreans to live up to their promises, we went long stretches without hearing from them at all. And when we did, they offered no substantive proposals.

Then, sometime in June 2019, a letter arrived from Chairman Kim. Its contents buoyed our hopes that a deal was still possible. The annual gathering of the leaders of the world's twenty richest nations—the G20—was about to take place in Osaka, Japan. This gave President Trump an idea. We decided to see if we could break the logjam with another in-person meeting. While in Japan, the president tweeted, "If Chairman Kim of North Korea sees this, I would meet him at the Border/DMZ just to shake his hand and say Hello(?)!" Hours later, the United States issued a formal notice of our intentions. Not long afterward, Kim returned the message, saying, essentially, "Happy to meet."

Summits often take months to pull off, or weeks if you rush. We had hours. Dan Walsh, the White House operations genius, began to work with my team on the logistics. For those who have not been to the North Korea–South Korea DMZ, it isn't much, apart from being one of the most heavily militarized parcels of real estate on the planet. We had to figure out who would meet, in what room, with what lighting, with what chairs, and everything else.

Everyone and his brother wanted to be part of this historic meeting, except for John Bolton, who upon learning of it immediately decamped to Mongolia. An American president setting foot inside North Korea—even if only for a few steps—had never happened before. It was decided that only four of us would meet—President Trump and Chairman Kim and me and my old pal Kim Yong Chol. This disappointed many on the president's team.

But the biggest challenge was the one we knew we would have to confront: South Korean president Moon Jae-in was going to demand to be part of this historic event. To make matters more complicated, we would be inside his country as we departed for and returned from the DMZ. President Moon called me directly multiple times, and my answer to him was well-rehearsed: Chairman Kim prefers to meet just with President Trump. Moon wasn't a happy camper, but we made the right call, as Chairman Kim had neither time nor respect for President Moon.

The next day I accompanied the president to the area of the DMZ, at the border of diametrically opposed worlds of light and darkness. With the world watching, he became the first American president to set foot inside North Korea. Walsh had pulled off a logistical miracle safely. He even threw a body block for me so I could push through the crush of North Korean reporters to get into the room where the four us would meet.

Once inside, President Trump and Kim put their cards on the table. Sadly, no breakthroughs were to be had. Kim was as immovable that day as he was in Hanoi. We at least could use this opportunity to make sure the intelligence community could watch and learn from this scramble on the North Korean side, and they did.

The truth is, we didn't get what we had wanted out of North Korea. But the personal touch of showing up at the DMZ solidified the Trump-Kim relationship, so much so that for the rest of the Trump administration's time in office, North Korea didn't test any nuclear weapons, nor did it perform any long-range missile launches. When you consider that President Obama told President-Elect Trump during the transition period that North Korea would be his greatest national security challenge, this was a pretty good outcome. It wasn't perfect, but it is one I think most Americans can welcome. And it happened in part because we knew the importance of showing up.

SHOWING UP MAKES ALL THE DIFFERENCE

Diplomatic trips may look grand on TV, but they are not vacations. They involve grueling schedules that lurch through multiple time zones, poorly pressurized government planes, and high stakes. Most of the time, you're on your way to or from somewhere to discuss a serious problem. But these trips are vital. They build relationships, trust, and respect. There's no substitute for accepting a guest's invitation, putting in the effort to make the trip, and letting them welcome you into their home. Zoom meetings aren't handshakes.

A big goal of mine was to deploy to places where a US secretary of state hadn't been in a while or perhaps ever. This wasn't about ego stroking. This was about playing to win for America in our era of great-power competition. China and Russia are striving on every continent—often in coordinated fashion—to knock the United States off the pedestal of global leadership and harm our interests. These trips focused my attention, and that of my hosts, on that problem. I could read all day about Huawei, but it really got my attention, for example, when I saw huge Huawei ads outside the airports in Colombia and Uzbekistan immediately telling visitors China was in town. They might as well have been Chinese Communist flags. Similarly, General Secretary Xi Jinping knows that high-level leader visits are crucial to signaling who a country's true friends are. He has been as active as any world leader has in the past decade traveling outside China to buddy up with everyone from African dictators to the mayor of Anchorage, Alaska. In our era of revived great-power competition, showing up matters more than ever before.

★ ★ ★

At the CIA, my travel was frequent but not often public. I'll never forget landing in a desert in the middle of the night in a helicopter—I hadn't seen the truest dark of night until I'd seen it in a remote desert. My coordinates were miles from the nearest man-made light. I needed to visit an elite team of about half a dozen folks doing important work in harsh conditions. Their ranks included an electrical engineer, a physicist, and four guys who told me, "Sir, we just get stuff done." While I can't discuss the stuff they got done, it was vital to our national security interests.

That stop was also memorable because when I set foot in the desert sand, the first person to greet me said, "Rock Chalk, Mr. Director." For the uninitiated, "Rock Chalk" is a salutation between graduates of the University of Kansas. But because my family is from Wichita, we are fans of the Wichita State Shockers, rivals of the Kansas Jayhawks. So, while I think this greeting was meant in friendship, it may have been a bit of a jab. Either way, it should remind us all that the men and women who serve in dark places come from ordinary American stock, and their anonymous excellence keeps us all safe in ways most of us will never know. The fact that I had shown up that night, simply to thank them for their work and listen to their challenges, traveled across Langley and the entire agency. Showing up matters.

At headquarters, I sometimes showed up in the dining area for lunch. I had become a CIA hero when I pushed forward the long-delayed opening of a Five Guys in the building. The old adage that an Army runs on its stomach turned out to be true for our spies as well. I can't tell you how many on my team would say, "Mr. Director, thanks for getting Five Guys open." I did it because I like hamburgers, but also because I wanted to show that our leadership cared about everybody. That simple act bought me more goodwill than any other single reversal of policy I can recall!

To hear what the team was really thinking, I showed up at meetings where I wasn't expected, in addition to planned sessions for anyone who wanted to come called "Meet with Mike," where Agency staff could fire away with whatever was on their mind. When Susan traveled with me, she showed up at medical facilities and at day care centers and at family gatherings and just listened. Her showing up mattered, too—the officers could see that just as their entire family was in it for America, so was the director's family.

I also showed up a few times with the president. In 2017, he went to Paris to celebrate Bastille Day and the hundredth anniversary of America's entry into World War I. There was no big agenda, but French president Emmanuel Macron wanted us all to be there. It was important to him, and we deepened our relationship by just showing up. The president's staff waited around for several hours for the program to get started, and we made small talk. I'll never forget when Dan Scavino, the keeper of the Trump Twitter account, said: "You know, Mr. Secretary, you'll write your interesting book, but I'll sell more copies of mine. I'm going to call it *You Should See the Ones I DIDN'T Send*." The president's team all roared with laughter at the thought of this immediate bestseller. I told him I would buy it for full price.

On the ground in Paris, President Trump sat beside President Macron. He was treated to a display of French military forces parading down the Champs-Élysées. It was an impressive show, featuring equipment from 1917 and 2017 paired together. Despite the reputation of the French military as "cheese-eating surrender monkeys," to borrow a quip from *The Simpsons*, the French today have one of the best-trained and most active militaries in Europe. Their work fighting terrorists in the Sahel region of Africa has allowed America to spend our resources elsewhere. We met with the French to discuss significant issues on that trip, but the real value was that our team showed up to pay respects to the sacrifices that had been made by French forces. It made the relationships I had with my French counterparts deeper and stronger, to America's benefit.

HITTING THE ROAD AS SECRETARY

Before becoming a true road warrior at the Department of State, I had to show up at Foggy Bottom and establish myself there. Morale was low following the departure of Secretary Tillerson, who had left it badly damaged due to poor personnel decisions. I also had to work on the vacancies that required Senate confirmation. I needed to surround myself with others who would show up for the jobs that were then empty.

Honoring the American people with my selection of trips was also important to me, so I took time to think hard about the most essential trip destinations. I wish I could say that my predecessor, John Kerry, had his priorities straight in terms of his own travel schedule. But it's hard to explain why he made thirty-four visits to France, twenty-eight visits to the United Kingdom, and twenty visits to Switzerland. Undoubtedly, some of those jaunts entailed what he regarded as important diplomatic business, even if it was for stupid objectives such as sealing the Iran deal and the Paris climate accords. But I think he was equally interested in rubbing shoulders with globe-trotting elites and climate activist celebrities such as Leonardo DiCaprio, as Kerry did on a trip to France in 2015. Other stories abounded inside the State Department of whimsical overseas excursions that seemed to serve no purpose other than that of his own entertainment, such as the hours he spent with world-renowned foreign policy expert James Taylor. Showing up to the salons of Europe once a month may be more fun than being in Vietnam or Indonesia or the Pacific Islands, but preferencing those destinations demonstrates a lack of seriousness about the true challenges that confront America. It belittles the value of showing up.

This critique is not to ignore the importance of our relationships with America's Western allies—it would have been diplomatic malpractice not to build them. I'll never forget being in Berlin on the thirtieth anniversary of the fall of the Berlin Wall. Stopping to commemorate this important historical event was a reminder that Communist regimes are brittle and that American strength can shatter them. That trip was also special for me personally as I reunited with former soldiers who had served with me in the days when that wall still stood. We walked through the German town of Mödlareuth ("Middletown"), a burgh that once had a wall running straight down its center, dividing families and communities on the line between democracy and evil.

On a trip to Italy, I had a few hours to squeeze in a visit to take in my family's roots in the tiny Abruzzo town of Pacentro. The Italian government loved having me travel there, and the people of that little community welcomed me as a returning hero. Several families opened their homes to show me where my great-grandfather had lived—Susan and I joked that he must have moved around a lot! Funny, too, was when the keeper of a tiny shop handed Susan and me a box to deliver to "Louise Ciccone," an American woman better known by her stage name, Madonna. The shopkeepers assumed that since Madonna and I shared roots in the same town, we must surely be close. We took the package and did our best to get it to her, laughing that I was the second-most famous American with connections to Pacentro. It was a very distant second, of course.

But I overwhelmingly concentrated my travel schedule on the places where American diplomatic presence was most desperately needed. Among other priorities, my air miles reflected a dedication to our Middle East strategy of bringing Israel into closer partnership with the Gulf monarchies. I visited Saudi Arabia seven times—tied with Belgium for the most of any country, and I went there only for NATO meetings, not mussels and beer. Six times I went to Israel and the UAE, essential American allies for the new Middle East emerging under the Abraham Accords.

I was astonished to learn that Secretary Clinton and Secretary Kerry had failed to visit countries that were most at risk from China's and Russia's predatory advances. I had to correct this deficit. In February 2019, I made my first real swing through parts of Europe—and my first destination was in its east, not its west. I booked stops in Hungary, Slovakia, and Poland. Later I flew to Iceland. China's sense that America didn't care about these places had emboldened its own efforts. No secretary of state had visited Slovakia since 1999 or Iceland since 2008, so I fixed that. Later that year, I became the first secretary of state to visit Montenegro since it gained its independence in 2006. This small Balkan country, plagued by corruption, was at the time suffering from a bad decision to let the Chinese build a little-used highway at an exorbitant cost.

As for Hungary, the Obama administration had shunned our NATO ally, treating it almost like North Korea and barely engaging at all. The last time a secretary of state had made a visit was in 2011. When officials did have contact, they gave lectures on democracy and human rights. The Russians and Chinese exploited this icy relationship, and sadly today Hungary is the EU country with the friendliest ties to both regimes. I spent several hours with Prime Minister Viktor Orbán when he and I attended the swearing in of Brazilian president Jair Bolsonaro on New Year's Day 2019. For more than two hours, we were holed up in an anteroom with Prime Minister Netanyahu of Israel. The conversation was, well, lively. Orbán was determined to root his time in office in his nation's history and Christian faith. He laid out for me, in exquisite detail, the inner workings of European socialist parties and the failures that had led to the decline of Europe—including the risk that France and Germany would never be the same after allowing massive migration from Islamic

countries. I showed up for a Brazilian inauguration but built a relationship with a neglected democratic nation and got to spend time with our
Israeli friend as well. Showing up truly mattered.

In January 2020, I became the first secretary of state in twenty-five
years to visit Belarus, a country led by a dictator for nearly thirty years,
which today is in a state of indentured servitude to Vladimir Putin.
For months, we had been getting signals that President Alexander Lukashenko was trying to create some distance from Russia. I wasn't in love
with the idea of meeting with a tyrant, but I'm not ashamed to say that
raw geopolitical interests are more important than the diplomatic fear of
"legitimizing" someone such as Lukashenko.

My meeting with Lukashenko was in some sense productive. I told
him that America was willing to supply natural gas to his country to
end his dependence on the Russians. We planned to appoint our first
ambassador there since 2008—a move that would also help reinforce the
brave skeleton crew manning the US Embassy in Minsk under constant
Belarusian and Russian surveillance. Then things went crazy. Deep inside his self-aggrandizing palace, he ranted. My staff thought our closed-
door meeting was running long because things were going so positively.
In reality, he was talking my ear off about various imagined enemies and
conspiracy theories. Months later, Lukashenko proved he was never serious about any reforms, and he remains unjustly entrenched in power
today. Maybe showing up hasn't yet delivered, but a secretary of state who
isn't willing to take a few risks won't enjoy much success.

The rest of the world beyond Europe was also a battleground. Nearly
every trip I took involved the threat of the CCP. Everywhere I went, from
the United Kingdom to the United Arab Emirates to Korea, I would seek
support on our various counter-CCP projects. The urgency of the China
challenge sometimes meant excursions to faraway places. Angola was
growing financially strained from bad Chinese loans, and I encouraged
the Angolans to extract themselves from Chinese deals. The tiny Pacific
Island country of Micronesia has approximately 1,500 miles of territorial
waters, which the Chinese would love to dominate. I became the first
secretary to ever visit this nation. It was quite a sight as our plane landed
at the country's airport, which was only big enough to keep one plane of

its size on the tarmac. As I descended the plane's staircase, I looked down to see my counterpart wearing a short-sleeved island shirt. This was no buttoned-up visit to London.

South America was crucial, too. As the first secretary of state to visit Paraguay since 1965, I wanted the people there to know that we applauded their courageous decision to be the only South American country to maintain diplomatic relations with Taiwan. Venezuela's tiny neighbor Suriname may not seem important, but my visit to that country—another first for a secretary of state—was critical to building American ties with a new leader in our hemisphere to whom the Chinese would soon be paying a visit, if they hadn't already.

I prioritized Brazil much more than my predecessors. The trade relationships between North and South America are underdeveloped and critical to American security and prosperity. President Bolsonaro had largely modeled his candidacy for president on President Trump's, so we knew if we got off on the right foot with his administration, we could get a whole lot done. My trip to Bolsonaro's inauguration on New Year's Day 2019 signaled that the relationship with South America's most populous country mattered enormously. His foreign minister, Ernesto Araújo, was a brilliant writer and thinker and knew America's founding history as well as I did, often speaking about it as a model for his country.

Araújo likewise understood the China challenge. Our countries enjoyed a massive influence on the soybean market. China needed access to what our farmers grew, and it had tried to play our countries against each other. We believed that together we had real supplier power and could use it to benefit our two countries. The like-mindedness between Presidents Trump and Bolsonaro greased the skids for several important accomplishments: We expanded and reformed trade ties, and Brazil became a Major Non-NATO Ally. After twenty years of negotiating, we also agreed to cooperate on space launches in Brazil in a way that would prevent the Chinese from stealing American missile technology.

People might wonder: "Mike, why should I care about tiny countries such as Montenegro, Micronesia, and Suriname? How is spending any time at all on those places serving an America First foreign policy?" It's a fair question, one which President Trump would ask me all the time. First,

American businesses deserve the chance to make money all around the globe, and our diplomacy in these countries creates opportunities for our people to prosper. Second, the scope of the challenge America is facing from China is monumental. The CCP wants to flip countries into their column so that China can expand its military and economic presence everywhere. We need friendly nations willing to let us use their water, air, and land rights to base and move our military. Economically, the CCP wants to create enough leverage over countries so that they ultimately deal only with China, thereby cutting the United States out of global trade and crippling our economy. And third, it's consistent with the American character and love of liberty to support the sovereignty and independence of other nations—especially small nations. When the secretary of state shows up, America stays strong and what we stand for is clear.

SHOWING UP HELPS AMERICA WIN ECONOMICALLY

The American economy is our greatest asset for achieving geostrategic victories. My most powerful tools were America's innovative technology, our capital markets, and our private sector's ability to solve complex problems in ways that the governments and private companies of other countries cannot.

America's economic power has been brought to bear several times in our history, to great effect. During World War II, America's arsenal of democracy cranked out airplanes and tanks and ships faster than the Axis powers did, and this made the difference in winning the war. In the 1980s, Reagan knew that the American capacity to innovate and create wealth would ultimately put the Soviet Union on the ash heap of history. Under President Trump, the United States became the world's largest producer of crude oil and maintained its lead as the world's leading natural-gas producer, giving me powerful economic cards to play in virtually any diplomatic engagement. In working to slash oil and gas production, Biden hasn't just curtailed a source of prosperity for American workers. He has rolled back a source of American power and goodwill at a time when energy shortages are plaguing the planet.

Historically, the United States has not used its full diplomatic power to scout and secure deals for American companies. This failure to show up has put our country at a disadvantage. China's gigantic state-backed corporations have powered China's economic rise. Along the way, Beijing has doled out bribes and loans, with other nations' national sovereignty as the collateral for nonpayment.

Less nefariously, Germany and France have never been shy about having their leaders call customers on behalf of their businesses. That kind of advocacy doesn't just give those nations an edge over the United States—it also has the potential to empower our rivals. Indeed, Germany's corporate sector—giant companies such as Volkswagen, Siemens, and BASF—has helped run European foreign policy on China into the ditch by lobbying for unlimited access to Chinese markets. For many years, the State Department wasn't eager to help our companies to the degree that it should, because of a poor sense of priorities or a fear that hustling on behalf of American firms was unethical.

We flipped this script, and it worked. President Trump understood that American economic power was crucial to creating good outcomes in foreign policy. I heard President Trump's axiom about wealth undergirding power rattling around in my mind time and again: "Mike, who's got the money?" We knew a poor America was an unsafe America—one unable to finance a robust defense apparatus and vulnerable to losing out to the Chinese. So, we redid trade agreements. We made economic deals a component of the Abraham Accords. And we fast-tracked hundreds of billions of dollars in weapons sales to partners such as Saudi Araba and Taiwan. Arms sales serve the dual purpose of sustaining American jobs and strengthening defense ties.

In my own diplomacy, the most common question other leaders asked me in my meetings was something along the line of "Why don't American companies do more business in my country?" The most common answer to this question was something like: "Your legal system needs to do a better job upholding the rule of law and intellectual property rights." But the frequency with which this question came up told me we needed to chase deals for American businesses harder than ever. I filled the normally sleepy role of undersecretary for economic affairs with high-energy Keith Krach and his team. Treasury Secretary

Steve Mnuchin and Commerce Secretary Wilbur Ross—both brilliant business leaders—wondered why State even had economics officers. But State has a unique capability. It has a permanent presence in almost two hundred countries, with our officers interacting with every nation's private companies. Showing up at the host nation's commercial businesses and chamber of commerce gatherings mattered to an administration that wanted to compete around the world for wealth for its own people.

Our work paid off. In addition to crushing Huawei, Keith was in full-on sales mode for America everywhere he went. The leadership throughout the "E" bureau—including Frank Fannon and Manisha Singh—understood that securing wins for American business was a priority. One enterprising E appointee, Dan Negrea, helped create 150 Deal Teams at our missions overseas—teams made up of folks from various federal government agencies dedicated to assisting US companies looking for opportunities around the world. In less than a year, the Deal Teams produced transactions valued at more than $76.5 billion. On top of that, they scouted out roughly 1,400 existing and potential export and investment opportunities, with an estimated value of more than $1 trillion. That's the dollar value of showing up.

I showed up to win for our businesses too. I constantly made calls in support of them. American leaders had previously often stayed away from making these pitches, viewing them as "beneath" governmental leaders. We see traces of this attitude in the words of the famous strategist George Kennan, posted to Moscow as a young diplomat in the 1930s. When approached by a Wisconsin machine manufacturer to help him win a contract in the Soviet Union, Kennan scoffed. It wasn't the job of the government "to push individual deals."

I took the complete opposite approach. I loved getting on the phone to help with a deal. A perfect example was a big power project in a country where many Americans had fought and died. I reminded that country's leader that his nation's very existence resulted from American sacrifice, and I sure hoped that a great bid from a great American company would be viewed with that in mind. I suppose that wasn't subtle, but the American company got the business. (I assume a good offer had something to do with it, too.)

Energy was a fixture of so many of my engagements. In recent years, the small South American nation of Guyana has discovered billions of barrels in energy reserves off its coast. Guyana needed our help to develop this opportunity that will change this poor nation forever. I went down and signed agreements with President Irfaan Ali to strengthen US investment and cooperation on energy and infrastructure. The prosperity that will flow from these oil deposits matters to Americans: increased supplies of oil will lower global prices, enhance our region's stability, and generate paychecks for the thousands of Americans who work at ExxonMobil, which is developing the reserves. And when small countries know America is behind them, it gives them confidence to take the necessary stand in other areas. Guyana is right next door to Venezuela, but Ali nonetheless said publicly on my visit: "We support and respect the need for free and fair elections in our hemisphere. With urgency, we believe the democratic values and principles should be respected in Venezuela as well."

THE LOWS AND HIGHS OF REPRESENTING AMERICA

As much as it was right and necessary to show up for America, certain visits were a gigantic waste, and there was no option but to simply endure them. Libya had been a dumpster fire ever since 2011, when Secretary Clinton led the charge to take out Muammar Gaddhafi in a way that resulted in chaos and exposed the world to greater risks from jihadis. Debate was contentious inside the administration over the Libya file. John Bolton wanted to get involved and support General Khalifa Haftar; I wanted nothing to do with wading into a civil war. The good news is that most days President Trump agreed with me. Alas, "most days" is the operative term. In January 2020, Merkel and Macron demanded that a gaggle of leaders come to Berlin for a Libyan peace-process meeting. My recommendation was to send no one. At Merkel's request, the president sent me at the last minute. To make matters even worse, I had to squeeze in this meeting immediately before a scheduled visit to Colombia, some 5,800 miles from Berlin.

The gathering was totally pointless for every leader there. First, the warring parties in Libya were not even present at the meeting. Second, many of the countries calling for peace and restraint were—at the very

moment we sat in that room—violating the UN embargo against exporting weapons to Libya. None of them had any intention of backing down.
We were one of the few countries not then currently running weapons
into Libya. Most of the other nations had squandered any credibility to
propose a constructive solution.

As the meeting was winding down, Merkel asked to see me and
Prime Minister Boris Johnson of the United Kingdom in private. She
said General Haftar had agreed to a set of conditions for peace that had
been laid out in a communiqué. I had the audacity to ask her if she had it
in writing or if she had spoken directly to Haftar. She said no, neither, but
that Sisi had spoken to someone who had spoken to Haftar. Boris almost
fell out of his chair laughing. The lesson here is that diplomats can't live
in a fantasy world. If a meeting won't accomplish anything, don't hold it.
And don't tout phony agreements.

Sometimes, showing up just flat out didn't yield any results, no matter how hard we tried. For many years, the Ethiopians have been building
the Grand Ethiopian Renaissance Dam (GERD) on the Blue Nile, one
of the major tributaries for the Nile River. The name is outrageous, as
neither will the dam guarantee an Ethiopian renaissance nor is it really all
that grand, being built largely by Chinese construction companies using
Chinese labor. But the dam is a massive structure designed to generate
huge amounts of energy for Ethiopia and lift the country into a new, elec-
trified era. Not surprisingly, Sudan and Egypt, which depend on stable
quantities of water from the Nile, were upset at the prospect of reduced
water flows. A massive legal, diplomatic, and commercial fight had been
brewing for years when President Sisi asked the United States to mediate
the dispute. Secretary Mnuchin led our effort, which ultimately failed.
The sticking point for a tripartite agreement was the rate at which the
dam's upstream reservoir would be filled. Demonstrating how central
water and power are to diplomacy, for thirteen months it was impossible
to speak with any of these three nations without "the GERD" at the top
of their list of complaints. It is anyone's guess as to whether, when, or how
this dispute will conclude.

But these episodes are barely worth mentioning in comparison to the
difficulty of showing up to the truly hardest place of all—Dover Air Force

Base in Delaware. This is where the US military receives the flag-draped caskets of heroes who had given their all for America on the battlefield. I traveled there whenever I could to honor their sacrifice and to express condolences to their husbands and wives, fathers and mothers, and sons and daughters. There wasn't anything to be said beyond expressing our gratitude and offering our prayers. And there certainly wasn't anything that could be done. But there was no more meaningful way to show up for America.

★   ★   ★

My time as secretary of state was also a special time in my marriage with Susan. In every job I've had since we've been married, Susan has been a force multiplier for whatever I'm trying to accomplish, and I was blessed time and again to have her. She was born in Iowa and moved to Kansas as a small child. She had never lived anywhere else before I became CIA director. Behind the scenes, she quietly labored to support me, my team, and America and enhance our diplomacy.

Sometimes she would accompany me on my trips. The ethics lawyers always wagged their fingers over it, but what we did was completely legal, and it advanced American interests. She helped assess the living and working conditions for our CIA and Foreign Service families and reported back to me how we could try to make life better for these folks. She took massive abuse from the press. Here was this woman—gracious, humble, brilliant, faithful to her Maker—going to really hard places such as Abuja, Nigeria, and the like, all for exactly zero dollars and zero personal benefit, yet facing allegations of illegal and unethical behavior. When the spouses of my predecessors had done this, they were lauded. Suffice it to say that Susan continued showing up and delivering for America.

I also showed up in as many countries as I could to meet with the entire embassy team. I would open it up and take any question. I got my fair share of arcane questions from Foreign Service officers about hiring freezes, pay rates, job-bidding criteria, and so on—but I don't blame them a whit for looking out for their paychecks. I gave pep talks and took lots of pictures with their children. I wanted them never to lose sight of the fact that they were doing meaningful work for America—and that they should do it with pride and excellence.

THE STATE DEPARTMENT'S FINEST HOUR

Once the COVID-19 pandemic descended upon the world, I knew that my travel would stop for a while. Indeed, between March 23 and July 20, 2020, I made only one brief trip overseas, to Israel. But America still had to show up, and we did.

One of the things the State Department does extraordinarily well is help Americans when they get in a bad spot overseas—whether they've lost a passport or encountered a legal or medical problem. The pandemic brought out the best in the entire department. When countries locked down and canceled flights, we had to move at light speed to bring Americans home, beginning with the staff at the US Consulate in Wuhan, China. Dr. Will Walters, our deputy chief medical officer for operations, led the effort. The son of a bricklayer, who started his career in the Army and at community college, Will is a razor-sharp medical doctor and logistician—and also one of the greatest American public servants of this century. In January 2020, he alerted Brian Bulatao to the reality of the pandemic and asked for permission to evacuate our people from Wuhan before they got caught in a Chinese lockdown. Brian agreed, and his response was classic Bulatao: "What are you still standing here for, then?"

Wuhan began to lock down on January 23. By the next day, Walters and his team had a plan in motion to send an aircraft with a biocontainment unit to Wuhan to bring home Americans. All we needed was the plane to fly into the Wuhan hotspot—easy, right? Like many remarkably patriotic American private citizens, a man named Ken Griffin was deeply invested in helping us figure out solutions to problems connected to the pandemic. He had a colleague in China as it was locking down; we had diplomats and other Americans stuck, too. Ken agreed to provide a plane to get them out. After much diplomatic wrangling, enormous resistance from US authorities ("Where are you going to bring these exposed people back to?"), and with the help of an amazing group of patriotic medical personnel with significant experience working around infectious outbreaks around the world, we got the first plane into China and then back to March Air Force Base in California. Because we couldn't carry everyone on that first flight, I went back to Ken and said we needed to return. Without hesitation, Ken said, "Whatever we need to get Americans back home." It is fair to say that, without his support, we would not have been able to repatriate these people in a timely fashion.

At one point, as American citizens with crying babies were waiting on the tarmac for their departure, the CCP held them up. But our team on the ground negotiated with the CCP, in tight coordination with senior officials back in Washington, and the Americans were eventually allowed to board. We evacuated 800 Americans from Wuhan in just seventy-two hours. Between January 28 and February 16, 2020, the department executed the largest nonmilitary evacuation of US citizens in its history, bringing home 1,174 Americans from Wuhan and the *Princess Diamond* cruise ship in Japan. Steve Biegun, by this time the deputy secretary, deserves great credit for helping bring home Americans in the early days of the pandemic, too.

This was just the beginning of a Herculean worldwide effort. We immediately set up a Repatriation Task Force under the leadership of Ian Brownlee. Their work will stand as some of the greatest ever undertaken on behalf of the American people. They worked around the clock coordinating flights, negotiating with foreign governments, and ensuring Americans had safe passage wherever they needed to go. Dozens of Americans deep in the Amazon jungle of Peru got to the nearest airport in time. An American double lung transplant recipient in Honduras needed to get home, and we did it. Diplomats starved of sleep in Morocco held a plane for a mother with a baby. And in probably the most complex medical evacuation in history, a COVID-positive individual on a ventilator deep inside the Himalayan nation of Bhutan was medically transported back to the United States, arriving home more than thirty hours after wheels up.

The level of coordination was unbelievable. To bring home sixty-four Americans from Serbia, the Repatriation Task Force once held a call at four in the morning between Embassy Belgrade, Air Serbia, Customs and Border Patrol, and the Transportation Security Administration to secure landing rights at Los Angeles International Airport for a plane full of passengers ready to take off from Belgrade. We received it. Ultimately, in five months, the State Department evacuated more than one hundred thousand Americans from 139 countries. I will be forever proud of how teams on the ground and in Washington put Americans first. Later, Walters and the Operational Medicine team were able to deliver 190,000 doses of the Pfizer-BioNTech vaccine—which must be kept in deep subzero temperatures—to 256 embassies and consulates worldwide. It's a great American story of showing up.

A FORCE FOR GOOD IN THE DEPTHS OF THE PANDEMIC

At the outset of the pandemic, our priority was to take care of our own people. But the spread of the virus also created a foreign policy opportunity we couldn't miss. The CCP was demanding credit for a skillful handling of the pandemic—a ridiculous idea. The good news for America was that the world saw right through China's laughably poor propaganda pushing this brazen and devious boast. By the late spring and summer of 2020, nations all over the world were calling for an investigation and slamming the Chinese for pushing the world's foreign ministries to repeat Beijing's lies on how it deftly handled the outbreak. US Embassy Riyadh reported that social media users in Yemen—Yemen!—ridiculed a Chinese donation of ten thousand N95 masks and trashed China for its role in the pandemic. The cumulative effect of Beijing's dishonesty was that countries the world over began to restructure their supply chains, reject Chinese censorship and disinformation, and awaken to the true nature of the CCP.

It wasn't enough for me to watch the party absorb the biggest public-relations blow it had taken in decades. I wanted to deploy a counternarrative of American goodness and generosity. More practically, the world had to see that America would lead to help clean up the mess—and we weren't interested in doing it as a quid pro quo. It was simply a continuation of the generosity for which Americans are famous. From 2000 to 2020, the United States provided nearly $500 billion in all forms of foreign assistance, by far the greatest level of any country on earth. That's not to mention billions in contributions from faith groups, NGOs, and private citizens. Our administration sustained this legacy during the pandemic by pledging more than $1.6 billion in State Department and USAID funds through August 2020 to help more than 120 countries fight and recover from the virus. I was fortunate that I got to work with a trusted advisor on the disbursal of humanitarian aid. My former chief of staff on the Hill, Jim Richardson, was then running the State Department's Office of Foreign Assistance. If he made a recommendation, I was confident I could accept it. This let us push aid out the door at high speed and show the world that America was showing up in the middle of this catastrophe.

The other major way America blessed the world during the pandemic goes far beyond the normal distribution of humanitarian assistance. Operation Warp Speed will be remembered as one of the most successful scientific undertakings of all time—precisely because it was not designed to operate as anything like a typical government program. When the COVID-19 outbreak began, it was obvious that a vaccine would be the best way to reduce hospitalizations and deaths. The problem was that America and the world could not afford to wait for the federal government to develop a vaccine and move it through the regulatory process on a standard timeline. In normal circumstances, development and approval can take up to ten years. President Trump's instinct was to go big, move fast, and ditch bureaucracy. The administration partnered with America's world-leading biotechnology firms to produce the vaccine. As Jared Kushner, Alex Azar, Adam Boehler, and others began to interview candidates to lead the project, only one of them, Dr. Moncef Slaoui, believed it was possible to create a vaccine in less than a year. We did it, and without lowering standards of safety and efficacy. Millions of people are alive today because of this accomplishment.

And in the meantime, the United States kept up our normal humanitarian assistance throughout 2020 as well. We sent life-saving food and medical assistance to Lebanon in the wake of a gigantic explosion at a port warehouse in Beirut. We contributed $25 million to help Somalia, Ethiopia, Kenya, Sudan, and Uganda avert famine caused by locusts. And in 2020, we provided 43 percent of the World Food Programme's budget, while China provided just .06 percent. I was very proud that near the end of the Trump administration, President Trump ordered that all US foreign assistance bear a single logo, thus putting an end to the kaleido-scope of US government insignias that could be found on forms of foreign assistance. A single logo would boost America's "brand," so that the world better understood exactly who was showing up to meet their needs.

MISSION COMPLETE

Sadly, there came a day when I could no longer show up as secretary of state. After months of legal wrangling, President Trump failed in his challenge to the outcome of the 2020 election. The fat lady had sung, but I was determined to drive as much good policy as possible over the finish line in those final days. We fired off a bunch of final actions, in-cluding sanctions related to Venezuela, Iran, Cuba, and the CCP's abuses in Hong Kong. And on the second to last day of our term we denounced the genocide in Xinjiang as such, as I've already described.

I also gave a speech I had been itching to give for some time. It detailed how Tehran had become a sanctuary for al-Qaeda's senior leaders. The world needed to know that the threat of Iran was so much broader than just nuclear weapons. With Tehran's permission, Iran had become the home base of al-Qaeda in the years since 9/11. One only needed to look at how al-Qaeda's number two man, Abdullah Ahmed Abdullah, whose nom de guerre was Abu Muhammad al-Masri, was living comfortably inside Iran on the day he was gunned down in August 2020. He died on the mean streets of Tehran, not in the Federally Administered Tribal Areas of Pakistan or eastern Afghanistan. I'll remind the world again: the killers of three thousand Americans are no longer conducting the bulk of their external plotting against America from Afghan soil. They are in Iran.

Just as the media cast suspicion on my claims that America had in-telligence indicating Qasem Soleimani was plotting more attacks against Americans, scores of headlines in response to this speech carried the same message. The New York Times? "Pompeo Says Iran Is New Base for Al Qaeda, but Offers Little Proof." Reuters? "Pompeo Says Iran Gives al Qaeda New 'Home Base,' Analysts Skeptical." Al-Jazeera? "Pompeo Says al-Qaeda's 'New Home Base' Is Iran, with No Evidence."

I used to assume reporters know how to use Google. They just had to look up the State Department's Country Reports on Terrorism to see I wasn't bluffing. The edition released in 2020 said, "Iran remained unwilling to bring to justice senior al-Qa'ida (AQ) members residing in the country and has refused to publicly identify members in its custody." The 2021 version released under President Biden had nearly identical language, but for one subtle change: "Iran remained unwilling to bring to justice senior al-Qa'ida (AQ) members residing in the country and has refused to publicly identify members *it knows to be living in Iran*" (emphasis mine). That small difference didn't happen because the Biden administration thinks I have my facts wrong. It's because they can't admit I was right that Iran is actively sheltering al-Qaeda operatives, probably because the administration wants to get back into the nuclear deal. They are playing politics with counterterrorism.

Another thing I wanted to do was document all the good work that we did, and we lined up a three-week tweetstorm from my official Secretary of State Twitter account. Mary Kissel and a team in the Bureau of Global Public Affairs wrote hundreds of tweets to mark what we had done. True to form, the media whined that I was using the account for political purposes. But by the end, there were so many misperceptions about what our administration stood for and accomplished that this was a good way to draw attention to our record of success.

On the final day of the administration, January 20, 2021, I exited public service the way I came into it—with Ulrich Brechbühl and Brian Bulatao by my side. David Hale had asked if he could walk out with us as well—that meant a lot to me, too. Traditionally, an outgoing secretary of state exits the main lobby to the applause of hundreds of State Department employees. I didn't want that fanfare, and COVID-19 had limited in-person gatherings inside the State Department, anyway. Instead, I simply asked Ulrich and Brian, my best friends, to walk out the main doors with me. For the final time, I climbed into the back of my usual ride: an armored Cadillac sedan waiting to take me home to Susan. I was exhausted, sad, relieved, and proud. Above all, I was confident I had left it all out on the field for America. We never gave an inch.

CONCLUSION

TODAY AND TOMORROW

As my time as secretary drew to a close, I received a note from a couple I did not know, Steven and Anna Chu. They are Americans, having both lawfully immigrated from Communist China. I was floored by what they sent along—a copy of their newborn son's US Social Security card. His name: Tristan Pompeo Chu.

The letter commended what we did to confront the CCP and protect their country, the United States of America. They then added that they would write me in eighteen years to seek my recommendation for Tristan to attend the US Military Academy. Consider it done.

The Chu family understands that we must be prepared to continue fighting for the America we love. They know we can never give an inch in defending its central, constitutional principles. My commitment to this cause was reinforced while leading the best spy agency in the world and, for all its faults, the world's most important diplomatic corps. I saw from new vantage points how adherence to our constitutional order remains foundational for unrivaled freedoms and prosperity here at home. I saw how adherence to these norms benefits people everywhere. I saw how our bureaucratic institutions, slow and cumbersome as they may be, must operate within the bounds of the law. And I saw what happens when those who call themselves nonpartisan civil servants within these institutions abuse their power and thus threaten the very idea of America.

There are of course times when compromise is not only possible but necessary. But we can never give an inch on America's main ideas, on the things that really matter: the dignity of every human being made in the image of God, the right to enjoy the fruits of our own labor, the family as the central organizing unit of all great civilizations, and government by the consent of the governed.

We each have a duty to deliver on those founding ideas and to get our nation closer to them every day. A man named Barry Takimoto owned the Baskin-Robbins in Costa Mesa, California, where I rose to the noble rank of assistant manager. While I was still officially a trainee, he once saw me heading out after my shift was over. Barry asked me something that sticks in my mind to this day: "Mike, what'd you do today to make this place better?"

Ever since, I've asked myself that question with respect to everything I've done, from serving in the Army, to owning a small business, to working in Congress. More recently, I've asked it about my service in the Trump administration. We built a sound economy and delivered hope to every American willing to work hard. We built friendships—in some cases more appreciated today than in the moment—with nations prepared to defend Western values and make America a better, safer, and more prosperous place. We led our friends and deterred our adversaries.

We put America first, and I have the scars to prove it: I am sanctioned by three countries—Russia, China, and Iran—and that last one is still trying to kill me. Another country has issued a summons for my testimony about an alleged assassination attempt. I can't even go buy a quart of milk without my security detail taking me to the store. Perhaps this is proof that our adversaries think I made America stronger. My sense is that these sanctions reflect their views that my work was both principled, not transactional, and stemmed from a deep belief in America, not animus to their people, and that I was strategic, not wild, in charting America's course.

We also opened eyes to the threats we face in a mean, nasty world. Indeed, I saw a study the other day showing that Americans have a less favorable opinion of China than they do of syphilis (OK, that's a joke). I'm proud that we led a dramatic shift in American (and global) opinion, because the CCP is far more dangerous than any venereal disease. We're going to see the Party's evil on display for many years to come.

It also sank in for me that, contrary to conventional wisdom, the influence of electoral politics on our foreign policy is an asset for our country. Pundits worry that American foreign policy swings dramatically every four to eight years, causing our allies to wonder whether our policies have durability or continuity. There is a quotation, perhaps apocryphal, that is often attributed to the British economist John Maynard Keynes: "When the facts change, I change my mind." When geostrategic realities change, so must America adapt its strategic approach. In 2016, America was done with the Bush-Obama foreign policy. We were done with timidly subordinating American interests within multilateral bodies. We were done with an endless war in Afghanistan. We were done with tolerating Chinese aggression, cheating, and promise breaking. The American people invested us with power to do things differently, and we did, to America's benefit.

In America, we can fix our mistakes because we have elections. It's how we hold our leaders accountable. Americans have an amazing capacity for self-renewal. This is yet another reason why, to use a financial concept, I am long on our country.

★ ★ ★

I've often been asked why I think I had so much ability to drive policy and execution in the Trump administration.

First, it was because my relationship with President Trump was sound. There was no magic formula: I told him the truth, respected the office of the presidency by never leaking our conversations for a personal or even a policy purpose, and executed on what he told me to do. I never returned to State after a meeting at the White House and told my team, "We have to do this because Trump says so." Even if the idea was not mine or I had a different view, I told the team, "Here is our mission, let's get after it." I wasn't fighting against him, as so many others who purported to be on our team did. I was fighting for America.

Second, I drove good outcomes because I worked my tail off. When

I was nominated to be the CIA director, the media, searching for dirt, chased down several of my high school classmates. The world now knows that I participated in school ditch day at Leo Carrillo Elementary (but that I did it with my mom's permission). Yet the most Pulitzer-worthy reporting turned up a man who was my teammate on the Los Amigos High School basketball team. He was willing to share an important secret. The reporter asked if I was a good player. My old teammate's response makes my son, Nick, laugh to this day: "He made the most of what he had."

He was right. Slow and under six feet tall, with a jump shot more likely to break the backboard than find the net, I wasn't the most talented guy on the team. But even then, I was fearsomely focused on doing everything I could with what the Lord had given me. I've never changed. In the Trump administration, I worked like a maniac.

Third, I got stuff done because I made the case for what was important. To quote one of my favorite Toby Keith songs, I favored "a little less talk and a lot more action." I focused on the highest priorities. And I did it all with the help of strong teams built on sound principles and with tightly focused missions.

Lastly, I was able to execute under President Trump for four years because it was never about me. The goal of never giving an inch is not to protect your place in history or your reputation. Never giving an inch matters because you have a once-in-a-lifetime chance to responsibly wield the immense power vested in the CIA director and secretary of state. Thus, I was vicious, relentless, manic, determined—you pick the adjective—on the highest priorities. Never giving an inch did not require me to make enemies of my colleagues or those who worked for me. Indeed, I took pleasure in sharing credit, working on the things they cared most about, and even sending them short notes when they were under fire. As I did this, I think President Trump could see that I was in it for America, every day, as part of his team.

Of course, the prevailing *New York Times* or *Washington Post* narrative offers a different reason I survived: "He was a suck up, sycophantic, former-Trump-hating, power-hungry hack." I'm summarizing, but they made clear that they would change their views and write of me approvingly if I would only sell out Trump and become, instantaneously, the

"Adult in the Room." Bit players in the Trump administration grand drama such as Miles Taylor, Nikki Haley, Gordon Sondland, and Stephanie Grisham know what I mean. The quid pro quo from the East Coast, liberal establishment was on display in every one of their cases: once you flip on Trump, glory and money from us, the elites, will be yours. The inverse message from the establishment, of course, is that if one stays and delivers, then you must surely be a yes-man intent on the destruction of our republic. I was a bit of an enigma for them because I didn't fit neatly into their categories. Surely, they reasoned, the guy who went to Harvard Law School and graduated first in his class at West Point is gaming everyone? "He has to be playing a strategic hand against that fool Trump," they believed. No. My effectiveness baffled them and my willingness to stay on the team infuriated them. Their made-for-cable-TV drama (literally) failed to capture that one could be an adult in the room, out of the room, around the world, and with his teams and deliver for our country in the Trump administration.

★ ★ ★

Since leaving office, I still think quite a bit about keeping Americans safe. As has always been the case, American leaders must be prepared to protect everyone. A willingness—or unwillingness—to do so sends its own particular message. Sadly, as this book goes to press, the current leadership team in the White House is failing at this.

Numerous Iran-led or Iran-supported episodes this past summer prove it. In July 2022, an Iranian-directed Chechen mook with a loaded AK-47 nearly killed the same Iranian American citizen living in Brooklyn who was previously the target of an IRGC kidnapping plot. In August, a Shia extremist and an IRGC fanboy attacked the author Salman Rushdie while he was giving a public speech. The attempted murder was designed to fulfill, on US soil, the ayatollah's 1989 fatwa demanding Rushdie's death.

And in that same month, the Department of Justice unsealed an indictment against an Iranian operative working at the IRGC's direction to perform contract killings targeting me for $1 million and Ambassador

John Bolton for $300,000. Their plan was not a hapless Wile E. Coyote scheme—the would-be attackers had cased homes and offices and were well on their way toward executing the plot. This threat is but one of many that my family and I have experienced since leaving office nineteen months ago, as of this writing. While details must be omitted here, other Americans—some former Trump administration officials, some senior American military leaders, and some ordinary Americans—remain on the Iranian kill list.

Most disturbingly for us and our families, Iran's assassination campaigns have no expiration date. Just look at Iran's track record of attempted and successful assassinations. It stretches as far back as 1979, when the former shah's nephew was gunned down in Paris. Over the years, American and Israeli personnel, among other nationalities, have been frequent targets, from Argentina to Azerbaijan to Bulgaria to Cyprus to Kenya to Thailand and everywhere in between. American counterintelligence teams uncovered a plot in 2011 to assassinate the Saudi ambassador to the United States while he was dining at an Italian restaurant in Washington, DC. Today Iran—a nation-state actor—is so bold as to plot to kill Americans on American soil. This is what spreading the Islamic Revolution looks like in 2022.

The response from the Biden administration should be a fierce display of deterrence—exactly the posture the Clinton administration took in 1993. When America's leaders discovered an Iraqi plot to assassinate former president George H. W. Bush on a trip to Kuwait, they imposed costs *before* the mayhem, not *after* it would have occurred. In June 1993, US Navy ships lobbed twenty-three Tomahawk missiles at the headquarters of the Iraqi Intelligence Service. In President Clinton's words, it sent a message: "We will combat terrorism. We will deter aggression. We will protect our people . . . From the first days of our revolution, America's security has depended on the clarity of this message: Don't tread on us."

President Biden has foolishly taken the opposite approach. Contrast President Clinton's response to Iraq's plot to Jake Sullivan's statement released after the DOJ indictments:

We have said this before and we will say it again: the Biden Administration will not waiver [*sic*] in protecting and defending all Americans against threats of violence and terrorism. *Should Iran attack any of our citizens, to include those who continue to serve the United States or those who formerly served, Iran will face severe consequences* [emphasis added]. We will continue to bring to bear the full resources of the U.S. Government to protect Americans.

The Biden administration's policy is to let Americans die first and respond later.

Even worse, the Biden administration is doing next to nothing because it craves a return to the Iran nuclear deal. Special Envoy Rob Malley continues to defend providing the Iranians billions of dollars of financial relief from sanctions. Even John Kerry has admitted that such money ends up in the hands of the IRGC and funds its global terror and assassination campaigns. Rob, why on earth would you reward these murderers while they are trying to kill your predecessor? Like me and my family, the great patriot Brian Hook and his family are now at risk because of your—and your administration's—personal jihad to restore a deal with Iran that will get Americans killed.

This blood money to Iran is for me, of course, both a policy matter and deeply personal. I am thankful for the security assistance that Secretary Blinken and the State Department security team have provided to me and continue to provide. This lifetime threat will require continued vigilance from me and my family and all those around me, too. I'm deeply aware that as I meet with large groups and travel around our great country, a hidden explosive device or an attacker on an Iranian-sponsored spree may well harm hundreds of people.

Adopting a policy where the enemy gets to kill an American former senior official before you act is obscene and dangerous for America. In fact, it is strikingly like responding in Ukraine after Ukrainians were dead. Biden's die-first, respond-later policy enhances the risks that America will suffer a very bad day at the hands of IRGC thugs on the streets of our nation. America deserves better.

★ ★ ★

Prioritizing the right agenda items will be the key to maintaining American primacy in the twenty-first century. I will not give an exhaustive list of every challenge and corresponding action that must be taken. More on that in the months ahead. But I will say that all other foreign policy challenges must be subordinated to the goal of stopping the CCP. It presents the single greatest external threat to our republic (the greatest overall threat to America is actually Randi Weingarten and the teachers' unions). The CCP is not serious about any kind of accommodation—they want 100 percent of the pie and on their terms. They will not give an inch on any issue we confronted them on. The promise breaking that occurred over the South China Sea and Hong Kong is for them a feature, not a bug, of the CCP. Witness, too, how the Chinese purchased almost none of the additional $200 billion worth of goods it promised to purchase under President Trump's 2020 Phase One trade deal. The web of China-related threats is limitless. The head of US Strategic Command has said China's intent is "to achieve the military capability to reunify Taiwan by 2027 if not sooner." Every day, billions of bytes of American data are exposed to Beijing. Chinese bribes—legal and illegal—flood the world. We must continue to compete in every domain with China—by separating our critical supply chains from their soil, guarding our technology and data from the CCP's clutches, and making sure the United States and our allies have ample and superior weaponry to defend ourselves.

Our institutions must also be properly adapted to focus on winning competition with China. This means, among other things, a State Department that is more aggressive and risk-accepting. It is much to my embarrassment that during my tenure we were unable to restructure the Foreign Service in a meaningful way. The State Department doesn't suffer from lack of numbers. It suffers from leaks, fragmentation, layers of bureaucracy, and a model for career advancement that disincentivizes risk-taking and ingenuity among the diplomatic corps. What the State Department needs is fundamental structural reform, something that I believe will take eight years to do the right way.

Finally, guarding our first principles and our place in the world is not exclusively the responsibility of those who vote in Congress, wear the uniform, or work at the CIA or State Department. It is for all Americans in all walks of life. Just as the book of James in the Bible reminds us that "faith without works is dead," so, too, is an admiration for America hollow without action to defend it. And there is no more urgent time to mount a defense than now. There are new forces arrayed against the American tradition that are already doing catastrophic damage to it. There are Marxist "intellectuals" teaching our kids that all of American history is a grim saga of racist oppression. Ideologues who have infiltrated American institutions are obliterating God-ordained gender categories and our unalienable right to free expression. Big tech overlords are happy to assist in these cultural suicide missions and muzzle those who disagree. And on foreign policy, too many inhabit a fantasy world about the challenges we face, and frequently postulate solutions to our problems that in one way or another call for an abrogation of American leadership.

The time is urgent, and challenges are many. But I take heart that patriots such as Steven and Anna Chu still abound—and I am sure Tristan Pompeo Chu will grow up to be a great American, too. The way forward is to hold on to our values, honor the will of the people, and never give an inch. I am confident that if we do so—if we all use our God-given talents for America—we will have another American century.

ACKNOWLEDGMENTS

I've done many things in my life, and I've read a lot of books, but this was my first time writing one. Conducting research, developing a structure and narrative framework, and telling a good story is an extensive and deeply collaborative project. I hope I've done it right.

My gratitude abounds to all who have assisted.

My beloved wife, Susan, encouraged this endeavor from the beginning. Just as she has sharpened me in every way since we first met, she also put her keen eyes on the manuscript, and made it better.

My son, Nick, never shies away from dishing out both praise and helpful criticism. I'm grateful to know he always has my back.

I could not ask for a better writing partner than David Wilezol. He was with me at State and wrote some of my best speeches. The bad ones were all mine. He has taken my random ideas and made them a book. This would not have been possible without him. Thank you, David.

John J. Miller did a masterful job adding polish to the draft.

My agent, David Vigliano, was a total professional in putting together a very fine proposal and securing the right publisher for me.

Eric Nelson at HarperCollins was a wise and patient editor who strengthened the material.

My two brothers—Ulrich and Brian, as well as Michelle and April—have sustained Susan, Nick, and me through much. I was grateful to be able to call upon them to help fact-check this work. Here's to another forty years.

Professor Mary Ann Glendon, on a flight back from Jakarta, looked

Susan and me in the eye and said, "You have to write." I hope I have done my friend and mentor honor with this work.

Peter Berkowitz, Kim Breier, Andy Kim, Mary Kissel, Keith Krach, David Stilwell, and Miles Yu proved they are true champions for America while at the CIA or the State Department. Careful recollections of whirlwind days and nights from several of them helped bring this story to life.

Ron Przysucha came through in the clutch with photos.

Jim Richardson has kept me organized and ready for everything for the past decade-plus.

Of course, this book would not be in your hands without the support of many friends who have encouraged and guided me in public service over the years.

INDEX

KIR TUBEN / THE POMPEO FAMILY

ABOUT THE AUTHOR

Michael R. Pompeo served as the seventieth secretary of state of the United States of America from 2018 to 2021. Prior to his service as America's top diplomat, Mike was the director of the Central Intelligence Agency from 2017 to 2018. He was proud to represent the Fourth Congressional District of Kansas in the US House of Representatives from 2011 to 2017. He is currently a distinguished fellow at Hudson Institute.

A native of Southern California, Mike graduated first in his class from the US Military Academy at West Point in 1986. He served as a cavalry officer in the US Army, with his first assignment leading small units patrolling the border between the Soviet bloc and freedom-loving people of the West. Mike left the military in 1991. He graduated from Harvard Law School, having served as an editor of the *Harvard Law Review.*

Following a brief stint practicing law, Mike headed to south-central Kansas, where his family had deep roots in Wellington, Winfield, and Wichita. As the CEO of two manufacturing businesses there—first in the aerospace industry and then in the oil field services equipment sector—he took pride in making products Americans need and providing jobs for hundreds of hardworking Kansans.

In 2010, Mike lost his mind and decided to run for Congress. He won and was reelected three more times to represent south-central Kansas—the heartland of America. In addition to the House Energy and Commerce Committee, Mike served on the House Select Committee on Benghazi and House Permanent Select Committee on Intelligence, working to keep American soldiers and diplomats safe and the American people more secure.

Mike and his wife, Susan, are proud parents of their son, Nick, and his lovely wife, Rachael, both of whom they consider to be the greatest blessings of their lives. The Pompeos dedicated many volunteer hours to their home church in Wichita, Eastminster Presbyterian Church, where Mike served as a deacon and where he is convinced that he became qualified to be secretary of state by teaching fifth-grade Sunday school alongside Susan and two other Christian couples. The playing schedules for Army Football and the Wichita State Shockers, LA Rams, and UCLA Bruins are always on Mike's calendar.